Ironies of Organizational Change

ELGAR INTRODUCTIONS TO MANAGEMENT AND ORGANIZATION THEORY

Series Editors: Cary L. Cooper, *Alliance Manchester Business School, University of Manchester, UK* and Stewart R. Clegg, *School of Management, University of Technology Sydney, Australia*

Elgar Introductions to Management and Organization Theory are stimulating and thoughtful introductions to main theories in management, organizational behaviour and organization studies, expertly written by some of the world's leading scholars. Designed to be accessible yet rigorous, they offer concise and lucid surveys of the key theories in the field.

The aims of the series are twofold: to pinpoint essential history, and aspects of a particular theory or set of theories, and to offer insights that stimulate critical thinking. The volumes serve as accessible introductions for undergraduate and graduate students coming to the subject for the first time. Importantly, they also develop well-informed, nuanced critiques of the field that will challenge and extend the understanding of advanced students, scholars and policy-makers.

Titles in the series include:

Elgar Introduction to Theories of Organizational Resilience
Luca Giustiniano, Stewart R. Clegg, Miguel Pina e Cunha and Arménio Rego

Theories of Social Innovation
Danielle Logue

Elgar Introduction to Theories of Human Resources and Employment Relations
Edited by Keith Townsend, Kenneth Cafferkey, Aoife M. McDermott and Tony Dundon

Organizational Project Management
Theory and Implementation
Ralf Müller, Nathalie Drouin and Shankar Sankaran

Elgar Introduction to Organizational Paradox Theory
Marco Berti, Ace Volkmann Simpson, Miguel Pina e Cunha and Stewart R. Clegg

Elgar Introduction to Organizational Improvisation Theory
António Cunha Meneses Abrantes, Miguel Pina e Cunha and Anne S. Miner

Elgar Introduction to Organizational Stress Theories
Kimberly E. O'Brien and Cary Cooper

Elgar Introduction to Designing Organizations
Miguel Pina e Cunha, Stewart Clegg, Medhanie Gaim and Luca Giustiniano

Ironies of Organizational Change
Introduction to Change Management and Organizational Theory
Richard J. Badham and Brenda M. Santiago

Ironies of Organizational Change
Introduction to Change Management and Organizational Theory

Richard J. Badham

Honorary Professor, University of Sydney and University of Technology Sydney, Australia

Brenda M. Santiago

Principal, Inspiring Change, Sydney, Australia

ELGAR INTRODUCTIONS TO MANAGEMENT AND ORGANIZATION THEORY

Edward **Elgar**
PUBLISHING

Cheltenham, UK • Northampton, MA, USA

Published by
Edward Elgar Publishing Limited
The Lypiatts
15 Lansdown Road
Cheltenham
Glos GL50 2JA
UK

Edward Elgar Publishing, Inc.
William Pratt House
9 Dewey Court
Northampton
Massachusetts 01060
USA

Paperback edition 2023

A catalogue record for this book
is available from the British Library

Library of Congress Control Number: 2023934058

This book is available electronically in the **Elgar**online
Business subject collection
http://dx.doi.org/10.4337/9781786437723

ISBN 978 1 78643 771 6 (cased)
ISBN 978 1 78643 772 3 (eBook)
ISBN 978 1 0353 2914 4 (paperback)
Printed and bound by CPI Group (UK) Ltd, Croydon, CR0 4YY

In Memory of Petra and Hector

Contents

Figures

Tables

Acknowledgements

Richard would personally like to thank his two lovely sisters, Diana and Sally, for making life so enjoyable along the way, Julian Woodbridge for his humour and affection, and Michael Zanko for being the best friend a man can have, and who grounds Richard and his work in reality, including the use of a biting irony that makes him the most deeply angst-ridden funny man I have ever met. Of course, there is also Richard's immediate family, Alec, Max, Christian and Mallory, who, as children and young adults, continue to teach him that giving is also receiving. From the academic side. Richard would like to particularly thank Professor Ian McLoughlin, an academic partner in ironic crime who, despite being younger, has long-lived irony even when Richard was in his cognitive nappies. Professors Peter Robinson and Norma Harrison whose mentoring and support have been crucial and remarkable. Professor Stewart Clegg for his intelligence, comradeship and support, Professor Dave Buchanan for his cutting insights and incredible collegial generosity, Professor Martin Kornberger for his affection and creativity, Professor Patrick Dawson for teaching me that change was not a 'non-subject', Professor Carl Rhodes for his recent support and ability to wear his radicalism with a light cloak, Richard Claydon for his insights, work and persistence in our struggles to make sense of irony, and the late Professor James March for his inspiration, kindness, and the twinkle in his eye. For their collegial collaboration in frequently challenging academic-industry projects, I owe much to Professor Paul Couchman, Richard Carter and Karen Garrety. For their life lessons in the workplace, I must particularly thank Neville Glennan of Ford, Garry Langton of BHP, Peter Robertson and the late Joe Pollard. They led me through the tangled entrails of institutional politics while also teaching me to be more human and enjoy the journey. For their comradeship, stimulation, and practical wisdom, I am especially indebted to consultant and idea entrepreneurs Allan Parker (Peak Performance) and Peter Fuda (The Alignment Partnership).

Beyond these specific acknowledgements, Richard's enduring gratitude goes to those industry partners and collaborators who over a period of 30 or so years allowed him into their worlds and provided him with so much insight, inspiration and companionship, as well as the more than 4,000 MBA students at the Macquarie Graduate School of Management who were so much part of the development of these ideas as unwitting guinea pigs, sources of intellectual ideas and practical wisdom and, for the most part, energized and enthusiastic partners-in-crime. Thanks to you all!

Brenda wishes to acknowledge and personally thank her family (bloodlines and chosen) across hemispheres and beyond, who are a constant reminder of the value of human connection. There is her father, Hector, whose limitless love opened the path for all possibilities and his mom, the unbridled Aba Fela whose spirit ignited all she touched. She is also grateful to her protective baby brother Eric and mother, Gloria, one of her greatest teachers. For inspiration, love and support Brenda would like to thank Pedro M Cardona-Roig, whose passions make her island of Puerto Rico and the world a better place. For their lessons in the workplace, a special note of gratitude to Dr Joe Collins whose energy and belief in her propelled each health initiative into a higher stratosphere. To the Jims (Gilmore and Catlett) who opened the world power and politics, Roman Velasco Gonzalez and Bruce G Herman who shed light on the challenges of labour reform and social justice, Ed Morrison who moves mountains through the power of human connection and Brooke Donnelly, whose drive gives her hope for our planet.

For his imagery, inspiration and remarkable flexibility, both of us are also very grateful to our professional cartoonist Jock McNeish.

On a final personal note, we would like to express our love and gratitude to each other, for the humour, unconditional love and joy that simply makes life better.

An invitation

Panta Rhei (Everything flows). No person ever steps in the same river twice, for it's not the same river and (s)he's not the same (wo)man. (Popular adaptation from Heraclitus Fragments)[1]

In this book, you are invited to re-imagine change and re-invent yourself. You cannot have one without the other. Organizations are living, breathing institutions, and change processes are complex, social, and unpredictable. Agents and recipients of change are human beings making sense and searching for meaning. Re-imagining change puts this at the forefront of any discussion of managing and leading change. Re-inventing yourself means taking this to heart in all your interactions.

One of the challenges we face in this enterprise is living under a shadow. The shadow is cast by a deeply ingrained yet overly rational view of how people and organizations think and act. This book is an invitation to step out of this shadow and into the light. As an illustration of what this involves, let's use the experience of COVID-19. How often have you heard people railing against mistakes, the lack of preparation, blinkered thinking, bull-headed arrogance, short-termism, and self-interested politics? If we prepare for change without fully understanding and considering such dimensions, we are preparing to fail.

COVID-19 AS A PREDICTABLE SURPRISE

In discussions on changes wrought by COVID-19, whether or not it should have been predicted and prepared for is a matter of debate and controversy. The same goes for the adequacy of institutional and political responses to its arrival and spread. Was its arrival a 'Black Swan' event, totally unpredictable, or more a 'Gray Rhino' that was predicted, predictable, yet ignored and neglected until it was too late (Avishai, 2020; Taleb, 2010; Wucker, 2020; Wucker, 2016)? In terms of Rumsfeld's famous remark, was it a 'known known', a 'known unknown' or an 'unknown unknown'?

> There are known knowns; there are things we know we know. We also know there are known unknowns; that is to say, we know there are some things we do not know. But there are also unknown unknowns – the ones we don't know we don't know. (Rumsfeld, D. (2002), *Defense Department Meeting*, February)

Given that we were warned about the likelihood and dangers of such a pandemic by influential and celebrated individuals such as Bill Gates, expert policy bodies such as the Obama Commission and authoritative institutions such as the World Health Organization, why were we so unprepared? Should we be similarly surprised or not by the delayed responses to its onset, the politicization of strategies for how it should be handled and the controversies surrounding its urgency and treatment? The controversies surrounding blame strategies for what was controversially stigmatized as 'Chinese flu', the notorious failures of many politicians and governments to initiate containment or 'lockdown' procedures, the inegalitarian 'roll out' and the disputed safety of the engineered vaccines were shocking to many. Yet are these something we should be startled and appalled by ('unknown unknown')? Although the details and degree are unpredictable, are they a predictable phenomenon ('known unknown')? Or are they something that anyone with knowledge of how change occurs would have expected and could have prepared for ('known known')?

These are critical change management questions. They address how we should handle what, in a sense, we all know. Unfortunately, people and institutions often ignore or deny challenges to routines, habits, and ways of living that they have become accustomed to or committed to. They then fail to notice or respond to the challenges effectively. As we will show in this book, developing change strategies or 'pushing' change without considering such factors results in mis-managing or mis-leading change.

Many responses to COVID-19 ignore these realities and repeat traditional change management formulae. The importance of mindful, attentive, and considerate leadership is emphasized, attending to communication, engagement, involvement and so on (Huron Consulting, 2021; Kalina, 2020; Maak et al., 2021). Motivating and supporting by attending to the predictable 'grief cycle' and challenging the 'valley of despair' is stressed (Lahri & Shankar, 2020; Offereins, 2020). Seeking out and aligning individual and organizational purpose is highlighted (Schaninger et al., 2020; Dhingra et al., 2020). The significance of creating agile and adaptive mindsets, cultures and structures cultures is re-emphasized (Amis & Janz, 2020; Faeste et al., 2021; Freeland, 2020). And so on, and so on. Sound advice. Conventional, predictable and reassuring. Yet this was all well known and widely recommended before the COVID-19 crisis! With a critical hat on, it is reminiscent of Greta Thunberg's (2021) recent condemnation of the 'Blah, Blah, Blah' of climate change rhetoric. If advice is restricted to such traditional formulae, the barriers to putting such advice into action remain untouched. These barriers are well known and entirely predictable. They only surprise us if we ignore, neglect or underestimate them. Ironically, we commonly do so, and to our cost.

So, thinking about how you have experienced the reaction of yourself, others, and institutions to the COVID pandemic, review the conditions drawn from Bazerman and Watkins' (2004) analysis of 'predictable surprises' (below) and reflect on the question: '*How far were they present in your COVID-19 experience?*'

PREDICTABLE SURPRISES: BARRIERS TO PUTTING ADVICE INTO ACTION

Source: Watkins and Bazerman (2003); Bazerman and Watkins (2004).

SELF-SERVING PSYCHOLOGICAL BIASES

- Illusions that things are better than they are, that we will 'get by'
- Greater weight is given to evidence that supports rather than challenges our preconceptions
- Too little heed is paid to what other people are doing, making us more vulnerable to their actions
- Dominance of short-term thinking, more committed to the present than the future, avoid incurring pain today for pleasure tomorrow
- Issue not previously personally experienced or vividly communicated, so individuals and institutions didn't feel compelled to address the problem

ORGANIZATIONAL BIASES

- Silos result in a fragmented approach to problems
- Silos mean that no one takes responsibility for the problem
- Hierarchies filter information, particularly that which is sensitive or embarrassing, so those at the top get incomplete or inaccurate data
- Hierarchy gives responsibility to one institution or area and does not fully consider others
- Decision-makers with an 'impact horizon' that is too narrow, neglecting major constituencies

POLITICAL BIASES

- Self-interests of powerful key decision-makers
- Imbalances of power favouring the interests of one group or groups over significant others
- Decisions made without considering the dynamics of political manoeuvring and governmental systems
- Inadequate consideration of the power and resources required to address the problem
- Presence of cultural and institutional fears of 'speaking up' restricted understanding of the problem and the ability to evaluate progress

If your honest answer is that these 'predictable surprises' were present, let's consider their broader relevance. Isn't it only reasonable to expect such conditions? Shouldn't you take these into account in preparing yourself for other changes? And, given that we often do not do so, what does this say about the real challenges of handling change effectively and meaningfully? If these questions intrigue you, then our invitation has been a success. Read on!

ACCOMPANYING WEBSITE AND ONLINE COURSE

This book draws on and aligns with the Coursera course *Leading transformations: Manage change* with over 30,000 active learners at the time of publishing. The course is a compact and accessible introduction to the subject with online lectures, selected readings, and short exercises. The subject material and reviews can be found at https://www.coursera.org/learn/change-management.

Our Reimagining Change website https://reimaginingchange.com supports and supplements this book with additional topic discussions, readings, exercises, stories, and video/internet links. It details how best to access and use the online course and is regularly updated to include recent literature, events, and experiences.

NOTE

1. We use the term '*Popular adaptation from Heraclitus Fragments*' since the origins and meaning of the pre-Socratic philosopher's comments on change are obscure and contested. However, commonly accepted are the (i) interpretations of the aphorism '*Panta Rhei*' as the only constant is change, (ii) references to the contextual and situational nature of change by stating no one steps into the same river twice, and (iii) statements about how we are also in a state of constant change, and how we experience the world changes over time (Graham, 2021; Rescher, 1996, p.9).

Prologue

It is a truth universally acknowledged that an organization in want of a change must be in need of a change management methodology. (Jane Austen (1813), *Pride and Prejudice*, modified first sentence!)

CHANGING CHANGE MANAGEMENT

'Change Management' is an Oxymoron

If management is about control and change is out of control, can you control the uncontrollable? The statement and the subject are contradictory and non-sensical, a topic for fools or charlatans. Or is it?

I first heard the phrase, 'change management is an oxymoron' from a fellow lecturer, damning the managing change topic I was teaching. At the time, I really didn't know what oxymoron meant. The part 'oxy' sounded OK, but 'moron' was not so appealing. Then, to my delight, the dictionary provided a meaning different to how it is commonly used. Oxymoron does *not* mean contradiction. Instead, it refers to juxtaposing two seemingly contradictory terms to create a deliberate rhetorical effect. For example, deafening silence, lonely crowd, awfully lucky, love-hate, agree-to-disagree, cruel-to-be-kind, and sweet sorrow. Oxymorons highlight tensions. They create opportunities to ponder and explore the complexity and meaning of apparently contradicting ideas. So, yes, change management *is* an oxymoron, but not in the way its critics think.

The phrase was first coined by Jim Clemmer (1995) in his delightful book *Pathways to Performance*, legitimated by Henry Mintzberg et al. (1998) in *Strategy Safari* and popularized by Gary Hamel (2018) in his video '*Why Change Management is an Oxymoron*'. The phrase was used to critique traditional views of change management as planned change. In an era of 'permanent white water' (Vaill, 1989), programmed change is often too little, too late, and ineffective. We live in a VUCA ('Volatile. Uncertain. Complex. Ambiguous') age, requiring agile structures, adaptive leadership, and light and fast organizations (Gibbons, 2015; Heifetz & Linksy, 2017; Hollingworth, 2016). Traditional top-down, pre-planned, and tightly managed change programs are too limiting, too slow and too demotivating to be effective. The old ethos was more like that of the fictional character in the Star Trek franchise Captain Jean Luc Picard, who set the course and said, 'make it so'! The new ethos is more akin to the television superhero Captain Leonard Snart in *Flash* (2017[2014]). To paraphrase, you create a plan, you follow the plan, you expect the plan to go wrong, and then you…chuck the plan!

Sound sensible? Even exciting? Many would agree. It appeals to all our prejudices against slow, top-down, tendentious formality. It feeds our romantic aspirations for embarking on a heroic quest against the dead weight of bureaucracy and the opposition of apparatchiks. But it is mis-leading and dangerously so. To understand why, we need to dig deeper into our change management oxymoron and its promise.

Whether or not the modern era is really different, modern organizations are *always* riven by an inherent and fundamental tension. We want and need to change as individuals and organizations, yet we find it very difficult in practice. It is common knowledge that organizations need to innovate and change to survive and thrive. They also need to proclaim and demonstrate to all their stakeholders that this is what they are doing. Still, it seems as if organizations are perfectly designed to ensure otherwise. Established frames of thought, embedded habits and vested interests all act against our aspirations and strategies for change being realized. The temptation is to view one of these elements as the main game and the other as a mere sideshow. We either fall into the naïve trap of thinking the latest 'magic bullet' will solve the problem or relapse into cynical resignation that real or beneficial change is impossible. Yet, as we will argue throughout this book, you will need to accept the tension and deal with it. That is, embrace the oxymoron and get on with the task of living with and working through it.

So, to return to our praise of the oxymoron. Our choice does not lie between old-fashioned, stable, top-down change management and a new era, dynamic and entrepreneurial leadership of change. That idea is attractive, and as we shall see, some of the points are valuable. Yet, ultimately, it fails to accept, creatively address, or even encourage us to enjoy the change management oxymoron. We want to control change to bring about what we desire, yet change cannot be controlled. As individuals and organizations, we aspire to bring about desired changes, but we are confronted by conditions making them difficult to achieve at every turn. So, our real choice is either accept the oxymoron and grapple with the tension or deny, ignore or avoid it. Which one would you prefer?

This is a strong statement, but not actually as radical or new as one might expect. The 'tension' embodied in the idea of managing change as an oxymoron was documented long ago in two well-known characterizations of how organizations innovate and change. In 1928, Joseph Schumpeter famously described innovation as a challenging process of 'creative destruction' (Schumpeter, 1928, pp.379–80). This underlay his argument that, in contrast to invention, bringing about innovation is a 'feat not of intellect, but will. It is a special case of the social phenomenon of leadership.' In 1970, in his Reith Lecture, Donald Schon (1970, pp.2, 8) pointed to similar challenges in the 'dynamic conservatism' of organizations which caused them to 'fight like mad to remain the same'. 'Significant change', he observed, 'requires sources of power and energy sufficient to combat the dynamic conservatism of institutions, and institutions are not vacuums [but] a dynamically conservative plenum...Change, therefore, is always in the nature of a fight.'

Schumpeter and Schon were champions of innovation yet felt compelled to emphasize its challenges and barriers. Their two oxymorons ('creative destruction' and 'dynamic conservatism') captured the duality well as they highlighted the importance of creativity, dynamism and innovation while acknowledging the barriers to making it succeed. How they embraced this tension is illustrated by comparing their approach to that of Nico Machiavelli four centuries earlier. In *The Prince*, Machiavelli ([1514] 2005, p.22) observes, 'there is nothing more difficult to execute, nor more dubious of success, nor more dangerous to administer, than to introduce new political orders. For the one who introduces them has as his enemies all those who profit from the old order, and he has only lukewarm defenders in all those who might profit from the new order.' For Machiavelli, with his eye on the realpolitik of retaining power, there is no tension in this statement. It is better to avoid trying to bring about change to retain or increase power. For Schumpeter and Schon, however, modern organizations cannot survive without innovation and change, so for them, the tension between forces driving innovation and change and those holding them back are front and centre.

Mis-leading Change

The long-established nature of this insight raises important questions. Why is the tension more often avoided than accepted? Even when acknowledged in principle, why is it not addressed in practice? The answers lie in the first horn of the dilemma or part of the change management oxymoron. Organizations must innovate and change strategically and effectively to survive and prosper. Part of this enterprise is *being seen to do so*. So, they are forced to deny the 'conservative' side of their nature.

One of the central ironies of organizational change is *situational irony*. The dominant myth of organizations as rational enterprises actually prevents them from acknowledging the tension between the aspiration and the reality of organizational life and how they struggle in practice to overcome the gap.

This irony persists because the publicly articulated logic of modern organizations is that they are efficiently and effectively pursuing innovation and change. The rational myth of organizations proclaims this as a fact, upholds it as an aspiration, feeds it as an expectation and idealizes it as a quest. The sociologist Zygmunt Bauman (1998) expressed this modernist ethos as 'without us, the deluge'. In the words of Chris Argyris and Donald Schon (1978), this is the dominant 'espoused theory' of how organizations operate and change. It is a mental map or model deeply entrenched and firmly embedded in how organizations and those within them view how they think and act. Yet, as Schon (1970, p.8) emphasizes, once we acknowledge the change management oxymoron, 'we explode the myth that change occurs in rational ways. The notion occurs by analysing problems, evaluating options, choosing the most effective one and implementing it – that notion doesn't work.'

The result of misunderstanding the nature of organizations and avoiding or denying their conservative side is what we call the systematic *mis-leading of change*. Organizations proclaim and are called upon to lead change efficiently and effectively. Yet what is commonly recognized and regularly experienced in practice is its mishandling. Locked into black and white either/or thinking, the tensions generated by the change management oxymoron are denied, ignored, or avoided. Organizations, and those within them, then espouse one view in public but acknowledge and experience another in private.

We learn to live with this *verbal irony* or what some call an *irony of manners*. As individuals and organizations, we formally and explicitly say one thing but informally and implicitly admit to or indicate another in our actions. And it can be risky and dangerous to call the game! As a result, the embedded tension is misrepresented or misunderstood. The consequence is organizations routinely, systematically, and persistently mishandle change, misunderstand and misrepresent why, and fail to lead change in an effective and meaningful way. Welcome to the mis-leading of change!

Using the word irony to describe how we think, talk and act in managing change is a gamble. As the critic Muecke (1980, p.3) once remarked, trying to pin down irony is a bit like 'gathering mist'. We know roughly what it means, but it is very tough to be definitive about it (for a quick, accessible introduction, see Kreuz, 2022, and for a now infamous comic assessment, see Byrne, 2006). Despite this challenge, in the face of overly rational views of managing change, we believe the term provides an important and valuable counterweight and guide. As a counter, referring to the ironies of organiza-tional change brings into question our dominant rationalized, controlling, and one-dimensional views of change. It surfaces and highlights what, in a sense, we all 'know', which is the stupidities and arrogance, chaos and multiple meanings, frustrations and accidents that abound in change. It also acts as a pragmatic guide through the often murky waters of change. It does so by highlighting the importance of adopting an ironic perspective, being adept at giving an ironic performance and developing an ironic temperament. A brief explanation of each is provided below.

Irony 1: Situational Irony and an Ironic Perspective

At the heart of any notion of irony is what is commonly described as situational irony. It refers to situations where events run contrary to our expectations. It occurs when we think and act in ways that have different or opposite effects to what we intend. The dominant irony of organizational change is the common belief and expectation that change will or can be managed rationally and stra-tegically. When things do not work out as we plan or believe they should, we create another plan or strategy to solve the problem. Yet the real challenge is that our strategies do not get implemented! In our search for and faith in rational solutions, we all too often avoid the uncertainty, deny the emotions, and ignore the politics – at our cost! The situational irony lies deeper than simply being mistaken, however. Our exaggerated faith in our abilities, over-confidence, blinkered neglect or defensive denial makes this situation ironic. Situational irony is created by our folly, our fallibility, and our persistence in believing in our God-like qualities of intelligence and foresight despite evidence of our limitations and feet of clay. An ironic perspective accepts this state of affairs and works with it rather than denying it or lashing out in frustration when things do not work out the way we hope and expect.

IRONY 1

In life: 'The more (s)he chased him (or her), the more (s)he ran away.'

In leadership: 'Aware that strategies do not get implemented change management experts and consultants often recommend a change strategy!'

Irony 2: Verbal Irony, Irony of Manners and an Ironic Performance

It is one thing to appreciate this ironic state of affairs. It is quite another to communicate it persuasively and constructively. If we are confronted by ignorance and denial, just 'telling it as it is' is a dubious recipe for success! What is required is an ability to recognize, appreciate and sympathize with our exaggerated and illusory rationalizations while also questioning and pointing beyond them. Verbal irony (in our speech) or irony of manners (in how we act) is a way of expressing these multiple viewpoints, the contradictions they embody and the ambivalence they create. Verbal irony is commonly understood as saying one thing and meaning another, often the opposite. But what distinguishes it from simply lying or crude sarcasm is the communication of multiple levels of meaning and sympathetic appreciation of the tensions in how we and others think and what we want. The second source of irony in organizational change is created by individuals and organizations espousing an image of unity, rationality and alignment in public yet displaying (and admitting to) the opposite in private. An ironic performance acknowledges the existence and sympathizes with both views while surfacing the tension between them without undermining credibility or creating a backlash.

IRONY 2

In life: The statement made by one person to another when suffering from wet or bad weather conditions, 'Nice weather we are having, isn't it?'.

In leadership: When confronted by an army giving voice to his exaggerated reputation, Mel Gibson, as William Wallace in *Braveheart* (1995), uses sympathetic and constructive self-mockery to maintain faith and loyalty yet avoid the negative effects of this inflated image. In his celebrated *Great Speech* to the Scottish army (*Braveheart*, 1995, 1.12.30–1.19.00 mins), Wallace nods his head in acknowledgement. But he then parodies himself to the point of ridicule by exaggerating his powers and using vulgar humour to emphasize the point – killing men in their hundreds, using fireballs and lightning to do so, and claiming the lightning coming out of his rear end!

Irony 3: Ironic Disposition and an Ironic Temperament

An ongoing appreciation of the situational ironies of change and communicating these in a nuanced ironic performance requires discipline and effort. The temptation to put one's faith in a rational solution or new magic bullet, as well as just 'tell it as it is', is real and ever-present. If we are not predisposed to expect, grapple with, and even enjoy the difficulties and tensions in how we act and communicate in change, then we are more prone to unhealthy stress, less likely to be effective and may end up severely disappointed or disillusioned. The third irony of organizational change is a stoic temperament that accepts and prepares for such eventualities and a tempered romanticism that finds meaning and purpose in the challenge. In contrast to popular stereotyped views of an ironic character as distant and cynical, the classic ironic temperament we describe and advocate is humble, playful, and constructively engaged with the challenges of change.

IRONY 3

In life: In Ancient Greece, Socrates was widely portrayed as possessing such a temperament, a motivated and knowledgeable educator who sought to instruct through feigning ignorance and asking questions.

In leadership: Gandhi, as dramatized in the movie of the same name (played by Ben Kingsley), reprimands his enthusiastic, somewhat violent young supporters when they visit him in his rural commune (*Gandhi*, 1983

1.00.47–1.02.08 mins). He makes the point that when our values are challenged and we perceive injustice, we often lash out ineffectively. We are more concerned to relieve our anger and punish those we see as 'sinners', than we are to actually change things. He emphasizes that he does believe in fighting against oppression but with discipline and strategic precision rather than egocentric knee-jerk acts of violence.

We are using the phrase and idea of ironies of organizational change to direct attention to these issues and bring the traditional *mis-leading* of change into question. To this end, we use the traditional weapons of irony to help shift established mindsets. In this book and our teaching and consulting, we employ popular images, stories, cartoons, movies, and theatre. We use humour, parody, and the insights of popular culture. These help shift us out of our overly rational machine mentality and surface and celebrate the lived experience of change and the pragmatic wisdom of those who can grapple with the real issues it raises.

The ambiguous and uncertain, emotive and personal, fluid and situational nature of the organizational world is often better captured through the aesthetic quality and poetic insights of popular and classic artistic creations than more standard, often plodding and frequently overly analytic cases and textbooks (Guillet de Monthoux & Czarniawska, 2005; Huczynski & Buchanan, 2006; March & Weil, 2005; Rhodes & Westwood, 2008). In addition, the use of humour, parody and irony of all forms to counter dominant overly rational narratives often provides a less threatening, meaningful, visceral and ultimately more engaging and effective way of challenging our conventional (lack of) wisdom (Czarniawska, 2017; Westwood & Rhodes, 2007; Badham & Hafermalz, 2019).

Let us be clear, however. In focusing on narratives, stories and ironic insights, we are not recommending the use of the term irony as a strategic discourse in change management. There are too many misunderstandings and narrow prejudicial uses of this word to do so. We are, however, using the term irony and the insights it provides to help introduce you to a theoretically informed and pragmatically mature approach to handling change – and hopefully excite and inspire you in the process!

A DIFFERENT KIND OF HANDBOOK

The primary purpose of the *Ironies of Organizational Change* is to surface and open up discussions of the change oxymoron and the dangers of mis-leading change. The second is to provide a theoretically informed and practically focused analysis of what can be done about it. We follow the views of Joseph

Schumpeter and Donald Schon in emphasizing the inherent tension in innovation and the inevitability of the mis-leading of change. However, we can dramatically improve how we handle it with the necessary insight, motivation, and discipline. The book provides you with the concepts, illustrations and tools needed to achieve this outcome.

As an introduction to change management and organization theory, *Ironies of Organizational Change* is theoretical, reflective, engaging, and practical. It is written to aid those wishing to achieve greater success or find meaning from studying, teaching or practising managing and leading change. It is based on learnings from delivering leading change programs to experienced executives over a few decades and learning from over 4,000 change initiatives taken by these professionals and guided by the framework, concepts and methods outlined in the book.

Throughout the book, we adopt the stance of the action researcher and the reflective practitioner. Rather than documenting multiple academic approaches or claiming to provide evidence-based laws, we present concepts, heuristics and guidelines to help support reflection and inform judgement. In addition, each chapter challenges established overly rational and naïvely humanistic mythologies of change. In this way, the book offers a down-to-earth, warts-and-all and sociologically informed handbook for the reflective practitioner.

For academics researching and teaching on this topic, the book introduces organizational theories and their relevance for change. It also provides a succinct and accessible overview of established change management theory and practice. These are brought together in an open and generative framework. This is supported by an internet course and website with tailored online videos, readings, exercises, and questionnaires.

For experienced professionals, the book provides a short and accessible introduction to the theory and practice of change management. It contains images, metaphors, illustrations, exercises, guidelines, and tools. These will help you reflect on your change experiences, improve your practice, enhance your career, and look after yourself in the process.

For less-experienced students, the book uses popular images, movies, and personal examples. These help you leverage your own experiences and cultural background in understanding the dynamics and exploring the challenges of change. It is intended to be entertaining as well as instructive. We hope you find it inspiring, informative, and of enduring value rather than an exam-focused textbook.

BOOK STRUCTURE

The book is divided into three main sections. These are described as 'Acts' for three main reasons.

First, change is popularly portrayed as a 'Three Act' Transformational Drama (Tichy & Devanna, 1997) or Transition (Bridges & Bridges, 2016). This idea draws on our common-sense notions of past, present, and future and reflects our cultural assumptions about 'transition rituals'. Anthropologists document these rituals as a sense of 'separating' from the past, passing through an anxious and exciting 'in-between' state, and then 'incorporating' a transition into a new normal (Badham et al., 2012a; Brown, 1998). This over-simplifies a complex reality but identifies some key features of change.

Second, we would be remiss if we failed to draw on such imagery when we challenge conventional wisdom in an introductory text on change theory and practice. We recommend *separating* from past images of change (Act 1: Re-Imagining Change), *guiding* through the anxiety-inducing 'difficult middles' (Act 2: The Cycle of Change), and then *incorporating* a sustainable new sensibility (Act 3: Leadership of Change).

Third, the book concludes that we need to step outside our self-narratives, reflect on how we dramatize change from our perspective, and adopt a lightness of thought, heart, and touch in interpreting and dealing with change.

Describing the main sections of the books as 'Acts' helps to keep all three in mind.

Each Act has book chapters divided into an Introduction, Head (Theory), Heart and Hand (Practice) and Resources. The Head section in each chapter addresses cognition and introduces the theory and overviews the topic. The Heart and Hand section addresses emotion and application and contains corporate cases and creative practice exercises illustrating 'change in action' as well as Change Habit exercises to help break dysfunctional habits and improve our chance of success. Finally, the Resource section includes chapter summaries and recommended further readings to supplement the Head section. A comprehensive list of chapter references can be found at the end of the book.

Act I. Re-imagining Change

The purpose of change management is commonly understood to be one of alignment. This has two parts. First, adapting the culture and structure of the organization to environmental demands. Second, ensuring the efficient and effective execution of the adaptation process. However, underneath this strategic 'rational' surface are deeper and more challenging views of the change problem and what is involved in addressing it. Exploring these issues is the purpose of this first Act.

Chapter 1. The change problem
The now cliched '70% of change projects fail' problem is presented as an evidence-based statistic and used to support new 'best practice' change consul-

tancy services. It opens up a deeper 'change problem', however. This is created by the vicissitudes of human action, the 'dynamic conservatism' of organizations, and the problematic 'bias' towards 'pushing' change. The chapter uses a favourite cliche of overly rational approaches to managing change to open up discussions of the fundamental challenges of influencing change and the ability (and inability) of the historical 'waves' of change management to capture and address these.

Chapter 2. Re-imagining change, re-inventing yourself
The rational image of organizations and how they change is identified as institutionalized mythology, one metaphorical image amongst many. Popular images of the organization as an 'iceberg' and change as a 'rollercoaster' are elaborated as resonant counter-metaphors. They invert rational system imagery and provide accessible and memorable alternative heuristics. The chapter elaborates and reinforces these counter-metaphors in the form of a practical **5M framework**. This framework details the re-imagining of change as an effective cycle and the re-invention of oneself as a leader. The framework is grounded in rational strategic models of the Plan-Do-Check-Act (PDCA) cycle and leadership expertise and roles. Yet it transforms thought and reflection by viewing and presenting these as a cultural process involving the *Mindful Mobilizing* of *Maps*, *Masks* and *Mirrors*.

Act II. Cycle of Change

In contrast to linear views of managing change as the planning and control of an 'N-step' change journey (Collins, 1998), the cycle of change builds on dynamic models of a continuous improvement and experiential learning process, popularly expressed in the PDCA cycle. It re-conceptualizes this in more general terms as an Orientation, Performance and Reflection cycle. The **5M framework** then extends the conceptual boundaries of change management by taking the traditional, mechanistic and task-based PDCA process of Planning, Execution and Evaluation and transforming it into a creative and fluid cultural process of applying *Maps*, donning *Masks* and deploying *Mirrors*.

Chapter 3. Maps and orientation
Building on the metaphor of change as a journey, the traditionally rigid planning of change is represented as an iterative sensemaking and sensegiving *Mapping* process. The 'mapping' metaphor extends the task-focused planning of change. It acknowledges and addresses the abstract, fluid, interpretive and ongoing nature of orienting and re-orienting change. This chapter takes the established tools of Gap Analysis, Force Field Analysis and the Stages of

Change (described as Route Analysis) and stretches and transforms them into key building blocks in a culturally and politically informed 'GPS'.

Chapter 4. Masks and performance

Plans have to be executed, and maps have to be followed. This chapter builds on, extends and transforms the idea of executing change strategies, implementing change plans and following maps. It presents the process and practice as a more or less successful performance in the exercise of influence. The embedded tensions within the performance metaphor point to pragmatic *and* theatrical success. The performance metaphor moves the discussion from executing planned tasks to the discipline of impression and expression management in interactions with others. This is extended into a discussion of the key dimensions of exercising influence. This involves 'controlling' people and events and addressing the paradoxes involved and donning the appropriate *Masks* in effectively undertaking these activities.

Chapter 5. Mirrors and reflection

For adherents to a rational change management model, evaluation and monitoring suggest a large degree of objectivity, measurement, and control. In this chapter, what constitutes adequate reflection is extended and expanded. It uses the metaphor of *Mirrors* to capture the importance of reflection yet extend it into recognizing the selective and partial nature of all 'mirrors'. This includes the challenge of overcoming political and cultural biases to 'see what one wants to see'. By shifting the discussion from evidence-based evaluation to the mindful use of mirrors, the chapter explores the challenge of being agile and adaptive in creating and using multiple mirrors, relevant measures, and creating trustworthy learning spaces.

Intermission

In between Acts II and III is a short intermission where you are introduced to the drama of *Jamie's School Dinners*. It illustrates the concepts covered and allows you to apply them to an emotional and chaotic case of change. The Intermission 'kick starts' a reflective application of the change mapping tools in an entertaining format. The Resource Guide at the back of the book provides a comprehensive review of key concepts and the relevant literature to deepen your understanding of mapping out the change terrain. It includes a thorough examination of the individual and organizational conditions that create readiness and resistance to change.

Act III. Leadership of Change

Effective cycles of change have to be implemented, so influence has to be exerted to overcome obstacles and realize opportunities for success. This section addresses this issue by extending and deepening the understanding of 'leadership'. The common contrast between 'management' and 'leadership' raises important issues. Yet, it often operates within a restricted strategic-rational model of what this involves. In this section, the scope and depth of leadership are explored. The **5M framework** extends discussion beyond change knowledge and formal roles and onto a *Mindful* appreciation of the complexities and barriers to change and the ability to *Mobilize* energy and resources to address them.

Chapter 6. Knowing–doing gaps

This chapter shifts and extends the discussion of management and leadership. It expands discussions of the knowledge and roles required of transformational leaders into the capacity to accept and grapple with inherent knowing–doing gaps in our ability to influence change. Practice, leadership and power gaps are identified. Being *Mindful* and effectively *Mobilizing* are explored as essential qualities in attempts to reduce or 'plug' these gaps.

Chapter 7. Paradoxes of change

This chapter captures and explores the three central tensions we confront in our attempt to think and act rationally in leading change. These are captured and described as paradoxes of rationality, performance and meaning. Next, we explore the leadership challenge in working with and through these embedded contradictions. This involves being *Mindful* and *Mobilizing* energy and resources in resolving and living with them.

Chapter 8. Ironies of change

The ironies of organizational change challenge change leaders to find and communicate meaning in the change enterprise. This chapter identifies and challenges a 'deficit thinking' approach to this problem. As an alternative, it advocates an ironic sensibility as a positive, resilient, and seriously playful 'strength-based' approach to change. This sensibility draws on and combines long and well-established insights into irony as a perspective, a performance, and a temperament. It is an intelligent and proactive stance that resonates deeply with leaders and followers. It does so through its *Mindful* attention to the genuine uncertainties and dangers of change and its generative *Mobilization* of energy and support to find and create meaning in the enterprise.

Epilogue

The Epilogue recommends what could be termed a desirable lightness of becoming in bringing together the re-imagining of change, the creation of a generative change cycle, and the effective and meaningful leadership of change. Lightness of thought, heart and touch are identified as key features of a desirable and bearable lightness of being in living with the gaps, paradoxes, and ironies of change.

Resource Guide: Force Field Analysis – A Comprehensive Guide to Forces, Fields and Analyses

We covered many key issues concerning the nature of change, drivers of change, sources of readiness and resistance in Act 1 and Act 2 Ch.3 Mapping Change. These issues and how to map them out were illustrated in the Intermission using the case of *Jamie's School Dinners*. For accessibility, this initial discussion did not introduce you nor try and capture the wide range of insights and discussions in the now voluminous change literature. The role of this Resource Guide is to provide you with an essential, comprehensive and yet accessible supplement. It covers the complex 'field' of change, the 'forces' within them, the individual and organizational factors that foster 'readiness' or create 'resistance' to change, and what type of 'analysis' is required. It does so in a way that will help you improve how you map out change, reflect on the assumptions you have made and evaluate progress.

* ON THE 'CHANGE HABITS'

We're all creatures of habit. Some habits are more easily changed than others, but we believe that even an old dog can learn new tricks. We're our own masters of change, and in each of the book chapters, you'll be introduced to new habits to put into practice. Each of the eight chapters introduces you to change habits or ideas in mantras to keep in mind when managing and leading change – to create a productive and effective change cycle.

We'll introduce you to two re-imagining change habits to prepare you for change, three cycles of change habits to guide you during change, and three re-inventing yourself habits to help develop your leading change capabilities.

The two re-imagining change habits are to **expect the expected** *and* **flip the iceberg***. These are 'jolts' and reminders to create a change mindset.*

The three cycles of change habits are to **be prepared***,* **play the part** *and* **be reflective***. These will assist you in the productive use of maps, masks and* *mirrors in the change process.*

*The re-inventing yourself habits are **mind the gap**, **work through tension**, and **keep steady**. These enhance your awareness of what is required to be effective and find meaning in leading change.*

*We've put all the habits on the access of an asterisk, forming what we call the Asterisk of Change. This little star derives its name from an Ancient Greek scholar who used similar characters **asteriskos** when proofreading Homeric poetry to mark the duplicated lines. The asterisk evolved, but its meaning as a symbol used to correct defects, and now highlight bullet points remain.*

The asterisk can be found above the eight on your keyboards [*] and can be used as an ongoing reminder of the Change Habits. These habits will help you correct the defects of the sloped playing field and improve the odds of getting things done and achieving your goals.

So, whether you're an experienced manager or early on in your career, we hope you'll work on applying these to your work and even daily life. Repetition is the key to learning and making them your own. Don't forget to reward yourself when you adopt them successfully. Recognize them and celebrate each win.

ACT I

RE-IMAGINING CHANGE

INTRODUCTION

Act I (Chapters 1 and 2) of this book is an exercise in *Imaginization* (Morgan, 1997). It is an invitation for the reader to re-imagine change, to *picture* organizational change and its management in a new way. It is an invitation to leave behind a drab and grey, one-dimensional outlook on organizations as systems and ourselves as functionaries, and to picture them (and us) as a smorgasbord of human creativity, with equal doses of idiocy and ingenuity. The outlook is far more fun, far more delightful and, somewhat ironically, far more practical. Without such a fundamental re-imagination of change, change management and change managers will fail to address the significant challenges of change or make the most of the opportunities it provides.

The challenge is a significant one. You see, we live in the shadow of a rational myth of how organizations operate and transform. As a result, management academics, gurus, consultants, and media analysts peddle a rational model of organizational life that is as inaccurate as it is widespread. It has become our reality and is taken for granted. It is the cultural air we breathe, but it is not impermeable. As the renowned sociologist Pitirim Sorokin once noted, a fish only notices the water it swims in when it finds itself on dry land. In many mundane day-to-day ways and through more or less frequent dramatic crises, we feel like a 'fish out of water'.

We confront 'life's little ironies', for example, when our plans go awry, non-sense rules, incompetence triumphs, or self-interest wins over common sense and decency. 'How can this be?' we ask ourselves. More dramatically, perhaps, we see our career going in directions out of our control, misdirected large-scale strategic initiatives foundering or abandoned, and a churnover of Fortune 500 companies as success breeds rigidity and complacency. We hope and expect people to be rational or behave rationally, that organizations will and should effectively pursue their strategic objectives, and that all our lives will progress in an orderly fashion. So, when these events occur, they inevitably raise the question: 'What does this all mean?'

From within our dominant rational world view, this is a major challenge of re-interpretation. In a fundamental sense, we live in organizational worlds that we imagine and construct, although we may not do so as we please or in ways we choose. We do not choose the established orthodox images, but we have to live with their implications. The rational myth dominates the mythology around how modern organizations operate and change. In traditional societies and organizations, custom and religious faith provide guidance and legitimation. In the modern era, the rational myth provides guidance and legitimation that rules and leaders should be followed because they are rational and strategic in thought and action. To question this myth strikes at the heart of how modern organizations and the people within them formally and publicly understand themselves and legitimate what they do and how they behave.

This myth, however, like all others, is inevitably partial. However, it dominates and shapes our beliefs, hopes and expectations. It also, like all perspectives, has built ways of avoiding, silencing, or encouraging polite discretion in not pointing out its limitations (Goffman, [1959] 2022; Meyer & Rowan, 1977; Morgan, 2006). It ignores, avoids, or represses the existence of routine, systemic and predictable irrationalities in organizational change.

Let's explore further how this works.

The rational myth legitimates and expects change to be conducted by:

- *rational actors* involved in
- *rational decision-making* in
- *strategically rational* enterprises.

Organizational structures, strategies and processes are expected to efficiently and effectively pursue the organization's strategic goals, survival, and growth. However, in theory and practice, these expectations are often shattered.

- Individuals are 'boundedly rational' (Simon, 1976) and predictably irrational (Ariely, 2009).
- Decision-making is frequently chaotic, symbolic, and political (March, 1994).
- Structures and strategies are legitimated as strategically rational. Yet they are often framed and produced in ways that are fragmented rather than aligned, symbolic rather than operationally effective (Bromley & Powell, 2012; Dick, 2015; Meyer & Rowan, 1977).

Yet, despite such evidence and experiences, we cannot address them effectively. This is because the rational myth dominates our 'taken-for-granted' view of organizations and how we can and should act within them. Its assumptions appear 'so reasonable, so much a part of the ideology of how management is practised, that most people take them virtually for granted' (Pfeffer & Salancik, 1977, p.17). It ensures we routinely expect and act on the expectation that organizations have:

- unambiguous performance criteria,
- objective information available about the environments they are in and the type of structures best suited for those environments,
- tight links to their environments, so the best designs will survive, and
- design choices and implementation processes that can be rationally planned and controlled.

Re-imagining change requires challenging this mythology at its core. But without underestimating its power and influence. It means being able to uncover and address:

- the ambiguity of and conflicts over performance criteria,
- the lack of objective data,
- the loosely coupled nature of organizations, and
- how to influence change when conditions do not allow for rational planning and control.

...and all the while, acknowledging the expectations of others, and indeed ourselves, that this enterprise can, will and should be rational!

However, re-imagination extends *even* deeper. Re-imagining change to overcome the limitations of the rational myth extends more personally and into our intimate lives. It requires re-inventing our identities and ourselves. When looking to make sense of the world, we interpret the situation we are in, the people we are and what people like us should do in such situations (Badham, 2017; March & Olsen, 2009). In this way, the rational myth encourages us to expect:

- change situations will involve rational actors in the pursuit of strategic goals,
- we are rational actors in this context, and
- we should use rational methods to plan, control actions and achieve strategic outcomes.

Yet what we encounter and experience is often:

- change situations in which misunderstanding, conflict, chaos and emotion are rife,
- we are restricted in our understanding, blinkered by established identities and biased by self-interest, and
- we require the creativity, reflexivity, and resilience necessary to influence ourselves and others in such conditions.

Re-inventing ourselves involves thinking through, acting within and finding meaning in a change enterprise that takes place in such conditions. This includes recognizing the inadequate and outdated images of our traditional identities as managers. It means transcending the view of ourselves as more or less well-fitted, well-oiled and high-performing cogs in a machine or expert and dedicated therapists integrating people into a purposeful living human system.

Act I provides you with a set of creative and playful images designed to support you in becoming a creative and reflective leader of change. It involves:

- Re-interpreting and deepening your understanding of the change problem and what is required to 'pull' rather than 'push' change in recognition of what is involved.
- Re-imagining organizations and how they change using resonant metaphors such as the 'iceberg' and the 'rollercoaster' to build on yet transcend traditional systems views.
- Re-inventing yourself as a mindful leader of change, sensitive to the barriers of change, and capable of mobilizing yourself and others to address the challenges.

1. The change problem

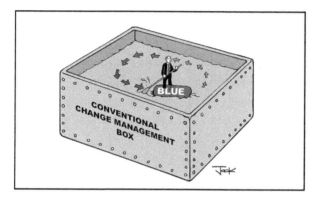

We can't solve a problem with the same type of thinking that we used in creating it.
(Albert Einstein)

Einstein was onto something! Traditional approaches to change management try to solve the problem of change by using the same tools that created the problem in the first place. They provide you with designs to implement designs and strategies for executing strategies. In *Act I: Re-Imagining Change*, you will discover the importance of stepping outside the box of conventional change management, colour in the white spaces in the organization chart, and navigate the messy and choppy waters of the change journey. In this chapter, you will critically analyse the nature and origins of the failure rate of change initiatives, examine how and why modern organizations systematically mis-lead change and learn what an alternative approach involves.

Learning objectives

Head (theory)

1.0 Introduction

1.1 On the surface

1.2 The deeper problem

1.3 Solutions that fail us, solutions that don't

1.4 Chapter summary

Heart and hand (practice)

1.5 Cases and exercises

Resources

LEARNING OBJECTIVES

- Examine conventional views of how the change problem is defined in the modern organization, its nature, cause, and solutions.
- Question and debate failure rates of organizational change initiatives and their systemic causes.
- Analyse and evaluate conventional change management approaches and how to build on their contributions.

HEAD (THEORY)

1.0   INTRODUCTION

There's a nagging reality in change management. And that is the knowledge that organizations do not manage change well. Despite all the rhetoric, attention and money that goes into managing change, the problem still remains. And there is no indication it's getting any better. To explore our options, let's view the choices in terms of taking a 'Blue Pill' or a 'Red Pill'. The idea of two pills comes *The Matrix* and is repeated in *The Matrix Resurrections*. In the *Pill Scene* from the earlier classic *The Matrix* (1999, 25.40–29.52 mins), the rebel leader Morpheus offers the hero Neo a choice between a Blue Pill and a Red Pill.

If he takes the Blue Pill, he'll wake up in his bed as he has always done. He'll stay in his comfort zone and continue his everyday life. But if he takes the Red Pill, he'll get to go beneath the surface and explore his nagging doubts. To paraphrase Morpheus, it means exploring how deep the illusions of what we take to be 'reality' go and uncover the 'wonders' that lie beneath – referring to Lewis Carroll's novel *Alice in Wonderland* (also see Heracleous & Bartunek, 2021; McCabe, 2016). So, the Red Pill promises a journey of discovery and finding truths. In this spirit, there are 'Blue Pill and Red Pill' approaches to change management.

The Blue Pill applies, and repeats established mantras – create readiness, craft a vision, build a coalition, and so on. If you do this, you cover yourself. No need to worry if the mantras don't appear to work. If the definition of insanity is continuing to do the same thing, and expecting a different outcome, then those who take the 'Blue Pill' may be somewhat insane! In contrast, a Red Pill approach recognizes and tackles the problem. It accepts the realities of a systematic *mis-leadership of change* and sets out to find its origins and see what can be done.

As the character Bugs observes in the *Red Pill/Blue Pill Scene* in *The Matrix Resurrections* (11.12–12.03 mins), the world is clearly more complex than such binary Blue Pill/Red Pill oppositions suggest. Most importantly, there is a sense in which taking the Red Pill allows us to see what, in a sense, we knew all along but did not pay attention to!

In this chapter, we'll examine what the change problem involves. We'll explore the failure rates of change initiatives and their systemic causes. Finally, we'll identify solutions and strategies that don't work and find others that do.

Are you ready for your Red Pill?

1.1   ON THE SURFACE

If you are still reading, you have taken the Red Pill! Congratulations.

Now let's look at that irritating 'splinter' in your mind referred to in *The Matrix*. This is the nagging awareness that all is not as it seems, or should be, in the land of change management. Think about yourself. In your own life, how many of your dreams, goals and New Year's Resolutions do you actually manage to bring about? How often do you tell yourself and others you are serious about projects you set yourself? But you know deep down you won't really follow them through! Author Paul Gibbons (2015) tells the story of himself as a student working in a cancer research laboratory. Paul would compile evidence on the effect of cigarette smoke on cancer in mice and then go out to the car park to have a cigarette. Unfortunately, he had a one-pack-a-day Marlboro habit. Welcome to the human race!

Why would we expect organizations to be different? Naturally, they are not. Organizations have visions they do not realize, strategies they do not execute, and reforms they do not deliver. Cynicism and distrust inevitably follow. This is not new. A famous quotation attributed to the Roman Gaius Petronius from the first century AD observed:

> We trained hard, but it seemed that every time we were beginning to form up into teams, we would be reorganised. I was to learn later in life that we tend to meet any new situation by reorganising; and a wonderful method it can be for creating the illusion of progress while producing confusion, inefficiency, and demoralisation.

Charlton Ogburn actually wrote this in 1957, but it is still 60 years old! It captures a long-established feature of organizational life! To go back to the individual, Richard's son once wrote to him saying, '*Dad, I know what you are – a "tids-optimist"*.' Richard looked it up, and it meant someone overly optimistic about how much they can fit into the time they have available! The Nobel Prize-winning behavioural scientist Daniel Kahneman (2011, p.215) highlighted the dangers of this optimism bias as it pervades individual and organizational life. We are mis-led, to our cost, by believing '*the world is more benign than it really is, our own attributes are more favourable than they truly are, and the goals we adopt are more achievable than they are likely to be*'. With projects, this overly optimistic bias was first identified by Daniel Kahneman and Amos Tversky (1982). While this bias may positively encourage us to embark upon enterprises and persist, it can also cause widespread error and incredible frustration.

At a fundamental human level, this *is* the change problem. There's a gap between what we wish and aspire to and what we *actually* achieve. There are obvious reasons for this. Yet, we persist and collude in avoiding or denying the gap. We mis-lead ourselves and others by talking and acting as if it isn't there. It is a recipe for disaster! Success requires taking the Red Pill, owning the gap and getting on with the real job.

Blue Pill change management, as promoted by global change gurus and consultants, has an answer to the problem, and one it hopes will re-assure us. Their 'MO' (or *modus operandi*) is to shock us with failure stories and then relieve us with packaged solutions and stories of success. The shock is created by survey after survey indicating '70% of change programs fail'.

Between 2006 and 2017, for example, McKinsey & Company – one of the world's most prestigious management consultancies – surveyed in total over 10,000 managers confirming the persistent result: two-thirds of change initiatives fail to achieve moderate or high-performance outcomes (Ghislanzoni et al., 2010; Isern & Pung, 2007; Isern et al., 2009; Jacquemont et al., 2015;

Keller et al., 2010; Lindsay et al., 2018; Meaney & Pung, 2008; Vinson et al., 2006).

Drawing on cases of the '30% that succeed', they provide a 'new and improved' set of principles, methods, and tools. We are assured that applying these will guarantee our organization is transformed into one of the chosen few! But how convincing is this, really? Given decades of using change management techniques, with little evidence of improved outcomes, how far are we prepared to trust the latest upgrade (Barends et al., 2014; Hughes, 2011)? If we go below the surface, where does a deeper insight into the problem take us? What does taking the 'Red Pill' involve? Well, it begins with noticing the 'splinter'.

In 2017, Prosci consultants documented that over 70% of large companies used structured change methodologies, down from 80% in 2013, yet still very high (Prosci, 2019). In the same year, the Boston Consulting Group (BCG) estimated that large companies spent $10 billion on change consultants in the US alone, and clearly, much more is spent on the change projects themselves (Tollmann et al., 2017). Yet, despite this spread of 'change management', PricewaterhouseCoopers, Bain and Company, BCG, and others have confirmed McKinsey's survey results: the majority of change programs are still seen as failing to deliver the goods (Aguirre et al., 2013; Bain, 2018; Fleming & Colizzi, 2017; Litre et al., 2018)! Disengagement, cynicism and distrust remain, and many indicators of workplace stress are on the rise!

Does this not indicate a major problem? Taking the 'Red Pill', and confronting this situation head-on, opens up a world of opportunity. You move out of a world of denial, delusion, and cover-up. You enter a world of acceptance, insight, and potential. 'Life', as the saying goes, 'wasn't meant to be easy'. But it can be creative, exciting and fun. When you learn to 'expect the expected', you can be both genuine and successful.

1.2   THE DEEPER PROBLEM

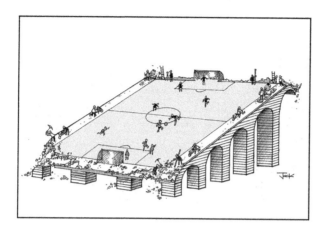

Cricket is one of the most popular sports in the world. Its 'home' is the Lord's Cricket Ground at St Johns Wood in London. Lord's is famous for its sloping outfield – the Lord's Slope! The southwest side of the ground is almost two and a half metres lower than the northwest side. This causes a huge deviation to the ball when bowling.

The ethics of fairness in sports demands a 'level playing field'. Yet, despite many controversies at Lord's, the slope remains – as in life. However, some batsmen have successfully adapted. When change programs appear to fail, the knee-jerk response is to blame individuals or hope better tools will solve the problem. But what if the cause lies deeper? What if we're on a sloped field, facing a *Lord's Slope*?

In the 1960s, American political scientist Eric Schattschneider (1975) introduced the idea that many organizations have a 'mobilization of bias'. It's evident in widespread institutional discrimination against women and minorities. However, one of the deeply embedded biases organizations have is against significant change. Radical change is routinely held back by what has been described as 'dynamic conservatism', 'structural inertia' or reacting against the losses from 'creative destruction'. We like to think of ourselves as innovative and progressive. We might even dedicate ourselves seriously to the task. Yet, we're often reluctant to change what we're used to. British author G.K. Chesterton summed it up nicely, 'New roads, new ruts'. And we all know what getting stuck in a rut feels like.

It is created by two sets of obstacles:

1. What gets us into a rut are entrenched ideas, values and interests.
2. What keeps us from getting out of it are the risks and uncertainties!

Why? Because change challenges threaten and even destroy much of what exists! Its complex, uncertain and unpredictable nature also makes it inherently dangerous. If you think about it, this is common knowledge. So, what stops us from adequately considering such issues and dedicating enough time and resources to addressing them?

The answer lies in four main biases:

1. for **the head** – over the heart and the hand
2. for **design** – over implementing
3. for **strategizing** – over executing
4. for **reform** – over results.

Let's go through each one briefly.

First, **head bias**. Our education system is biased towards science, technology and mathematics. It also places intellectual skills and abilities over practical knowledge and experience (Robinson, 2011). Around the world, STEM education (science, technology, engineering and maths) is held in higher regard than arts or language. Practical trade and vocational education are deemed a lower form of training than education at high school and university.

Our organizations reflect this bias towards the head in:

*   how they define and reward achievement,
*   what they focus on, and
*   the language they use to describe what they do.

Underlying this bias is a view of organizations as completing tasks and aligning functions. Not people in search of meaning. Organizations are described or treated as machines and organisms – to the relative neglect of culture and politics (McCabe, 2016; Morgan, 2006). Despite any rhetoric of prioritizing people and purpose, our deep-seated prejudices and practices ensure we do not do so.

Second, **design bias**. Across all professions, attention, status and rewards go to creativity and ingenuity in design – NOT practical knowledge or persistence in getting it done (Badham, 2000). Politics reinforce it. In modern organizations, those responsible for advising or implementing designs have less status, power and voice.

As a result (Clegg, 1993; Perrow, 1983):

- design gets priority over maintenance,
- creating technologies and systems has priority over how to operate them, and
- development has priority over implementation.

Third, **strategy bias**. There's a widely recognized phenomenon in strategy known as the 'strategy gap'. It's the difference between the number and range of strategies developed and those that are actually realized (Martin, 2010; Sull et al., 2015). Excelling in strategy execution is routinely under-rated as compared to strategy development.

It is entrenched in three standard practices (Mankins, 2017):

- The responsibility for developing strategy lies with senior managers. Responsibility for executing it goes to lower or middle managers.
- Lengthy, siloed and sequential 'Plan–Do' processes are favoured over rapid iterative 'Plan–Do/Refine–Do' cycles.
- Hierarchical strategy execution is the focus. Not enough attention is paid to ensure horizontal cooperation and impact.

Fourth, **reform bias** (Brunsson, 2009; Buchanan & Badham, 2020; March & Olsen, 1983). Organizations are under immense and constant pressure to improve their performance and to show they are doing this by initiating reforms. It's expected and even demanded by customers, clients and stakeholders.

The pressures this bias creates have predictable outcomes:

- talk is favoured over action,
- developing and initiating reforms gets more attention than achieving real results,
- serious program evaluation is routinely avoided or postponed, and when this occurs
- finding excuses, allocating blame and 'clearing up' gets more time than properly preparing in the first place.

These biases are endemic in modern organizations. If change managers do not acknowledge and creatively respond to the sloped playing field they create, then the same disappointing results are predictable. Creating change programs without considering the Lord's Slope is a recipe for frustration and disaster. Wisdom begins when we learn to live with what cannot be changed and focus on what we can.

Here's an idea:
Smile when you face these conditions. Then, whisper quietly to yourself and your team, 'Lord's Slope', and get on with the actual job.

1.3   SOLUTIONS THAT FAIL US, SOLUTIONS THAT DON'T

The American author and motivational speaker Jim Rohn said:

> *We must all suffer from one of two pains: the pain of discipline or the pain of regret. The difference is discipline weighs ounces while regret weighs tons.*

How do we discipline ourselves in change and travel light, with little to no regrets?! Change management is often presented as a discipline, a body of knowledge, and a set of protocols to be managed by an expert change agent. We need to understand this discipline. Those not aware of history often unintentionally repeat it, warts and all. But, we need to use it, not be trapped by it. Thus, there is a need for discipline in applying the discipline of change management.

Let's begin by going back to the 1930s and 40s when the German-Jewish émigré Kurt Lewin planted the seeds of what is now called change management (Burnes & Bargal, 2017; Lewin, 1947b). Many of his insights are now firmly embedded in the discipline, yet at the time, they ran counter to scientific management ethos. They also ran up against the biases that slope the playing field of change.

Underlying Lewin's extensive body of work, four main sets of insights and recommendations have shaped the field of change management (for a similar view, see Burnes, 2004b):

1. To understand the whole field
2. To prepare, support and reinforce change
3. To pull rather than push change
4. To learn in action.

Let's briefly go through each one in turn:

1. Understand the Whole Field

Change is often viewed as a technical or structural solution to a performance problem. But if you're to find the real source of the problem and create valuable solutions, you'll need to go below the surface. Leonardo da Vinci once said, *'everything connects to everything else'*. What may appear to be a structural or technical challenge on the surface is often either a cultural or political issue or intertwined with such issues.

2. Prepare, Support and Reinforce Change

Momentum to create, maintain and sustain change requires paying attention to meaning and motivation. It involves destabilizing established ideas, interests and habits. It also requires transitioning people through interim states that are anxious and exciting, a source of loss and gain. Finally, it also demands action to prevent slipping back by embedding change in a new set of norms and habits.

3. Pull Rather than Push Change

Similar to interactions in a physical force field, if you 'push' such changes upon the existing field of forces, you will likely get an 'equal and opposite reaction' against it. Traditional management seeks to overcome resistance by more or less 'pushing' its agenda. Yet, a more effective way is to create readiness by working with people and using forces within the field for 'pulling' change.

4. Learn in Action

Former US Secretary of State for Defense Donald Rumsfeld once said change includes both 'known unknowns' and 'unknown unknowns'. There are and will be uncertainties and differences, so we need to adapt and learn as we go. This is what Lewin meant by 'action research'.

Each of these insights and recommendations by Lewin has been taken up and developed within the discipline of change management.

As you can see in Figure 1.1 *The Tree of Change Management,* Lewin's work was picked up by organizational development or 'OD' consultants in the 1960s and 70s (Burnes & Cooke, 2012) who:

- addressed the challenges of group dynamics,
- highlighted the value of participative leadership, and
- provided the expert consultant with a set of 'process' tools and methods.

The 1980s and 90s added two new key elements (Caldwell, 2003):

- principles and practices for entrepreneurial change agents and transformational leaders, inspirational, energizing and powerful, and
- a greater understanding of strategic transformation and different corporate leadership styles, including handling emergence and conflict.

The early twenty-first century added four additional sets of insights from the following:

1.   Complexity and Process Theory

Highlights the importance of uncertainty, fluidity and context. It advises greater experimentation and improvisation.

2.   Behavioural Theory

Identifies the 'predictable irrationality' of people in organizations. It provides advice on how to use this understanding as a basis of influence.

3.   Distributed Leadership

Focuses on and emphasizes the significance of informal as well as formal leadership and its multi-levelled and relational nature. It draws on this to recommend a less formal and less 'heroic' view of change agency.

4.   Drama, Discourse and Storytelling

Identifies the interpretive, narrative and performative dimensions of change. It explores and advises on the role of translation, drama and storytelling.

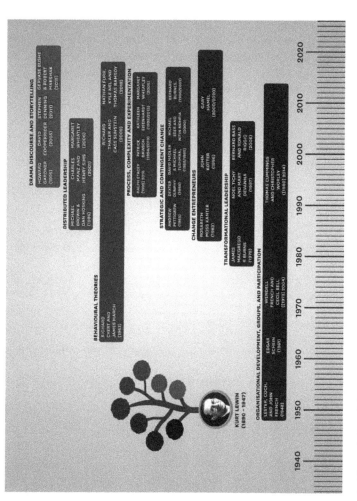

Source: Reproduced with permission of the authors and Edward Elgar in the Coursera/Macquarie University online course *Leading Transformations. Manage Change.*

Figure 1.1 Tree of change management

(For examples see: Bartunek & Jones, 2017; Burnes, 1996, 2004a; Bushe & Marshak, 2015; Stouten et al., 2018.)

All of these developments are now intertwined and inform the theory and practice of change management academics, consultants and practitioners (Szabla et al., 2017).

As inheritors of Lewin's legacy, however, the original four principles have been pushed in two directions. On the one hand, they have been used to advocate more expert system-based views of leading change. On the other hand, they have informed more interpretive culture-based approaches (Bushe & Marshak, 2015; Hughes, 2019).

The left-hand column of Figure 1.2 outlines the more systems-based approach:

- provides expertise on unfreezing, moving and refreezing change,
- highlights the role of heroic formal change agents, and
- advocates an agile, re-engineering approach to achieving change in turbulent environments.

The right-hand column outlines the more culture-based approach:

- provides advice on preparing, supporting and reinforcing transitions,
- highlights the importance of re-interpretation, translation and distributed agency, and
- advocates an adaptive approach to meaningful transition in uncertain and emerging situations.

Both approaches have upsides and downsides.

- Expert system views resonate with many managers but can be mechanistic and formulaic.
- Interpretive culture-based views give meaning and appeal to many creative leaders, yet they can be fluffy and impractical.

1.4   CHAPTER SUMMARY

In *Chapter 1, The Change Problem*, you have learned:

1.1   On the Surface

- Individuals and organizations have a shared change problem: we aspire to more than we achieve. We then avoid or deny this to be the case.

Source: Reproduced with permission of the authors and Edward Elgar in the Coursera/Macquarie University online course *Leading Transformations. Manage Change.*

Figure 1.2 *The Discipline of Change Management diagram summarizes these differences*

- The change problem is packaged up by many change management consultants as a 70% failure rate that can be solved by applying the latest models
  and techniques.
- The problem lies deeper than this, and so does the solution. Finding out
  what this involves is where we go next.

1.2   The Deeper Problem

- Change management does not take place on a level playing field.
- There are four significant biases or causes of the Lord's Slope (head,
  design, strategy and reform).
- Effective approaches to change management accept the slope is there and
  adapt to it.

1.3   Solutions that Fail Us, Solutions that Don't

- Kurt Lewin established the discipline of change management by planting
  four seeds: (1) understand the whole field; (2) prepare, support, and reinforce change; (3) pull rather than push change; and (4) learn in action.
- The *Tree of Change Management* captures how these seeds have been
  nourished and developed within different branches of change management.
- The *Discipline of Change Management* spans more systems-based and
  more culture-based approaches to leading change.

HEART AND HAND (PRACTICE)

1.5   CASES AND EXERCISES

1.5.1   Ripples from the Zambezi

In his books and talks on international aid and enterprise development, Ernesto
Sirolli (2012, 2015) introduces us to a fun and creative variant of what has been
described as a 'positive deviance' approach to achieving behavioural change in
communities (Pascale et al., 2010). The approach is based on bringing about
change by seeking out and supporting 'outlier' ideas, practices and advocates
already present in communities (see also Abrahamson, 2004).

Sirolli argues that international aid agencies often impose inappropriate
externally defined views of what development should occur and fail to get
the buy-in and support needed from champions inside the community. In this

playful 'warm-up' case, we use Sirolli's anecdotes to illustrate and explore the meaning of a 'Red Pill' approach to change management in our lives.

Case material

Kogod, T. (2021). The Matrix Resurrections reveals the Red Pill's secret truth. 31 December 2021. https://www.cbr.com/matrix-4-revealred-pills-true-meaning/ (accessed 21 July 2022)

Sirolli, E. (2012). *Want to help someone? Shut up and listen!* TED Talk (YouTube) (27 November). https://www.youtube.com/watch?v=chXsLtHqfdM (accessed 30 May 2022)

Sirolli, E. (2015). *The new Victorians the millennial revolution* (21 August). https://www.youtube.com/watch?v=I3YbwLhOWLA (accessed 23 May 2022)

The Matrix (Directors: Wachowski, L. & L.) (1999). *The Matrix – tumbling down the rabbit hole*. 2 April 2009. https://www.youtube.com/watch?v=TbYirSi08m4 (accessed 30 May 2022)

The Matrix Resurrections (Director: Wachowski, L.) (2021). Red Pill Blue Pill scene (11.12–12.03).

Task 1

Watch Sirolli's first TED Talk (2012), in which he tells the story about an Italian NGO teaching Zambians to grow food. Then, consider what you know about initiatives to bring about internal change in modern organizations, and address three questions:

1. How do Sirolli's (2012) stories capture how and why managers often 'push' change?
2. What are the problems this 'push' creates?
3. Why is it desirable to 'pull change' by 'asking them'?

Task 2

Watch the first 3.5 minutes of Sirolli's second talk (2015) and consider these issues:

1. Why do you think Sirolli's first case of international aid led to people 'coming out of the closet' and 'confessing', in Dilbertian style, about their own stupidities and those of the organizations they work for?
2. What view of the world underlies Sirolli's humorous anecdotes about individual and collective folly? If we believe in the possibility that 'Stonehenge was an International Aid Project!', what does this say about how organizations operate? What does it mean to look back at projects and appreciate that 'At least we fed the hippos!'?

Ernesto Sirolli initially intended his book *Ripples from the Zambezi* (1999) to be titled something like 'The Butterfly Effect' to capture the somewhat chaotic, unintended and creatively open effects of projects in complex environments. However, his talented graphic artist, Roland Butcher, pushed him into using an alternative metaphor in the title and cover page to capture the same idea – a hippos-in-the-Zambezi version of the unending ripples created by throwing a stone into a pond. It aligns very nicely with his famous story of the tomato-eating hippos.

If the world is not as sensible and predictable as we are often led to believe, what does this say about the nature and importance of how we motivate ourselves and others? How do we learn to travel light and surf on the waves of irrationality and unpredictability?

Task 3

Watch the clip '*Down the Rabbit Hole* – from the Matrix'. It dramatizes the choice between 'Red Pill' and 'Blue Pill' approaches to life (and, in our case, 'change'). Also, watch the updated reference in *Matrix Insurrections* and the explanation by Kogod (2021).

Discuss the degree to which how Sirolli tells his stories reflects his specific form of 'Red Pill' approach. Is there also a sense in which our laughter reflects what we already implicitly know about how institutions operate? After discussing the 'Red Pill' approach implicit in Sirolli's anecdotes and those who responded, try out the new world view in *Habit 1: Expect the Expected*.

Further material

Sirolli, E. (1999). *Ripples from the Zambezi*. Gabriola Island, BC: New Society Publishers.

1.5.2   The 70% Failure Debate

The claim '70% of change projects fail' has become an urban legend and a controversial statistic. In this exercise, we focus less on the accuracy of the statement and more on what the debate reveals about how we approach change.

Case material

Barends, E., Janssen, B., ten Have, W., & ten Have, S. (2014). Effects of change interventions: What kind of evidence do we really have? *Journal of Applied Behavioral Science, 50*(1), 5–27.

Frahm, J. (2016). Of myth busting, babies and bathwater. *Conversations of Change* (1 May), 1–11. https://conversationsofchange.com.au/of-myth-busting-babies-and-bathwater (accessed 30 May 2022)

Frahm, J. (2017). *Conversations of Change: A Guide to Implementing Workplace Change*. Melbourne: Jennifer Frahm Collaborations.

Hughes, M. (2011). Do 70 per cent of all organizational change initiatives really fail? *Journal of Change Management, 11*(4), 451–464.

Leith, J. M. (2017). *'70% of organizational change initiatives fail' – how the myth evolved.* http://jackmartinleith.com/70-percent-organizational-change-initi (accessed 30 May 2022)

Task 1

Reflect on what 'the controversy' reveals? Different change management 'experts' support, dismiss or call for a more nuanced account of high failure rates. In what ways do you think the perspectives of consultants, academics and others reflect their different vested interests and professional environments? What insights do they provide, and what blinkers do they impose? Do you find yourself getting irritated with any of these views? If so, what does this say about your approach to valuable knowledge about change?

Task 2

If the 70% statistic is correct, you are 2.5 times more likely to survive Russian Roulette unscathed than a change program! The Russian Roulette Myth is what we are dealing with here, and we have a choice. As outlined in Frahm's (2016) blog and subsequent book on *Conversations of Change* (2017), we can become 'myth debunkers', preoccupied with the evidence base (Barends et al., 2014) or spend our time understanding and using this myth as an archetypal story and warning. For this exercise, think through the second approach. The idiomatic expression of 'throwing out the baby with the bathwater' (losing any gains by going too far) was used by Frahm (2016) to describe the dilemma. What valuable baby should you cherish and further develop from the '70%' debate? What is the 'bathwater' in the '70%' debate that it is desirable to show up, criticize and avoid? And why?

1.5.3   Nudging and Predictable Irrationality

Over the last few years, businesses have begun to consider the insights of behavioural economics on the predictable irrationality of those who work in organizations and consume their products. McKinsey's and others recommend establishing 'Behavioural Insight Units' in organizations to 'nudge' people's behaviour (Buchanan & Badham, 2020).

Case material
Ariely, Dan. (2008). *Are we in control of our own decisions?* US: Ted Talks. https://www.youtube.com/watch?v=9X68dm92HVI (accessed 30 May 2022)
Bhattacharjee, D., Gilson, K., & Yeon, H. (2016). Putting behavioral psychology to work to improve the customer experience. *McKinsey & Co* (March). https://www.mckinsey.com/business-functions/marketing-and-sales/our-insights/putting-behavioral-psychology-to-work-to-improve-the-customer-experience (accessed 30 May 2022)

Buchanan, D., & Badham, R. (2020). *Power, Politics and Organizational Change* (3rd edition). London: Sage.

Business Balls. (2019). *Nudge theory: A complete overview*. https://www.businessballs .com/improving-workplace-performance/nudge-theory/ (accessed 30 May 2022)

Thaler, R. (2011). *Nudge: An overview* (30 July). US: YouTube. https://www.youtube .com/watch?v=xoA8N6nJMRs (accessed 30 May 2022)

Thaler, R. (2015). *Misbehaving. The Making of Behavioral Economics*. New York and London: W.W. Norton.

Thaler, R. (2019). *A closer look at nudging* (4 June). US: YouTube. https://www .youtube.com/watch?v=nQ_9m7yERUw (accessed 30 May 2022)

Thaler, R., & Sunstein, C. (2008). *Nudge. Improving Decisions about Health, Wealth and Happiness*. New Haven and London: Yale University Press.

Task 1

Watch Richard Thaler's two videos (Thaler, 2011, 2019). Note his examples of nudging people's eating habits through cafeteria layout/calorie information and driving speed through painted lines on the road. Brainstorm how you might 'nudge' people during change.

Task 2

Watch Dan Ariely's TED Talk (Ariely, 2008) and focus on his examples of how the *framing of choices* can influence decisions (e.g., using 'default' and 'third-way' options, presentation, etc.). Using these insights, what do you think is the role of a 'choice architect' in organizational change? For popularized information on applying this approach, see the McKinsey 'Choices' framework presented by Bhattacharjee et al. (2016) and Business Balls 'Nudge Theory Toolkit' (2019).

Task 3

The 'nudging' fashion suggests we are prepared to acknowledge and predict irrationalities in ourselves and others. But what if Ariely is right, and we find it difficult to accept that we are not 'in the driving seat' and routinely default to an overly rational view of what to expect? How do we remain mindful to avoid ineffective action and unnecessary frustration? Is Ariely's reflective humour a necessary component of a change mindset?

1.5.4   Leading Change: Haier

Haier has rapidly grown to become the world's largest home appliance manufacturer. It has been widely heralded as a world-leading example of successful innovation and transformational leadership. The CEO, Zhang Ruimin, has clearly been able to combat the 'sloped playing field'.

Case material

Fischer, B., Lago, U., & Liu, F. (2013). *Reinventing Giants: How Chinese Global Competitor Haier has Changed the Way Big Companies Transform.* San Francisco: Jossey-Bass.

Joost. (2019a). *Picking the brain of the world's most radical CEO: Zhang Ruimin.* https://corporate-rebels.com/interview-zhang-ruimin/ (accessed 30 May 2022)

Joost. (2019b). *The world's most pioneering company of our times.* Corporate Rebels. https://corporate-rebels.com/haier/ (accessed 30 May 2022)

Knowledge@Wharton. (2019). *For Haier's Zhang Ruimin, success means creating the future.* https://knowledge.wharton.upenn.edu/article/haiers-zhang-ruimin-success-means-creating-the-future/ (accessed 30 May 2022)

Task 1

Read the Haier case materials: Joost, 2019b, 2019a; Knowledge@Wharton, 2019. For additional information, see Fischer et al., 2013.

Task 2

Test out your understanding of Lewin's four disciplines of change management by applying them to Haier by briefly describing (in dot point format) how Ruimin led rather than mis-led change through his intelligent application of (i) understanding the whole field; (ii) learning through action; (iii) pulling rather than pushing change; and (iv) preparing for, supporting and reinforcing change.

1.5.5   Change Habit 1: Expect the Expected

*When Richard orders a takeaway coffee from a barista, he doesn't like them to put the plastic cap on the cup because it removes the froth as he walks along. In the past, when he ordered, he would ask, 'Can you please not put a cap on!' They always, always put the cap on. For a while there, he would get really frustrated. He'd ask them to take it off or hand it back to them. Now THAT irritated them to no end. He'd say to me, '**You** heard me, right?!' I just knowingly nodded my head. In his mind, he couldn't help thinking why they'd kept putting the cap on despite his specific and polite request not to do so. Perhaps it was because they were required to do it for some occupational safety reasons?! But when pressed, the standard reply from DIFFERENT baristas was, 'No, sorry. It was just automatic. I wasn't thinking'. After some time, we both learned from this. He stopped asking. Now, he looks for a recycling bin while he's placing his order. Then once he's got the coffee, he throws the cap into the bin. He learned to 'expect the expected'.*

*In a real sense, '**Expect the Expected' is the biggest change habit**. Let's call it 'the Master-Habit' above all the rest. The 'I just wasn't thinking'*

*reminds us that organizations and individuals often act without fully un-
derstanding what they do and why. In particular, we expect and hope for
logical and rational actions. Yet, we commonly experience behaviour that's
blinkered, emotive and self-serving. Despite such experiences, we still get
shocked and frustrated, rather than expecting and adapting to it. Why would
it be any different during change? In fact, given the uncertainties and emotions change generates, we might reasonably expect this type of behaviour
and our unreasonable reaction to be even more prevalent!*

*Study after study reveal this paradox: It's **only reasonable and rational**
to expect that individuals and organizations will **not act** reasonably and rationally. Meaning, we humans aren't as logical, rational, nor as intelligent
as we'd like to think we are. Yet, while we may understand this in theory,
we often neglect or forget it when under threat or pressure in the heat of the
moment. So, to help you remember, keep the mantra in mind, and try to build
this into a habit: 'Expect the Expected!'*

Task 1

Experiment with two little 'I just wasn't thinking' experiments to illustrate and
'kick start' the habit of 'expecting the expected'. Undertake one experiment
with a colleague and another with a friend or family member. In each case, find
an irritating pattern of behaviour you and others have gotten into. Meaning,
one that usually results in the other person (and you) getting a little upset or
frustrated because the other doesn't behave how one wants them to or thinks
they should. It must be something simple, like not being punctual, not cleaning
up after yourself, using someone's parking spot.

Task 2

Try to have an honest conversation with them about it. Discuss your perceptions of the pattern of behaviour and its outcomes. Ask 'why' they do what
they do and how they see you and your actions. See what you find out! Given
what you've learned, how might you respond in future when you see such
patterns emerging? Think about how the other person responded to how you
presented the issues. How might you better consider their perceptions and
emotions when having conversations on difficult topics in the future?

RESOURCES

The Change Problem

Taking the 'Red Pill' approach to influence change requires going below
the surface of overly rational views of organizations and how we 'manage'

change. When we abandon the 'official story', we can see 'how deep the rabbit hole goes' as encouraged by Morpheus in 'The Matrix', inferring to the tale of Alice in Wonderland. Within organizational studies, Darren McCabe (2016) uses the 'Wonderland' metaphor to exhort researchers and practitioners beyond the dominant rational image of how we organize and change.

McCabe, D. (2016). 'Curiouser and curiouser!': Organizations as Wonderland – a metaphorical alternative to the rational model. *Human Relations*, *69*(4), 945–973.

The ineffectiveness of traditional 'Red Pill' approaches to managing change is the subject of various polemical overviews and critiques of the field. In challenging, if somewhat academic, introductions, Chris Grey (2003) gives us a radical critique of the 'fetish of change' and Robert Chia (2014) a set of reflections on required 'changefulness' in the face of unpredictable and emergent change processes. In a more recent and accessible provocation, Dave Buchanan (2015) makes a case for why 'I couldn't disagree more' with current and fashionable change management research and advice.

Buchanan, D. (2015). I couldn't disagree more: Eight things about organizational change that we know for sure, but which are probably wrong. In B. Burnes, & J. Randall (Eds.), *Perspectives on Change: What Academics, Consultants and Managers Really Think about Change* (pp.5–22). London and New York: Routledge.
Chia, R. (2014). Reflections: In praise of silent transformation – allowing change through 'letting happen'. *Journal of Change Management*, *14*(1), 8–27.
Grey, C. (2003). The fetish of change. *Tamara: Journal of Critical Postmodern Organization Science*, *2*(2), 1–19.

1.1   On the Surface

The debate around 70% failure (see 1.5.2) is a useful introduction to the issue of failure rates. Mark Hughes' (2011) article triggered the critical academic and then more popular debate. The *McKinsey Quarterly* article by Carolyn Aiken and Scott Keller (Aiken & Keller, 2009) provides a classic consultancy packaging of the statistic and its 'lessons' for change management. Peter Gibbons' (2015) discussion of failure provides a nuanced pragmatic discussion of how to conceive of and address the issue.

Aiken, C., & Keller, S. (2009). The irrational side of change management [4]. *McKinsey Quarterly*, (2), 101–109.
Gibbons, P. (2015). *The Science of Successful Organizational Change*. Pearson.
Hughes, M. (2011). Do 70 per cent of all organizational change initiatives really fail? *Journal of Change Management*, *11*(4), 451–464.

An important recent *Human Relations* Special Issue on 'Organizational change failure: Framing the process of failing' further explored the issues around how failure is interpreted and the emergent dynamics of success and failure over time. The article by Heracleous and Bartunek (2021) is of particular interest in extending the discussion of Wonderland as a metaphor for deepening our understanding beyond surface, overly rational, interpretations of the phenomenon.

Of additional interest in sensitizing us to the contested and controversial nature of defining, admitting to and denying failure is a Reflection piece on the Special Issue by Mark Hughes (2022). Consider, in particular, Hughes' (ibid., p.19) '7 hopes for organizational change studies in the future' in grappling with how to usefully explore the challenges and failures of change.

Heracleous, L., & Bartunek, J. (2021). Organization change failure, deep structures and temporality: Appreciating Wonderland. *Human Relations, 74*(2), 208–233.
Hughes, M. (2022). Reflections: How studying organizational change lost its way. *Journal of Change Management, 22*(1), 8–25.
Schwarz, G. M., Bouckenooghe, D., & Vakola, M. (2021). Organizational change failure: Framing the process of failing. Special Issue: Introduction and Overview. *Human Relations, 74*(2), 159–179.

1.2   The Deeper Problem

The analyses of the systemic biases on what makes change so difficult vary from deep social and economic investigations to consultancy problem/solution packages. It is advisable to start from a serious analysis and question the overly rational view of individuals and organizations. Within organization studies, a classic and still relevant critique by Jeffrey Pfeffer and Gerald Salancik (1977) questions the 'rational model' of organizations. Darren McCabe (2016) made a more recent intervention in his argument for an alternative 'Wonderland' metaphor of organizations. The irrationality of individuals is comprehensively addressed by Daniel Kahneman (2011), Richard Thaler (2015), and Dan Ariely (2009); the TED Talk by Ariely (2008) used in Practice 2 is probably the best and most valuable introduction. In *A Primer on Decision-Making,* James March (1994) provides a comprehensive, if somewhat dry, introduction to the patterned irrationality of individuals and organizations. And again later, a more succinct yet equally dry talk at HEC in Paris (2007). These analyses consider the non-rational (or arational) dimensions of individual and organizational life. Once we have internalized the possibility and presence of such dimensions, we can explore the biases created by 'predictable irrationalities'. The publications cited in the 'Deeper Problem' highlight several important ones.

Ariely, Dan. (2008). *Are we in control of our own decisions?* US: Ted Talks. https://www.youtube.com/watch?v=9X68dm92HVI
Ariely, D. (2009). *Predictable Irrationality: The Hidden Forces that Shape our Decisions.* New York: Harper-Collins.

Kahneman, D. (2011). *Thinking Fast and Slow*. New York: Farrar, Straus and Giroux.

March, J. (1994). *Primer on Decision-Making*. New York: Free Press.

March, J. G. (2007). *Management and Don Quixote*. France: HEC, YouTube. https://www.youtube.com/watch?v=bztgYMoTEjM

McCabe, D. (2016). 'Curiouser and curiouser!': Organizations as Wonderland – a metaphorical alternative to the rational model. *Human Relations, 69*(4), 945–973.

Pfeffer, J., & Salancik, G. (1977). Organization design: The case for a coalitional model of organizations. *Organization Dynamics, 6*(2), 15–29.

Thaler, R. (2015). *Misbehaving. The Making of Behavioral Economics*. New York and London: W.W. Norton.

1.3   Solutions that Fail Us, Solutions that Don't

With this in mind, Bernard Burnes (2004b) and David Rosenbaum et al. (2018) provide useful reviews of Kurt Lewin and his ongoing influence on change management. In addition, Jeroen Stouten et al. (2018) provide an overview and academic assessment of prescriptive consultancy 'stage' models, Raymond Caldwell (2003) summarizes models of change agency, and Gervase Bushe and Robert Marshak (2009) outline the shift over time from systemic 'diagnostic' to interpretive 'dialogic' approaches to organizational development and change.

Burnes, B. (2004b). Kurt Lewin and the planned approach to change: A re-appraisal. *Journal of Management Studies, 41*(6), 977–1002.

Bushe, G. R., & Marshak, R. J. (2009). Revisioning organization development. *The Journal of Applied Behavioral Science, 45*(3), 348–368.

Caldwell, R. (2003). Models of change agency: A fourfold classification. *British Journal of Management, 14*(2), 131–142.

Rosenbaum, D., More, E., & Steane, P. (2018). Planned organizational change management. *Journal of Organizational Change Management, 31*(2), 286–303.

Stouten, J., Rousseau, D. M., & De Cremer, D. (2018). Successful organizational change: Integrating the management practice and scholarly literatures. *Academy of Management Annals, 12*(2), 752–788.

Thaler, R. (2015). *Misbehaving. The Making of Behavioral Economics*. New York and London: W.W. Norton.

2. Re-imagining change, re-inventing yourself

Education is not filling a bucket but lighting a fire. (W.B. Yeats)

You already have the knowledge necessary to manage change in your head, heart and hands. This knowledge is embedded in the cultural images and counter-images of what managing change involves. In this chapter, we help you appreciate the degree to which this is true and support you in applying what, in a sense, you already know.

Learning objectives

Head (theory)

2.0 Introduction

2.1 Images of change

2.2 Re-imagining change

2.3 Re-inventing yourself

2.4 Chapter summary

Heart and hand (practice)

2.5 Cases and exercises

2.5.1	Change Agents: *A Bug's Life* v *Chicken Run*
2.5.2	Sing a Different Tune: *Love Actually* v *Bohemian Rhapsody*
2.5.3	Are You a Leader of Change? A Self-test
2.5.4	Tell a Compelling Story: ACME
2.5.5	Change Habit 2: Flip the Iceberg

Resources

LEARNING OBJECTIVES

- Develop the reflective capacity to stand on the 'balcony' and take a 'third position' when confronted by different and conflicting images of change.
- Recognize and transcend overly rational models and myths of change through the generative use of two counter-metaphors: 'iceberg' and 'rollercoaster'.
- Understand the nature and appreciate the importance of the 5M framework as a practical and meaningful guide to re-imagining change and re-inventing yourself.

HEAD (THEORY)

2.0   INTRODUCTION

In the last chapter, we promised a rich and colourful journey using stories, film and art to capture the human dimension of change. Now we look to unleash your creative juices and encourage you to creatively imagine and explore new ways of thinking about change and your approach to it. You'll learn about the many images and stories of the change journey. There will be epic sagas, romantic tales of heroic achievements, as well as tragic and ironic stories of decline and fall.

How we see and re-imagine change is never separate from how we invent and re-invent tales of who we are or should be. Some stories are 'fairy tale' versions of organizations as responsible and effective systems for achieving common goals. Others are highly critical of the simplicity, naïvety and hypocrisy of such views. We enter organizations as living and breathing cultural beings, not simple minions or hired hands. Inevitably we are influenced by these images.

This chapter draws on such images in arguing for re-imagining change and re-inventing yourself. We will also draw on established cultural stories of change to provide you with images and advice that is simple enough to be useful yet sophisticated and deep enough to resonate.

You will be shown how to re-imagine change as a **Cycle of Change** and re-invent yourself as a **Leader of Change**. To help capture the personal nature of this journey and provide a memorable set of images, you will be introduced to the **5M Framework** for managing and leading change – *the Mindful Mobilizing of Maps, Masks and Mirrors*.

The cycle of change entails you becoming:

- adept at Mapping out the change journey,
- using Masks to influence others in its performance, and
- deploying Mirrors as a reflective guide along the way.

This change cycle is creative, dynamic and cultural. To help embed this in your memory and understanding, you will also be presented with images of the organization as an iceberg and the change journey as a rollercoaster. You will also learn how this involves you in re-inventing yourself as a leader of change. This requires developing your ability to be Mindful of the challenges of change and Mobilize yourself and others to overcome the barriers. These are the last 2Ms of the **5M Framework**.

In this chapter, you will learn how to achieve this by '*Re-imagining Change*' and '*Re-inventing Yourself*' in the Mindful Mobilizing of Maps, Masks and Mirrors. So, get ready for the journey. It will be what the German philosopher Schlegel called 'seriously playful'!

2.1   IMAGES OF CHANGE

Source: Reproduced with permission from Brett Wood, Creative Wisdom.

Figure 2.1   *Duck v. Rabbit*

Inscribed in the forecourt of the Temple of Apollo at Delphi is '*Know thyself*'. Our advice from this ancient Greek oracle is that 'wisdom and knowledge begin when we better understand ourselves, how we interpret the world and the position we take towards it' (for further insight into 'practical wisdom', see Schwartz & Sharpe, 2011).

Have a look at Figure 2.1. What do you see?

Did you see a duck or a rabbit? Now, imagine that before showing you this image, you were having a deep conversation with a friend about ducks or rabbits. Imagine if they even said, 'This is a picture of my duck (or my rabbit)'? How much would it have influenced what you saw?

Change is much like the picture of the duck or the rabbit. Different people see different things. Locked into one way of seeing, it becomes difficult to see another. If other people do not see what we see, we become frustrated. *Are you ready to see the duck **and** the rabbit?*

Our modern culture is a rich storybook of images, metaphors and narratives. If we're to re-imagine change, we need to be aware of the nature and power of these images. If we are to re-invent ourselves, we must consider how our identities are wrapped up in the storylines.

One foundational story of change permeates the ideas and practices of many managers and organizations. It is an overly rational approach to change. Organizations are viewed as machine-like – we're 'cogs in the machine' (March, 1994; McCabe, 2016; Morgan, 2006, Ch.2). In its eyes, change is a simple two-step process of identifying what's not working well and then improving it. Change is then an instruction. Let's call this 'The Nike' approach to change management – adopting their 'Just Do It' slogan. The end result is much like the American comedy *Groundhog Day*, where a cynical TV weatherman finds himself reliving the same day over and over again. We live and repeat this rational change story every day.

Other familiar stories of change challenge this Rational Story. Managers and champions of Organizational Development provide us with narratives of Transitions (Bridges & Bridges, 2016. Organizations are regarded as more like living organisms, and people are not merely 'cogs' (Morgan, 2006, Ch.3). Change is viewed as a three-step process (Brown, 1998; Cummings et al., 2016).

1.   persuading people to 'let go' of the past,
2.   guiding them through the 'difficult middles', and
3.   ensuring they don't slip back after initial triumphs and enthusiasm wanes.

MIT Professor Peter Senge (Senge & Roth, 1999) said the traditional or rational image of change is like a manager standing in front of a plant issuing the instruction 'Grow'! Champions of the Transition story advocate nurturing, watering and feeding.

You'll also hear a collection of stories by promoters of Agile and Adaptive organizations (Gibbons, 2015; Heifetz et al., 2009a, 2009b; Heifetz & Linsky, 2017). In these narratives, tales are told of rapidly changing environments and organizations working to keep up (Abrahamson, 2004). Leaders and the led are exhorted to 'thrive in chaos', 'embrace uncertainty', and 'experiment' in the face of these challenges (Crainer, 1997, Ch.7.; Du Gay & Vikkelso, 2017, Ch.3). Change is viewed as a turbulent learning cycle, not a predictable shift between two stable states. Leaders are regarded as heroic champions in an entrepreneurial quest (Buchanan & Badham, 2020; Collinson et al., 2018).

Finally, the most recent stories present pictures of deeper and more profound complexity and chaos. The 'hero's journey' is less epic. These stories are less about heroism and more about Humility and Resilience in the face of adversity (Boyatzis & McKee, 2003; Pirotti & Venzin, 2017; Seville, 2016; Weick, 1996). Some of these stories are tragic and cynical in tone, telling tales of organizational incompetence, worsening conditions, fatally flawed heroes and failing initiatives (Alvesson & Spicer, 2017; Fleming, 2013; Hughes, 2019; Tourish, 2013). Others are more romantic and inspiring with stories of personal triumph over individual failings and mobilizing others through humility and authenticity (Alvesson & Einola, 2019; Fuda, 2013; Ibarra, 2015a, 2015b; Uhl-Bien & Ospina, 2012). Then others are more stoic, less cynical and less romantic. They're more about endurance in the face of inherent struggles and uncertain outcomes. They praise elegance and artistry in creating meaning amidst the troubles (March & Weil, 2005; Rhodes & Badham, 2018).

The entire storybook of change narratives draws on long-established cultural images. They provide us with perspectives we believe are essential to consider. However, many individuals and organizations' knee-jerk reaction is still dominated by the Rational Story. Stories of Transition, Agility and Resilience challenge this story and open alternatives. You will need to consider them all in learning how to re-imagine change. In the discourse of change, 'snake-oil' salesmen simply draw on 'received images' (Czarniawska & Joerges, 1996, p.14) and uncritically reproduce 'reassuring narratives' (Buchanan, 2015, p.11). In contrast, we side with Barbara Czarniawska and Dave Buchanan in recommending critical reflection on established imagery in focusing on the challenges of 'making change happen' in practice.

In this book, we expand on this rich imagery and set of stories in presenting a new perspective on managing change. This perspective is open, comprehensive and reflective in the way it draws on established imagery. It is also practical in its focus on how to make use of these images in preparing for, conducting and reflecting on getting change done. Over the next couple of chapters, you'll see how these images and stories can be effectively combined in an image of a 'Cycle of Change' and the 'Leadership of Change'.

The Cycle of Change image aligns with the scientific problem-solving methods of W. Edwards Deming (Deming, 2000): his (Plan–Do–Check–Act or Plan–Do–Check–Adjust) or PDSA (Plan–Do–Study–Act) approach drawn from the earlier work of Walter Shewhart. Project management literature presents this process as the strenuous task of pushing this cycle uphill, using a 'chock' to prevent it from slipping back – as in Figure 2.2 the Leadership of Change is the mindset, motivation, energy and intelligence required to improve the chances of succeeding in this task.

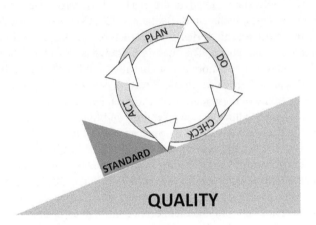

Figure 2.2   PDCA cycle

The Cycle of Change is an iterative and challenging one, with an ever-present danger of slippage. It is grounded in a three-part cycle of planning, executing and evaluating tasks, but it's more than this. It's a cultural or transition cycle. It re-imagines change as a meaningful cycle of orienting ourselves (with Maps), performing (using Masks) and reflecting (in Mirrors).

The Cycle of Change has both utility and appeal since it aligns with:

- the planned change bias in the Rational story,
- the motivational challenges identified in the Transition story,
- the turbulence and experimentation in the Adaptive and Agile story, and
- the stress on humility, openness and persistence in the Resilience story.

In *Re-Imagining Change*, you are provided with popular and accessible imagery of what change involves to support the activities involved in the Cycle of Change. In *Re-Inventing Yourself*, you are introduced to the mindset and motivations required to establish and perpetuate this cycle.

2.2   RE-IMAGINING CHANGE

Drawing on the Merriam-Webster Dictionary (Mish et al., 2020, p.206), change can be defined as '*the act or process of making or becoming different*'.

- What is it for an organization to become 'different'? What counts as 'different' depends on our perspective and values. In defining what 'different' means, we must ask ourselves what the purpose of a change is.
- What's involved in 'acts of making' or 'processes of becoming'? In deliberate organizational change, our 'acts of making' inevitably involve the exercise of influence. However, we have to ask ourselves how we might best exercise influence. This consists in exploring our capabilities as well as our effects on others.

In addressing these questions, change management is part of everything we do, regardless of whether we are formally designated as change managers. It goes far beyond applying expert change methodologies. It also requires discipline in responding constructively and creatively in sometimes uncertain conditions and in the face of significant opposition. To capture these themes, in this book, we define change management in a general and inclusive manner as *the discipline of influencing oneself and others to achieve a purpose*.

As we have learned, the many stories of change provide various answers to questions about 'difference' and what is involved in the 'act of making' or 'process of becoming'. The Cycle of Change integrates major insights from these stories. It's an easy guiding image. However, if we're not careful, we default to the Rational Story, and a comprehensive view of the Cycle of Change will shrink to a task-focused Plan–Do–Check cycle. To short-circuit this response, we provide you with simple, memorable and evocative counter-images. These will assist us in applying our new 'discipline'.

This chapter introduces you to two such images as an ongoing reminder and guide.

1.   The organization as an 'Iceberg'.
2.   The process as a 'Rollercoaster Ride'.

The Iceberg

First, the Iceberg. The formal view of organizations includes:

- systems and structures,
- processes and procedures, and
- roles and responsibilities.

Organizations are regarded as more or less functional systems that deliver the products and services they create. As the Nobel Prize-winning economist Richard Thaler (2015) said, people are expected to behave as rational 'Econs' and organizations to deliver. Leaders proclaim this, clients demand it, employees expect it and consultants advise it.

Yet, this is only a partial view of the surface or 'tip of the iceberg' (Badham et al., 2020; Senior et al., 2020). Below the surface, there's an informal and more personal dimension to organizations. It's a world of ambiguity and chaos, emotion and intrigue. You'll find diverse sub-cultures and competing political interests. Organizations give a public performance of unity and rationality but indulge in very different activities below (Buchanan & Boddy, 1992). They're much like ducks 'calm on the surface but paddling like hell underneath'.

Re-imagining change requires us to 'flip the iceberg'. What is made or becomes 'different' includes the messy, emotional and political dimensions of organizations. Instead of ignoring or denying these underlying realities, we surface and focus on them. Rather than being fooled by public appearances and the rational 'tip' of the iceberg, we learn to appreciate the informal dimension of organizational life and dedicate time, resources and attention to it.

The Rollercoaster Ride

Since the eighteenth century, our dominant image of the 'acts of making' or the 'process of becoming' is one of progress in two stages. It's a 'black and white' story of moving from a 'bad' non-rational past to a 'good' and rational future.

Counter-images of change challenge this image as a three-stage process. Our storytelling minds (Buchanan & Badham, 2020, Ch.6; Storr, 2019) are also familiar with a three-step plot:

1. a past state of affairs,
2. a journey involving challenges and struggles, and
3. a future of 'happy' or 'tragic' endings.

Our cultural awareness of 'rites of passage' identifies this with a three-stage transition (Badham et al., 2012b; Brown, 1998). As the anthropologists van Gennep and Turner first highlighted, we expect and practice:

1. a 'separation' from the old cultural attitudes, beliefs and roles,
2. entrance into a 'liminal' state of anxiety and excitement in between, and
3. 'incorporation' of new identities and behaviour on the 'other side'.

One popular yet partial view of the three-step process is the 'Valley of Death' or 'Death Valley' image of change. Here the focus is coming to terms with 'loss', as in the popular Elisabeth Kubler-Ross' 'grief cycle' (Elrod & Tippett,

2002). This image highlights the denial and anger at the start of the change journey and the descent into what Rosabeth Moss Kanter (2020) describes as the 'difficult middles' of change – the anxieties, depression and inability to cope, perform and 'move on'.

An alternative, equally partial, image is one of excitement, challenge and opportunity in 'taking the plunge'. Here the focus is on 'gain', opportunities and benefits for growth and development, as in Carol Dweck's (2017) popular image of the 'growth mindset'. It admits fears but focuses on the exhilaration and thrill of the ride. It celebrates the delight that comes from facing up to fears and transforming oneself and others. It extols the rewards of reaching a higher stage of achievement.

The metaphor of the 'rollercoaster' ride (Schneider & Goldwasser, 1998; Smollan, 2014) allows us to combine both of these images.

It captures:

1. the anxiety and the excitement,
2. the challenges of leaping into the unknown and being 'out of control' in the 'Big Dipper', and
3. the many unexpected twists and turns as well as ups and downs on the journey.

The rollercoaster image helps us expect the fears of loss, anticipate the joys from the gains, and appreciate the temptation yet discomfort of rigidly gripping tightly onto the sides of our change carriage. There is a lovely brief excerpt from a popular novel (Dessen, 2009, p.323) that is worth checking up on. The excerpt captures the experience of speed, uncertainty and fear that overcomes us and makes us want to hold on tight but recommends relaxing, releasing and going along for the ride!

The Cycle of Change and the Change Journey

With the help of the iceberg and rollercoaster images, you can re-imagine the cycle of change. They'll assist in preventing the knee-jerk reactions and false expectations built into the overly rational story. However, the lesson is not that the 'iceberg' and 'rollercoaster' are *real* descriptions of organizations and change. Like all images, they're partial. The point is that they can be *useful* as a simple and appealing reminder and guide. In Re-Imagining Change, they help us leave our reactive culture of complaint – complaining things don't happen as our 'rational' story says they should – and move on to a constructive world of creativity and enterprise.

At the risk of sounding like a fortune cookie, let me say, 'when you learn to live outside yourself, life becomes richer'! You're well on your way by learning how to re-imagine change. Now we'll go deeper. Let's talk about you.

2.3   RE-INVENTING YOURSELF

To succeed and not default to comfort zones, you need to work on yourself. If you're to re-imagine change as the application of maps, masks and mirrors, you need to know the person behind the mask, what has to be done and who you need to be. Two capabilities are critical to re-inventing yourself as a leader of change:

* To be fully **mindful** of the issues and barriers you face, and
* To be effective in **mobilizing** energy in yourself and others.

These are the final 2Ms in the **5M Framework** – the mindful mobilizing of maps, masks and mirrors, and we explore them further in Chapter 6.

Being Mindful

In *One Second Ahead* (Hougaard et al., 2016), Jacob, a large European financial company senior manager, describes 'being mindful' as 'one second ahead'. In the past, he had been the victim of his automatic responses and prejudices. Being 'one second ahead' meant he could now respond intelligently and creatively to events, not react mindlessly. In the face of uncertainty and challenge, being mindful short-circuits unproductive fight or flight responses. A core capability in change.

Being mindful requires moving beyond 'rigid' or 'fixed' thinking and 'mindless' thought and action, being ready to challenge our own assumptions and 'think outside the box' (Langer, [1989] 2009). This involves adopting a 'flexible' and 'growth' mindset (Dweck, 2017; Zerubavel, 1991) and being capable of 'third-order' thinking or 'triple loop learning' (Bartunek & Moch, 1987).

What this means in practice is:
First, being able to work on problems without requiring a change in our assumptions. Second, being ready to question those assumptions and explore different viewpoints when the old ones no longer work. Third, being prepared and even enjoying a life in which this is an ongoing activity.

This process begins with the 'head' but doesn't end there. It involves the heart. It's one thing to be ready to change one's mind, and it's quite another to alter how you feel, open yourself up to others and handle emotional conflict. The stories we tell ourselves and others are rife with prejudice. This is what makes them so interesting. To stand outside our stories, consider other people's emotions and viewpoints, and work creatively with them is not easy (Badham & King, 2021; Buchanan & Badham, 2020; Kegan & Lahey, 2016; King & Badham, 2019). When they're not like you and may not even like you, it's essential to be aware and considerate of their feelings and your own, and even share a sense of humour!

Finally, being mindful means being aware of the complexities and barriers to change that go beyond you and your personal interactions. It demands strategic attention to the problems these barriers create. You'll need to act to address them and accept it as part and parcel of the change journey.

Mobilizing Energy

Being mindful in your head and heart is one thing. Being able to mobilize energy and resources in practice is another (Bruch & Vogel, 2011; Buchanan & Badham, 2020; Kanter, 1985). Sheryl Sandberg (2013) refers to this as 'leaning in'. That is, being able and willing to overcome the internal and external biases that hold us back. Her favourite question? 'What would you do if you weren't afraid?' Motivating ourselves and others to overcome anxieties and fears is essential. London Business School Professor Herminia Ibarra (Ibarra, 2015a) says it requires 'stepping up'. Learning to lead demands moving outside your comfort zone as an 'expert manager'. It requires embracing the skills and opportunities to influence others outside the arena of formal authority. This goes beyond self-reflection and leadership training to develop what Ibarra calls 'outsight'. To grow as leaders, we must challenge ourselves in our jobs, develop networks, draw on mentors, and develop by 'acting ourselves into becoming better leaders'. As the renowned organizational scholar, Karl Weick put it, 'How can I know who I am until I see what I do!' (Weick, 1995, cited in Ibarra, 2015a, p.6).

Ibarra, like Sandberg, emphasizes the importance of handling barriers outside as well as inside ourselves. As we have learned, there's a 'Lord's Slope' in change. It's far from being a level playing field. We love the old joke about the couple driving through Ireland who stop to ask a farmer the way to Cork. His reply was timeless *'If I were going to go to Cork, I wouldn't start from here!'*

In an ideal world, we'd have all the time, resources and support necessary for a productive change cycle. In reality, they're often missing. The ability to mobilize the energy and resources required is a crucial change capability (Bacharach, 2016). Developing these skills and acting in this way is personally challenging. As one senior change manager put it, 'change always requires you to put in that extra bit to make sure things get done.' That 'extra bit' can be exhausting and the enterprise risky. It's essential, therefore, that you're able to mobilize yourself. So, as a general rule, do whatever you can to pursue changes that align with your values and enhance your career. Your personal resilience, persistence and ultimately, your fate will depend upon it.

You're now prepared to delve into the details of managing change in practice. Over the following three chapters, we'll take you through the tools and actions you need to create a productive Cycle of Change. Then, we return to the topic of Re-Inventing Yourself in Chapter 6 when we explore the Leadership of Change.

2.4   CHAPTER SUMMARY

In *Chapter 2, Re-Imagining Change, Re-Inventing Yourself*, you have learned about:

2.1   Images of Change

- The different images, metaphors and stories of change frame how we see it, as illustrated through the image of the duck and the rabbit.
- We have a rich storybook of change narratives – the dominant one is Rational, but it is challenged by stories of Transition, Agility and Resilience.
- We draw on these stories in re-imagining change as a cyclical process of orientation, performance, and reflection in an ongoing Cycle of Change.

2.2   Re-imagining Change

- Images of change are based on views of the organization and the process of change.
- The 'iceberg' and the 'rollercoaster' are valuable and appealing images. These images are to be used creatively as a reminder and a guide to avoid slipping into an overly rational view of change.
- Re-imagining change as a change cycle requires you to re-invent yourself.

2.3   Re-inventing Yourself

- 'Re-inventing Yourself' has two main elements:
    - being mindful of the challenges of change in the head, hand and heart, and
    - being able to mobilize oneself and others, to overcome the barriers.

You're now prepared to delve into the details of managing change in practice. In the following section, we'll take you through the tools and actions you need to create a productive **Cycle of Change.** Then, we return to the topic of *Re-Inventing Yourself* in Chapter 6 when we explore the **Leadership of Change**.

HEART AND HAND (PRACTICE)

2.5   CASES AND EXERCISES

2.5.1   Change Agents: *A Bug's Life* v *Chicken Run*

Change agents need to address factors 'below the waterline' of the organizational iceberg to be effective. However, as one wit pronounced, 'after all is said and done, more is said than done!' For this reason, lightweight and amusing fictional video clips may be more useful than programmed case studies in stimulating reflection. There are three reasons for this. First, while it may seem obvious to be 'mindful' of what is going on beneath the surface of the iceberg, it's often less easy to notice and apply this recommendation in practice. Second, fictional representations often succinctly capture 'what we all know' in a very clear and precise way. They are not 'real' incidents, but how the writers represent the incident reflects their intuitive understanding of what we all look for and notice in actions and events. Third, incidents often capture issues much better than longer case studies and, if they are amusing, it encourages us to be more open and creative in understanding and using them.

Case material
Chicken Run (Directors: Lord, P., & Park, N.). (2000). A better place scene (16.37–18.45). https://www.youtube.com/watch?v=GKjA8F4ruvg
A Bug's Life (Director: Lasseter, J.). (1998). Going around the leaf scene (2.00–2.30). https://www.youtube.com/watch?v=qTQJdGp4F34

Task 1
Watch the two video clips and contrast the style and achievements of the different 'change agents' Mr Soil, in *A Bug's Life* (1998), and Ginger, in *Chicken Run* (2000).

Task 2
After watching the scene in *A Bug's Life*, address the following:

1. What is the state of mind of those affected by the leaf, and how do we pick this up?
2. How does Mr Soil, the 'change agent', respond? Note things such as speed, acknowledgement and reassurance.
3. What did the 'change agent' do to 're-frame' the situation in a way that would make those affected more optimistic or confident?
4. When the 'change agent' made suggestions that those affected by the leaf did not initially accept or act on, how did he respond?
5. How did the 'change agent' use tone, body language and a balance of influencing styles to bring about change?
6. What lessons might you draw from this – jot down three principles about how one might think and act mindfully in addressing the iceberg issues in organizational change.

Task 3
After watching the scene in *Chicken Run*, address the following:

1. When Ginger points to the empty nest, what is the audience's response? How does she dismiss or criticize the reactions?
2. When the audience member says, 'It's a living', what did the 'change agent' say in response, and what was her tone and mannerisms?
3. After painting a visionary picture of an ideal future, how did the audience respond, and how did she react to their views?
4. How did Ginger end up, what did she say, and how did she feel?

Task 4
Reflect on and address the following questions:

1. How did *Chicken Run* differ from *A Bug's Life* in interactions and outcome?

2. What lessons might you draw from this? Jot down three principles, keeping in mind the importance of appreciating the 'iceberg' of non-judgemental appreciation of perspectives and the ability for self-appraisal.

2.5.2 Sing a Different Tune: *Love Actually* v *Bohemian Rhapsody*

Being mindful of the perspectives and prejudices you and others hold is crucial in developing your capabilities to address the cultural and political forces beneath the surface of change initiatives. To help build and test your understanding of what is involved, this exercise consists in applying Dunoon and Langer's (2011) view of mindful leadership to two dramatic incidents of attempts at change persuasion in two movies, *Love Actually* (2003) and *Bohemian Rhapsody* (2018).

Case material
Bohemian Rhapsody (Director: Singer, B.) (2018). Queen meeting with Ray Foster scene (43.00–46.50). https://www.youtube.com/watch?v=C1XOQTcW5f4 (accessed 23 May 2022).
Dunoon, D., & Langer, E. (2011). Mindfulness and leadership: Opening up to possibilities. *Integral Leadership Review*, *11*(5), 1–15.
Love Actually (Director: Curtis, R.). (2003). Billy Mack – Christmas is all around (first scene). https://www.youtube.com/watch?v=_-aMV2xXdpsv

Task 1
Read Dunoon and Langer's (2011) view of mindful leadership.

Task 2
Watch the scene from *Love Actually* (2003) when the manager (Joe, played by Gregor Fisher) of a pop singer (Billy Mack, played by Bill Nighy) succeeds in shifting Billy out of his old habits and, with a 'smile', successfully records a very different album to what he has done in the past.

Task 3
Analyse and discuss:

1. What initial mindsets of Joe and Billy put them at odds?
2. How does Joe handle Billy's first 'mistake'?
3. How do Joe and Billy respond to the second 'mistake'?
4. What really makes them both 'smile' at the end?

Task 4
Watch the scene from *Bohemian Rhapsody* (2018) when the band Queen and their lead singer Freddie Mercury (played by Rami Malek) try to persuade the

record executive Ray Foster (played by Mike Myers) to agree to produce and promote their 7-minute single 'Bohemian Rhapsody'.

Task 5
Analyse and discuss:

1. What are Freddie's and Ray's initial mindsets that put them at odds?
2. How do they assert themselves and respond to each other?
3. How does their approach contrast with those of Queen's lawyer (Jim Beach, played by Tom Hollander) and their manager (John Reid, played by Aiden Gillen)?
4. What can you learn from both movie clips, *Love Actually* (2003) and *Bohemian Rhapsody* (2018), about attending to others' perspectives, responding at the moment and using verbal, intonation and body language?

2.5.3 Are You a Leader of Change? A Self-test

Prepare to enter the mobilizing dimension of 're-inventing yourself' by first reading Schneider and Goldwasser's (1998) article on the '*Classic Change Curve*' and then take the 'Self-Test for Change Leaders', drawn from the paper, to see how well you mobilize others to face up to the challenges of the rollercoaster ride.

Case material
Schneider, D., & Goldwasser, C. (1998). Be a model leader of change. *Management Review*, *March*, 41–45.
'Self-Test for Change Leaders' (below)

Task 1
Read Schneider and Goldwasser's (1998) paper on the '*Classic Change Curve*' and the role of the model leader.

Task 2
Complete the 'Self-Test for Change Leaders' below. Use the questionnaire to think through a change project you are responsible for at work. If you do not have one, be a bit creative and apply the questionnaire to any change you have attempted or might attempt to promote in your personal life or at work.

Read each question, answer with (A) 'Not really' [0 points], (B) 'Almost' (1 point) or (C) 'Absolutely' (2 points), and tally your score.

Self-test for change leaders

QUESTIONS	ANSWERS (A) 'Not really' (B) 'Almost' (C) 'Absolutely'	SCORE (A) **0** points (B) **1** point (C) **2** points
1. Am I fully committed to the success of the change?		
2. Do my verbal and non-verbal messages demonstrate my commitment to the change?		
3. Can I clearly articulate the business case for the change?		
4. Have I freed up my time enough to be an effective leader of change?		
5. Have I arranged for the necessary resources to be provided for the change initiative?		
6. Have I ensured that change management activities are built into the change plan?		
7. Am I participating in a political and communication campaign to address the interests of all stakeholders?		
8. Do I search out and address sources of resistance among key stakeholders?		
9. Have I empowered the change team to be creative and resilient in thinking 'outside the box'?		
10. Have I motivated change agents to remain committed?		
11. Am I sure that line managers understand their role in the change process?		
12. Do I understand how this change relates to the organization's strategy and other initiatives?		
	TOTAL SCORE	

Task 3

Reflect on your scores and act on your results.

0–6: You are not fulfilling the role of an effective change leader. Re-assess your actions and abilities. Re-assess your commitment level and role.

7–15: You are doing some things right. Consider improving in areas where you scored low.

16–24: You are well on the way to becoming an excellent change leader. Congratulate yourself on a good start and keep it up!

2.5.4 Tell a Compelling Story: ACME

Case material

McKinsey and Co. (2019). *McKinsey transformation: Tell a compelling change story to inspire your organization.* https://www.youtube.com/watch?v=4FlP1-5WMyo (accessed 22 May 2022)

Rick, T. (2014). *Organizational culture is like an iceberg.* http://www.torbenrick.eu/blog/culture/organizational-culture-is-like-an-iceberg/ (accessed 22 May 2022)

Rick, T. (2015). *The iceberg that sinks organizational change.* https://www.torbenrick.eu/blog/change-management/iceberg-that-sinks-organizational-change/ (accessed 22 May 2022)

Task 1

Read Torben Rick's (2014, 2015) short blogs on *Organizational Culture is Like an Iceberg* and *The Iceberg that Sinks Organizational Change.*

Task 2

With the ideas from **Task 1** in mind, now watch the *McKinsey Transformation: Tell a Compelling Change Story to Inspire your Organization* (2019) video, which tells what they believe is a compelling change story for ACME.

Task 3

Reflect on and discuss the following:

1. In what ways do you think McKinsey believes it is telling an emotive and compelling story?
2. How far do you think McKinsey's ACME change story goes 'below the waterline' of the organizational iceberg, or does it remain 'above the surface'?
3. The two public comments on the view are diametrically opposed: one views it as 'corporate jargon'/'BS' and the other as 'great tips' that 'works for clients'. What is required to create a genuinely compelling story that considers the prejudices underlying these viewpoints?

2.5.5 Change Habit 2: Flip the Iceberg

In an attempt to make the fastest possible crossing between the UK and America, the Titanic set sail in the belief that it was unsinkable. Its fate is now a matter of myth and legend, sunk by the 'below the surface' bulk of an iceberg. We all have our 'Titanic moments'. You know, those times when in our rush to get on with things, we're overconfident in our knowledge and capabilities. Our hopes and plans are dashed on problems we'd failed to consider and had not expected.

For example, in the celebrity TV show Jamie Oliver's School Dinners, *the chef Jamie Oliver tries to get schoolchildren to eat more healthily. He worked with the cafeteria staff or 'dinner ladies' to cook 'healthier' meals. Unfortunately, the children wouldn't eat his food. Some just threw it away, preferring to keep their 'pizza, burgers and chips'. Halfway through the show, they show Jamie sitting in his car, reflecting on his frustrating journey. Recognizing that the change isn't just about food and menus but 'brainwashing and retraining kids', and he doesn't know whether he is up to it! You see, it wasn't about food – it was about getting kids interested in healthier food options. So, Jamie, welcome to the Iceberg of Change!*

Task 1

Let's play a little game we call '***Flip the iceberg***'. You're going to experiment with recognizing what really lies beneath the surface so that you can address it upfront in the future. Take **two change projects** you are working on or want to do with other people: one in your work life and one in your personal life. If you're not currently working, two in your personal life are just fine.

1. For each change, draw out the 'iceberg'.

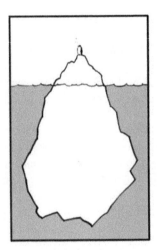

Iceberg

2. Look at the 'tip' of the iceberg (everything above the surface), and now without giving too much thought to it, quickly jot a couple of bullet points on the tasks you need to do to make it happen.

3. Now, give your project a punchy short title – one that captures your 'to-do' list.

Task 2

Now, Flip the Iceberg! Yes, turn the iceberg upside down so that the 'bulk' beneath the surface is now on top.

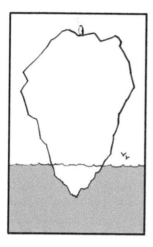

Flipped iceberg

1. Write down a list of behaviours that you and others would need to change but may be reluctant to do so.
2. Now, think through what you *actually* have to do to make the change happen.
3. Write down a short new title for the project that captures the realities and challenges before you.

Task 3

Compare your titles – do they suggest a different type of change project? How much do they suggest an overlap? What percentage of the project's success depends on doing the tasks you described in the 'tip', and what percentage addresses the behavioural issues depicted in the 'bulk' beneath the surface? Given what you've learned, does this affect how you might begin to think about changes you are planning to undertake in the future?

RESOURCES

For more on this view of change and the 5M framework, a useful overview is provided in Badham (2013):

Badham, Richard. (2013). *Short Change: An Introduction to Managing Change.* Suny: Business Perspectives.

2.1   Images of Change

There are multiple articles and books on metaphors, narratives and stories of change, with some tension between accessible and popular yet lightweight overviews and valuable and critical yet inaccessible academic analyses. A useful overview is provided in:

Buchanan, D., & Badham, R. (2020). *Power, Politics and Organizational Change.* London: Sage, chapter 5, Telling tales.

Our focus in this chapter is on the dominance of the rational image of change, the development of counter-images and the importance of taking a reflective and creative stance on how we imagine and recount change. For this purpose, some classic papers that show the influence of the rational image are central. See:

Marshak, R. J. (1993). Managing the metaphors of change. *Organizational Dynamics,* *22*(1), 44–56.
Morgan, G. (2006). *Images of Organization.* London: Sage, chapter 2, Mechanization takes command: Organizations as machines.

For a creative approach to how to deal with contemporary images, see:

Marshak, R. (2004). Morphing: The leading edge of organizational change in the twenty-first century. *Organization Development Journal,* *22*(3), 8–21.
Oswick, C., Grant, D., Michelson, G., & Wailes, N. (2005). Looking forwards: Discursive directions in organizational change. *Journal of Organizational Change Management,* *18*(4), 383–390.

2.2   Re-imagining Change

This chapter points to the value of the iceberg and rollercoaster images as an accessible contrast to the established rational image. The following provide an overview of the ups and downs, emotion and lack of control captured by the rollercoaster image, the challenges of the 'dip' into 'Death Valley' and the energy and creativity required to get out of it.

Elrod, P. D., & Tippett, D. D. (2002). The 'death valley' of change. *Journal of Organizational Change Management,* *15*(3), 273–291.

Hindshaw, I., & Gruin, A. (2017). *Reenergize change programs to escape the valley of death.* Forbes (Bain Insights) (Vol. 10, pp.4–7). https://www.forbes.com/ sites/baininsights/2017/06/27/reenergize-change-programs-to-escape-the-valley-of -death/#31a929ce5bbe (accessed 22 May 2022)

Rendle, G. (2017). *Gil Rendle – The rollercoaster of change* (3 March). US: YouTube (Albany Institute). https://www.youtube.com/watch?v=jFXX7OeoTI8

Smollan, R. K. (2014). Control and the emotional rollercoaster of organizational change. *International Journal of Organizational Analysis, 22*(3), 399–419.

The origin, multiple uses and potential of the 'iceberg' image are captured in the following:

Badham, R., Bridgman, T., & Cummings, S. (2020). The organization-as-iceberg as a counter-metaphor. In M. Maclean, S. Clegg, R. Suddaby, & C. Harvey (Eds.), *Historical Organization Studies: Theory and Application* (pp.55–77). London and New York: Routledge.

2.3   Re-inventing Yourself

An accessible run through, and introduction to Herminia Ibarra's book *Act Like a Leader, Think Like a Leader* can be found in:

Ibarra, H. (2015b). The authenticity paradox. *Harvard Business Review, Jan–Feb,* 53–59.

A useful introduction to the type of mindfulness needed in change can be found in the following conversation with Karl Weick. As we shall explore further in Chapter 6, elements of this mindset are captured by Ellen Langer (Ibarra, 2015b) in her studies of the positive effects of overcoming mindfulness and multiple treatments of mindful and resonant leadership (Langer, [1989] 2009). However, Weick's analysis points most clearly to the requirements of handling uncertainty, complexity and challenge. Please note that you have to take Weick's ideas on high reliability organizing and apply them to be mindful of change.

Coutu, D. L. (2003). Sense and reliability: A conversation with celebrated psychologist Karl E. Weick. *Harvard Business Review, April,* 84–90.

The broad literature on mobilizing covered more extensively in Chapter 6 is captured in Buchanan and Badham (2008, 2020). A valuable and accessible introduction can be found in:

Bacharach, S. (2016). *The Agenda Mover: When Your Good Idea is Not Enough.* Ithaca: Cornell University Press.

ACT II

THE CYCLE OF CHANGE

INTRODUCTION

Becoming is about the discipline and persistence, faith and hope required to continue on a journey when you are uncertain about the exact destination and what is involved in getting there. (Michelle Obama elaborates it nicely, and puts it far better, in the Epilogue of her recent book *Becoming* (2018, p.419). It is well worth reading.)

Act II (Chapters 3, 4 and 5) of the book reminds us the world, other people, and ourselves are continuously *changing*. Experiences and circumstances are fleeting, and it is an illusion to think we can grasp everything taking place or fix and control all that occurs and affects us. In the words of the Ancient Greek philosopher Heraclitus, '*You can never step into the same river twice because it is not the same river and you are not the same person.*' Yet, we often forget or deny this when faced by or working on the *changes* most valuable to us. Our reflex response *is* to attempt to fix and control. Our instinct is to try and lock in what we want and remove, stop or control what we don't. None of us wants to get older, so many try to eat healthily and exercise regularly. We do what we can do but are not able to do more.

Faced with this reality, many philosophers and organization scholars wax lyrical, and sometimes not so lyrical, about 'process' and 'becoming' as our fundamental experience (Chia & Langley, 2004; Chia, 2014; Dawson, [2003] 2019; Helin et al., 2014; Langley et al., 2013; Langley & Tsoukas, 2017; Pettigrew et al., 1992a, 1992b; Tsoukas & Chia, 2002; Weick & Quinn, 1999). Using and extending Heraclitus' metaphor of water and the river may help flesh out some of the fluidity, complexity and challenges any attempt to influence change must take into account.

THE RIVER METAPHOR

Lewin (2009, p.74) famously viewed social life as a river with a particular direction and velocity. Pettigrew (1997, p.340) extends the process image by pointing to change as an interaction between many fields or rivers – more like a river basin than a single stream. Fineman, Gabriel and Sims (2010, p.1) point to similarities between organizations and rivers. Both appear static and calm from a distance, on a map, from a helicopter or even on the surface. However, they are far less tidy and controlled when caught up in the stream. Cohen and March (1986, p.214) compare the navigational choices we have to those of drifting with the current: using a powerful motor to drive the boat in one direction or using the sails and rudder to harness the power of the wind and help us get to where we want to go. Rather than floating along, the rudder and sails support us in exploring the options we have. Vaill (1989) extends the issue of turbulence even further by encouraging us to view the modern change environment as 'permanent white water'. It leads to images of white-water rafting rather than traditional boat racing on calm rivers. When it comes to navigating the 'river' of change, Quinn (1988, p.164) observes how many people cling to the bank, afraid to let go and risk being carried by the current. He directs our attention to the boulders and snags, the many canals and branches. Rather than 'simply messing around in boats' as they do in *The Wind and the Willows* (Grahame, 2022, p.7), Dopson (1997, pp.47–48) compares the challenge to Edgar Allan Poe's *Fisherman in the Maelstrom*, searching for flotation devices in the fear and the chaos. As an end note, Nietzsche ([1913] 2011, note 394 p.175) cautions us against our over-confidence, egoism, and hubris in observing.

The small force that it takes to launch a boat into the stream should not be confused with the force of the stream that carries it along: but this confusion appears in nearly all biographies.

Seeking to depict such fluidity, Karl Weick famously advocated using verbs rather than nouns to capture the lived experience of life in modern organizations (Bakken & Hernes, 2006). He made a case for seeking to understand and explore organizing rather than organizations, changing rather than change. Moreover, in a world of ambiguity and uncertainty, ambivalence, and equivocality, he appealed to managers to match this complexity in the world with the requisite complexity in their own mindsets. 'Complicate yourself!' was his appeal. What is less well known was in his later works, he continued this theme in spirit but partially retracted the claim. Drawing on the work of William Schutz, Weick (2007) argues for moving from 'superficial simplicity' in our understanding of the world through 'confused complexity' to 'profound sim-plicity'. In addressing this 'profound simplicity', he advocated not replacing nouns with verbs but appreciating them both, as one morphs into another in how we experience and represent the world. To come to terms with the fluidity and uncertainty of change, we need to navigate with mindful simplifications and heuristics, ready to impose order on our perceptions, experiences and actions while being sensitive to the fact they are partial, artificial and must be renewed regularly.

In *Act I: Re-Imagining Change*, we used the generative metaphors of the *Lord's Slope*, the *Iceberg* and the *Rollercoaster* to help us understand the lim-itations of the rational myth of how organizations operate and change. These images are designed to inspire and support a more fluid and politically and culturally sensitive approach to change. As outlined in Badham et al. (2020), the images are carefully crafted to build on established views of organizations as systems (Morgan, 2006) and change as an 'N-step' process (Collins, 1998). Yet, they are used to go beyond them in capturing the messy, complex, and contested nature of change.

Act II: The Cycle of Change takes us further by elaborating what it means in practice to re-imagine change. As a framework aspiring to 'profound simplicity', it addresses our ongoing need to orient ourselves, deliver perfor-mances and reflect on how we are going. In doing so, it builds on an estab-lished and resonant Plan-Do-Check-Act (PDCA) cycle, yet goes far beyond it. Evidence-based Planning is replaced by constructive and creative Mapping, task-based Execution is extended into the delivery of cultural Performances, and the self-critical use of multiple Mirrors supersedes objective Evaluation. In this way, the Cycle of Change provides us with a cultural GPS designed to help us navigate the fluid, turbulent and often treacherous processes of change.

3. Maps and orientation

The map is not the territory. (Alfred Korzybski)

If change is a journey, what type of journey is it? And what do we need to guide us along the way? This chapter on Maps and Orientation provides you with the tools necessary to map out the path you need to take and revise this map along the way. You will learn to apply the three essential mapping tools: 'gap analysis', 'force field analysis' and 'route analysis'. In combination, these three provide you with a GPS for navigating the complex and often treacherous journey of change.

Learning objectives

Head (theory)

3.0 Introduction

3.1 Gap analysis

3.2 Force field analysis

3.3 Route analysis

3.4 Chapter summary

Heart and hand (practice)

3.5 Cases and exercises

    3.5.1   Apply Mapping Tools

    3.5.2   Define the Problem: *Moneyball* (2011)

    3.5.3   Streamline Chaos: Jamie Oliver's School Dinners

    3.5.4   Inconvenient Truths: Five Multinational
                   Corporations (MNCs)

    3.5.5   Change Habit 3: Be Prepared

Resources

LEARNING OBJECTIVES

- Prepare a gap analysis to define the change by detailing the distance you have to travel between 'where you are' and 'where you want to be'.
- Conduct a force field analysis of the conditions and forces you will encounter on the journey and which need to be considered in planning your route.
- Create a route map for the change journey, charting your progress through the standard stages of change (beginning, middle and end) and adapting this to the conditions at hand, conditions that are identified in the gap and force field analyses.

HEAD (THEORY)

3.0   INTRODUCTION

Individuals and organizations often set off excitedly on a change journey without really understanding what is involved or how to motivate people to get there. In this sense, they put the 'cart before the horse'. We all know the adage, 'If you fail to prepare, you are preparing to fail' (Quote Investigator, 2018). The first stage in effectively **preparing** for change is to orient yourself on the journey.

This chapter introduces the tools you will need to guide you in this task. The tools are simple enough to be practical yet complex enough to be insightful. In the last chapter, you were introduced to the metaphor of change as a journey, and in this chapter, we build on this by exploring the preparation or planning of change as 'mapping a journey'.

Why do we use this term? Well, mapping a journey is different from creating a project plan (Ingold, 2007). Project plans are more like creating an itinerary for a short trip. Journeys are longer, less predictable, and more exploratory than trips (Dunn, 1990; Inns, 1996; Lakoff & Johnson, 1999). Guidance on a journey requires something more flexible and more open than a rigid 'plan' or a fixed itinerary.

Mapping is a better term than planning, which has strong connotations of rationality, precision, logic and data-driven analysis. In contrast to planning, mapping provides you with a much-needed orientation without being too rigid. Most people understand that maps are often inaccurate, get rapidly outdated and require interpretation (see Further Reading: Maps). And we all know that map reading skills are not the only capability needed to be a good traveller!

By the end of this chapter, you will be able to apply three essential Mapping tools as the first step in the Cycle of Change:

1. **Gap analysis** to determine where you are and where you are going. It defines the particular change under consideration.
2. **Force field analysis** to capture the conditions that you will face. It identifies the specific forces that influence the nature and dynamics of the change journey.
3. **Route analysis** works out how you will get to where you want to go. It identifies the activities you plan to undertake and the sequence in which you decide to take them.

The Mapping process is the application of the tools that act as your guide and will orient you on your change journey. In theory, you apply the three simple tools in sequence. However, in reality it will be more iterative, overlapping and messier than this suggests.

Mapping is more akin to the use of a GPS than defining and following a fixed itinerary, drawing on multiple perspectives (Bennett, 2009) and, as popularly understood, involving regular feedback on whether one is on track and, where necessary, what is required to get back on track. As famous and experienced Generals have emphasized, plans rarely survive an encounter with the enemy ([Von Moltke], Ratcliffe, 2016).

This chapter provides you with what you need to know about mapping change to better understand and influence it more effectively. We are now in the first 'Orienting' Phase of the Cycle of Change.

3.1   GAP ANALYSIS

We do not embark upon change for the sake of change. In response to a request to change, the nineteenth-century British statesman Lord Salisbury famously said, 'Why change? Aren't things bad enough already?!' This points to a key feature of our 'do management' approach to managing and leading change. Our focus is *not on change per se* but on the **changes we need to bring about to achieve a purpose**.

In the first Orienting Phase of the Change Cycle, the first mapping tool is called a 'gap analysis' (Kim & Ji, 2018). As you can see in *Figure 3.1, 'Gap Analysis'*, it usually has two columns. The left-hand column lists existing conditions where you are ('As Is'). The right-hand column describes where you want to go ('To Be') (for example, see SlideTeam, 2019).

"As is" CURRENT STATE	"To be" FUTURE STATE
1.	1.
2.	2.
3.	3.
4.	4.

Figure 3.1   Gap analysis

Many strategy exercises add another column – actions to be done. But, STOP! This is premature! Leaping into what to do before you are clear about where exactly you are and where you want to go is dangerous. *Fools rush in where angels fear to tread.*

The first challenge in mapping out our journey is **whether to begin with the destination.** Do we start by clarifying where we want to go? In a sense, yes. Defining our vision and purpose is essential (Covey, 2020, 'Habit 2: Begin with the End in Mind'; Senge et al., 2010, Chapter 9, 'Personal Mastery'). The Australian golfer, Greg Norman, stressed the importance of focusing on a goal. As he put it, 'If you don't know what you're aiming at, you will hit it every time!'

It may seem obvious. But think for a moment. How often have you made big decisions in your life without *really* considering the outcome? If you had thought them through more or with the benefit of hindsight, would you have embarked on the change?

Then again, have you ever got to the end of a change and realized you were wrong about what you really wanted? Should you have been trying to achieve something different? Unless you have clarity on where you want to go, your efforts may be misdirected. Lewis Carroll (2009, p.57) brilliantly captures this in *Alice in Wonderland*:

> 'Would you tell me, please, which way I ought to go from here?'
> 'That depends a good deal on where you want to get to,' said the Cat.
> 'I don't much care where—' said Alice.
> 'Then it doesn't matter which way you go,' said the Cat.

Principle 1: when mapping out a journey, spend time clarifying where you want to go.

The second challenge is facing the fact that **a change journey is *more than* a destination**. It's just as much about where we're starting from (Liberman, 2013). Think about it. If you're lost in a city, what's the first thing you need to know? Where you are! When you finally find the city map displayed, what do you look for?! The big red dot that says, 'You are Here!'

Again, it may seem obvious. Yet, how often have you made the wrong turn by being wrong about where you are? Have you ever been so convinced you knew where you were, that you didn't listen to other people or pay attention to signs warning you might not be right? How often have you arranged to meet someone on an event or trip and agreed on a meeting point only to find out you had misunderstood each other and were standing in separate areas?

Principle 2: if you're planning your route, you need to have a pretty accurate idea of where you are or where you need to start your journey.

This now leads us to the third challenge. When asked about the nature of a change, many people begin by describing the goals. So, they usually refer to formal goals and explicit intentions. But change is ultimately not about the destination or where you are. It is about *getting from where you are to where you want to be* (Lesser et al., 2011, p.24 and chapter 7). If you're very close to where you want to get to, then it is a short trip. If you're very far away, then it is another type of journey. In a very real sense, the 'journey is the thing'. That's what we're interested in! To focus on the end goal without considering the journey needed to get there is to put the strategic cart before the change management horse.

Principle 3: the keystone in mapping change is understanding the difference between where you are and where you want to go.

In completing a Gap Analysis, four additional issues need to be addressed:

1. ***Uncertainty*** – How much information is needed? Over what period? How much quantitative or qualitative data (Schutz, 1943)?
2. ***Different perspectives*** – Complex change has many stakeholders. Each may have different views on the 'To Be' and the 'As Is' as well as vested interests in pushing forward or holding back information (Badham, 2003).
3. ***Complex processes*** – In the face of uncertainty and disagreement, how do you create working compromises on the initial 'Gap'? How can you prepare to modify the Gap as new information becomes available and new conditions arise during the change (McLoughlin et al., 2005)?

A fourth theme cuts across all three. It's the temptation to understate or ignore the:

1. ***Cultural and political dimensions of change*** – It can be technically, emotionally and politically easier to focus on the 'tip of the iceberg' of change. As we have argued, doing so is mis-leading and dangerous (Badham et al., 2020).

Figure 3.2 depicts a more sophisticated form of Gap Analysis that captures these factors as well as the distance to be travelled into a 'radar chart' or 'spider diagram'.

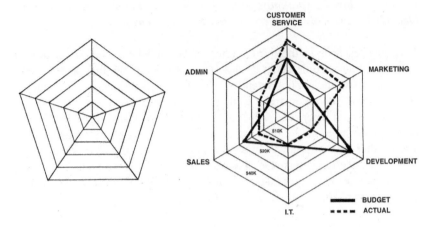

Figure 3.2   Radar or spider gap analysis

3.2   FORCE FIELD ANALYSIS

Far too many individuals and organizations set off on a journey to a destination without seriously considering what the conditions will be like along the way. Yet taking our eyes off what lies, or will lie, beneath our feet can be hazardous!

After running a Gap Analysis, we use the Force Field Analysis to map out the ground we have to cover or the terrain we have to cross. The terrain is often fluid and shifting. It's made up of many forces that determine how much of the journey will be uphill climbs and how many downhill runs. It covers the resources you have to use and the obstacles you have to navigate to get to where you want to go.

A force field analysis begins with, again, a deceptively simple two-column table (Figure 3.3) (e.g., MindTools, 2019):

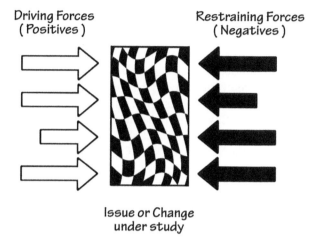

Figure 3.3   Force field analysis

The list of promoting/pushing/positive forces for the change is on the left-hand side.

All the resisting/restraining/negative forces against the change are on the right-hand side.

For ease of communication and discussion, it's good to rank each force in terms of degrees of strength (on a 1–5 scale) and mark the stronger forces on each side with thicker and longer lines.

The initial value of the force field analysis tool is that it gives you a comprehensive yet accessible visual picture of the forces affecting any change. This has particular significance for both individuals and groups:

1. it stimulates and *encourages reflection by individuals* into thinking through all the factors affecting the change they are planning or involved in, and
2. it *assists a group to map out,* appreciate and discuss what they consider the main factors affecting a change.

Applying the force field analysis mapping tool requires you also to address some additional dimensions and undertake further work. To complete an insightful force field analysis, you need a better understanding of (1) the makeup of a 'field', (2) the nature of the 'forces' involved, and (3) the character of your analysis.

These insights come from the work of the founding father of modern change management, Kurt Lewin. Two features of the makeup of the **'field'** of forces can be illustrated by comparing Lewin's force field with that of the physicist Sir Isaac Newton.

First, Newton's force fields are a set of interconnected energy flows with positive and negative charges. They are not a fixed static set of elements. Similarly, the forces you'll encounter along the journey are not clearly identified, separate and independent factors. In an important sense, they are a 'field' of forces – interdependent, systemic, dynamic and shifting in nature (Burnes & Cooke, 2013; Cronshaw & McCulloch, 2008; Swanson & Creed, 2014).

Second, remember Sir Isaac's third law of physics? 'For every action, there is an equal and opposite reaction' – that applies in change too! When you 'push' a force field, you can get 'push back': an equal and opposite reaction. The force field analysis suggests that any attempt to influence change has to work with the balance of forces within the 'field' rather than 'steamroll' over all opposition (Oreg & Sverdlik, 2011; Watson, 1971). Remember Richard Beckhard's aphorism (cited by Senge & Roth, 1999, p.14) 'people don't resist change, they resist being changed'.

The insightful use of the force field analysis also needs to consider the nature of the 'forces' at play and do so with care. Let's return to the iceberg metaphor of change. The forces 'above' the waterline are the formal, overt, rational 'tip'. These commonly refer to organizational structures and systems set in the context of market changes or government legislation. The forces 'below the waterline' are the informal, covert and non-rational forces. These are the recognizable yet not so easily talked about arenas of organizational culture and politics. They capture the forces of emotion and feeling, diversity of perspectives and patterns of power and influence (Badham et al., 2020; Senior, Swailes & Carnall, 2020, pp.132–133). These are frequently ignored or underestimated in overly rational plans of change.

Finally, the character of the force field analysis. In conducting such an analysis, you need to be

- open and mindful,
- balanced, and
- constructive.

Rather than getting caught up on categories

- be open to creating your own, and
- be mindful of simplistic stereotypes and debilitating complexity.

Make sure you give enough thought to *all* the forces and how they may work for and against change. Cultural and political forces are, at least, as important as structural and systems ones. Recognizing all such issues is part of the *change mindset* of skilled individuals and change teams. It allows for sharing perspectives, forging agreements, and creating a practical basis for informed and constructive discussions.

An extensive analysis of the Forces of Change is provided in the *Resource guide: force field analysis – a comprehensive guide for forces, fields & analyses* at the end of this book. This supplement outlines their characteristics and what are widely identified as the standard forces promoting 'readiness to change' and creating 'resistance to change'. Textbook introductions to change often have separate chapters on such topics. From a force field analysis perspective, these are most usefully viewed as preliminary generalizations about factors promoting and hindering change. A considered and relevant force field analysis places these in context and treats them as heuristics.

3.3 ROUTE ANALYSIS

Many change management solutions continue to put the cart before the horse. As we have learned, strategists often make the mistake of focusing on the goal without considering the journey. What concerns us in this chapter is that some change managers compound this error by prescribing *one fixed* route to a destination without considering the specific conditions along the way. The prescribed plan or Route Map takes the form of a fixed itinerary or a set of stages to be followed.

Harvard Professor John Kotter (2007, p.97) stated, '*The change process goes through a series of phases that, in total, usually take a considerable period of time ... Skipping steps only produces the illusion of speed and never produces a satisfying result'* – and this has become for many the North Star, or what is known in many cultures as a 'guiding star' in managing change.

As outlined in Table 3.1, there are various prescriptive models of that guiding light. They all offer their version of what David Collins (1998) described as 'N-step' models of change – where 'N' serves as a placeholder for the various steps in prescribed models. Yet, they all stem from Kurt Lewin's original insights into change as involving phases of unfreezing, moving and re-freezing. In recent years, this idea of preparing, supporting and reinforcing change is most clearly captured in William Bridges and Susan Mitchell (2000) and William Bridges' phases of 'letting go', transitioning through the 'neutral zone', and establishing 'new beginnings' (Bridges & Bridges, 2016). Scratch the surface of sequential models since Lewin's original formula, and you will find similar themes (Cummings et al., 2016; Weick & Quinn, 1999).

For example, in Kotter's 8-Step Process of Change reading, you will see that the first three stages: creating a sense of *urgency*, building a *coalition* and creating a *vision* and strategy – are all components of what Lewin identified as preparing for change. When Kotter argues that 50% of change programs fail in the first stage – not creating enough urgency – he points us to the genuine challenges of preparing properly for change. As a heuristic guide, this can be useful. This mis-leads us, however, when these insights are placed within a rigid itinerary of three stages of 'unfreezing', 'moving' and 're-freezing' and context-free prescriptions of fixed sequences of actions.

The ability to capture these predictable challenges without taking the form of a rigid itinerary is made possible using our third Mapping tool in the Orientation Phase: The Route Analysis. This analysis:

1. creates a route map as a provisional plan for preparing, supporting and reinforcing change, and
2. adopts a flexible, iterative, and pragmatic process.

The Route Analysis works as **a suggestive GPS** and not a set of commands to be followed on a forced route march. It raises issues to be considered, but the *form, degree* and *order* are fit-for-purpose. How, what and when we tackle issues depends on the context and conditions revealed by the Gap and Force Field analyses – creating an inherently fluid mapping process (Lesser et al., 2011, pp.24, 101).

Once the Gap and Force Field analyses are done, a route analysis details a desirable route. Once defined, however, you may find there are practical barriers or insufficient resources for what is proposed. For example, 'Is this initiative unrealistic? Is the timing right?' Raising such questions calls for re-examining the gap, a new force field and a revised route map. It's an iter-

Table 3.1   Stages of the change journey

Lewin (1947b)	Lippitt et al. (1958)	Schein (1961, 1996)	Kübler-Ross (grief) (1969)	Prochaska, Prochaska & Levesque (addiction) (2001)
UNFREEZE	Develop Need for Change Establish Change Relationships	Disconfirm/Destabilize Learning/Survival Anxiety Psychological Safety	Denial Anger	Pre-Contemplation (not ready) Contemplation (getting ready) Preparation/Determination (ready)
MOVE	Work Toward Change	Redefinition & Role Models Mind & Behaviour Modification Personalized Learning/T. & E. Mystical Manipulation Eliciting Confessions	Depression Bargaining	Action/ (change behaviour) Willpower
RE-FREEZE	Stabilize Change Achieve Terminal Relations	New Normal No Disconfirming Evidence	Acceptance	Maintenance (maintain behaviour) Termination or Relapse

Kanter (1985)	Tichy & Devanna (1986)	Bridges & Bridges ([1991] 2016)	Rogers (diffusion) (2003)
Project Definition gather information (tech/pol) manageable & saleable needs/scope definition Coalition Building build consensus top-level support acquire resources	Recognize Need for Revitalization Create New Vision	Saying Goodbye • letting go	Knowledge Persuasion Decision

Action mobilize/protect team counter mis-information communicate progress midcourse corrections	Mobilize Commitment Transition	Neutral Zone uncertain confused	Implementation
	Institutionalizing Change	Moving Forward • letting come	Confirmation
Kotter (1996)	**Brown (1998)**	**Luecke (2003)**	**Scharmer (2009)**
Creating Urgency Building Coalitions Developing Vision & Strategy	Rites of Separation rites of questioning rites of rationalization & legitimation	Mobilize Energy joint identification of problems Shared Vision competition & organization Identify Leadership	Sensing suspending redirecting
Communicate the Vision Remove Obstacles Create Short-Term Wins	Rites of Transition rites of degradation & conflict rites of passage & enhancement	Focus on Results not activities Start Change at Periphery then spread not top down	Presencing letting go letting come
Consolidating Improvements Institutionalize the Change	Rites of Incorporation rites of integration and conflict reduction	Institutionalize Success Monitor and Adjust	Realizing crystallizing prototyping institutionalizing

ative process to be done at the start of the change cycle but also one to repeat throughout the cycle as conditions unfold (Appelbaum et al., 2012; Chia, 2014; Dawson, 2019; Kotter, 2014; Liberman, 2013; Tsoukas & Chia, 2002; Weick & Quinn, 1999).

When going through this process, remember that the Route Map is a provisional plan for a complex cultural transition. Consider the scholar Alfred Korzybski's famous phrase 'the map is not the territory'! – it metaphorically illustrates the difference between belief and reality – just as the menu is not the meal or the painting of a pipe is not the pipe. A considered Route Analysis gives us the flexibility needed to adapt any Route Map to the terrain to be crossed since it reminds us of three realities in mapping change:

First, vagueness. Stages are not distinct. They are blurry and general in character. 'When' and 'how' issues are treated as a creative part of the route analysis. It's not a given (Badham et al., 2012b; Collins, 1998, chapter 4; Zerubavel, 1991).

Second, sequence. In reality, change does not happen through a rigid sequence of stages. Despite a logical coherence, stages actually overlap, are iterative and even occur in reverse! Given this complexity, you'll need to be flexible in applying and reapplying the route analysis (Kanter et al., 1992; Kanter, 2011; Lok et al., 2022).

Third, level. Different parts of change and areas of an organization will progress at different rates in addressing the many issues associated with the various stages. Therefore, the route analysis must adopt a multi-level understanding and approach (Bartunek & Jones, 2017; Stouten et al., 2018).

A sophisticated route analysis output is a realistic and flexible route map or provisional plan. It guides us through the storms of change while not distracting us from attending to the changing weather and treacherous waters.

Such a **Route Map** provides:

1. A framework for group communication and discussion.
2. A 'plan of action' to guide and track change activities.
3. An 'early warning system' alerting us to potential problems and remedial actions.
4. A 'motivational' device to capture progress and identify and allow the celebration of 'small wins'.

Table 3.2 outlines some well-known guidelines for leading change focusing on key issues and iterative cycles rather than a rigid sequence of stages.

Table 3.2   *Issues and cycles in the change journey*

Ancona (2005; et al., 2007)	Lawrence, Dyck, Maitlis & Mauws (2006) (champions)	Kanter (2011) (change wheel)	Fuda & Badham (2011) (metaphors)
Sensemaking	Use influence	Common theme & shared vision	Fire
Relating	(evangelists)	Symbols & signals	Snowball
Visioning	Use authority	Governance & accountability structure	Mask
Inventing	(autocrats)	Education, training, action tools	Russian Dolls
	Embed change	Champions & sponsors	Chef
	(architects)	Quick wins & local innovations	Movie
	Manage culture	Communications, best practice	Coach
	(educators)	exchange	
		Policy, procedures, systems alignment	
		Measures, milestones & feedback	
		Rewards & recognition	

3.4   CHAPTER SUMMARY

In *Chapter 3, Maps and Orientation*, you have learned about three mapping tools in the **Orientation Phase** of the Cycle of Change:

3.1   Gap Analysis

- Change is not the destination. It is the journey from where you are ('As is') to where you want to be ('To be').
- A simple gap analysis captures this journey in a two-column table. A more complex one is a 'spider diagram'.
- The analysis is a challenging process of creating a practical, workable and revisable view of the gap.

3.2   Force Field Analysis

- A *simple force field analysis* identifies the forces for and against change that must be considered when planning your change journey.
- An *advanced force field analysis* considers the complex interactions between forces, the full range of forces involved, and how to analyse to ensure these are adequately considered.

3.3   Route Analysis

- Adopts a flexible and enabling three-stage (preparing, supporting and rein-forcing) view of issues and challenges to be considered.

- Uses the 'gap' and 'force field' analyses to determine which issues are the most significant and when and how they should be addressed.
- Is the revisable output of an ongoing mapping GPS.

HEART AND HAND (PRACTICE)

3.5 CASES AND EXERCISES

Studying or intervening in organizational change requires balancing the *complexity* needed for realism and credibility and the *simplicity* needed to be useable and practical. Mapping a change journey requires the knowledge of where one is and where one is going ('gap analysis') and the conditions along the way ('force field analysis') *before* determining the best road or path to take ('route analysis'). Mapping also needs to be sensitive to the complexity vs simplicity trade-off. Uncertainty, conflict and change mean a gap analysis has to be sensitive to its, at least in part, artificial nature. Complex intertwining, limited information and changing circumstances make a force field analysis more akin to informed guesswork than objective reporting. Route analysis is, then, always a rough sailing guide rather than a fixed route march. The degree to which effort must be put into different types of actions depends on circumstances and context, and stages are vague, overlapping and shifting. As we have said, what this means is an ongoing need to be mindful that the '*map is not the territory*'.

Continuous mapping is essential for orientation and reorientation on the change journey. In exercise 3.5.1, we begin with a review of conventional wisdom and standard consulting assumptions about conducting a 'gap', 'force field' and 'route' analysis. Exercises 3.5.2 and 3.5.3 dig deeper into critical discussions of avoiding over-simplification. Finally, in cases 3.4, 3.5 and 3.6, you will find two additional cases to continue practising and using the mapping tools (*Jamie's School Dinners, An Inconvenient Truth*).

3.5.1 Apply Mapping Tools

Case materials
Levinson, E. (2015). *Thriving on change: Creating a gap analysis.* https://www
  .youtube.com/watch?v=uc3m_yWAbSk&feature=youtu.be (accessed 23 May 2022)
Riley, J. (2016). *Lewin's force field analysis model.* https://www.youtube.com/watch?v
  =X9ujAtYAfqU (accessed 23 May 2022)
Tanner, R. (2022). *Unfreeze, change, refreeze: Is this a child's game?* https://
  managementisajourney.com/unfreeze-change-refreeze-is-this-a-childs-game/
  (accessed 23 May 2022)

Part A: Gap Analysis

Task 1
Watch the Levinson (2015) video.

Task 2
Reflect upon:

1. What are the elements of a 'current state' or 'starting point'?
2. What are the elements of a 'future state' or 'desired outcomes'?
3. What is a 'Road Map', and why is it essential to conduct a Gap Analysis first?

Part B: Force Field Analysis

Task 3
Watch the Riley (2016) video.

Task 4
Reflection:

1. What are the most critical forces required to promote change?
2. What are the most critical forces that hinder change?

Part C: Route Analysis

Task 5
Read the blog and watch the Tanner (2022) video.

Task 6
Reflect upon and answer:

1. On what grounds does Tanner (2022) argue that Lewin's three-stage view of 'unfreezing', 'moving', and 're-freezing' is not a 'child's game' but a 'simple and powerful' model?

3.5.2   Define the Problem: *Moneyball* (2011)

The 2011 sports film *Moneyball* (Director, Bennett Miller) is based on a true story about Billy Beane (played by Brad Pitt), the new General Manager of the Oakland Athletics baseball club and his attempts to assemble a competitive team (Lewis, 2004). The movie relates the challenges he faced in taking a poor, underperforming club and making it a success by shifting its established 'experience-based/talent scout' model of player recruitment and selection to a statistics-based model.

Billy Beane's interpersonal challenges are captured in three selected scenes, where he challenges the established habits and perspectives of the scouts. We use this case to explore the interpersonal dimension of the 'changes' we are mapping.

Case material

Moneyball (Director: Miller, B.) 3 Scenes: (1) 08.25–12.38, (2) 31.26–36.48, (3) 46.48–49.23

In short form can be accessed via:

Moneyball (Director: Miller, B.) (2011a). Scene 1 from Moneyball – What is the problem? https://www.youtube.com/watch?v=pWgyy_rlmag (accessed 23 May 2022)

Moneyball (Director: Miller, B.) (2011b). Scene 2 from Moneyball – Science vs scouts. https://www.youtube.com/watch?v=DtumWOsgFXc (accessed 23 May 2022)

Moneyball (Director: Miller, B.) (2011c). Scene 3 Moneyball – Adapt or die. https://www.youtube.com/watch?v=ugN5aD5p2NU (accessed 23 May 2022)

Task 1
Watch Scene 1 from *Moneyball*.

Task 2
Discuss:

1. How do Billy Beane and the scouts differ in their views of the nature of the 'problem' and its causes?
2. What do you think is the change 'gap'?

Task 3
Watch Scenes 2 and 3 from *Moneyball*.

Task 4
Describe:

1. The *political forces* at play (*Hint*: who decides, who do they answer to, and what coalitions are in conflict?).
2. The *cultural forces* at play (*Hint*: how does the way Billy Beane and the scouts talk about the problem affect how they act and their fortunes, what are seen as legitimate sources of advice for the different parties and how do they demean others?).

3. The *structural forces* at play (*Hint*: how do Billy Beane and the scouts differ over the solution lying with the replacement of players they have lost on the advice and experience of the scouts? Note the sharp emotive conflict of powerful rhetorics).
4. What do you think is the *change force field* at Oaklands?

Further reading
Lewis, M. (2004). *Moneyball: The art of winning an unfair game*. New York: W.W. Norton.

3.5.3   Streamline Chaos: Jamie Oliver's School Dinners

Jamie's School Dinners was a landmark four-episode documentary series broadcast on Channel 4 in the UK from 23 February to 16 March 2005. The series features the TV chef Jamie Oliver attempting to improve the quality and nutritional value of school dinners at Kidbrooke School in the London Borough of Greenwich, followed by the whole Borough. The initiative led to a broader campaign (called Feed Me Better) to improve school dinners throughout Britain and was followed up by several other initiatives and documentaries, including *Jamie's Return to School Dinners* (2006); *Jamie Oliver's Ministry of Food* (2008); and *Jamie Oliver's Food Revolution* (2010–11).

While dramatized as a 'reality-tv' show, the director signed a contract with Jamie Oliver to release *Jamie's School Dinners* despite some of his reservations. The case captures in video-documentary form the 'below the surface' drama and emotion, turbulence and emergence, errors and recoveries involved in change. It arguably does this better than any other available. It is arguably the best in a series of increasingly popular documentaries on chefs using celebrity status and skills to help restaurants transform (e.g., Gordon Ramsey) or address contemporary food and health issues (e.g., Heston Blumenthal).

Case materials
Jamie's School Dinners (Directors: Gilbert, G., & Oliver, J.) (2005). S01 – Ep01. https://www.stan.com.au/watch/jamies-school-dinners & https://www.justwatch .com/au/tv-show/jamies-school-dinners/season-1 (accessed 22 May 2022)

Task 1
Watch *Jamie's School Dinners* S01 – Ep01.

Task 2
Apply the mapping tools (gap, force field, route analyses) to the case. You can check on your analysis of the coverage of *Jamie's School Dinners* in the Intermission.

Further reading
Jamie's School Dinners (Directors: Gilbert, G., & Oliver, J.) (2005). S01 – Eps01–4.
https://www.amazon.com/Jamies-School-Dinners/dp/B00099BISK/ref=sr_1_1
?keywords=jamie%27s+school+dinners&qid=1579731543&sr=8-1 (accessed 23
May 2022)

3.5.4   Inconvenient Truths: Five Multinational Corporations (MNCs)

Between 2015 and 2017, Christopher Wright and Daniel Nyberg (2015, 2017b,
2017a) publicized their findings on the outcomes of climate change strategies
in five major Australian corporations over ten years. Their findings? In each
case, companies began with a radical and impassioned agenda for addressing
climate change (*Phase 1: Framing*) and proceeded to translate this into a set
of implemented practices, internal measures and active proselytizing of the
benefits (*Phase 2: Localizing*) and then in the face of increasing challenges
and growing criticism, wound back the changes and re-prioritized market
concerns (*Phase 3: Normalizing*). The case allows you to explore the broader
institutional and political context of organizational change objectives, barriers
and outcomes in matters of great social significance.

Drawing on Wright and Nyberg's account of the phases of 'framing',
'localizing' and 'normalizing', use the classic 'unfreezing', 'moving' and
're-freezing' route analysis to map out and evaluate the change undertaken
by these companies. 'Route analysis' is where the 'rubber hits the road' in
the mapping process. It involves applying the general types of phases/issues
identified in stage theories of change to either design a desired path of change
or evaluate and adapt to the progress of change so far. For a precise and useful
analysis, it is important to include both 'gap' and 'force field' analyses within
the case when applying the 'route analysis' tool to the change journey Wright
and Nyberg documented.

Case material
Wright, C., & Nyberg, D. (2015). *Climate Change, Capitalism, and Corporations.*
Cambridge: Cambridge University Press.
Wright, C., & Nyberg, D. (2017a). An inconvenient truth: How organizations translate
climate change into business as usual. *Academy of Management Journal, 60*(5),
1633–1661.
Wright, C., & Nyberg, D. (2017b, 22 November). How bold corporate climate change
goals deteriorate over time. *Harvard Business Review*, 2–4.

Task 1
Read Wright and Nyberg (2017a, 2017b).

Task 2
Describe what the organizations did to 'unfreeze', 'move' and 're-freeze' the change. You may find it helpful to use Kotter's breakdown of these phases into: create urgency; establish coalition; define vision and strategy ('unfreezing'); communicate the vision, empower action and create short-term wins ('moving'); and embedding in the culture and structure ('re-freezing').

Task 3
Evaluate how well you think organizations moved through these stages, considering the nature and degree of change required ('the gap') and the forces affecting the change ('the force field'). What did you uncover?

3.5.5   Change Habit 3: Be Prepared

It's no secret. Brenda is a list maker. It's because she's a doer and loves that feeling of accomplishment when she scratches things off her list. However, she doesn't plan out one area, and that is her holidays. Whether she's just too tired by the time she actually takes one or what, but she seriously resists creating itineraries.

Recently, this beautiful friend invited her to share in a very planned holiday. Brenda had a 'quiet freak out' when she looked at the minutia on the itinerary. The trip organizers had all activities packaged up, event by event, day by day, hour by hour. Brenda does not do 'mandatory fun' well. But she ended up having a great time and is incredibly grateful for the experience! Had she not been given 'the plan', she would've never seen so many incredible places in a short time. She and her friend also found themselves with more free time than expected and got ideas from locals and social media on the best food and private events.

But, despite all the planning, her travel agent made a mistake. The boat trip ended in Budapest, but he had her returning to Australia by plane from Prague. She'd never been. So, she took a train, and booked a hotel using Wi-Fi, Uber-ed from the Prague train station and fell in love with one of her now most favourite cities in the world. A place that wasn't on her original route became one of the highlights of her trip.

Lessons from this? As her father – a colonel in the army – would say, 'Proper Preparation Prevents Piss Poor Performance'. But this means leaving space for creativity. Supplement it with exploration when things do not go according to plan. And never underestimate the value of mapping technologies as a supportive GPS!

So, to help you get used to the idea of how you might use maps as a form of flexible and creative planning, we'd like you to try two exercises: 'Be

Prepared' and 'Micro-Managed v Free Bird'.

Task 1

'Be Prepared'. Imagine you have 15 minutes to leave your house. What five things do you take with you? Do not overthink! Just list. Take no more than 5 minutes to complete this exercise.

Note: Usually, the things we pick reflect what's most important to us and how we prepare for the unexpected. This is a great game to play amongst friends at a dinner party: notice the differences and what it says about you and them. It also gives you something to ponder when considering how you and others view the future, priorities, and prepare. Some of us take practical things; others take things with emotional significance. Some focus on financial and identity things and documents, others on people. One of our friends said she would take her cats but didn't mention her husband! Others go into 'Survivor'-mode bracing for a catastrophe. These decisions reflect how you and others prepare for events, what you think is essential, and how you approach the future. Reflect on what your choices said about you and what you need to prepare for change. Then reflect on how others' choices are similar or different and what this says about what you should prepare if you were trying to influence them!

Task 2

'Micro-managed vs Free Bird'. Think of your next two calendar days as types of journeys. Use whatever mechanism you usually use – an electronic device, calendar, actual paper planner or even post-it notes.

For the first day, **Create a 'Micro-Managed Diary'**. List out the activities you believe you will or should do, and fit them into a plan for the day. Include all main activities, both personal and work. Then, try to stick to the plan!

For the second day, **Create a 'Free-Bird Diary'**. List only the key activities that absolutely must be done. Provide a rough sequence only and leave as much open as possible. In this case, try to do these key activities as well as you can.

Now, reflect on your experiences with these two styles of preparation.

- How did you **benefit** from either or both?
- What did you see as the **limitations** of the styles?
- Think about how you allocated your time.
- How much were you able to do? How well did you do them etc.?
- Which made you happier?
- What do you think are the implications for how you might best prepare for and 'map out' change?

RESOURCES

3.0   Mapping

Ever since Alfred Korzybski coined his classic phrase, 'the map is not the actual territory', there has been a recurring interest in the advantages and yet limitations of maps, how they are deployed in practice and their reflective use. In advocating and conducting mapping, we need to be mindful of this. As a classic organizational studies introduction to the practical and thoughtful use of maps see Weick (1983). For a web-based accessible run-through of the map is not the territory see Farnham Street (2015).

Bookstein, F. L. (2015). *The map is not the territory.* https://fs.blog/2015/11/map-and -territory/ (accessed 23 May 2022)
Weick, K. (1983). Misconceptions about managerial productivity. *Business Horizons, July–August,* 47–52.

3.1   Gap Analysis

Simple introductions to 'gap analysis' are rarely followed by a critical and reflective discussion of its nature, value and complexities. However, one of the best classical discussions is provided by Beckhard and Harris (1985) in their somewhat stylised 'transition model': 'defining the future state'; 'assessing the present: benchmarks for change'; and 'getting from here to there: transition management'.

Beckhard, R., & Harris, R. (1985). *Organizational Transitions: Managing Complex Change.* Reading, MA: Addison-Wesley, chapters 5–7.

3.2   Force Field Analysis

There is a trade-off in the force field readings. Accessible introductions and illustrations are useful to grasp what is involved yet are often too simplistic, while critical reflections on avoiding over-simplification often become rather abstract. Practical classic examples of the former are:

Hustedde, R., & Score, M. (1995). *Force-Field Analysis: Incorporating Critical Thinking in Goal Setting* (No. ED 383 712). *Collected Works.* New York. https://files.eric.ed.gov/fulltext/ED384712.pdf (accessed 23 May 2022)
Thomas, J. (1985). Force field analysis: A new way to evaluate your strategy. *Long Range Planning, 18*(6), 54–59.

In terms of the latter, Burnes and Cooke (2013) argue that 'force-field analysis' is a 'watered down' version of Lewin's original field theory (see pp.416–8).

When combined with Lewin's other insights (into group dynamism, action research and the three-step model), they believe it's part of a 'powerful approach to bringing about change' (p.421). Swanson and Creed (2014) argue that there is a 'creeping simplification' in the use of force field analysis (see pp.28–34) and illustrate their point with two examples of initiatives in health and waste management. While their analyses and cases are sometimes hard to follow, they sensitize us to the importance of grasping shifting perceptions of change and its complex, contested and contextual nature.

Burnes, B., & Cooke, B. (2013). Kurt Lewin's field theory: A review and re-evaluation. *International Journal of Management Reviews, 15,* 408–425.

Swanson, D. J., & Creed, A. S. (2014). Sharpening the focus of force field analysis. *Journal of Change Management, 14*(1), 28–47.

While Burnes seeks to go beyond restricted 'force field analysis' by arguing for 'field theory', Cronshaw and McCulloch (2008) make a case for 'organization field assessment'.

Cronshaw, S. F., & McCulloch, A. (2008). Reinstating the Lewinian vision: From force field analysis to organizational field assessment. *Organization Development Journal, 26*(4), 89–103.

3.3   Route Analysis

Badham et al. (2012b) argued that the creative and reflective use of a three-stage view of change is extremely valuable **if** viewed as a flexible heuristic.

In contrast to overly rational and managerial two-stage views of change, this three-stage model highlights the importance of non-rational and rational factors in guiding people through what can be a difficult 'transition'. This involves preparing them for change, guiding and supporting them through the 'difficult middles' and reinforcing change to prevent slippage back to earlier established habits and outlooks. The sophisticated application of Kurt Lewin's three-step model of organizational development and the ritualistic nature of any process of guiding people through transitions are of immense value. Much of this supportive literature was covered in Chapter 1, Tree of Change (see Tichy & Devanna, [1986] 1997); Chapter 2, Re-Imagining Change ('The Rollercoaster') and Further Reading ('Re-imagining Change'). In addition, the use of John Kotter's 8-stage theory and its alignment with Bridges' managing transitions model is covered above in Chapter 3, Cases and Exercises ('Thinking Through Route Analysis: The Kotter Model). Additional 'feel' and insight can, however, be gained from reading the following:

The discussion of the *rollercoaster ride* in:

Badham, R. (2011). *Experiencing Change: The Death Valley Roller-Coaster*, Leaflet 2 Location: Ironies of Organizational Change: Book Website @ https://reimaginingchange.com/

Badham, R. (2013). *Short change: An Introduction to Managing Change*, Introduction (section: 'This course and the book it introduces') and chapter 2, The 5M Framework (section 2.3, Experiencing Change).

The extension of Kurt Lewin's three-step model in a series of works and interventions by Edgar Schein on 'coercive persuasion' and organizational change-facilitation, in:

Schein, E. H. (1996). Kurt Lewin's change theory in the field and the classroom. *Systems Practice*, 9(1), 27–47. Particularly section 2, There is nothing so practical as a good theory: Lewin's change model elaborated.

Schein, E. H. (2008). From brainwashing to organization therapy: The evolution of a model of change dynamics. In Thomas Cummings (Ed.), *Handbook of Organization Development* (pp.39–53). Thousand Oaks and London: Sage. Particularly the section: Brainwashing or Coercive Persuasion (1952–1961).

For a critique of unreflective 'undersocialized' stage theories of change and a 'grand foundation' of 'change-as-three-steps' (CATS) from Lewin's initial 'sketchy idea' (Cummings et al., 2016), read:

Collins, D. (1998). *Organizational Change: Sociological Perspectives*. London and New York: Routledge. See chapter 4, N-step guides for change.

Cummings, S., Bridgman, T., & Brown, K. G. (2016). Unfreezing change as three steps: Rethinking Kurt Lewin's legacy for change management. *Human Relations*, 69(1), 33–60.

4.   Masks and performance

All the world's a stage, and we are but players on it. (William Shakespeare, *Hamlet*)

Knowing what to do to manage change is one thing. Knowing how to do it is another. While the route map outlines what you need to do, you have to decide *how to do it* in context and with others. How change plans are executed is always a performance, the artful exercise of influence in time, space and conditions that are often not of our choosing. In this chapter, you will discover the *performances* you will have to give, the *masks* you will need to wear, the tensions and dilemmas you will encounter, and why *influencing yourself* is central to your ability to influence others.

Learning objectives

Head (theory)

4.0 Introduction

4.1 Practice and performance

4.2 Control through influence

4.3 Tensions, dilemmas and paradoxes

4.4 Chapter summary

Heart and hand (practice)

4.5 Cases and exercises

Resources

LEARNING OBJECTIVES

- Discover and critically analyse the frontstage and backstage performances that are required in the practice of managing change.
- Examine and contrast models of management and leadership as alternative styles of influence and control.
- Apply and critically assess the costs and benefits of alternative means for influencing events.

HEAD (THEORY)

4.0   INTRODUCTION

In this chapter, we move from the **Orientation Phase** to the **Performance Phase** of the Change Cycle. When we perform the actions we have mapped out, we put the exercise of influence into practice.

The language of 'managing' or 'executing' tasks fails to capture this exercise of influence's dramatic nature and requirements. So, we're asking you to view your managerial and leadership practices *creatively* as **masks and performances**. We do so because we want you to appreciate and value the artistry involved in assuming the roles you have to play, the masks you have to wear and the performances you have to give.

Your guide to using masks and giving performances is Janus, the Roman God of transitions (Figure 4.1). He's the god with two faces. One looks back to the past – the other points towards the future. Janus symbolizes the ambiguities and tensions we experience when we're on the verge of taking on

Figure 4.1   Janus

something new. He's also a symbol of **creativity** in the face of these tensions. Albert Rothenberg (1979), Professor of Psychiatry at Harvard Medical School, describes 'Janusian thinking' as not about being 'two-faced'. It's about not being restricted to looking and acting *through* particular masks but being able to look *at* and use them. This chapter is about learning to be *creatively* **'Janusian'** in playing roles, adopting masks and performing change.

We all wear masks in dealing with others. We express ourselves through these masks, and through these masks, we leave an impression on others. But some of us can control our masks, while others are controlled by them. Performing change involves using a variety of masks. In the following pages, you will be introduced to the masks of the Roman God Janus and those associated with the Greek mythological figure of Prometheus and the notorious Italian philosopher Niccolò Machiavelli. You will learn about their uses but also be warned about their flaws.

Traditional management has one of the most established masks – the mask of the rational controller. Those unaware of its artificial character often act as if they are in an emotion-free zone. They are unable to recognize and unwilling to admit to the mask they wear. This carries over into managing change, as the Mask of the Planner and the Technician. However, effectively influencing others in change means knowing when to use this mask, drawing on its strengths, and avoiding its weaknesses. An endless element of artistry is involved in playing such roles, wearing these masks and giving such performances. Welcome to the art of leading change!

In this chapter, you will learn:

1. turning 'maps' into actions involves donning masks in the exercise of influence,
2. the exercise of influence is a frontstage and backstage performance, and
3. successfully influencing others means being aware the masks you wear as a manager or leader have both a 'dark' and a 'light' side.

4.1 PRACTICE AND PERFORMANCE

The famous Austrian economist Joseph Schumpeter (1968, p.88) once said, 'Innovation is a feat, not of the intellect but will'. We must go beyond ideas and talk to get things done.

Maps outline the territory, but they are not the territory. Maps need to be read and used along the way. It's one thing to plan how to change. It's another to make it happen. Plans need to be put into practice. Intentions have to be realized. Decisions must be made and followed through. In the case of change, follow-through means influencing people. More specifically, it's about influencing them to change their thoughts, feelings and actions to realize the purpose. Anyone who has tried to influence another person knows it can be complex and challenging. The performance is everything, and it must be right on opening night.

Most of us grow attached to particular roles or personas. As a result, we find it difficult to move outside and reflect on them. In a sense, we are controlled by the masks we wear. Yet, influencing people, in time and context, involves taking on and taking off a variety of masks. Bringing about change requires adopting many fit-for-purpose influencing styles and giving credible performances. A vital aspect of this requires standing back from the parts we play to show ourselves and our concerns as more than the functionary or the zealot. As a discipline, it involves a balancing act. This means being both in and out of the roles we play. In a sense, it involves living in an uncomfortable liminal zone 'betwixt and between' comfortable roles, personas and certainties.

What does this performance involve?

The Harvard Business School Change academic and consultant John Kotter (1990, pp.4–6 & Postscript) argues that leading change involves four main activities:

1. establishing an agenda,
2. developing a human network to realize this agenda,
3. executing the agenda, and then finally
4. achieving the outcomes.

It's about deciding what to do *and* getting things done.

As a manager, it involves traditional 'command and control' tasks such as planning and budgeting, organizing, staffing, controlling and problem-solving. This produces a degree of predictability and order in achieving stakeholder demands. This classical project management approach is essential. Establishing and running efficient processes is a necessary change management discipline. As a leader of change, however, much more is involved. Leadership means working with or creating a community with a purpose. It consists of establishing direction, aligning people, motivating, inspiring, and ultimately producing sustainable change. Leadership means winning hearts and minds, mobilizing energy and motivation. This requires more than disciplined processes.

Whether we understand, act or present ourselves as managing or leading, the exercise of influence means we have to perform on-stage and backstage. We have to act formally, upfront and in public, as well as informally, behind the scenes and in private. On the surface, change programs are presented as rational and efficient enterprises. It is the view shown in official policies and procedures, statements to customers and the public, as well as written up and verbalized in meetings, agendas and minutes. The sociologist Erving Goffman ([1959] 2022) described it as the 'frontstage' public performance of organizational life. It is the view we present, and like to present, to stakeholders and ourselves about rationality and efficiency.

As managers, we have to make a formal case for change, create legitimacy, and build confidence by acting and talking with certainty about our plans and the outcomes these will generate. As leaders, we motivate through unifying and inspirational visions of a common and higher purpose. We ignore all such activities at our peril.

On another level, change initiatives involve a range of what Goffman described as 'backstage' activities (Buchanan & Boddy, 1992). In this realm, we find a distinct language spoken. It's what the decision-making experts James March and Johan Olsen (1983) describe as the '*rhetoric of realpolitik*'. It's a world of commentary upon the formal organizational performance, a realm in which tales are told of confusion, intrigue, incompetence, vested interest and even chaos. It's what is talked about in bars, over the water cooler, and during the coffee breaks in ritualized meetings.

More than talk, these backstage activities are inevitable and essential. They involve all the pragmatic, emotional and political behind-the-scenes work needed to prop up the public performance and make it successful. For example, in our personal lives, we get ourselves ready before we go out, prepare before parties and events, and gossip and debrief with our intimate friends afterwards. We all do this, hidden from public view. We know how important it is, but we don't let others in on the act. While it may seem more real and informal than actions on the formal stage, it makes its own demands on how we need to appear. Those managing change must not only be pragmatic, but they must also *appear to be so*. Leaders must not only cater to division and conflict but must be seen to do so. They must reveal themselves as a person behind the mask, a 'beating heart' behind the 'stuffed shirt'. Again, managers and leaders ignore such realities and appearances at their peril.

The practice of change is the performance of influence. As managers and leaders, we have to do this on the frontstage and backstage. The following two sections will address how this is to be done and the tensions and dilemmas we confront.

4.2　CONTROL THROUGH INFLUENCE

Knowing there was a right mask for each performance,
Richard began to worry.

In the Performance Phase of the Change Cycle, we exercise influence and control. Debates over how best to exercise control over people and events have preoccupied humanity long before 'change management' came onto the scene. How far is the use of force or manipulation required or justifiable? To what extent are we the victims of bigger movements and events? To what degree are individuals really able to influence them?

In 1670, the French mathematician and Christina philosopher Blaise Pascal famously remarked:

> The nose of Cleopatra: had it been shorter, the face of the entire world would have been changed. (Pascal & Krailsheimer, 1995, p.120)

So, would Marc Antony and Julius Caesar *still* have fallen under her spell? And would the history of the Roman Empire have been different?

Management has always been regarded as being about control. It is based on a belief in control and a quest for control. However, control, like power, is a complex and contentious term. It has many nuances and interpretations – none of them neutral. The word 'management' originally comes from the Italian *maneggiare*, 'to handle, touch', as in 'to control a horse'! So, the theme of control is always present whether it is seen as a general practice or an organizational elite (Williams, 2015).

What's more subtle is *what one means* by control (Child, 2015). What does it mean to 'control' change?

1.   Old-style management is essentially '*controlling*', e.g., **'managing of'** oneself, others and organizations.
2.   New-style leadership is more about '*influencing*', e.g., **'managing to'** get things done (just managing, managing to get by etc.).

Think, for a moment, of the separate mental images created by using the phrase 'managing to change' rather than 'managing of change'. Attempts to dominate people and events more strongly is a particular level or form of exercising control – and not the most effective. We may more effectively influence people and events by being less controlling!

What's the best form of control over events?

Do we always have to be one step ahead to influence events? Does it require anticipating and planning every move and regulating everything? Or, given the volatility, uncertainty, complexity and ambiguity in the world, does success require room for emergence and improvisation? Not surprising, there are separate established schools of thought on the matter.

One school stresses planning and anticipation. It reflects traditional organization development's (OD's) concern with **planned** change (Burnes, 1996, 2017). It means anticipating and addressing 'people issues' upfront, mainly motivation and resistance to change. This is where expert HR/OD staff break out their diagnostic tools and intervention and planning techniques to deal with 'the people side' of change.

The second school of thought points to the importance of **emergence and improvisation**. UK Change Professors Andrew Pettigrew (2011) and Patrick Dawson (2019) have challenged the static and artificial nature of planning change. Instead, they have taken the 'processual' or process-like nature of change and focused on flexible adaptation to changes. These are described as inevitably complex, iterative and contextual.

Much of the debate over **planning versus emergence** comes from the claims and counter-claims about the dynamics or nature of change itself (Tsoukas & Chia, 2002; Weick & Quinn, 1999). Views conflict over the degree to which change is orderly and predictable or chaotic and out of control. Distinct personality types and managerial philosophies are partial to influencing strategies that are more planned or more emergent in siding with one view or another.

For example:

1. People with a more bureaucratic, rule-governed, orderly personality – the ISTJ in the Myers–Briggs framework (see Garrety et al., 2003) or the 'Box' in the Psycho-geometrics typology (Dellinger, 1996) – tend to prefer the more law-governed view of change. They also prefer planned approaches to change programs.
2. Those with a more flexible, creative and innovative mindset – the Myers–Briggs ENFP or Psycho-geometrics 'Squiggle' – select the more interpretive, chaotic, emergent view of change. They also prefer the more flexible and creative ad hoc approach to mobilizing energy for change.

So, what's the best form of control over people?
Old-school management prefers to control through structure and systems, using formal authority and incentives. It has a military ethos, 'do your task and take your rations'. The German-born American sociologist Amitai Etzioni (1975) described it as 'low intensity' management. It involves setting rules, processes and giving instructions. It also monitors results and relies on financial payment for influence and control.

However, in uncertain and challenging times, people also need to be more engaged in finding solutions to problems. It requires a distinctive style of management. One that involves winning hearts and minds through 'high intensity' management, inspiring hope where possible, and creating urgency when necessary. This management style uses confronting and emotive methods described as either *coercive* or *normative*. The coercive method uses threats and instils fear. Etzioni (in March, 1967, p.651) describes this as using the 'gun, lock, and the whip'. It scares, bullies and shames people. The normative methods seek to engage rather than impose, building consent rather than forcing compliance. It uses the carrot, not the stick. It inspires through charisma and appeals to deeply held values, identities and loyalties (for an overview, see Etzioni, 1975, p.12).

Advocates of planned and gradual change often prefer normative methods. Supporters of rapid transformation when in crisis often admit to the need for coercion. Each approach has its upsides and downsides. In the next section, we shall explore the tensions in adopting these various masks.

4.3   TENSIONS, DILEMMAS AND PARADOXES

The Irish playwright Bernard Shaw once said, 'Life is not meant to be easy, my child; but take courage: it can be delightful'.

Performing on the stage of change isn't easy. It's a challenging balancing act. There are no easy answers. Each of the masks we're required to adopt has benefits and costs!

1.   Planning can be too rigid.
2.   Improvisation can be too chaotic.
3.   Participation can be frustrating and distracting.
4.   Coercion can create resistance and backlash.

But the artistry in balancing these tensions and the satisfaction of success when things are effectively addressed can be life-changing. So, let's explore the two central tensions and how we might handle them.

The first major area of tension concerns the degree of control we should try and exert over events. We call this the 'Promethean paradox' – for the classical Greek imagery of Prometheus (Figure 4.2). He was the Titan who defied the gods by stealing fire and giving it to humanity, thus enabling progress and saving civilization (Franssen, 2014). Zeus punished the immortal Prometheus for this theft by being chained to a rock and having his liver eaten out by an eagle, only to have it grow back overnight to be eaten the next day again.

Figure 4.2   *Prometheus*

The myth in *Prometheus Bound,* by the Greek dramatist Aeschylus (2012), is symbolic of the degree to which humanity should be given knowledge and technology. Just like in the stories of Frankenstein and Dr Jekyll and Mr Hyde (Badham, 1985, 2016; Schillinger, 1984), the myth raises the questions:

Is humanity's pursuit of greater technical capability a salvation or a curse? A source of progress or a dangerous tool?

The main issue (the controversy, the paradox and the drama), is **the degree to which one should try** (and can succeed) to control the world, events and other people. The classic 'mindful' Buddhist response would be 'such an attempt is doomed to fail and causes much needless suffering'.

No matter the stance, the central issue remains:

1. How far should one attempt to control and regulate people and events?
2. How much should one plan and stick to it, and how much expect the unexpected and be willing and able to improvise?
3. Are there limits beyond which it's immoral, unsustainable or self-defeating to tread in our quest for knowledge and control?

Our second major area of tension is over the **forms of control we should try and exert over people**. We call this the 'Machiavellian paradox' – for the Italian philosopher Niccolò Machiavelli (Figure 4.3). Since distributing his political 'handbook' (*The Prince*) in 1514, Machiavelli has been a controversial figure (Jackson & Grace, 2018). In the popular mind, Machiavelli has been demonized for recommending manipulation, fear and deceit in political affairs. His work was even initially banned by the Pope. Since then, Machiavelli has become a symbol for using the 'black arts'.

Figure 4.3   Machiavelli

Recently, that view has been challenged. Machiavelli has been praised for his 'brutal honesty' and the pragmatic advice he offers to those grappling with the realities of power (Buchanan & Badham, 2020). Now, Machiavelli is celebrated for 'calling the game'. Something is appealing about his exposing the hypocrisy of leaders who pretend to be principled and act for the greater good, yet behind the scenes, they act in their own self-interest indulging in manipulation, coercion and deceit.

Machiavelli is renowned for posing the central question regarding how to influence others:

> ... whether it is better to be loved than feared, or the contrary. The answer is that one would like to be both one and the other. But since it is difficult to be both together,

it is much safer to be feared than loved, when one of the two must be lacking. (Machiavelli, [1514] 2005, pp.57–8)

The importance of 'winning hearts and minds' to bring about sustainable change is commonly accepted. Yet, what's more debatable is what's required to achieve this (Collinson et al., 2018; Dunphy & Stace, 1988; Tourish et al., 2009).

Is it better to inspire through hope or create fear? A charismatic appeal or dictator's threat?
*Are people, ultimately, motivated by running **to** what they idealize and aspire to?*
Or
*Running **from** what they're scared about and threatened by?*

We prefer to believe the former. But is this what we would like to think, or what is indeed the case? When you feverishly get an assignment or proposal in at the last minute, is this inspiration or fear of missing the deadline? If we go beyond our preferences and cultural prejudices, we can recognize and creatively respond to these issues and tensions. We don't have to be trapped by them. It's not a question of 'either/or', but 'both/and' (Lüscher & Lewis, 2008; Smith et al., 2016; Smith & Lewis, 2022).

The Promethean paradox (cf. Ohana, 2019, 'Prologue') leaves us knowing the importance of 'planned emergence' or 'emergent planning'. We're not fated to demonize planners and celebrate improvisers, or vice versa. We can draw on their strengths while appreciating their weaknesses. The Machiavellian paradox leaves us knowing about the value of inspiration and hope yet also the power of fear and urgency (Beavan, 2013; Jackson & Grace, 2018; Kanter, 2003). We are not restricted to either/or. We're not limited to vilifying coercion and praising participation, or vice versa. 'Whatever it takes' can be a creative pragmatic enterprise (Buchanan & Badham, 2020), as much about stimulating collaboration and inspiration as it is about the use of manipulation and fear. Those who successfully influence people to change use these masks selectively, strategically and appropriately. They're effective performers on the stage of change.

4.4   CHAPTER SUMMARY

In *Chapter 4 Masks and Performance*, you have learned about the Performance Phase of the Change Cycle:

* turning 'maps' into actions involves donning masks to exercise influence,
* the exercise of influence is a frontstage and backstage performance, and

- successfully influencing others means being aware that the masks you wear as a manager or leader have both a 'dark' and a 'light' side.

4.1   Practice and Performance

- Following maps and executing change is a performance.
- This involves acting and appearing as managers and leaders.
- It occurs on the frontstage and backstage of the organization.

4.2   Control through Influence

- Managing change is about influencing people and events.
- Influence is an exercise of control and can be achieved by being less 'controlling'.
- There are different methods and preferences on how to control people and events.

4.3   Tensions, Dilemmas and Paradoxes

- There are tensions to be managed in how we influence others to change.
- The Promethean and Machiavellian paradoxes capture the key tensions.
- Successful performance is the art of balance, deploying masks while being aware of their uses and flaws.

HEART AND HAND (PRACTICE)

4.5   CASES AND EXERCISES

4.5.1   Frontstage and Backstage Performances: *Hot Fuzz*

To improve our ability to influence others (and ourselves), we need to develop the capability to reflect on how we adapt and present masks in interaction with others. In organizations, we frequently have to juggle formal, public, rational and strategic performances with informal, private, social and political ones. This can be very challenging for some and easier for others. To influence organizational change successfully and effectively, it is necessary to handle multiple masks in the workplace effectively. To illustrate this, we'll be using *Hot Fuzz* (2007), a buddy cop action-comedy film directed and co-written by Edgar Wright, co-written by and starring Simon Pegg.

Case materials

Hot Fuzz (Director: Wright, E.) (2007a). Hot Fuzz opening scene (22 January). https://www.youtube.com/watch?v=7Lqd-UwZmJ4 (accessed 23 May 2022)

Hot Fuzz (Director: Wright, E.) (2007b). Hot Fuzz good luck Nicholas scene (28 June). https://www.youtube.com/watch?v=faMh6OYfuNE (accessed 23 May 2022)

Warburton, N. (2015). Erving Goffman and the performed self. 15 April. Narrated by Stephen Fry, BBC Radio 4. https://www.youtube.com/watch?v=6Z0XS-QLDWM (accessed 23 May 2022)

Task 1

Watch the BBC Radio 4 video clip, 'Erving Goffman and the performed self', then discuss the following questions:

1. Erving Goffman once observed that not only do we 'play many parts' but 'with every uniform they issue a skin'. What do you think he meant by this?
2. How do you think many feel obliged to wear a 'managerial' mask at work? How do you think this affects our ability to handle change?
3. Erving Goffman notes the discomforts created by the requirement to perform differently to different audiences. What do you think are the typical audiences in change? What kind of masks does this require us to wear?

Task 2

Watch the two *Hot Fuzz* video clips (2007a, 2007b), then discuss the following questions.

1. What do the scenes reveal about the formal and informal ('frontstage' and 'backstage') 'skills' required to be effective in the police force? What does it mean to be a 'team player'?
2. In what ways did PC Angel's mask prevent him from effectively juggling the multiple masks required?

Task 3

Answer the following questions:

1. What masks are commonly used in promoting or responding to change?
2. Are there any similarities between PC Angel's mask and fate and overly rational 'management' masks and approaches to change?
3. What masks do you have to deploy to influence others in change?
4. What does the effective art of juggling masks involve?

4.5.2   Influencing: *Bandits* and *Braveheart*

In moving beyond the rational and restrictive models of traditional 'manage-ment', you will inevitably be giving leadership *performances* that are more or less effective in handling the issues and tensions surrounding the Promethean ('planned v emergent') and Machiavellian ('participatory v coercive') dimen-sions of leading change. In this two-part case study we will focus on the perfor-mances required to influence the targeted audiences effectively. To highlight and help capture the inevitably dramatic nature of change performances, we use two movie clips, from *Bandits* (2001) and *Braveheart* (1995), as the basis for study and analysis.

Part A

Case material
Bandits (Director: Levinson, B.) (2001). Bandits 2001 vs RED 2010. 20 October 2016.
    https://www.youtube.com/watch?v=VrSscuReTQA (9.00–12.30) (accessed 21 May
    2022)

To complete Part A, watch the Bank Robbery scene (9.00–12.30) from the criminal comedy movie *Bandits* (2001, director Barry Levinson) and answer the questions below. Joe (played by Bruce Willis) and Terry (played by Billy Bob Thornton) have just broken out of prison and recognize they need money. So, Joe decides they should rob a bank. Observe how the characters approach the robbery and its immediate aftermath.

Task 1
Reflect on the differences and interactions between Joe and Terry as they improvise during the robbery. Answer the following questions about what it takes to be a successful *improviser*:

1. What makes Joe (i) effective and (ii) credible as a bank robber? Which characteristics do you think you require and need to display as a change agent able to successfully deal with the challenges that arise during change?
2. What makes Terry (i) ineffective and (ii) lacking credibility as a bank robber? Which characteristics do you think you need to avoid possessing or displaying to deal with the challenges that emerge during change?

Task 2

1. Reflect on your preliminary analysis. While you should not view the list below as a final or authoritative list, which of the following characteristics did you identify?

    a. Confidence and certainty
    b. Clarity of goals and commitment to them
    c. Resourcefulness
    d. Speed and timing
    e. Demonstrated experience
    f. Positive language
    g. Strength and forcefulness
    h. Poise, calm and lack of stress
    i. Polite, friendly and humorous demeanour
    j. Luck.

2. Reflect on what you picked up on and what you didn't, then consider the following:

    a. What are your feelings about these ten characteristics?
    b. What preferences and abilities do you think you (and your colleagues) possess?
    c. Which ones do you feel you (and they) have to work on improving in dealing with the uncertainties and risks of change?

Part B

Case material
Braveheart (Director: Gibson, M.) (1995). (1.12.30–1.19.00 mins)

Can be accessed in short form at: *Braveheart Leadership Speech* https://www.youtube.com/watch?v=hyqoC3wHMwY (accessed 5 January 2022)

In Part B, you will work with this scene from the romantic epic *Braveheart* (1995, 1.12.30– 1.19.00). In this scene, William Wallace (played by Mel Gibson) gives a dramatic speech in which he seeks to build up the confidence of the Scottish warriors at the Battle of Stirling when faced by a much larger and better equipped English army. This case analysis aims to illustrate and discuss what is required from the leader to energize and motivate enthusiastic *participation* in difficult and threatening conditions. Watch the video clip and answer the questions below to complete Part B.

Task 1
Watch the *Braveheart* scene, and answer the following two sets of questions:

1. What were the main differences between the words and actions of Wallace ('the leader') and those of the nobles ('the managers')? Second, what does this say about how you need to talk and act to inspire others to change?

2. What inspirational rhetoric did Wallace employ ('the words'), and what other elements of the performance (staging and props, actor credibility,

timing, tone and body language, etc.) are essential? How might you use these methods yourself in influencing people to change?

Task 2

Review your analysis, and consider 'rhetoric' and 'performance dimensions':

1.   Which of the following uses of *rhetoric* did you notice?
     a.   Purposeful and committed display of his identity and worthiness (*Hint*: how does he assert who he is)
     b.   Appeal to 'higher and broader' community (*Hint*: beyond their identity as conscripted serfs)
     c.   Acceptance of their concerns, but reframing them (*Hint*: answering the question about their fear of being killed)
     d.   Humility and humour break down barriers and unite in a common cause (*Hint*: self-mocking vulgarity).
2.   Just as importantly, but for many less intuitively, what other *performance dimensions* did you notice?
     a.   Timing (*Hint*: not too early, not too late – imagine if he had arrived half an hour earlier or later?)
     b.   Display of strong and prepared followers (*Hint*: arrived with his team, armed with long spears – imagine if he turned up alone!)
     c.   Dress and demeanour (*Hint*: warpaint, stares over the battlefield, armed for battle); lack of self-interest in symbolic challenging of 'managerial' authority (why do they leave …)
     d.   Staging and amplifying his presence (*Hint*: the horse, Mel Gibson is not tall, and note how the horse speeds up when he makes a major point – imagine if he had been walking …)
     e.   Use of tone and body language (*Hint*: try turning off the sound and see the importance of his physical acknowledgement of concerns, an intense stare and word emphasis to strengthen his points and raising his hand and sword in the air).
3.   Now, consider the following questions:
     a.   How often do you and others take time and effort for rhetoric and performance to influence others to contribute or participate?
     b.   What might you now do differently?

4.5.3   Delivering a *Braveheart* Speech

In *The Arts of Leadership*, Keith Grint (2000) argues leadership is 'an array of arts' (see Kruger, 2012). We can draw on this framework in exploring how to act out the leadership of change. Grint mainly focuses on the importance of 'philosophical', 'fine', 'performing' and 'martial' arts in addressing the critical questions leaders must answer in their attempts at influence: 'who', 'what', 'why' and 'how'.

In this exercise, you are asked to address these questions in scripting and acting out your version of the '*Braveheart* speech' previously analysed. This exercise can be done individually or in groups. Each individual or group works to prepare and deliver an inspirational speech designed to motivate a group who is uncertain and scared about the complex challenges they are being asked to face. The challenge can be work, personal, or a sports or political situation.

Case material

Grint, K. (2000). *The Arts of Leadership*. Oxford: Oxford University Press.

A summary of the above is found in: Kruger, M. (2012). *The Arts of Leadership by Keith Grint: An Executive Book Summary*. https://keithdwalker .ca/wp-content/summaries/1-c/Arts of Leadership.Grint.EBS.pdf (accessed 23 May 2022)

Task 1

Read the Grint (2000) article.

Task 2

Craft your own *Braveheart* speech. Ensure to address the 'who', 'what' and 'why' questions raised by Keith Grint:

* appeal to the identities of the audience,
* present a vision that is compelling to the audience, and
* use techniques for persuasive communication.

Hint: You may find the analysis of the *Braveheart* speech rhetoric and stage-craft in the previous case study valuable in addressing these questions.

After briefly setting the scene (work, personal, sports or political situation), the motivational performance should take no longer than 2–3 minutes. If it's a group activity, it should involve as many of the group as possible. The performance should be followed by a class discussion of 'what went well' and 'what did not go so well'. In this discussion, pay less attention to the quality of the acting. Instead, consider what the actors intended to do and discuss their actual impact and reasons behind it.

To make this activity more fun and interesting, create two types of *Braveheart* speeches. The first is a standard attempt at creating a motivational speech and try to make this as convincing as possible. The second is the creation of speeches that, while they have the intention and trappings of a motivational performance, are actually profoundly demotivating in their effects. The latter version is often more fun, generates more laughter and the debrief of what took place even more enlightening.

4.5.4   Strategic Change: GE and ASDA

The paradoxical nature of organizational change and its management has been recognized (Sparr, 2018). Within this literature, the tensions and dilemmas in handling 'planned' and 'emergent' strategies for change as well as the 'participative' and 'collaborative' means for achieving these are well established. Bernard Burnes (1996), in 'No Such Thing as a "One Best Way" to Manage Organizational Change', discussed the trade-offs between planned and emergent approaches to change. Dexter Dunphy and Doug Stace (1988), in 'Transformational and Coercive Strategies for Planned Organizational Change: Beyond the OD Model', discussed the appropriateness of collaborative and participative strategies for incremental and transformational change. Finally, Dexter Dunphy and Andrew Pettigrew revisited these choices and tensions in Michael Beer and Nitin Nohria's (2000a) edited volume *Breaking the Code of Change*.

This exercise aims to explore how these dimensions and tensions are handled in Michael Beer and Nitin Nohria's (2000b) classic article on 'Cracking the Code of Change'. Beer and Nohria distinguish between 'Theory E' and 'Theory O' approaches, with 'leadership' and 'process' in Theory E being 'top-down' and 'plan and establish programs', while Theory O recommends 'bottom-up' and 'experiment and evolving'.

Case material
Beer, M., & Nohria, N. (2000b). Cracking the code of change. *Harvard Business Review*, *78*(3), 133–141.

Task 1
Read the Beer and Nohria (2000b) article and answer the questions below.

1. Beer and Nohria praised Jack Welch at GE for sequencing an initial Theory E with a later Theory O. How far do you think the Welch/GE sequencing approach is a valuable heuristic or an overly simplistic and mis-leading guide?
2. Beer and Nohria also praised Archie Norman at ASDA for 'setting direction from the top and engaging people below' and 'planning for spontaneity'. To what extent do you think these are valuable guidelines or superficial or unhelpful generalities?

Further reading

Beer, M., & Nohria, N. (Eds.) (2000a). *Breaking the Code of Change*. Boston: Harvard Business Review Press.

Beer, M., & Nohria, N. (2000b). Cracking the code of change. *Harvard Business Review, 78*(3), 133–141.

Burnes, B. (1996). No such thing as … a 'one best way' to manage organizational change. *Management Decision, 34*(10), 11–18.

Dunphy, D. C., & Stace, D. A. (1988). Transformational and coercive strategies for planned organizational change: Beyond the O.D. model. *Organization Studies, 9*(3), 317–334.

Dunphy, D. (2000). Embracing paradox: Top-down versus participative management of organizational change: A commentary on Conger and Bennis. In M. Beer, & N. Nohria (Eds.), *Breaking the Code of Change* (pp.123–136). Boston: Harvard Business Review Press.

Pettigrew, A. (2000). Linking change processes to outcomes: A commentary on Ghoshal. In M. Beer, & N. Nohria (Eds.), *Breaking the Code of Change* (pp.243–253). Boston: Harvard Business Review Press.

4.5.5 Change Habit 4: Play the Part

Brenda is what's commonly referred to as a military brat. Her family is Puerto Rican, and her father served in the US Military. She was born in Germany and spent most of her childhood between European and American bases and Puerto Rico, speaking different languages. So, she was sensitized to the issues around roles and translation at an early age. In her adult years, she was appointed as a senior political adviser to the government of the day in Puerto Rico. A key part of her liaison role was to bridge federal and state issues while helping Spanish- and English-speaking governments to understand each other – politically and culturally.

Even with this broad view of translation, it's still possible to misunderstand what it really involves. The translation goes far beyond language, ideas and communication. It's also a personal and political performance. Ideas do not travel without someone to carry them. People are not heard if they're not credible or don't have access to a stage upon which to perform. We compete with others for attention.

When Brenda was asked to address over 500 workers at a closing plant on behalf of the governor, she knew she'd have to dig deep. Delivering a message of hope and resilience in her first week on the job wasn't easy. However, that particular performance and the impact on the audience energized her subsequent performances to the government actors. Over 9000 jobs were lost that year, and she had to deliver that message more times than she wished to remember. She does, however, recall switching between the roles of advocate, champion, analyst, adviser, strategist and translator. It required creating meaningful connections across sectors, political camps and cultures. It was not a stage for the faint-hearted.

Those who seek to influence others effectively need to be aware that we wear such masks and their effect. You also need to be willing and able to adapt the masks you wear and the performances you give to the audience and context. This shift to an influencing/performing mindset will challenge many. The traditional role of the manager is simply to adopt the mask of the task-focused expert in control and issuing instructions and not recognize or admit to it as a mask. This doesn't prepare you well for the role of the translator. Nor does it prepare you to adapt your mask to the context and the audience. And so, our focus in this chapter is on becoming more aware of our masks and how we might use them. Finally, we would like you to reflect upon your experiences and jot down your answers to two questions.

Task 1

The first question is: **how many masks have I worn today?** Write them down for both personal and work life. Now reflect: How did the masks work for you? Were you comfortable and get the desired reactions? Or did you find it was an effort to hold a mask? Did some work better than others?

Task 2

The second question follows: **what kind of masks do you think you need to wear to influence others in a change process**? Reflect on: the masks you're more comfortable using and those which will require more practice wearing. How can you use them more effectively in future?

RESOURCES

We use the term Janus to help capture and memorize the creative performances required from those seeking to implement change. Looking to the past and the future, Janus symbolizes the tensions involved in transitions, the creativity needed to handle them and the push-and-pull of facing in different directions, adopting contrary perspectives, and donning contradictory masks. Within organizational studies, the image of Janus has been used as a guide to help understand creative thinking, struggling with the paradoxes of participation, combining authoritarian and benevolent leadership and the ambidexterity required from innovators looking to the past and the future. A useful guide to many of these issues and tensions is provided in Isaksen and Tidd (2006):

Isaksen, S., & Tidd, J. (2006). *Meeting the Innovation Challenge: Leadership for Transformation and Growth.* Hoboken, NJ: Wiley.

4.1   Practice and Performance

In the execution phase of the change cycle, we are centrally concerned with how people actually implement the plans that have been 'mapped' out. This is a practical form of knowledge, what Ryle (2009) referred to as 'knowing how' and has, from classic Greece onwards, been regarded as 'practical wisdom' (Schwartz & Sharpe, 2011). As a discipline of influencing oneself and others, the tasks of executing change are, in many ways, akin to a performance. They are all about '*ex*pressing' oneself in a way that leaves an '*im*pression' on the audience. In this chapter, we have emphasized the importance of influencing others by effectively playing the roles of 'manager' and 'leader' on both the 'frontstage' and the 'backstage' of organizational life.

The focus on those involved in change as playing roles, donning masks, acting out scripts and delivering performances 'on stage' plays a vital role in allowing us to look beneath the surface of the 'iceberg' of organizational change. It helps focus our attention on the key significance of human inter-actions, how influence is exercised, how people make sense of the world and the ways they try to influence how others do so. In addition, the use of the 'organization-as-theatre' metaphor helps to highlight the handling of ourselves and others in giving influential performances, how we follow and yet impro-vise upon scripts, and how we set up or are the victims of the 'stages' on which we are required to play our 'part'.

Looking at the practice of change through this lens has a long history. It is var-iously described as the 'organization-as-theatre' or 'organization-like-theatre' view and as a 'dramaturgical' or 'performative' perspective. For a quick introduction to this viewpoint, see the short, entertaining video used above on Erving Goffman narrated by Stephen Fry and used in the *Hot Fuzz* (2007) exercise.

Warburton, N. (2015). Erving Goffman and the performed self. 15 April. Narrated by Stephen Fry, BBC Radio 4. https://www.youtube.com/watch?v=6Z0XS-QLDWM (accessed 23 May 2022)

An introduction to this as an academic perspective on change can be found in Badham et al. (2012b, pp.195–199). This chapter has the advantage of setting this perspective in the history of change management and the view of managing and leading change as a practice. It is, however, somewhat dense. Accessible general introductions to 'organization-as-theatre' are provided in introductory guides to images of organizations and the frames we use (Bolman & Deal, 2017; Carlson, 1996), as well as sociological introductions to 'life as drama' or 'life as theatre' (Berger, 1986; Edgley, 2013).

Badham, R., Mead, A., & Antonacopoulou, E. (2012b). Performing change: A dram-aturgical approach to the practice of managing change. In D. Boje, B. Burnes,

& J. Hassard (Eds.), *Routledge Companion to Organizational Change* (Vol. 1, pp.187–205). London and New York: Routledge.

Berger, P. L. (1986). *Invitation to Sociology: A Humanistic Perspective.* Harmondsworth: Penguin.

Bolman, L. G., & Deal, T. E. (2017). *Reframing Organizations.* San Francisco: Jossey-Bass.

Carlson, R. V. (1996). *Reframing and Reform: Perspectives on Organization, Leadership, and School Change.* New York: Longman.

Edgley, C. (Ed.) (2013). *The Drama of Social Life: A Dramaturgical Handbook.* London: Ashgate.

One of the most interesting and easily grasped features of executing change as performance is the idea that organizational actors have to perform effectively on both the 'frontstage' and 'backstage' of organizations. Again, there is no simple, comprehensive introduction to this, but Erving Goffman in *The Presentation of Self in Everyday Life* provides a valuable initial statement.

Goffman, E. ([1959] 2022). *The Presentation of Self in Everyday Life.* New York: Anchor Books, Doubleday.

Applied to organizations and change, valuable introductions and reviews are provided by the following:

Buchanan, D., & Badham, R. (2020). *Power, Politics and Organizational Change* (3rd edition). London: Sage, pp.157–8, 282–4.

Buchanan, D., & Boddy, D. (1992). *The Expertise of the Change Agent.* New York: Prentice Hall.

Burns, T. (1961). Micropolitics: Mechanisms of institutional change. *Administrative Science Quarterly, 6*(3), 257–281.

March, J., & Olsen, J. (1983). Organizing political life: What administrative reorganization tells us about government. *American Political Science Review, 77*(2), 281–296.

The idea that 'managers' and 'leaders' represent different sets of activities, roles and personas is a popular and useful way of addressing some of the influencing activities and performances managers must give. Probably the most popular presentation of the difference and the need to combine these two is provided in a series of works by John Kotter (see in particular Kotter, 1996, chapter 2, pp.17–33). Storey (2004, pp.1–39) provides a valuable introduction and critical assessment of the distinction. If you want an updated view that links these discussions to broader debates on change agency, see Caldwell (2003) and Hughes (2019, pp.237–56).

Kotter, J. (1996). *Leading Change.* Boston: Harvard Business School Press.

Storey, J. (2004). *Leadership in Organizations: Current Issues and Key Trends.* London and New York: Routledge.

and

Caldwell, R. (2003). Models of change agency: A fourfold classification. *British Journal of Management, 14*(2), 131–142.
Hughes, M. (2019). *Managing and Leading Organizational Change.* London and New York: Routledge.

Arguably the most interesting and detailed elaboration of what could be termed the 'N functions' of managing and leading change is provided in a series of reviews by Malcolm Higgs and Deborah Rowland summarized in their FramCap (Framing and Capacity building) model, and in a popular representation by Rosabeth Moss Kanter of the ten elements of systemic change in what she describes as the 'Change Wheel'. Both of these are described and reviewed in more detail in the Reimagining Change website accompanying this book.

Higgs, M., & Rowland, D. (2000). Building change leadership capability: The quest for change competence. *Journal of Change Management, 1*(2), 116–130.
Higgs, M., & Rowland, D. (2005). All changes great and small: Exploring approaches to change and its leadership. *Journal of Change Management, 5*(2), 121–151.
Higgs, M., & Rowland, D. (2011). What does it take to implement change successfully? A study of the behaviors of successful change leaders. *Journal of Applied Behavioral Science, 47*(3), 309–335.
Kanter, R. M. (2011). *The Change Wheel : Elements of Systemic Change and How to Get Change Rolling.* Harvard Business School Background Note 312–083, November.
Rowland, D., & Higgs, M. (2008). *Sustaining Change: Leadership that Works.* San Francisco: Jossey-Bass.

4.2   Control through Influence

For an overview of the links between different views of control and management and leadership ideas, see the discussion of the contrast between 'managing organizational change' and 'leading changing institutions' (Badham, 2006).

Badham, R. J. (2006). Mudanças not removalists: Rethinking the management of organizational change. *Human Factors and Ergonomics in Manufacturing, 16*(3), 229–245.

For summary overviews of the debate between more planned/controlling and more emergent/process views of how to control events in change, see in particular the references:

Burnes, B. (1996). No such thing as … a 'one best way' to manage organizational change. *Management Decision, 34*(10), 11–18.
Weick, K., & Quinn, R. (1999). Organizational development and change. *Annual Review of Psychology, 50*(1), 361–386.

For probably the best classic description of the contrast between more participatory and more coercive approaches to controlling people in change:

Dunphy, D., & Stace, W. (1988). Transformational and coercive strategies: Beyond the O.D. model. *Organisation Studies, 9*(3), 317–334.

For more extended and contemporary reflections on both sets of issues:

Buchanan, D., & Badham, R. (2020). *Power, Politics and Organizational Change.* London and New York: Sage, chapters 1, 2 and 8.
Chia, R. (2014). Reflections: In praise of silent transformation – allowing change through 'letting happen'. *Journal of Change Management, 14*(1), 8–27.
Dawson, P. (2019). *Reshaping Change: A Processual Perspective,* second edition. London and New York: Routledge.

4.3   Tensions, Dilemmas and Paradoxes

The tensions involved in exercising control are further elaborated in works exploring the paradoxes of change, the intertwining of participative and coercive activities and ethics and the arts of leadership as a performance. See, in particular, the following references:

Beer, M., & Nohria, N. (Eds.) (2000a). *Breaking the Code of Change.* Boston: Harvard Business Review Press.
Beer, M., & Nohria, N. (2000b). Cracking the code of change. *Harvard Business Review 78*(3), 133–141.
Grint, K. (2000). *The Arts of Leadership.* Oxford: Oxford University Press.

For quick summaries of Beer and Nohria (2000b) and Grint (2000):

Hart, C. (2003). Summary of Beer & Nohria (2000). Cracking the code of change. *Management and Accounting Web.* https://maaw.info/ArticleSummaries/ArtSumBeerNohria2000.htm (accessed 22 May 2022)
Kruger, M. (2012). *The arts of leadership by Keith Grint: An executive book summary.* https://keithdwalker.ca/wp-content/summaries/1-c/Arts of Leadership.Grint.EBS.pdf (accessed 22 May 2022)

For an interesting discussion of the coercive features of purportedly participative change strategies, see:

Tourish, D., Collinson, D., & Barker, J. (2009). Manufacturing conformity: Leadership through coercive persuasion in business organisations. *Management, 12*(5), 360–383.

5. Mirrors and reflection

Life is lived forwards but understood backwards. (Soren Kierkegaard)

Leaders of change initiatives are faced with known unknowns but also *unknown unknowns*. Uncertainty is endemic, complexity is unavoidable and denial is widespread. How do you evaluate your progress and adjust your course before it is too late in such contexts? How do you create early warning signals? In this chapter, you will discover the value of experimentation and evaluation, examine and critically analyse methods for monitoring intellectual, emotional and practical capabilities and progress (the head, hand and heart), and learn how to create effective and practical learning spaces within change initiatives.

Learning objectives

Head (theory)

5.0 Introduction

5.1 Reflection and agile learning

5.2 Changing measures

5.3 Learning spaces

5.4 Chapter summary

Heart and hand (practice)

5.5 Cases and exercises

    5.5.1   On the Balcony and the Dancefloor: *Invictus*

    5.5.2   Mirrors In Leadership Transformed

    5.5.3   Create Learning Spaces

    5.5.4   Barriers to Learning: NASA

    5.5.5   Change Habit 5: Be Reflective

Resources

LEARNING OBJECTIVES

- Discover and critically assess the requirements for improvisation and experimentation in complex, uncertain and confrontational change environments.
- Examine and apply measures for monitoring the intellectual, emotional and practical (head, heart and hand) capabilities and state of those involved in change projects.
- Analyse and critically assess strategies for creating effective learning spaces during change.

HEAD (THEORY)

5.0   INTRODUCTION

During any change journey, the question is always raised: '*How are you going?*' And to follow up, '*How are you doing, really?*' These are the critical questions of the **Reflection Phase** of a Change Cycle.

As you navigate through the change terrain, you find yourself second-guessing what people are thinking and feeling and, of course, what they are up to. You'll need to test influence tactics and reflect on assumptions about the situation you're in. Every action is an experiment. We all decide the best way to act based on our fallible theories about conditions and impact. So, expect or at least be ready for things to go awry and events not going according to the 'best-laid plans of mice and men'. You'll need to have timely and real feedback on how things are going, about your assumptions, and the impact of your actions – so you can influence them.

The **managerial 'plan–do–check' cycle** views change as a task-based re-engineering process. The 'check' is a rational technical step of monitoring and evaluating. It confirms if tasks are done and checks how well they are completed. We are comforted by the fact that surgeons, pilots, and engineers raising skyscrapers all use checklists. It rarely ends well when they don't. And this ends up in your newsfeed and on the evening news! Managing change also requires checklists. But just ticking the boxes is not enough.

The **leadership 'maps–masks–mirrors' cycle** goes beyond this. It captures the nature of change, and its evaluation, as a meaningful transition process. Within this process, the term 'mirrors' highlights the artificial and challenging nature of how we reflect on ourselves and our actions.

Many of us have a love/hate relationship with mirrors. Sometimes we want the truth, yet at other times we don't. We sometimes deny what we see in mirrors but still can't resist looking into them. We might even have that favourite mirror in the house. We want to see a flattering image that reaffirms a 'preferred' picture of ourselves and our activities. Remember Snow White's evil stepmother's, '*Mirror, mirror, on the wall, who is the fairest of them all?*' We are particularly sensitive to those mirrors that tell us what we are like and how others see and judge us. As the social scientist Charles Cooley ([1902] 2009) once noted, we are a 'looking-glass self' very much concerned with keeping up appearances. In checking up on how we look, and deciding how we should act, we use multiple mirrors and in different ways. For example, we use both side-view and rear-view car mirrors to capture what is beside and behind us to help us act appropriately when looking forward. When we delight in halls of mirrors, this comes from our playful appreciation of how partial and distorted mirrors can also be. Remember the warning on car side mirrors: 'Objects in the mirror are closer than they appear'!

In this chapter, you learn to use the metaphor of using mirrors in social interaction to help capture the key elements of feedback and reflection in the third and final phase of the Cycle of Change: Reflection.

In this chapter, you will learn how to build a house of mirrors to enable:

1. agile learning,
2. measurement of change, and
3. creation of learning spaces.

5.1   REFLECTION AND AGILE LEARNING

When someone tells you, '*Make time for reflection and learning*', you most probably want to scream, '*WHEN*?!!' But then, you nod your head because you know you should be taking this on board. The Reflection Phase is not an 'add-on' at the end of an outdated step-by-step change model but a capacity for ongoing agile learning in a constant iterative change cycle throughout the change journey.

In a world of constant change, competitive environments and increased pressure, it seems there's just not enough time and space to reflect and learn (Hougaard et al., 2016). Yet, we need to. As the retired lieutenant general and US Congressman Bergman noted, it is as if '*There is never enough time to do it right, but always enough time to do it over*'. Unfortunately, this is *not* a recipe for success. So how do we keep our balance and learn to improve continuously while travelling at the speed of change?

Thus far, you've learned that a **change mindset** involves being:

- Creative, entrepreneurial, and prepared for learning and growth. Embracing this is essential to adapt and survive emerging situations and demands.
- Aware that the map is not the territory, and maps are often inaccurate and don't get you there.
- Mindful that planning is essential, yet also expects actions and events will not always go according to plan.
- Ready to don different masks to influence people and events through the change journey.

Now we'll explore how to be clever in our use of 'mirrors' to guide us on this journey and help us review how we are going. We address this as the third Reflection phase of the Cycle of Change but note this is an ongoing process and is genuinely 'cyclical'. It means being ready at every stage to:

- Ditch the autopilot and re-assess plans and perspectives (Hougaard & Carter, 2018; Ie et al., 2014; Langer, 2009; Sinclair, 2016).
- Release outdated yet often preferred images of ourselves and our programs, variously described as the 'planning fallacy' or 'optimism bias' (Sharot, 2011, 2012).
- Take the initiative and keep the train on the tracks rather than just observing or waiting for the train wreck (Barton & Sutcliffe, 2017; Covey, 2020; Fraher et al., 2017).

All of this requires rapid, ongoing, agile learning. It involves the adept use of multiple mirrors in addressing what MIT Professor Donald Schon described as the three main components of reflection (Schon, 1987, pp.26 & 115; Yanow & Tsoukas, 2009):

- **Reflection-in-action**: reflecting in the moment, during the action,
- **Reflection-on-action**: in regular reviews of capabilities and progress, and

- **Reflection-on-reflection-on-action**: in evaluating practices for reflecting in and on action.

All three are required in *responding proactively* to unpredicted and emerging challenges and opportunities. It needs us to not only reflect on our thoughts and beliefs (***head***) but also on how we feel (***heart***) and how we act and perform in situ and in practice (***hand***). It means becoming more agile in our heads, hearts and hands (Hemerling et al., 2018; Kehr, 2017; Thornhill Associates, 2018). To explore this further, let's view ourselves through the eyes of three different creative mindsets.

The first is the **Explorer** – driven by the unknown. The explorer is a pioneer, throwing away old certainties and diving into the unknown. The explorer is not a discoverer. Explorers like Galileo or Richard Branson are not looking for what they already know is there. Instead, they are curious and fascinated by what they don't know. They courageously seek to push out 'final frontiers' and are resilient in their pursuit. They encourage and involve others to contribute to the journey. Also, they try to learn and profit from it. The mindset of the explorer is one who enjoys, celebrates and benefits from encountering and wandering through the unknown (Boorstin, 1983, 1992, 1998; Fischer, 2016; Gino, 2018; Martin, 2009, chapter 6; Robinson, 2020).

The second is the **Experimenter** – trialling, testing and learning as they go. There is no fun in failing, but the truth is that you'll absolutely learn much more from your failures than your successes – although it may not feel as good. Recent work on change 'failure' stresses this importance of reflection in adopting a positive and proactive response. Redefining failure as a learning opportunity (De Keyser et.al., 2021; Heracleous & Bartunek, 2021), experimenters are ready to 'fail forward fast'. They are always looking ahead, building on the useful and valuable experiences of prior attempts. An experimenter is the opposite of someone who looks backwards, holding onto mental commitments and vested in the interests of the past (whether they're habits, old programs or plans). Experimenters like the Polish physicist Marie Curie and basketball legend Michael Jordan persevere. Michael Jordan's reflection captures this:

> I have missed more than 9,000 shots in my career. I have lost almost 300 games. On 26 occasions, I have been entrusted to take the game-winning shot, and I missed. I have failed over and over and over again in my life. And that is why I succeed.

This is the mindset of the experimenter – proactive and forward-looking, focusing time, energy, commitment and resources on rapid experimentation and using what is learned for the next step (Brown & Eisenhardt, 1998, chapter 5; Duckworth, 2016; Dweck, 2017; Liedtka, 2018; Martin & Golsby-Smith, 2017; Peters, 2018).

Finally, the **Jazz Musician** is the third creative to inspire us – creatively improvising (Barrett, 2003; Leybourne, 2005, 2006; Weick, 1998). The jazz musician is provocative. Geniuses like Dizzy Gillespie saw the potential in people better than they saw it themselves and loved disrupting routines, forcing people to think in new ways. Jazz musicians are open and enthusiastic about their ability to improvise. Professor of management and jazz pianist Frank Barrett (Barrett, 2012b) talks about this in *Yes to the Mess*. He tells us how jazz musicians act their way into the future by trying different things and being open and receptive to people and events. They take turns to lead, stretching each other, and are seriously playful in contributing to the flow of action. In brief, they '*listen*', and not just with the head – they listen with their ears but also with their eyes, hearts and hands (Barrett, 2012a). In your readings and practice exercises, you will draw on these creative images in **creating *simple rules*** – for applying their capabilities and insights to how you reflect and learn in change projects (see Sull & Eisenhardt, 2012, 2015).

5.2   CHANGING MEASURES

Back to our original question for the **Reflection Phase of the Change Cycle**, '*How are you doing, really?*' Let's return to when we discussed creating Route Maps or alternate paths for the change journey to help guide you. We said Route Maps worked like a GPS, informed by the Gap and Force Field analyses. They are always the provisional end result of an iterative mapping process.

The Route Map is a crucial part of the overall Change Cycle. It tells us what kinds of performances we have to give, and when. But it does not tell us how we are going. This is where Reflection and measuring come in. It allows us to check on how we are progressing. When we create initial Route Maps, we are not clairvoyant. Although we often think or hope we are!

Measuring how we are progressing along the Route allows us to discover how well informed we were. And it gives us the ability to adjust to complex and changing situations (Accenture, 2018; Perry, 2015; Vargas & Conforto, 2019). Remember that we are now all experimenters, explorers and jazz musicians – in training – able and eager to learn. When we look back, it is always to help us see and move forward. Measuring helps us. Rather than a linear waterfall 'Plan–Do' model, however, learning requires an *agile 'Plan–Do/ Refine–Redo'* approach (Mankins, 2017). Make no mistake, this iterative, agile approach requires discipline and practice. It uses metrics yet goes beyond the metric.

Like in most domains in life, it's about the process, not the endpoint. The measures chosen to reflect the progress of change are vital. When relevant and used correctly, they capture our 'vital signs' and help us 'take our pulse'. If they are not, they only distract and distort. They become a 'Procrustean Bed' – after Procrustes, the bandit from Greek mythology who stretched or amputated travellers' limbs to make them conform to the length of his bed. The danger lies in force-fitting our actions to meet artificial measures. This does not help us to learn and adapt. The Economist Intelligence Unit (2008) has confirmed that the 'lack of clearly defined and/or achievable milestones and objectives to track progress' is the #1 factor in determining the failure of change initiatives!

Why is relevant measuring so important? Because it does three things: tracks, alerts and motivates.

1. *Tracks progress* (Prosci, 2018). Measuring allows us to establish what is to be done, what we have done and what is left to do.
2. *Alerts us to problems and opportunities* (Govindarajan, 2016; Weick & Sutcliffe, 2011). Measuring acts as an early warning system, allowing us to pick up 'weak signals' of potential problems and catch them in time or identify possible improvements.
3. *Motivates stakeholders* (Amabile & Kramer, 2011; Kanter, 2015; Kotter, 2014). Measuring achievements provides a basis for retaining and increasing confidence, reassuring stakeholders, and chunking up 'small wins' for staff to celebrate.

Many change initiatives focus on the tip of the iceberg, and their measures follow suit. Abstract indicators are used for how far we have moved from 'old' to 'new' **structures and systems**. Less attention is paid to the **context and**

meaning of change. Yet, we need to measure actual behaviour and how people make sense of what is happening: how far they have let go of old ways, how they are coping with the transition, and how much they have adopted the new ones. Also, the route map highlights that we measure progress in a three-phase triathlon and our pulse checks must capture this!

Let us illustrate this using Kotter's (2007) eight-step model. For example, if we are in **Stage 1 and Unfreezing**, we need to shake things up and build momentum. So, we must gauge how we are progressing in:

- creating levels of urgency,
- building effective coalitions, and
- providing an engaging vision and credible strategies.

In **Stage 2,** we are in **Moving** and creating support for momentum in the face of adversity. So, we'll be measuring how well we are:

- communicating the vision,
- empowering individuals and groups to overcome hurdles, and
- creating and celebrating small wins.

In the final leg of the challenge, **Stage 3 Refreezing**, we seek to avoid 'slippage' or reverting to old ways and come to embrace the 'new normal'. We'll be interested in how well change is embedded in:

- new structures, processes and systems, and
- new cultural assumptions, behaviours and habits.

Even when these deeper change issues are addressed, there is still a tendency to focus more on *strategic objectives and performance outcomes*, or **the 'head'**. Often, relatively less attention is paid to the *state of implementation* (**the 'hand'**) and even less to inspiring and empowering those *living the journey's pressures and experiencing the emotional 'rollercoaster'* (**the 'heart'**). As the Boston Consulting Group noted in their transformation report, the 'hands and heart are neglected' in most change initiatives (Hemerling et al., 2018). When measuring progress along this journey, it is essential to use a holistic and balanced set of measures and criteria. These include the 'head', the 'heart' and the 'hand' and, in addressing an issue such as 'urgency', incorporate the following:

1. The **cognitive-rational** dimensions of change (the 'head') (e.g., whether people *think* change is 'urgent – their ideas about what is urgent').
2. The **emotional-feeling** dimension of change (e.g., whether people *feel* urgent, i.e., scared or inspired by the change – their feeling of urgency or not).

3.   The **practical** dimension of change (the 'hand') (e.g., whether people can *act* on the urgency – their ability to respond in practice to what they see as urgent).

In the face of the challenges of change, staying motivated and energized is essential. Professor Hugo Kehr notes that over-emphasizing the 'head' and neglecting the 'hand' and the 'heart' is insufficient (Kehr, 2017). So, it's not the case that any old measure will do. Measures need to capture critical issues. And as conditions, tactics and objectives shift, we may need different ones – but that's part of the learning process, isn't it?

5.3   LEARNING SPACES

Do you ever expect to see a black swan? Probably not. The financier Nassim Taleb (2010) tells the story of how Europeans once believed black swans did not exist. They had only experienced white swans. So, Europeans encountered them for the first time when they came to Western Australia, much to their amazement. His point? One that financiers had ignored at a great cost: *We don't believe things can be other than what we think and expect, or different from what we've experienced in the past. Until the unexpected happens, and then we're not prepared for it.*

There will be many 'black swans' in complex situations such as change initiatives. How do we learn to 'expect the unexpected' and react to 'unknown unknowns'? How do we create 'learning spaces' that prepare us to deal with them? Our starting point in creating learning spaces needs to be realistic. We need to begin not with learning (which everyone agrees with, in principle), but with the harsh reality that learning so often fails to take place. Organizational change is no exception. Remember the 'iceberg'? It reveals its dangerous underside in learning about change as well. How? Well, once plans are created and gain momentum, they often seem to take on a life of their own. This can prevent learning and adaptation.

Champions who promote the initiative have a vested interest in good news stories. Those under pressure to deliver don't have enough time to stand back and reflect. Therefore, questioning plans, activities and progress can appear 'negative' or 'disruptive'. It can cause embarrassment, extra work and risks a political backlash. Let's face it. The 'learning playing field' is not a level one. To develop a **'learning mindset'**, you need to be aware of the challenges and barriers to learning. MIT Professor Chris Argyris warns against falling victim to such 'organizational traps' (2010).

Being aware of two traps is essential. First, we become routinely blinded by what Harvard social psychologist Ellen Langer describes as 'premature cognitive commitments' or PMCs (Ie et al., 2014; Langer, 2009). It just means individuals and organizations tend to 'see what they expect to see and ignore or deny what they do not want to see'. Questioning and criticizing change objectives and plans is often rejected as 'ill-informed' or 'improperly moti-vated'. Uncritical supporters and those with a vested interest in the appearance of 'success' often dismiss evidence of problems as a 'temporary hiccup' or 'inconclusive'. They prefer focusing on self-confirming data or positive outcomes.

Second, surfacing problems may cause embarrassment or pose a threat, prompting reflex responses like avoidance and denial. It triggers what Argyris describes as 'defensive routines' (Argyris, 1986, 1993; Jordan & Johannessen, 2014; Noonan, 2011). While we may present ourselves as being 'open' with others, the 'elephants in the room' remain – problems that people know but dare not voice. Not only are they undiscussable, but the fact they're undiscuss-able is also undiscussable! Being the 'Devil's advocate' or speaking 'truth to power' can be dangerous.

It's not enough to simply know these traps are there. It's also crucial to address them. We tackle this by building productive learning environments and creating the space to learn. We'll hold that space in time, in place and our lives. Here are four base elements and principles to consider in designing such spaces (Sense, 2004):

1. **Learning Styles.** Cater to different personalities and their preferences for different types of learning.
2. **Learning Relationships.** Spend time creating safe and trusting relation-ships allowing for difficult conversations.

3. **Learning Systems.** Develop methods and systems to stimulate creativity, capture outcomes, accumulated knowledge and insights and make them accessible.
4. **Learning authority and power.** Work on establishing official authority and the informal political will to learn. Why? Because it's essential to cover the costs and handle the controversies arising from critical analysis and active experimentation.

Learning during change is not academic; it is a **contact sport**. It is experiential, uncertain, and often upsetting and controversial. It is also practice-based, outcome-oriented and 'up close and personal'. So, it needs to take place as close to the action as possible. MIT Professor Peter Senge and his colleagues use the metaphors of the 'practice field' and the 'rehearsal' as a guide (Kofman & Senge, 1993; Senge, 1990; Senge & Roth, 1999). Where do sports teams practise? Not 'offsite' but 'on the field'. Where do actors rehearse their performances? Not just in scripting studios, but 'on stage'. Let's use two images and metaphors to shine the light on what's involved in learning spaces, first **the kitchen** and then **the playing field**.

Our colleague Dr Peter Fuda and Richard have argued that the practice of change resembles a chef. Change has its own ingredients, tools and recipes (Fuda, 2011, 2013; Fuda & Badham, 2011). It also occurs in a highly pressured environment, much like a 'kitchen'. But, just as the case in a real kitchen, the place where we prepare and serve up change may or may not encourage people to learn. Let's look at some of the UK celebrity chefs in their attempts to bring change. We can see advantages and disadvantages in how they set up their kitchens – from the chaos of Jamie Oliver, the precision of Heston Blumenthal, to the confrontational aggression of Gordon Ramsay (Badham, 2013). Who do you think provides the best learning environment?

As Senge illustrates in his discussion of 'practice fields', sportspeople practise on the same field they play on. Sports are often physical, confrontational, interactive and contextual. 'Practical skills' are intellectual, emotional and alive. They are 'up close and personal'. We test our skills and knowledge in real-life settings. To apply these principles to change initiatives implies that our learning should also:

- take place close to the action, e.g., 'timeouts' in a meeting, reflection at the end,
- involve experiments and testing in real life, real time and real contexts, e.g., in a 'pilot site', trialling experimental ideas.

Although management simulations and gamification are good tools – nothing beats learning in the thick of it!

5.4   CHAPTER SUMMARY

In *Chapter 5. Mirrors and Reflection*, you learnt about the Reflection Phase of the Change Cycle. You discovered how to build a house of mirrors to bring about:

- agile learning,
- measurement of change, and
- creation of learning spaces.

5.1   Reflection and Agile Learning

- Creating time for learning and reflection and being clever in using mirrors is essential.
- Being agile learners means bringing together reflection in and on action while working with the head (cognitive), the heart (emotional) and the hand (practical).
- Reflecting and learning while travelling at the speed of change combines the creativity and skills of the explorer, the experimenter and the jazz musician.

5.2   Changing Measures

- The Reflection Phase of the ongoing Change Cycle is about measuring, not just the measures.
- Why we measure is to track progress, alert us to potential problems and motivate staff and stakeholders.
- What we measure is above and below the waterline of the iceberg. It captures the state of our hands, our hearts and our heads. It monitors progress along the challenging triathlon as we let go of the old way, transition, and bed in the new.

5.3   Learning Spaces

- There are predictable barriers to learning. Be ready for people to be blinded by their commitments and reluctant to surface undiscussables.
- Learning spaces require time, physical space and commitment. Basic principles need to be followed, and deliberate action taken to implement them.
- Learning spaces are practice fields. Place them as close to the action as possible and expect learning to be personal and confrontational.

HEART AND HAND (PRACTICE)

5.5   CASES AND EXERCISES

5.5.1   On the Balcony and the Dancefloor: *Invictus*

The challenges of leadership are considerable when the change involves solving 'adaptive' problems for which there are no technical solutions. Sometimes discomforting behavioural change is needed. In 'A Survival Guide for Leaders', Heifetz et al. (2002) emphasize the difficulties for the leader in operating 'in and above the fray', 'courting the uncommitted' and 'cooking the conflict'. But how is this to be done? How do you handle your vulnerability and look after yourself in the process?

Case material
Heifetz, R., Grashow, A., & Linsky, M. (2002). A survival guide for leaders. *Harvard Business Review, June*, 65–74.
Invictus (Director: Eastwood, C.) (2009a). *Scene 1. Mandela's team motivation. First day in the office*. YouTube. https://www.youtube.com/watch?v=gqhS7t2dyEY (accessed 23 May 2022)
Invictus (Director: Eastwood, C.) (2009b). *Scene 2. Forgiveness*. YouTube. https:// www.youtube.com/watch?v=CYSKHgEwkfA (accessed 23 May 2022)

Task 1
Read the Heifetz et al. (2002) article and watch the two scenes from *Invictus* (2009a, 2009b).
   Scene 1. First Day in the Office. Mandela enters his office as the newly established President.
   Scene 2. Forgiveness. The head of Mandela's security, Jason Tshabalala (played by Tony Kgoroge), is confronted by former white Special Branch operatives being allocated to his detail.
   These two scenes illustrate how Nelson Mandela (played by Morgan Freeman) seeks to create a supportive yet challenging learning environment to transition to the 'rainbow nation'.

Task 2
Reflect upon and discuss the questions below.

1.   How does Mandela operate on 'the balcony and the dancefloor' and 'court the uncommitted' by, first, noticing and, second, addressing insecurities and fears and encouraging contribution?
2.   Do you think his approach will work?

3. What lessons might you draw from all of this?
4. How does Mandela create a 'vessel' that allows conflicts to 'freely bubble up' while not 'boiling over', i.e., 'cooks the conflict' and 'places the work where it belongs'?
5. After noting how differences and conflicts within the new security manifest themselves, what tactics do you think Jason should adopt to live up to Mandela's example?
6. If you think Jason will be unable to address the issues, and Mandela has gone a 'step too far', how would you recommend Mandela deals with the 'fallout' (if it occurs?). Again, what lessons might you draw from all of this?

5.5.2   Mirrors In Leadership Transformed

What does it take for leaders to transform themselves and their ability to influence and inspire others when they attempt to bring about organizational transformation? This question was tackled by Peter Fuda and Richard Badham (2011; Fuda, 2013). The case materials highlight the results of their in-depth interviews with seven successful transformational CEOs. Their extensive experiences with these CEOs and others revealed some common themes captured in seven metaphors for leadership transformation. Animated videos also illustrate each of these images. Three of these seven metaphors are about learning and how leaders use mirrors to monitor and adjust their mindsets, behaviour and relationships. These images and associated animated videos are *Master Chef, Movie* and *Coach*.

Case materials
Fuda, P. (2011b). *Movie: A leader's process of self-awareness and reflection.* YouTube & The Alignment Partnership. https://www.youtube.com/watch?v= QFX6UDtYW0M (accessed 23 May 2022)
Fuda, P. (2014). *Master Chef.* TAP. Ironies of Organizational Change Book. www .reimaginingchange.com (with permission)
Fuda, P. (2016). *Coach: In the context of sport and how it applies to business transformation.* YouTube. https://www.youtube.com/watch?v=0cHTfZ6xyX8 (accessed 23 May 2022)
Fuda, P., & Badham, R. (2011). Fire, snowball, mask, movie: How leaders spark and sustain change. *Harvard Business Review, 89*(11), 145–148.

Task 1
Read Fuda and Badham (2011).

Task 2
Watch the videos with the following relevant questions in mind:

1. For '*The Master Chef*' video: When attempting to influence others and bring about change, what recipes do I tend to follow, what tools do I tend to use, and what methods do I tend to follow? How well are these working for me? Do you see patterns in others as well?
2. For the '*Movie*' video: Do I find myself caught in a Groundhog Day of predictable frustrations in my interactions with others? How might I 'slow the action down' for oneself, take time out to 'edit' the scripts that govern my performance, attend to how I am coming across in any situation, and be ready to adapt on the spot? Do you find similar patterns in others, and what strategies might you advise?
3. For the '*Coach*' video: What are the advantages and disadvantages of using a 'head coach' (consultants), 'team members' (colleagues and subordinates) and 'supporters' (family)? How might I (and others) bring these sources of advice together in a way that makes it possible for you to receive criticism without this creating resentment?

Further reading
Fuda, P. (2013). *Leadership Transformed: How Ordinary Managers Become Extraordinary Leaders*. Las Vegas: Amazon Publishing.

5.5.3 Create Learning Spaces

Establishing an environment for genuine learning is an essential component in creating 'mirrors of change'. As Peter Senge et al. (2007) emphasize, there is a need to 'create space for change'. Senge et al. (2010) stress the metaphors of a sporting 'practice field' or 'rehearsals' for an artistic performance as helpful images for stimulating thinking about what learning spaces need to be.

Case materials
Kofman, F. & Senge, P. (1993). Communities and commitment: The heart of learning organizations. *Organisation Dynamics*, *22*(2), 5–23.

Task 1
Read Kofman and Senge (1993) and reflect upon the questions below.

1. What principles can you derive from the sporting 'practice field' or theatrical 'rehearsals' for establishing effective mirrors of change?
2. How would you apply the seven principles identified by Kofman and Senge (1993) as essential in setting up learning spaces?
   a. identify key issues

    b.   involve operational managers

    c.   create a safe, playful environment

    d.   slow down and speed up time

    e.   compress space

    f.   make the practice field like the regular workplace familiar to managers, and

    g.   seamlessly integrate the practice fields into managerial work so that reflection, experimentation, and action can be combined.

3.   Would you add anything else to the idea of practice fields for a meaningful contribution to learning for and about change? How much freedom would you give people? How would you surface issues that people find uncomfortable to discuss? How would you address issues of politics and power?

Further reading

Fulop, L., & Rifkin, W. (1999). Management knowledge and learning. In L. Fulop, & S. Linstead (Eds.), *Management: A Critical Text* (pp.14–48). Basingstoke: Macmillan.

Hemerling, J., Kilmann, J., & Matthews, D. (2018). *The head, heart, and hands of transformation. BCG Henderson Institute* (Vol. November). https://www.bcg.com/en-au/publications/2018/head-heart-hands-transformation.aspx (accessed 23 May 2022)

Kehr, H. (2017). *Motivate yourself with visions, goals and willpower.* YouTube. https://www.youtube.com/watch?v=iuIisjRIcVI (accessed 23 May 2022)

Rifkin, W., & Fulop, L. (1997). A review and case study on learning organizations. *The Learning Organization, 4*(4), 135–148.

Senge, P., Kleiner, A., Roberts, C., Ross, R., & Smith, B. (2010). *The Fifth Discipline Fieldbook: Strategies and Tools for Building a Learning Organization.* London: Nicholas Brealey.

Sense, A. J. (2004). An architecture for learning in projects. *Journal of Workplace Learning, 16*(3), 123–145.

5.5.4   Barriers to Learning: NASA

A series of mistakes and errors of judgement underlay two major fatal incidents in the USA's NASA Space Shuttle Program: the *Challenger* (1986) and *Columbia* (2003) disasters. In both cases, technical problems (*Challenger*'s now-infamous faulty 'O-rings' and *Columbia*'s 'pieces of foam') were responsible for crashes killing seven astronauts each. Investigations into these accidents uncovered that in both cases, individuals and units within NASA had warned about the technical problems and their potentially catastrophic consequences well before the 'go-ahead' was given for their launch.

In this case study, we will be using these incidents as a basis for exploring (i) the conditions required for learning to take place in organizations and (ii) barriers that must be addressed when attempting to create and sustain such conditions. NASA provides us with what is academically described as a 'counter-factual' case, one that throws light on what is required by revealing the causes and effects of their absence.

Case materials
Heracleous, L., Yniguez, C., & Gonzalez, S. A. (2019). Ambidexterity as historically embedded process: Evidence from NASA, 1958 to 2016. *The Journal of Applied Behavioral Science*, *55*(2), 161–189.

Palmer, I., Dunford, R., & Buchanan, D. A. (2017). *Managing Organizational Change: A Multiple Perspectives Approach* (3rd edition). New York: McGraw-Hill.

Smith, D., & Elliott, D. (2007). Exploring the barriers to learning from crisis: Organizational learning and crisis. *Management Learning*, *38*(5), 519–538.

Task 1
Draw on the case materials above and, if you have time, the further reading. Accessible content is freely available to inform the discussion, as well as many YouTube clips with relevant background information:

1. *Challenger* Question

    As documented by Mahler (2009) and summarized by Palmer et al. (2017), several structural and cultural conditions present in NASA made the *Columbia* disaster likely, even predictable. What were the organizational factors responsible for failing to take heed of warning signs before the *Challenger* crash, with the consequent disastrous results? A summary outline of many of these features can be found in Heracleous et al. (2019, pp.165–78).

2. *Columbia* Question

    When changes in NASA were put in place to address identified problems in accident prevention, why did these not prevent the *Columbia* crash? As illustrated in Denis Smith and Dominic Elliott (2007), there are several reasons why organizations do not learn from a crisis. What reasons do you think best apply? What could or should organizations such as NASA do to overcome them?

Further reading
Mahler, J. (2009). *Organizational Learning at NASA: The* Challenger *and* Columbia *Accidents*. Washington, DC: Georgetown University Press.

McCurdy, H. E. (1993). *Inside NASA: High Technology and Organizational Change in the U.S. Space Program*. Baltimore, MD: Johns Hopkins University Press.

McCurdy, H. E. (2001). *Faster, Better, Cheaper: Low-cost Innovation in the U.S. Space Program*. Baltimore, MD: Johns Hopkins University Press.

5.5.5   Change Habit 5: Be Reflective

As a little girl, Brenda was terrified of the wicked Queen in Walt Disney's Snow White and the Seven Dwarfs. *You know, the Queen summons the slave in the magic mirror and asks: 'Magic Mirror on the wall, who is the fairest one of all?'*

Well, imagine, if the Mirror shot back: 'Famed is thy beauty, Majesty. **But whether you are the fairest of all, well, it all depends!'**

You see, promoters of change believe they're fairest. They're the ones with the great new ideas. They're working hard to make things better. They know they need to check progress but want to hear and tell 'good news' stories. And those they ask know it!

Meanwhile, some people on the receiving end, the targets, or recipients, may be looking and hoping for the same stories, enthusiastic about the opportunities, and keen to receive the benefits. Others may differ. The 'fairest of all' is the 'good old days'. So, they may hear and circulate different types of stories about the change – stories of incompetence, insensitivity and chaos. Which one is correct? Well, it all depends – on how events are unfolding and the perspective you take upon them.

Proponents of negotiation theory often argue for the value of standing back and reflecting from the 'third position' to proactively resolve problems and tensions between different views and interests. In this case, it means rather than being locked into the claim made for and against a change, stepping back and looking at both sides, finding virtues in each, identifying overlaps, and seeking synergies. However, the first step is to find out what the different positions are, their evidence for their perceptions, and their arguments. Hence the importance of understanding the use of mirrors in change. Seeking reflection while being aware of the partiality of all mirrors and avoiding the temptation to seek self-affirming beliefs that you **are** *the* **fairest of all**.

We would like you to carry out a short '**It all depends**' exercise. Take a case of a recent change you have experienced or read about. It may be work-related or personal but try to find one where you have seen the change unfold over a period of time.

Now explore three issues:

1. **What did you or they think would happen?** What type of thinking and assumptions were behind the initial planning?
2. **What went wrong?** What did not go to plan, and how did people's perceptions of the change differ from what was expected?

3. **What could have been done to prevent it?** In what ways might the out-
    comes and perceptions have been improved if appropriate 'mirrors' had
    been put in place?

RESOURCES

The literature on individual and organizational learning is vast. For our present
purposes, the main focus is on what is required for ongoing and effective
monitoring, evaluation and adjustment in the change process. Our interest is in
the necessary ingredients for the creation of accurate and useful 'mirrors' that
make this possible.

The classic statements of the importance of reflective individual and organizational learning are provided by Chris Argyris (1993) and Donald Schon
(1987). The commitment to reflective experiential learning has been clarified
and extended in David Kolb's work on experiential learning, the learning
cycle and what is required to set up a valuable learning spiral (Kolb & Kolb,
2009; Kolb, 2015). In recent years, more considerable attention has been paid
to recognizing the role of power and emotion in learning (Vince, 2001) and
the organizational dynamics that can promote or hinder individual and organizational learning (Vince & Reynolds, 2009). For academic overviews, see
Armstrong and Fukami (2009) and Easterby-Smith & Lyles (2011).

5.0   General

Argyris, C. (1993). *Knowledge for Action: A Guide to Overcoming Barriers to
    Organizational Change*. San Francisco: Jossey-Bass.
Armstrong, S., & Fukami, C. (2009). *The SAGE Handbook of Management Learning,
    Education and Development*. London and Thousand Oaks, CA: Sage.
Easterby-Smith, M., & Lyles, M. A. (Eds.) (2011). *Handbook of Organizational
    Learning and Knowledge Management* (2nd edition). Oxford: Blackwell,
    pp.453–476.
Kolb, A., & Kolb, D. (2009). Experiential learning theory: A dynamic, holistic
    approach to management learning, education and development. In S. Armstrong, &
    C. Fukami (Eds.), *The SAGE Handbook of Management Learning, Education and
    Development* (pp.42–69). London and Thousand Oaks, CA: Sage.
Kolb, D. A. (2015). *Experiential Learning: Experience as the Source of Learning and
    Development*. Upper Saddle River, NJ: Pearson Education.
Schon, D. A. (1987). *Educating the Reflective Practitioner*. San Francisco: Jossey-Bass.
Vince, R. (2001). Power and emotion in organizational learning. *Human Relations*,
    54(10), 1325–1351.
Vince, R., & Reynolds, M. (2009). Reflection, reflective practice and organizing reflec-
    tion. In S. Armstrong, & C. Fukami (Eds.), *The SAGE Handbook of Management
    Learning, Education and Development* (pp.89–104). London and Thousand Oaks,
    CA: Sage.

Valuable overviews of such forms of individual and organizational reflection as a 'mindful' enterprise are provided by Yeganeh and Kolb (2009), Jordan and Johannessen (2014) and Jordan et al. (2009).

Jordan, S., & Johannessen, I. A. (2014). Mindfulness and organizational defenses: Exploring organizational and institutional challenges to mindfulness. In A. Ie, C. T. Ngnoumen, & E. J. Langer (Eds.), *The Wiley Blackwell Handbook of Mindfulness* (pp.424–442). Chichester: Wiley-Blackwell.
Jordan, S., Messner, M., & Becker, A. (2009). Reflection and mindfulness in organizations: Rationales and possibilities for integration. *Management Learning, 40*(4), 465–473.
Yeganeh, B., & Kolb, D. (2009). Mindfulness and experiential learning. *OD Practitioner, 41*(3), 8–14.

5.1   Reflection and Agile Learning

As part of an iterative change cycle, ongoing monitoring, evaluating and adjusting of change initiatives requires improvisation and experimentation. The following books and articles provide essential insights into both. They view improvisation through the lens of jazz and theatrical rehearsal. Experimentation involves prototyping, creating exploratory probes, and being mindful in fast-moving, complex and risky environments.

Barrett, F. J. (2003). Creativity and improvisation in jazz and organizations: Implications for organizational learning. *Organizational Improvisation, 9*(5), 605–622.
Barrett, F. J. (2012b). *Yes to the Mess: Surprising Leadership Lessons from Jazz.* Boston: Harvard Business Review Press.
Brown, S., & Eisenhardt, K. (1998). *Competing on the Edge: Strategy as Structured Chaos.* Boston: Harvard Business School Press.
Kanter, R. (2002). Strategy as improvisational theater. *MIT Sloan Management Review, 43*(2), 76–81.
Leybourne, S. A. (2006). Managing change by abandoning planning and embracing improvisation. *Journal of General Management, 31*(3), 11–29.
Mankins, M. (2017). 5 ways the best companies close the strategy–execution gap. *Harvard Business Review, 13*(3), 1–6.
Weick, K. E. (1998). Improvisation as a mindset for organizational analysis. *Organization Science, 9*(5), 543–555.
Weick, K., & Sutcliffe, K. (2011). *Managing the Unexpected* (2nd edition). San Francisco: Jossey-Bass.

5.2   Changing Measures

Creating comprehensive measures for monitoring and evaluating change requires consideration of the head, the hand and the heart. Kehr (2017) addresses the importance of each element for motivation and their operationalization as a set of measures are captured in consultancy methods by Thornhill Associates (2018) and BCG (Hemerling et al., 2018).

Hemerling, J., Kilmann, J., & Matthews, D. (2018). *The head, heart, and hands of transformation. BCG Henderson Institute* (Vol. November). https://www.bcg.com/en-au/publications/2018/head-heart-hands-transformation.aspx (accessed 23 May 2022)
Kehr, H. (2017). *Motivate yourself with visions, goals and willpower.* https://www.youtube.com/watch?v=iuIisjRIcVI (accessed 23 May 2022)
Thornhill Associates. (2018). *Thornhill Leadership Survey 3.1.* https://www.thornhill.co.za/wordpress/wp-includes/images/resources/Thornhill Leadership Survey 3.1 (TLS) fact sheet.pdf (accessed 23 May 2022)

5.3   Learning Spaces

The creation of learning spaces builds on and extends the work of Peter Senge and his associates in practice fields (see section 5.4.3). These ideas have been extended in analyses of the nature of 'holding environments' for adaptive leadership and transformation, experimentation, learning loops and safe spaces as central to 'strategic doing' (Morrison et al., 2019); and moving beyond 'learning environments' and 'organizational learning' in addressing the key role of power-politics and diverse perspectives in creating genuinely dialogic 'learning spaces' (Fulop & Linstead, 1999; Rifkin & Fulop, 1997). For a series of articles exploring the creation of a 'structure that reflects' and collective learning environments as a key component of learning, see the collection of articles in *Organizing Reflection* (2016), edited by Michael Reynolds and Russ Vince (particularly chapter 1 'Organizing Reflection: An Introduction' by the editors and chapter 6 'In Search of the Structure that Reflects' by Davide Nicolini et al.

Fulop, L., & Linstead, S. (1999). *Management: A Critical Text.* Basingstoke: Macmillan.
Heifetz, R., & Linsky, M. (2017). *Leadership on the Line: Staying Alive through the Dangers of Leading.* Boston: Harvard Business Review Press.
Morrison, E., Hutcheson, S., Nilson, E., Fadden, J., & Franklin, N. (2019). *Strategic Doing: Ten Skills for Agile Leadership.* Hoboken, NJ: Wiley.
Reynolds, M., & Vince, R. (Eds.) (2016). *Organizing Reflection.* Abingdon and New York: Routledge.
Rifkin, W., & Fulop, L. (1997). A review and case study on learning organizations. *The Learning Organization, 4*(4), 135–148.

Intermission: *Jamie's School Dinners*

In Chapter 3, Maps and Orientation, you were introduced to the docu-drama *Jamie's School Dinners*. The first episode was used as a case study to test your understanding and application of gap, force field and route analysis. In this Intermission, we draw on this case in more detail, illustrating the insights a force field analysis provides.

BACKGROUND

Jamie's School Dinners is a landmark four-episode 'docu-drama' recorded between the spring to winter of 2004 and broadcast on Channel 4 in the UK from 23 February to 16 March 2005. The first episode shows celebrity chef Jamie Oliver attempting to improve the quality and nutritional value of school dinners at a typical British comprehensive school, Kidbrooke, in the London Borough of Greenwich. In the second episode, he travels to Eden Primary School in Durham, an area designated as the unhealthiest in Britain, to test out his recipes and ideas on younger children. Finally, in the third and fourth episodes, Jamie tries to build on the lessons he has learned to transform the dinners of all schools in Greenwich.

In 2005, the *British Medical Journal* stated, 'Jamie Oliver has done more for the public health of our children than a corduroy army of health promotion workers or a £100m Saatchi & Saatchi campaign' (Spence, 2005). The series inspired a broader change campaign (*Feed Me Better*), persuading the Labour government to commit an extra £280 million over three years to school dinners in the UK (2005–2008). In 2010 the Universities of Oxford and Essex produced a report confirming the positive impacts on education because of Jamie Oliver's initiatives (Belot & James, 2011; Williams, 2010). Nora Sands left Kidbrooke but has gone on to help other dinner ladies, and others have undertaken further initiatives (Weale, 2015). In 2010 Jamie Oliver was also awarded the TED Prize for his visionary work sparking significant social change. His scope expanded from working with parents on their cooking (*Jamie's Ministry of Food*, 2008) to schools in the US (*Jamie's Food Revolution*, 2010) and even the entire 'sugar' industry and its influence on the modern diet (*Jamie's Sugar Rush*, 2015).

However, there has been a backlash from various quarters, including parents, children, teachers, dinner ladies, and the government agency, the Office for Standards in Education, Children's Services and Skills (Ofsted). A third docu-drama (*Jamie's Return to School Dinners* (2006) revealed the limitations, challenges, and breakdowns. Nora Sands, the dinner lady protagonist, resigned from Kidbrooke School in 2007, reputedly frustrated and demoralized by the lack of promised government funding and training. The terms in which the discussion was carried out have also been criticized, with Jamie Oliver criticized for his self-centred cult of celebrity, lack of consideration for parental authority, public shaming of those who do not conform to an ideal type of diet and physique, social stereotyping, and insensitivity towards those who could not afford healthy meals (Cook, 2008; Pike & Kelly, 2014; Piper, 2013; Warin, 2011). In 2015, Jamie Oliver asserted that the project had in many ways failed, foundering on the class divide in Britain (healthy eating was 'posh' middle-class fare) (see references in Flowers & Swan, 2015; Furness, 2015).

Superficial treatments of Jamie Oliver's successes and failures either simply praise his skills and capabilities as a change agent (TransitionCulture, 2006; Video Arts, 2012, 2015, 2020 – for a critique, see Kelly & Harrison, 2009, p.33) or condemn his initiative as self-interested and unproductive (Slocum et al., 2011). In this book, we take a different stance. We view Jamie Oliver as an ambiguous, contradictory, ambivalence-generating, and polarizing figure, as are the change initiatives he has been involved in (Cook, 2008; Pike & Kelly, 2014; Taddeo & Dvorak, 2010). As a result, *Jamie's School Dinners* provides a helpful case study since it is not a simple one-dimensional view of the change process and its actors. While it is important to appreciate the limitations of reality TV docu-dramas, *Jamie's School Dinners* also captures the emotion, politics, anxieties, excitement, challenges, and frustrations of change in a rarely seen way. There were reputed conflicts between Jamie Oliver and the director of the series over what was desirable and permissible viewing, as the director sought to portray a more nuanced view of Jamie's personality and actions. The series also interweaves the personalities and practices of individuals with the broader forces and conditions within which they operate in a way that is both engaging and informative. For these reasons, it is of considerable value as a case study illustration to apply some of the mapping tools described in Chapter 3. From a personal perspective, it is simply the most emotive, exciting and interesting change documentary we have been able to find over the last 20 years!

> Jamie's School Dinners is an extraordinarily rich (and contradictory) document of British society, politics, and television. (Leggott & Jochsherf, 2010, p.60)

> Jamie Oliver is fundamentally an ambiguous figure…intersections of contemporary celebrity culture and social (moral) entrepreneurship are complex and ambiguous spaces. (Pike & Kelly, 2014, pp.26, 34)

JAMIE'S SCHOOL DINNERS FORCE FIELD ANALYSIS

To generate thought and inspire reflection, the following are what we regard as the multiple forces at play in Jamie's change initiative. We would also like to take this opportunity to recognize the insights of managers and students who, over a decade, have added richness and depth to these reflections. The tables below summarize the multiple and complex forces (of strategy-structure, technology-innovation, leadership-power and culture-meaning) ***promoting*** (left-hand columns) and ***challenging*** (right-hand columns) Jamie's change initiative in Greenwich in 2004.

Table I.1   *Forces of strategy-structure*

External Environment	**External Environment**
International competitiveness demands a skilled and healthy workforce	The central government, council and school restricted budgets for school dinners
Centralized and managerialized government monitors educational performance and student well-being	Fragmentation of responsibility for children's health and educational performance
Government's regulation of health and risks	Legally binding contracts with school catering suppliers
'Health trends' in the food supply, fast-food, and overall restaurant industry (including celebrity chefs)	Lack of coordination and collaboration amongst healthy food suppliers
Increased health care costs, e.g., chronic illness	The proliferation of the fast-food industry, cheap junk food and their advertising campaigns
Local government responsible for public health and improved measurement of outcomes	Relative lack of coordinated government support for preventive and health-based education performance improvements
Government and council funding for school meals and kitchens	Professional medicine associations have prevention (nutrition) as a relatively low priority
Growth and proliferation of preventive medicine companies, associations and groups	Professional education associations have child's diet as a low priority
Parental responsibility for children's health	Parental challenges in prioritizing children's health through healthier, sometimes costlier and more time-intensive meals
Internal Structure	**Internal Structure**
Comparative lack of academic success in education, failure to achieve baseline standards	Food costs come from other educational budgets
Increased child poverty and associated educational and health costs	Food and catering are not part of the responsibility of staff or represented in the governance structure
Low-quality care for long-term and chronic child illnesses	Remuneration of dinner ladies as part-time, cheap, sub-contract labour
Comparatively high violence, drug use and mental problems amongst children	
Incentives for schools to improve academic and health performance	
Strategic Framing & Intent	**Strategic Framing & Intent**
Government child and chronic health initiatives	Low priority of school food in health and education ministry strategies
Government education initiatives to enhance performance and health and improve rankings	Schools have a cost-focused school dinner strategy
Independent school initiatives to increase education and health performance	Council's lack of attention to health-based educational attainment in their priorities and budgeting
Public health initiatives from concerned groups (alternative medicine, exercise, diet & weight)	

Table I.2   *Forces of technology-innovation*

External	External
Increased nutritional knowledge and professional expert advice	Lack of skill and training for sub-contracted kitchen staff
Growth in healthy food supply knowledge, equipment and processes	Cheap and tasty mass-produced fast food
	Available reliable supply of junk food
High rate of diet-related disease diagnosis and publicly available advice	Lack of knowledge, skill, equipment and money in the population (notably, here, dinner ladies and parents) for healthy food and cooking
Government regulation and advice on food and health standards	
Increase in packaged and takeaway healthy food	
Increased supply of organic and healthy food ingredients	
Healthy food menus from celebrity chefs, diet companies, vegetarian/vegan promoters, and organic food companies and associations	

Internal	Internal
Head dinner ladies and part-time chefs with cooking experience	Lack of equipment for preparation or storage of healthy foods
Availability of school kitchens, with equipment, processes and staff	Sub-contracted part-time staff, with little knowledge about or motivation to cook healthily
Jamie Oliver's recipes, knowledge and staff support	Highly regulated processes for unskilled dinner ladies, restricting content, tasting etc.
	Little time available for the preparation of healthy foods

Technology Frames and Strategies	Technology Frames and Strategies
Commitment to providing food to help children with their education	Aim to make children feel full and get a free meal rather than a healthy one
Commitment to children 'in need'	Routine and standardized thoughts and habits about how and what to cook
Jamie Oliver's challenging of the mass catering frame and attitudes and conditions supporting it	Lack of attention to health in the life and work of dinner ladies
	Good food as a cost rather than a value or a lifestyle

Table I.3   *Forces of leadership=power*

Promoting Sponsors	Resistant Stakeholders
Political parties in an election period	Political parties when there is no or negative
Government ministers with interest in publicity and	publicity
profile	Government ministries or sections within them
Sections of Ministries of Education and Health were	committed to existing budgets, policies and
concerned with student well-being, education and	practices
preventive medicine	Councillors and staff when over-budget or faced
Local councillors concerned with reporting and	with controversy
reputation	Governors and head teachers who went over budget
School governors and head teachers promoting	faced complaints or negative publicity
school's performance and reputation	Parents adhering to fast food, wishing to avoid
Parents committed to healthy eating and child's	children's complaints and/or anti-Jamie Oliver
well-being and education	Fast food companies and mass advertising
Media outlets supporting film and heroic stories	
Champions	**Resistant 'Targets'**
Jamie Oliver as a celebrity chef committed to	Stressed dinner ladies faced with extra work and no
healthy eating and advancing his profile	more pay, and the unions who support them
Nora as a head dinner lady, committed to doing	Children habituated to junk food and unwilling to
things right, the good of the children and her status	try alternatives
Dinner ladies interested in children, cooking, career	Caterers and parents, when asked to adjust their
'Converted' children participating in events and	offerings and behaviour
dissemination	
Change Team	**Change Team**
Jamie and his company (publicists, accountants,	Jamie's arrogance, lack of change skills, being
menu creators, family, film crew)	time-poor, and need for only positive publicity
Nora and supportive head dinner ladies &	Nora and other head dinner ladies, when faced
Kidbrooke staff	with Jamie's lack of planning, self-centredness and
Institutions mobilized to provide resources and	possible lack of focus
work on the project (e.g., army)	Jamie's wife Joules, against negative publicity and
Co-opted children working on the project (e.g.,	work taking him away from the family
sandwich boy)	School children's resistance, when faced with
	negative peer pressure

Table I.4   *Forces of culture-meaning*

Parents, educators and health promoters are concerned with the children's well-being and the ensuing anger/ guilt when it does not occur	Lifestyle, eating habits, and mores of many of the ('working class') dinner ladies and parents, as well as children
Suspicion and critiques of mass production, artificiality and the food industry variant	Advertising of mass food producers
Governments, ministries and councils concerned with status in health and education rankings	Working-class parents are financially strapped and view 'healthy' food as a 'posh' or 'middle-class' concern
Increasing popularity and commercialization of exercise, diet, healthy food, and preventive medicine	Children's aversion to authority (particularly when older) and peer group pressure to conform to established mores and behavioural habits
Children's desire to please (particularly when younger) and peer group pressure once the healthy diet has become the 'new normal'	The value of parental choice and responsibility for their own family in the face of intrusion from experts and institutions
Cult of celebrity and the celebrity status of Jamie Oliver as a chef	The instrumental view of work, and suspicion of authority, from dinner ladies (typical of lowly paid, sub-contract, part-time, unskilled labour)
Media promotion of the campaign, including this documentary series	Bureaucrats suspicious and resistant when faced with Jamie Oliver's flamboyant improvisation and contempt for rules

MAPPING *JAMIE'S SCHOOL DINNERS*: BRINGING IT ALL TOGETHER

Mapping a force field of change is no simple task. It is beset with challenges and risks. Common mistakes are to stereotype forces or examine them in isolation. In mapping, the concept of GIGO (Garbage In, Garbage Out) applies. An over-simplified or mis-leading force field analysis does not help us prepare the route map. It may even be counter-productive. If we can capture the multiple and complex forces involved and how they interact, then we are halfway there.

Reflection (Individual or Group)

After reviewing the above outline of the forces affecting Jamie Oliver's change initiative, how illuminating did you find it? Were there forces you did not consider? On reflection, which are the most significant? Were there distinctive gaps in your initial appreciation of the forces? What might this say about your existing mindset in approaching change? What might you do to improve? Clearly, you do not have to take the above list as 'gospel'. Be ready to discuss and debate whether you think they are correct, their relative importance and so on. Do this, however, from an open-minded learning perspective. Ask yourself: 'What might I learn from this?'

Let's explore how the force field analysis is intertwined with a gap analysis and route analysis in a change mapping process:

*   ***Gap Analysis***: how we identify and characterize the 'gap' influences the forces we consider. Also, once we have explored the forces in some detail, this often affects how we define the 'real' gap!
*   ***Route Analysis***: how we define the force field shapes our view of a possible and desirable 'route'. If the 'route' appears to be impractical or unfeasible, we need to return to the 'gap' we wish to address, reconsider the forces related to it, and map out a new route.

REFLECTIONS ON THE GAP ANALYSIS AND ITS IMPLICATIONS FOR A FORCE FIELD ANALYSIS

Scope Affects the Forces

The definition of the scope of the change not only defines the change but determines the forces affecting it. Is *Jamie's School Dinners*, for example, an initiative to create a 'healthier, happier, cooler nation' in which 'children do not die before their parents' (UK), 'changing school dinners in a borough' (Greenwich), or 'changing school dinners at one school' (Kidbrooke Comprehensive)?

Each one of Jamie Oliver's stated objectives is a different change project, even if they are nested within each other, and he would like to achieve each. Whether initiatives are perceived as successful or failures depends on how change is defined and the ability to influence the forces relevant to the different initiatives.

It is interesting to observe Jamie Oliver's rhetoric and broader political campaigns as a celebrity chef over time. Fundamentally he is concerned with the overall health of the public in general and children in particular. He begins his heavily publicized initiatives by seeking to deliver better school dinners (*Jamie's School Dinners*, 2005) and mobilize for the United Kingdom government's funding of school dinners (*Feed Me Better* campaign, 2004). Next, he looks to influence what and how parents cook (*Jamie's Ministry of Food*, 2008) and then expands his reach to eating habits in the United States (*Jamie's Food Revolution*, 2010). Finally, he campaigns against what he believes is the core issue, excessive sugar and obesity in the West (*Jamie's Sugar Rush*, 2015).

Reflection (Individual or Group)

So, what do you think Jamie's 'real' change project is? First, consider how different views of the scope change the nature and strength of the forces under consideration. Then, consider the validity and value of defining Jamie's primary change project as we do: *the transformation of school dinners in the borough of Greenwich as a demonstration site designed to influence the government.* The documentary, we believe, strengthens this demonstration site project, exerts a broader cultural influence within the UK, and helps to cement his career as a celebrity shift committed to healthy food.

Forces Influencing the Depth of the Gap

Once a comprehensive analysis of the force field affecting the change is done, attention is drawn to various factors that may not have been as visible in a 'first cut' view of the gap (often perceived primarily in terms of structural and technical issues). Is, for example, *Jamie's School Dinners* a technical project about 'creating a menu under 36p' (as per the Greenwich budget), a political project to 'get more money on the plate' (in the UK), an enterprise in 'brainwashing and retraining kids' or a broader socio-economic and cultural initiative to shift a UK class system in which healthy eating is a 'posh' middle-class concern? As a celebrity chef influenced by his start-up at Kidbrooke to cook more nutritious meals, Jamie may be forgiven for initially thinking this is a technical 'cooking' project. But we soon find out it is far more! Beneath the unhealthy eating 'iceberg surface' lies a whole set of cultural mores, group pressures and political interests perpetuating a 'junk food diet' amongst UK school children. As we dig deeper into the forces affecting the change, our view of the 'gap' and the 'route' begins to change.

REFLECTIONS ON THE ROUTE MAP AND ITS IMPLICATIONS FOR A FORCE FIELD ANALYSIS

A.   Route Maps: A Refresher

Chapter 3 introduced the change 'rollercoaster' as a heuristic guide to a 'three-phase view' of the change route taken in deliberate transformation initiatives. Additionally, we learned there are different slants on the processes of preparing, supporting and reinforcing change:

- 'unfreezing/moving/refreezing' (Lewin, 1947b)

- 'separation/liminality/reincorporation' (Turner, 1991)
- 'saying goodbye/shifting into neutral/moving forward' (Bridges & Bridges, [1991] 2016)
- 'sensing/presencing/realizing' (Scharmer, 2009)

As we have emphasized, this is a handy heuristic for typical tasks and rough sequences. It is not to be mistaken for a rigid route map, for that would be counter-productive, even silly (Cummings et al., 2016). The designated activities vary in significance, may overlap, and are often iterative and interdependent. Rather than a fixed plan, the heuristic allows initial speculation on 'what needs to be done' and means of evaluating 'where one is at'. It also informs and is informed by our force field analysis. That is because the nature and strength of the forces change over time, depending on the stage of the change process and the opportunities and challenges that arise.

John Kotter's (1996, 2014) popular books *Leading Change* and *Accelerate*, present a view of the key phases that can be employed as a helpful heuristic:[1]

Phase 1. Unfreezing

1. Creating a Sense of *Urgency*
2. Building a Guiding *Coalition*
3. Forming a *Vision, Strategy* and Set of *Initiatives*

Phase 2. Moving

4. *Communicating* the Vision
5. *Enlisting* a Change Hero Army
6. *Enabling* Action by Removing Barriers
7. Generating *Short-Term Wins*

Phase 3. Refreezing

8. *Sustaining* Acceleration
9. *Instituting* Change

B.   Jamie's Route Map

Phase 1. Unfreezing
Step 1: Creating a Sense of Urgency
     Jamie needed to create a widespread sense of urgency around the importance of transforming school meals in Greenwich.
Step 2: Building a Guiding Coalition
     Jamie needed to build a formal and informal coalition of support to transform school meals in Greenwich.

Step 3: Forming a Strategic Vision and Initiatives

Jamie needed to create an inspirational vision, form strategies for its realization, and develop initiatives to make the strategy and vision a reality if implemented fast and well enough.

Phase 2. Moving

Step 4: Communicating the Vision

Jamie needed to use every vehicle possible to communicate the new vision, strategies and initiatives to the key stakeholders, using words, symbols, images and exemplary actions.

Step 5: Enlisting a Change Hero Army

Jamie needed to enlist a network of motivated volunteers to help mobilize energy, resources and people for the change.

Step 6: Enabling Action by Removing Barriers

Jamie needed to remove obstacles to change, change systems or structures that undermined the vision and encourage risk-taking and non-traditional ideas, activities, and actions.

Step 7: Generating Short-Term Wins

Jamie needed to plan for visible improvements and successes, create these and recognize and reward those involved.

Phase 3. Refreezing

Step 8: Sustaining Acceleration

Jamie needed to keep up the momentum after sustaining a win or two.

Step 9: Instituting Change

Jamie needed to institutionalize changes achieved into the processes, including procedures and behaviours of the groups and organizations involved, ensure that the connections between the new behaviours and persuasive outcomes were shared and embedded and create the means to provide effective leadership development and succession to maintain the change.

C.   Route Map and the Force Field

This route map is created by applying the general 'stage' theories of change issues and required actions to the *Jamie's School Dinners* case. The result is a description and prescription of the challenges and initiatives to be undertaken. Change, and recommendations on how to achieve it, is always complex, however, and while we would like to 'do all of it', we have to be selective and focus on key issues and challenges. This focus requires serious analysis and attention to what we view as the force field! How can we decide the precise route if we don't consider the terrain we have to cross? In what follows, pay attention to both how your view of the Gap affects your analysis of the Force

Field (and vice versa) **and** how your analysis of the forces informs what you regard as crucial actions and initiatives in the Route Map (and how your analysis of the Route also shapes consideration or reconsideration of the forces at play).

This may sound somewhat complex, but don't be too daunted. The following exercises should be quite self-explanatory.

EXERCISE 1: WARM UP: 'JAMIE, MIND THE GAP!' (INDIVIDUAL OR GROUP ACTIVITY)

Part A. Define the Gap

Start by writing down a view of the 'gap' as Jamie appeared to see it at the start. Focus on technical and structural issues (e.g., menus, diet, health etc.). Then, discuss and write down a deeper view of the change based on a recognition of the degree to which the technical change in the nature and preparation of school dinners in Greenwich is embedded within a set of technical, economic, cultural and political conditions that include:

- skills and equipment in school kitchens and contracts with food suppliers,
- school budgets and the level and responsibility for funding school dinners,
- expectations of children about desirable food and dinner ladies about the nature of their work (in a context of the expectations and conditions of parents, mass food companies, organic and healthy eating movements, and contract labourers), and
- different, conflicting and fragmented interests of school heads, councils, food suppliers, education and health ministries and the government.

Part B. 'Sweet & Sour'

Have one group (or yourself if you are doing this alone) make a case for how excellently and even somewhat heroically Jamie addressed the 'standard' prescribed change actions in addressing this Gap ('the sweet'). Have another group (or yourself) make a case for how badly, even counter-productive, Jamie managed these change requirements ('the sour'). Following this exercise, you might provide a list of the 'pros' and 'cons' of the stance and initiatives he undertook. This will prepare you for the following exercise, in which you link your conclusions with the Jamie force field analysis provided earlier.

EXERCISE 2: YOU ARE THE CONSULTANT: 'HELPING JAMIE' (INDIVIDUAL OR GROUP ACTIVITY)

For this exercise, you will refine your understanding and analysis through a more detailed reading and applying the key mapping techniques.

Part A: 'Jamie's Force Field and Route Map'. The Appetizer

Read through, and have a preliminary discussion about:

- your view of the Gap based on your earlier reflections,
- the above Force Field Analysis of Jamie's School Dinners, and
- the Route Analysis provided for you.

Any initial ideas and insights you had not thought about? Feel free to modify, elaborate or add to our guides. These are intended as a discussion starter, not a rigid template, and your discussion will be as valuable as our suggestions in developing and reinforcing your understanding.

This initial reading and discussion will prepare you for the following two parts of this 'consultancy' exercise:

(i)   Reviewing and evaluating the route Jamie took, and
(ii)   Recommending to Jamie what he could or should have done better.

Part B: 'Jamie's Rollercoaster'. The Main (Group or Individual Exercise)

Review and evaluate Jamie's role as a change agent and the overall change initiative at Kidbrooke using Kotter's recommended steps.

1. For *each of the nine steps*, evaluate:
    a. In what ways and to what extent was Jamie successful in performing this step?
    b. To what extent do you attribute Jamie's success to the structural, technical, cultural and political forces promoting and hindering that particular step?
    c. How were these factors intertwined, repeated and changing over time, and what implications does this have?
2. Would you argue Jamie was more successful at Unfreezing, Moving, or Re-freezing? Why?

Part C: 'Jamie's Change Consultant'. The Dessert (Group or Individual Exercise)

Acting as advisers to Jamie, follow your retrospective evaluation of the route he took and how well he did by creating a new route map outlining what you believe could and should have been done, and conclude with a statement of the relevance of this analysis for anyone else considering healthy eating change initiatives in the future.

NOTE

1. In both *Leading Change* and *Accelerate*, Kotter focuses on eight (8) sets of activities, characterized as essential steps in *Leading Change* and more broadly as accelerators in *Accelerate*. We have modified this to include nine (9) steps for this exercise, as Kotter added 'Enlisting a Change Hero Army' accelerator to the *Leading Change* steps. In considering this blending of Kotter's different works, note:
    *   Urgency: is not just fear based, but includes excitement around a Big Opportunity.
    *   Coalition: includes a formal Executive Team or Stakeholder Group, Change Team and a mobilized Change Army.
    *   Vision and Strategy: includes setting up a series of strategic initiatives to realize the strategy.
    *   Communicating: omitted in Accelerate, clearly still important so retained as a phase.
    *   Enlisting: Change Hero Army is a new focus, emphasizing mobilizing an informal network.
    *   Enabling: previously described as empowerment but same content.

ACT III

LEADERSHIP OF CHANGE

INTRODUCTION

While accepting his American Film Institute (AFI) Life Achievement Award, Sir Thomas Sean Connery reflected on his experience, 'making movies is either a utopia, or it's like shovelling s*** uphill'. Few would argue that creating a productive and effective change cycle is any different. On the change rollercoaster, there are times when the wind is behind you and the sun on your back. Things get done, goals are achieved or even exceeded, your ideas work out, and your career advances. At other times, it is a hard, frustrating, and dispiriting struggle uphill. Confronting the Lord's Slope's systemic challenges can seem too hard.

In Act II, we identified the features of a productive Cycle of Change. In Act III, we explore how to act as leaders when confronted with the highs and lows, ups and downs of trying to implement this Cycle. In the face of such challenges, there is a temptation to look for and provide instruction manuals for heroic leadership. In his book *Accelerate* (2014), Harvard Professor John Kotter advises on '*Building Strategic Agility for a Faster-Moving World.*' In *Leading Transformation* (2018), INSEAD Professor Nathan Furr and his colleagues give instructions on '*How to Take Charge of Your Company's Future.*' The challenge, however, is not merely one of 'building' or 'taking charge'. What we offer is something, somewhat ironically, more pragmatic and more idealistic.

Rather than deifying leaders and romanticizing leadership, we are concerned with the mundane realities of getting things done in practice. We are also concerned with finding meaning and purpose in an uncertain and often hazardous enterprise. It is a matter of both *being effective* and *finding meaning*.

This requires an appreciation of what James March describes as the *plumbing* and the *poetry* of leadership (March & Weil, 2005).

The *plumbing* part of leadership is the capacity to apply known techniques. It is all those operational management tasks needed to achieve our goals and desired outcomes. It is the practice of 'plugging the gap' between our intentions and aspirations and what we attain. As March remarks, it 'involves keeping watch over an organization's efficiency in everyday tasks, such as making sure the toilets work and that there is somebody to answer the telephone' (March & Weil, 2005, p.98). But it goes far deeper than this. It requires competence at the top, as well as throughout the organization. It is a capacity to master the context and take initiatives based on delegation and follow-up. It entails creating a sense of community and trust. It means establishing unobtrusive methods for coordination, ensuring people understand their roles sufficiently to integrate into the overall process and adjust it. These features are essential for effective operations and change. They do not occur spontaneously, nor can they be achieved by applying a rule book. The successful plumber is a master-craftsperson and a dedicated professional able to get things done in sometimes uncertain and contested environments. 'Plumbing' plays a critical role in creating, supporting, and defending effective cycles of change, as you will see in *Chapter 6, Knowing–Doing Gaps.*

Leadership also calls for the gifts of the poet, able to forge visions, appreciate life and be aware of reality. The *poetry of leadership* includes attaining and maintaining elegance, balance, and poise in the face of conflict and hardship. An appreciation of this dimension of leadership is more than a craft. It is a process of self-discovery. It explores meaning and purpose for oneself and others. In often complex, uncertain and contested situations, it requires the ability to recognize paradox, be intellectually playful and foster an enabling humility. The poetry of leadership explores the meaning of 'living with the gap' between our aspirations and achievements. In the life and work of master-craftspeople and inspirational artists, plumbing and poetry intertwine. We explore the poetry of leadership not only for its own sake but also because it informs and assists the life of the plumber.

Leadership is an art, not a science (Grint, 2000). Actions and events shape our world, but it is also constructed by the language we use and the perspectives we adopt (Sinha, 2010; Weick, 2011). We create rather than find meaning in what we do and how we talk about it (Cunliffe, 2002; Ramsey, 2018; Shotter, 1996; Weick, 2004). And we do not do this alone or according to a plan. We construct the world we live in in interaction with others as well as in quiet reflection, in flashes of insight and inspiration as well as analysis and application. This insight is empowering and creative, practical as well as poetic. It is not a matter of 'anything goes', because we live in a world of limited resources and power plays. But if, as 'practical authors' (Cunliffe, 2001), we impose meaning, then what kind can, and should we fashion for ourselves and others? What lived experiences do we wish to evoke through the images, metaphors, myths, and narratives we create? This is a practical question, as well as a poetic one. We determine what we can achieve in practice, pursue beauty, and consider aesthetics in how we act and what we aim for. When an interviewer asked the celebrated anthropologist Clifford Geertz why he left journalism to study philosophy, he replied, 'I wanted to do something more practical.' We agree.

In *Chapter 1, The Change Problem*, we advocated taking the 'Red Pill' of change management and exploring 'how deep this rabbit hole goes'. *Chapter 7 Paradoxes of Change* and *Chapter 8 Ironies of Change* take you there. Chapter 7 reveals the embedded paradoxes in our change enterprise and the leader's role in accepting, living with, and working through contradictions and dilemmas that cannot be avoided or wished away. Chapter 8 follows this up by introducing the ironic perspective, performance and temperament required in leadership. In the concluding *Epilogue*, we argue this alternative view of leadership creates a lightness of being which is more pragmatic, more joyful, and simply more human than found in managerial manuals for success.

6.   Knowing–doing gaps

The road to success runs uphill. (William Henry (Willie) Davis, NFL Title and Superbowl champion)

While the principles underlying the change cycle are widely recognized, they are often not implemented. There is never enough knowledge and resources to do what individuals and organizations know needs to be done. This chapter explores the leadership, practice and power gaps that underlie these problems and discovers and examines how leaders mind these gaps and mobilize energy and resources to overcome them.

Learning objectives

Head (theory)

6.0 Introduction

6.1 The leadership gap

6.2 The practice gap

6.3 The power gap

6.4 Conclusion

    1. Being Mindful

    2. Mobilizing Yourself and Others

    3. Beyond Mindful Entrepreneurs

6.5 Chapter summary

Heart and hand (practice)

6.6 Cases and exercises

    6.6.1   Act Like a Leader: *Borgen*

    6.6.2   Change Masters: Rosabeth Moss Kanter

    6.6.3   Symbolism in Action: 'I Have a Dream'

    6.6.4   Turnaround at Starbucks?

    6.6.5   Change Habit 6: Mind the Gap

Resources

LEARNING OBJECTIVES

- Examine the nature and sources of the three main 'knowing–doing gaps' hindering the effective implementation of change cycles ('Leadership Gap', 'Practice Gap' and 'Power Gap').
- Develop an appreciation of the leadership skills required to overcome these 'knowing–doing' gaps that stop effective change implementation.
- Be able to analyse and evaluate the leader's role in being mindful of these gaps and mobilizing energy and resources to address them.

HEAD (THEORY)

6.0   INTRODUCTION

One evening after a day of work at a large multinational steel company, Richard met up on a tennis court with Peter, a manager from the local steel-works. The conversation went something like this:

> Peter: 'What is it that you do?'
> Richard: 'Researching and advising on change management'.
> Peter: 'Change management?' 'We don't need change management. We have tons of change management. But nothing changes! What we need is **do management!**'

Peter's frustration reflects what many managers experience as part of their everyday life – the *knowing–doing gap*. That is, knowing or having a general idea of what **should** be done but not being able to get it **done**.

Stanford Professor Jeffrey Pfeffer (1992, pp.12 & 30) asserts managers and organizations need more advice on 'the skills of getting things done' than on 'the skills of figuring out what to do'. He tells the story of a consultant offering strategic advice to a bank. His first presentation slide summarized the recommendations of the previous four consultants, each having provided much the same advice. Then he asked, 'Why do you need a fifth?!' He then offered assistance with implementation and change. He got the job.

Getting things done is genuinely difficult. Making things happen requires us to be both *mindful* of the knowing–doing gap *and mobilize* energy, resources and support to overcome it. Over the past few weeks, you've been presented with what you should do to create an effective Cycle of Change. This chapter introduces you to the **Leadership of Change** and what it takes to implement an effective Cycle. So **how** do we influence others to actually *get done* what we know *should be done?* In the words of Jeffrey Pfeffer and Robert Sutton (2000), how do we overcome the 'knowing–doing gap'?

In the following pages, you will become familiar with three 'knowing–doing gaps' a leader confronts in change:

1. The leadership gap,
2. The practice gap, and
3. The power gap.

Your first task is to be ***mindful*** of these gaps. Your second task is to ***mobilize*** yourself and others to address them. Up to this point, you have been encouraged to '**Re-imagine change**'. Now, you are asked to step up and '**Re-invent yourself**' to become an adaptive leader and a resourceful political entrepreneur.

6.1   THE LEADERSHIP GAP

Harvard Professor John Kotter begins many of his sessions with the question: 'In percentage terms, how important are management and leadership in successful change?'. The answer from the audience remains routine and predictable: '80% Leadership & 20% Management'. Then Kotter asks, 'In percentage terms, how much time is spent on management vs leadership?'. The consensus is the opposite: '80% Management & 20% Leadership'. It's safe to say then that the experience of many managers is that changes are most often over-managed and under-led. But what does this mean?

John Storey (2004, p.6) nicely outlined the contrast between management and leadership. He says **management** is mainly transactional, it:

- operates and maintains,
- accepts given objectives and meanings,
- controls and monitors,
- focuses on tasks,
- adopts a short-term orientation, and
- focuses on detail & procedures.

Leadership, on the other hand, is more transformational, it:

- challenges and changes,
- creates new visions and meanings,
- empowers,
- seeks to inspire and transcend,
- adopts a long-term orientation, and
- focuses on the big picture.

The **leadership gap** is the difference between the ideal or desired levels of this form of leadership and the actual levels of leadership in change. Two important facts about this leadership gap:

- leadership is often absent in change programs, and
- those attempting leadership often interpret it as management.

Why is this the case? You've already learned managers and organizations routinely focus on and prioritize:

- design over implementation,
- strategy development over execution, and
- establishing projects and programs over their successful completion.

The result? We don't give enough thought, value or attention to *how change is led*. The default managerial state is often egocentric, reactive and impulsive. As Greg Dyke, Director-General of the BBC, put it, 'Cut the crap. Make it happen' (Spicer, 2018). Even when leadership is recognized, it's often simply construed as another level of management. The focus is on predictability and control, not motivation and innovation. Leading change involves setting goals and priorities, staffing teams, allocating resources, and monitoring progress to ensure predictability and control. It manages change by checklist! In so doing, it underplays the degree of behavioural change needed.

To illustrate this, Kotter often advises managers to write down the parts of the organization affected by a change, the number of people in each section, and then list the total numbers whose behaviour needs to change. Unfortunately, based on his consulting experience, the knee-jerk response by managers under-estimates the degree of behavioural change required by a factor of 10!

The origin of this bias lies in the history of modern large-scale organizations and the management education and training provided. Early in this history, predictability and control became the dominant concern of management. Organizations learned to handle the complexities of scale over multiple locations and diverse countries. Business education followed. Managers and organizations now default to what they know best and are trained to do (Kotter, 2012).

The lesson here is **not** that management is bad and leadership is good. This would fail to recognize the genuine importance of the traditional project management role in change projects or programs. Nor should we regard managers and leaders as two different types of people. This ignores and disrespects managers' daily leadership activities to 'get things done'.

What **is** important is a deep awareness of our key advice in tackling the leadership gap: **expect the expected!** You will encounter situations where leadership is trivialized or ignored. **Accept** these conditions for what they are. Then, be creative and entrepreneurial in overcoming the barriers they create.

For many, this will be challenging. It means letting go of traditional mindsets and securities. We often expect and feel more comfortable dealing with the 'tip of the iceberg' rational stuff. We are more practised in handling matters of the head than affairs of the heart. We confront the leadership gap in ourselves as well as outside.

Back to our core theme, managing change is the discipline of influencing oneself as well as others to achieve a purpose. We need to be mindful of this state of affairs and focus on mobilizing ourselves and others to address it.

6.2   THE PRACTICE GAP

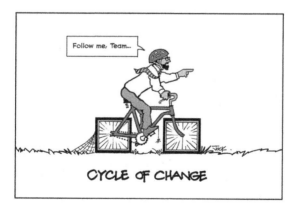

'How do you get to Carnegie Hall? Practice, practice, practice!'

The punchline of this old joke also applies to those seeking to manage change effectively. Why is this important? Because there is always, and we mean *always*, a gap between *your knowledge* and *what you need to know* to get change done. No matter how well-researched and packaged your methods, however well-informed your plans, and however well-meaning and sensible your intentions, the practice gap is always there.

The practice gap can be captured in various ways. In figurative terms, there's the difference between the map and the territory, or the menu and the meal. In technical terms, there is a gap between filling out checklists and making things happen or what rules prescribe and what situations demand. The implications for you as a change agent are quite profound. No matter how much knowledge you collect or sophisticated the methods you apply, more is always required.

The English philosopher Gilbert Ryle (2009) spoke of the fundamental difference between 'knowing that' and 'knowing how'. *Knowing that* we have tools available doesn't add up to 'practical knowledge' or *knowing how* to apply these tools and make things happen in complex and challenging situations (De Ven & Johnson, 2006).

There are three sources of this practice gap:

1. **uncertainty,**
2. **limits of prescription, and**
3. **unpredictability.**

Let's explore these further.

First, there's the challenge of *uncertainty*. Information is always limited and provisional (March, 1994). Collecting information on thoughts and feelings is tricky and subjective. The same applies to politics and power. We mistake motives, and people lie to us. Things change along the way.

Second, there's the *prescription* **challenge**. Techniques and rules always require other tools and methods to apply them (Tsoukas, 2005, p.112). Kotter advises us to create a sense of urgency. How? Pay attention to the heart as well as the head? How? Inspire hope or create fear. How do I inspire hope without appearing 'soft'? How do I create fear without fostering resentment and opposition? How much of each is required? 'Not too little, not too much' is the clichéd Goldilocks response. This doesn't really cut it. And so, the questions go on.

Third, there's the challenge of unpredictability (Brown & Eisenhardt, 1998; Stacey & Mowles, 2016). No matter how intelligent or well-intended our actions, outcomes are never guaranteed. We're not clairvoyant. There's a level of complexity and emergence in human affairs that means there's always an unavoidable degree of uncertainty and risk.

In a significant change program, the terrain will shift during the journey. Allies become opponents; unpredicted events will occur, contexts change and so on. What kind of thought and action *is* needed to face and *adapt* to these changes during the change journey? In the words of the warning on the London Underground and now elsewhere, 'How do we "Mind the Gap"?'

We begin by being *aware* of the existence of the gap, paying *attention* to its effects, and *accepting* its inevitability (King & Badham, 2019). We may be tempted to deny or avoid these issues, but arrogance, ignorance and complacency can create disaster. When successful, being mindful provides you with what the CEO of General Mills, Janice Marturano (2014), describes as the 'space to lead'. Mindless leaders react in a knee-jerk manner to uncertainty and threat by over-simplifying problems and unthinking decisiveness. Mindful leaders, in contrast, respond creatively and with care and consideration.

Once mindful of the practice gap, you are in the position to work on addressing it. This requires mobilizing *yourself, others* and your *organizations*. We need to increase adaptability and resilience, overcome the fear of uncertainty and failure, and learn to be confidently entrepreneurial and experimental.

In the language of social psychology, this involves proactivity, the ability and will of 'making things happen'. As Parker and Bindl (2017, p.1) put it, 'taking control to make things happen rather than watching things happen. It involves aspiring and striving to bring about change in the environment and/or oneself to achieve a different future.' What creates such a capability includes three sets of motivations: 'can do' (e.g., self-efficacy, perceived costs of proactivity), 'reason to' (e.g., intrinsic motivation at work, flexible role orientation) and 'energized to' (e.g., 'hot' feelings of enthusiasm and inspiration at work).

To foster these capabilities in yourself and others, consider:

1. *Creating a cultural ethos* that encourages self-development and open questioning. One that acknowledges failure, is wary of risks and ready to experiment (Kanter, 2012; O'Toole & Bennis, 2009).
2. *Establishing institutional supports* that recognize the value of innovation and the possibility of error. These need to create and maintain the trust necessary to admit uncertainty and mistakes. These are embedded in systems, practices, relationships and supportive forms of leadership (Edmondson, 2011, 2018).
3. *Building holding environments* that inspire experimentation and career advancement. These provide security while guiding and supporting an evolving balance of pressure and safety (Heifetz et al., 2009a, 2009b; Heifetz & Linsky, 2017).

And finally,

4. ***Developing sustainable resilience*** that encourages and stimulates. One that cares for and supports ongoing attention to all these activities by individuals, groups and organizations (Beer et al., 2009; Weick & Sutcliffe, 2011).

6.3   THE POWER GAP

Have you ever experienced a situation where you can clearly see a problem, but you just can't get others to see it? Have you ever offered suggestions and then wondered if anyone actually heard you? Have you ever thought you put things in place, even got agreement from people about what to do, but things just don't get done? Instead, everything seems to stall or bog down? Welcome to key elements of what we call the 'power gap'.

We all encounter and have to live with such frustrations. Anyone attempting to bring about change gets them by the bucketful! When faced with these conditions, we suggest tapping into the great American writer, Kurt Vonnegut (1980, p.469), who said, '*Laughter and tears are both responses to frustration and exhaustion. I myself prefer to laugh since there is less cleaning up to do afterwards.*'

All managers face a basic power gap. It's another level of 'expect the expected!' A power gap exists between what managers are expected, requested or required to do and the time, people and resources they're given or have available to get their job done. Why does this happen?

There are four main causes:

1. diversity and interdependence,
2. power and powerlessness,
3. structural inequality, and
4. over-promising and under-delivering.

We will consider each of these in turn.

1. Diversity and Interdependence

How much does your change initiative depend on the actions and support of interdependent people? Do they hold divergent views? How much control do you have over them (Buchanan & Badham, 2008; Kotter, 1985)?

As complexity, interdependence and divergence increase, initiatives may become unmanageable. It results in what we call 'lightweight' change management. If you're running around desperately trying to convince people to assist you because 'you're there to help them', – then that's you!

2. Power and Powerlessness

How many individuals or groups in positions of power are opposed to the change? Expect their opposition. How many affected by the change, have little autonomy and discretion in their jobs? Expect them to have a debilitating sense of powerlessness and a tendency to cling desperately to what they have (Buchanan & Badham, 2020; Kanter, 1979). As Rosabeth Moss Kanter (2010, p.36 put it, 'Power corrupts, as Lord Acton famously said, "but so does powerlessness".'

3. Structural Inequality

How many of the people you're trying to mobilize are at the bottom of society's totem pole? We live in a world of class, gender and racial inequality. Those most disadvantaged, inside and outside the organization, often become fatalistic, resentful and distrustful of authority (Buchanan & Badham, 2020, p.205; Clegg, 1989; Fox, 1974).

Readiness to change means believing the change is relevant to you. The odds are such people are far from 'ready'. They are not easily persuaded, and they have little faith leaders will live up to their promises.

4. Over-Promising and Under-Delivering

To what degree are those promoting a change strongly committed to the aspirations yet unaware or uninterested in the problems that must be addressed to realize them? As we saw in Chapter 1, over-promising and under-delivering is a major flaw in the systematic 'mis-leading' of change. So, if you find yourself in situations where there's never enough time to do things properly, but plenty of time to clear up the mess, take care!

It is essential to be mindful of these factors and mobilizing time, energy and resources to address them. You need to act as what I and my colleague Dave Buchanan (2020) term a 'political entrepreneur'. It entails avoiding the temptation to spend time complaining about what you do not have and focusing instead on creating what you require. Shift from a negative win–lose mentality to a positive win–win approach! An entrepreneurial growth mindset believes 'We do not have the power and resources … *yet*' (Dweck, 2014, 2017). To obtain this power and resources, you need to:

1. Acquire a Power Base.
2. Develop and Maintain a Network.
3. Look after Yourself.

Let's explore these further.

1. *Acquiring a power base* means you do not leave politics up to chance. It involves (Kotter, 1985):
    *   collecting political information,
    *   developing and applying interpersonal skills,
    *   creating good working relationships, and
    *   establishing and promoting your credibility and track record.
2. *Developing and maintaining a network* to mobilize energy and resources (Kanter, 1985; Kotter, 1985). This involves establishing and maintaining the support of three key groups (Badham, 1990; Briner et al., 1990):
    *   a 'steering' group' (for strategic resourcing and legitimation),
    *   a 'working team' (for resourcefulness and persistence in the face of challenges), and
    *   an 'invisible network' (for all the additional advice and help that you will need to get things done).

Finally,

3. **Looking after yourself**, your health, your personal life and your career. Ensuring the change initiative is strongly aligned with your career interests and reflects your values and social principles is vital in supporting you in the face of frustrations and setbacks (Boyatzis & McKee, 2003; Fuda, 2013; Ibarra, 2015a).

6.4   CONCLUSION

The leadership attitudes and practices of mindfully mobilizing provide a creative and proactive response to the three knowing–doing gaps. Adopting such a stance requires stepping outside our default reflex response to instruct ourselves and others to 'just do it'. Instead, it means being proactively mindful of the uncertainties, complexities and barriers the gaps create and creatively mobilizing the energy and resources necessary to overcome or grapple effectively with them.

1.   Being Mindful

Being mindful prepares us for the challenges we face and allows and encourages us to respond to them deliberately, proactively and effectively. In the face of uncertainty and complexity, it helps us be reflective and experimental with the frames we adopt and the stories we enact. It fosters resilience, realism and equanimity when confronted by practically irreconcilable differences and irremovable obstructions. It supports us in being reasonable in the face of irrationalities, retaining a cosmopolitan outlook in the face of diversity and difference, and being seriously playful in the face of the vicissitudes of fate.

Yet, there can be a dark side to mindfulness. An over-emphasis on questioning one's values and assumptions can be demobilizing. Spending excessive amounts of time on surfacing and preparing for potentially risky encounters can be costly and disruptive. Surfacing tacit, disturbing and repressed emotions, conflicts and denials may fan the flames rather than resolve the issues. The process needs to be undertaken with consideration, care and political nous. The dominance of narrow, instrumental self-centred views of mindfulness can also stymie deeper reflection on the meaning and purpose of change initiatives for others and oneself (Badham & King, 2021; King & Badham, 2019, 2020; Purser, 2019). Being mindful needs itself to be treated mindfully! It must also be supplemented by the entrepreneurial energy and enthusiasm necessary to make things happen.

2.   Mobilizing Yourself and Others

Mobilizing yourself and others is a proactive, growth-oriented and confident entrepreneurial endeavour. It provides energy, stimulates excitement, and fuels creativity and resourcefulness. Yet, there can also be a dark side to the entrepreneurial enterprise. It can become intolerant and dismissive of 'resistance' and 'bureaucracy', with little or no appreciation of the validity of objections to the cause or the value of some established rules and practices (Du Gay, 2000).

It can encourage obsession and exploitation, with little consideration for the health and well-being of oneself and others (Brockling, 2016; Miller & Rose, 2008; Oldham, 2018). It can lend itself to fostering cult-like cabals with fanatical dedication to a cause and irresponsible destruction (Stokes & Clegg, 2002). Therefore, mobilization as an entrepreneurial quest needs to be tempered and supplemented by a mindful appreciation of its limitations and downsides (Buchanan & Badham, 2008, chapters 7 & 8; Badham & King, 2021).

3.   Beyond Mindful Entrepreneurs

If you type 'mindful entrepreneur' into Google, you find multiple sources of advice on how to be 'present' and 'take care of yourself and others' in the entrepreneurial quest for wealth and success (Gerschman et al., 2017). This is a useful and valid concern. Yet what we recommend is broader and deeper. Mindful mobilization is an embodied mindset that is aware of the complexities, uncertainties and barriers to change, accepts their inevitability and attends to them. It combines an awareness of challenges (combining reflexivity, wariness, prudence and care) with enthusiasm for 'getting things done' (creatively, energetically and positively mobilizing oneself and others).

6.5   CHAPTER SUMMARY

In *Chapter 6. The Knowing–Doing Gaps* you have:

- Become familiar with three 'knowing–doing gaps' a leader confronts: (1) the leadership gap, (2) the practice gap, and (3) the power gap.
- Appreciate the leadership quality of being willing and able to mindfully mobilize energy and support to take up opportunities and overcome obstacles to address these gaps.
- Been encouraged to build on your ability to '*Re-imagine change*' and step up to '*Re-invent yourself*' as an adaptive leader and a resourceful yet mindful political entrepreneur.

6.1   The Leadership Gap

- Change initiatives are largely over-managed and under-led.
- The leadership gap is the difference between the ideal or desired levels of leadership and the actual level of leadership in change.
- Real leadership of change means being mindful of these realities and mobilizing yourself and others to overcome them.

6.2   The Practice Gap

- A practice gap exists between what rules prescribe and what situations demand. It's the gap between 'knowing that' and 'knowing how'.
- The practice gap is created by the uncertainties in our knowledge, the limitations of tools and the unpredictability of events and outcomes.
- We address these conditions by being mindful of their existence, mobilizing energy to cope with them and creating an ethos, supports and environments that foster these capabilities.

6.3   The Power Gap

- A power gap is the difference between what managers are required to do and the time, people and resources available to them.
- Leading change requires being mindful of the sources of the power gap (e.g., diversity and interdependence, power and powerlessness, structural inequality and systemic over-promising).
- Mobilizing resources to address this gap requires: (1) acquiring a power base, (2) developing and maintaining a network, and (3) looking after and developing yourself and your career.

HEART AND HAND (PRACTICE)

6.6   CASES AND EXERCISES

6.6.1   Act Like a Leader: *Borgen*

The difference between management and leadership is regularly discussed, and there is widespread awareness that organizations need to exercise a greater degree of leadership than they actually do. But how do we overcome this gap? In her work *Act Like a Leader, Think Like a Leader*, Herminia Ibarra (2015a, 2018) argues that *as an individual*, you need to 'act your way into a new way of thinking' in 'stepping-up' and 're-inventing' yourself as a leader.

Case materials – Part A
Ibarra, H. (2015b). The authenticity paradox. *Harvard Business Review*, *Jan–Feb*, 53–59.
Ibarra, H. (2018). *Act like a leader*. HR Congress, Brussels, 28–29 November. https://www.youtube.com/watch?v=4pk9TkHRZmI (accessed 23 May 2022)

Ibarra, H., Ely, R., & Kolb, D. (2013). Women rising: The unseen barriers. *Harvard Business Review*, *91*(9), 60–66.

Case materials – Part B
Decency in the Middle: Applying *Act Like a Leader* & 'Women Rising'.
Borgen: Series 1 Episode 1, 'Decency in the Middle' (58.30): Election Debate: 'Vote for a New Denmark' (46.10–48.25 mins). https://www.youtube.com/watch?v=Y3eLn3JHcjw&list=PLVIshZFGP-z2KQ1sP9q7R6QqQOHzQJyE8 (accessed 23 May 2022)

Further material
Ibarra, H. (2015a). *Act Like a Leader, Think Like a Leader*. Boston: Harvard Business Review Press.
Ely, R. J., Ibarra, H., & Kolb, D. M. (2011). Taking gender into account: Theory and design for women's leadership development programs. *Academy of Management Learning and Education*, *10*(3), 474–493.

Part A

Task 1
Watch Ibarra (2018) and read Ibarra (2015b). Consider how you might develop yourself as a change leader in overcoming what Ibarra identifies as the three main traps:

1. What is the 'competency trap'? How do you overcome it? *Re-define your Job*.
2. What are the 'narcissistic and lazy' and 'echo chamber' traps? How do you overcome them? *Expand your Network*.
3. What is the 'authenticity' trap? How do you overcome it? *Don't, just 'Be Yourself'*.

Task 2
Read Ibarra et al. (2013) and answer the questions below.

In 'Women Rising: The Unseen Barriers', Ibarra et al. (2013) identify the organizational barriers preventing women from 'stepping up' and overcoming these traps (based on Ely et al., 2011). Building on Ibarra's talk on individual challenges, use this article to reflect on the organizational obstacles to overcome.

1. Keep three questions in mind while reading:
   a. What do the authors define as the 'pipeline problem'? What are its causes?
   b. What is the 'second generation' gender bias against women becoming leaders?

    c. How is this problem addressed through: education about the 'second generation' bias; creating safe 'identity' workspaces; and focusing on individual and social purpose?

2. After this reading, reflect on the following:

    a. Is there a 'pipeline problem' and 'second generation' bias against the development and promotion of leaders, in general?

    b. How far do Ibarra's suggested solutions help?

Part B

Borgen (2010–2013) is a Danish political thriller made for television and is available on DVD with English subtitles. The title, Borgen or 'The Castle', is the nickname of Christiansborg Palace, home of the government of Denmark. The first episode of the first series ('Decency in the Middle') follows Birgitte Nyborg (played by Sidse Babett Knudsen) in her electioneering as a leader of a minor centrist party. In the selected incident, we are taken to the final live TV debate between the leaders of the contending parties before the election. Birgitte, scripted by her 'spin doctor' Kasper Juul (played by Pilou Asbaek), goes 'off script' with dramatic results.

Task 3

Watch Birgitte Nyborg's speech in the above clip from *Borgen* Series 1, Episode 1 and reflect upon the following questions:

1. What makes it appear Birgitte is speaking and acting authentically? What grabs you emotionally about her speech?

2. How do Birgitte's language and actions address what Ibarra and her colleagues characterize as 'central issues' – questioning old-fashioned and masculinist leadership imagery and focusing on individual and social purpose?

Task 4

Drawing on Birgitte Nyborg's example, what few principles might you apply to (i) act authentically and influence others in change, and (ii) challenge 'unseen barriers' that prevent you from acting like a leader in the future?

For follow up

Two other 'cases' from the movies illustrate leaders going 'off-script' in a manner perceived to be authentic and influential:

• *Bulworth* (1998): American political satire comedy film co-written, co-produced, directed by, and starring Warren Beatty.

- *The Adjustment Bureau* (2011): American science fiction romantic thriller film, directed by George Nolfi, based on the 1954 Philip K. Dick short story 'Adjustment Team'. See minutes 6.11–14.16 (frontstage/backstage and being 'authentic' as a politician).

6.6.2 Change Masters: Rosabeth Moss Kanter

Rosabeth Moss Kanter is arguably the leading world authority on mobilizing power to address the challenges of corporate innovation and change. While reading the prescribed article (Kanter, 1999) and watching Kanter's (2012) video presentation, pay attention to the lessons that may assist you in becoming enterprising and resourceful in overcoming the 'power gap'.

Case material
Kanter, R. M. (1999). The enduring skills of change leaders. *Leader to Leader*, *13*(Summer), 15–22. https://doi.org/10.1002/ltl.40619991305 (accessed 23 May 2022)
Kanter, R. M. (2012). *Creating a supportive environment for innovation to flourish*. https://www.youtube.com/watch?v=MPmQLsRInc0 (accessed 23 May 2022)

Task 1
Read Kanter (1999) and watch Kanter (2012) and focus on:

1. the main elements of an 'entrepreneurial spirit',
2. how a leader rallies people, builds and maintains coalitions, and
3. what is required to handle the 'difficult middles' of innovation and change.

Further material
Two case studies and self-assessment exercises on Kanter's 'seven skills of change agents' (2006) and 'six keys to leading positive change' (2012) are provided on this book's website.

6.6.3 Symbolism in Action: 'I Have a Dream'

In this exercise, we explore what is involved in being mindful of the complexities and challenges of change while creatively working to mobilize energy and commitment to the change. To do so, we will be watching and drawing on the symbolic actions and politics illustrated by the actions and performance of four iconic leaders. These are Dr Martin Luther King, Jr, Nelson Mandela as portrayed in documentaries and the movie *Invictus*, Mahatma Gandhi and Birgitte Nyborg, a fictional PM in the series *Borgen*. We begin with Dr King below. The other cases are found in this book in Exercises 6.6.1 'Act Like a Leader:

Borgen' and 8.5.4 'Poise and Performance: Gandhi' and on the book's website 'Exercise The Springboks Jersey (Mandela and Invictus)'.

Part A

Dr Martin Luther King, Jr
The American civil rights activist Dr Martin Luther King, Jr is known for his strategy of 'nonviolent' protest and rhetorical appeal for civil and economic rights and an end to racism in the United States (as exemplified in his '*I Have A Dream*' speech to the March on Washington for Jobs and Freedom on 28 August 1963).

Martin Luther King, Jr was faced with 'white supremacy' through control of the police and military, votes, and ideology. He had some cultural resources he was able to work with, however. The democratic culture of the US espoused values of equality, liberty and human rights. Yet, these were routinely and visibly betrayed in systemic illegal discrimination practices against disenfranchised 'African Americans'. This allowed him to present the 'black' problem as a 'freedom' problem and acts of protest as patriotic.

Case materials
History Channel (2018, 13 January). Martin Luther King, Jr.: Leader of the 20th-century civil rights movement – Biography.
King, Jr., M. L. (1963, 28 August). *I have a dream* speech, Lincoln Memorial, Washington DC, USA. [Video file]. Historic Film Archive.

Task 1
While watching the biography of Dr Martin Luther King, Jr (History Channel, 2018), reflect on the following questions below.

1. How was the use of 'non-violent' protest both necessary and symbolic?
2. How did Dr King use protests and boycotts to draw on the potential power invested in parts of the US legal system?
3. How was putting his life on the line instrumental to ensuring his influence then and his symbolic power today?
4. How might change leaders use similar tactics?

Task 2
While watching the '*I Have a Dream*' speech, reflect on:

1. How did Dr King appeal to espoused and emotively held US values to challenge an equally embedded set of beliefs upholding the institutionalized racism and discrimination he sought to end?

Task 3
Use Dr King's strategic actions and rhetoric as a thought-provoking example
to define:

1.   What actions and rhetoric might you use to lead change when there are
     significant cultural obstacles and political opposition to the changes you
     champion?
2.   In what ways does this require thinking and acting mindfully?
3.   How do you attend to the mobilizing of energy and support?

6.6.4   Turnaround at Starbucks?

Following his takeover as CEO and major shareholder in 1987, Howard
Schultz led a small Seattle-based freshly brewed coffee company, Starbucks,
through a decade of rapid expansion, from six stores employing under 100
people to 1,300 stores with over 25,000 employees. Starbucks' expansion into
an international coffee brand is now pretty well known and documented.

Starbucks' proclaimed mission was and is 'to inspire and nurture the human
spirit – one person, one cup and one neighbourhood at a time' with a vision 'to
establish Starbucks as the premier purveyor of the finest coffee in the world
while maintaining our uncompromising principles while we grow'. By 2002, it
had expanded into four continents, serving an average of 18 million customers
daily with sales of $2.6 billion. The heroic-origins story is aptly captured in
Howard Schultz's (1999) biography, *Pour Your Heart into It*, and in 'The
Barista Principle: Starbucks and the Rise of Relational Capital', the case study
by Ranjay Gulati et al. (2002).

However, by the end of the first decade of the twenty-first century, the
Starbucks story had taken a different turn. For its many external critics,
Starbucks' image had become severely tarnished. In the face of increased criticism, the phrase 'Starbucked' was coined to reflect its purportedly predatory
nature (Clark, 2007) and critical attention directed towards the 'Starbucks
moment' (Simon, 2009). Early warning signs of weaknesses in its expansion
were followed by consternation over its subsequent collapse in share price,
with Howard Schultz making a dramatic return as a CEO committed to resusci-
tating and re-orienting the brand. Again, the following crisis-turnaround story
is well documented by Howard Schultz (2012) in his second book *Onward:
How Starbucks Fought for Its Life without Losing its Soul*. It is also captured
in Nancy Koehn et al.'s (2014) HBS case study *Starbucks Coffee Company:
Transformation and Renewal*.

In the turnaround literature, Trahms et al. (2013) emphasize the central
importance of senior leadership's 'response'. In the short case study above

and the more extended case on the website, we focus on the leadership role of Howard Schultz in the crisis-turnaround phase.

Case material

Gulati, B. R., Huffman, S., & Neilson, G. (2002). The barista principle: Starbucks and the rise of relational capital. *Strategy + Business, 28*(3), 1–12. https://www.strategy-business.com/article/20534?gko=eb786 (accessed 23 May 2022)

Kanter, R. M. (2003). Leadership and the psychology of turnarounds. *Harvard Business Review, 81*(6), 58–67.

Koehn, N. F., McNamara, K., Khan, N., & Legris, E. (2014). *Starbucks Coffee Company: Transformation and Renewal* (Harvard Business School Case Study No. 9-314–068).

Task 1

Read the above case material and answer the following three-part question:

To what degree was Schultz successful in reversing the 'cycle of decline' by:

1. showing himself to be a mindful leader,
2. being open to and aware of uncertainty, complexity and barriers to change, and
3. being capable of effectively mobilizing the energy and building coalitions to bring about the change?

See also

Clark, T. (2007). *Starbucked: A Double Tall Tale of Caffeine, Commerce, and Culture.* New York and London: Little Brown and Company.

Fellner, K. (2008). *Wrestling with Starbucks: Conscience, Capital, Cappuccino.* New Brunswick and London: Rutgers University Press.

Schultz, H., & Gordon, J. (2012). *Onward: How Starbucks Fought for Its Life Without Losing Its Soul.* New York: Rodale.

Schultz, H., & Yang, D. J. (1999). *Pour Your Heart into It: How Starbucks Built a Company One Cup at a Time.* New York: Hyperion.

Simon, B. (2009). *Everything but the Coffee: Learning about America from Starbucks.* Berkeley, Los Angeles and London: University of California Press.

Trahms, C. A., Ndofor, H. A., & Sirmon, D. G. (2013). Organizational decline and turnaround: A review and agenda for future research. *Journal of Management, 39*(5), 1277–1307.

6.6.5 Change Habit 6: Mind the Gap

Nearly 300 people fell through gaps between the platform and the train in New South Wales, Australia, in 2016. It's a real issue. We found that people are visually and audibly warned to literally 'Mind the Gap' across major transportation systems in the world! It's obviously a gap no one really thinks is there. If we're careless, we become a global statistic. Some change problems are like that.

There's another side to minding the gap. With the right mindset, the gap can be energizing and motivating. MIT Professor Peter Senge speaks of the creativity and enthusiasm generated by being committed to a vision and knowing there's a gap to conquer to get there. Minding the gap involves mobilizing energy and support for change. It's not just being aware of a gap but being able and willing to do something about it!

We would like you to explore 'minding the gap' when dealing with differences. If you're familiar with the sport of track and field, it's the equivalent of what is known as 'Volzing' in pole-vaulting terms. Pole vaulting is an event where an athlete uses a long flexible pole to jump over a bar. This Olympic sport has been around since the ancient Greeks and Celts. Volzing – which is now, by the way, illegal – is a method of holding or pushing the bar back onto the pegs while jumping over a height. The American David Volz used the space between going up and down and made it an art form. It's that type of moment many do not realize exists, but in which you actually have a choice about how to respond, grasp an opportunity or recover before it is too late.

No, we don't want you to pole vault! But what we'd like you to do is still a bit of a challenge. It's to see how you can make the best out of an exchange with someone very different to yourself. It's not just about 'walking a mile in their shoes'. It's also what it reveals about you and how you handle differences at the moment – a crucial change capability.

In its basic form, we begin with the 'Empathy Walk' exercise developed by MIT Professor Edgar Schein. Although it's something you could do by yourself or with a friend or colleague, it can be more creative and fun with another.

Task 1

So first, find someone you consider most different from you. It requires thinking about what similarities you share and how you differ. Second, establish a relationship with that person so you can spend a while getting into that person's world. Use whatever questions or methods you think appropriate to find out how similar and different you are and what this means. Third, after the discussion, capture and write down the issues you uncovered and the stories you picked up.

Many people find the differences between them and 'their target' to be greater than between them and a friend. They realize how insulated their lives and perspectives are or how privileged their position is and experience the challenge of dealing with someone with a different social status. In every case, it opens people up to becoming more inquiring and sensitive to others.

Task 2

Now, part 2 – back to 'Volzing'. How well did you handle the uncertain dynamics and differences of your encounter? Were there moments when you and the other person were more or less ready to discuss the issues that made you different? Did tensions, prejudices or frustrations surface, and how did you respond? In future changes, what might you do to prepare yourself to get the most out of encounters with those different from you?

RESOURCES

6.0 The Knowing–Doing Gap

Arguably the best work done on this issue is by the Stanford Professor Jeffrey Pfeffer. His most notable works addressing this matter in a way that is both comprehensive and politically astute are the following:

Pfeffer, J. (1992). *Managing with Power: Politics and Influence in Organizations.* Boston: Harvard Business School Press.
Pfeffer, J., & Sutton, G. (2000). *The Knowing–Doing Gap: How Smart Companies Turn Knowledge into Action.* Boston: Harvard Business School Press.

6.1 The Leadership Gap

There is a well-established debate on whether desirable leadership capabilities are universal or vary depending on contingencies or context. We explored some of these issues in discussing the multiple masks that the leader of change must adopt in the performances they must give to influence others. The discussion implied that leadership involves a degree of pragmatic flexibility in adapting one's style to effectively influence others in context (Buchanan & Badham, 2020).

In recent years, however, increased attention has been paid to the general importance of 'authentic leadership' and being 'positive' ('appreciative inquiry', 'positive psychology' etc.) in leading change. In line with this argument, we made the case in Chapter 4 that *appearing authentic* is a crucial motivational device. Goffman argues that we must go beyond our role, not being a 'stuffed shirt', and the 'role distance' is not the 'individual' but is a carefully crafted form of expression and impression (Goffman, 1961; Peterson, 2005). However, being authentic, with assumptions of a true self that must be realized in all cases, is a highly problematic notion and can be debilitating (Alvesson & Einola, 2019). Similarly, 'being positive' can be, and often is, a desirable motivational stance, yet it can also be superficial and trite (Buchanan & Badham, 2020; Cunha et al., 2013).

Alvesson, M., & Einola, K. (2019). Warning for excessive positivity: Authentic leadership and other traps in leadership studies. *Leadership Quarterly, 30*(4), 383–395.

Buchanan, D., & Badham, R. (2020). *Power, Politics and Organizational Change* (3rd edition). London: Sage.

Cunha, M. P. e., Clegg, S., & Rego, A. (2013). Lessons for leaders: Positive organization studies meets Niccolò Machiavelli. *Leadership, 9*(4), 450–465.

Goffman, E. ([1959] 2022). The presentation of self in everyday life. New York: Anchor Doubleday.

Peterson, R. A. (2005). In search of authenticity. *Journal of Management Studies, 42*(5), 1083–1098.

For a more in-depth discussion of what this means for developing oneself as a leader, the work of Herminia Ibarra is probably the most in-depth and accessible, exploring the intertwining of identity, transitions and power in adopting leadership qualities and roles. Key readings from her work include:

Ibarra, H. (2015a). *Act Like a Leader, Think Like a Leader.* Boston: Harvard Business Review Press.

Ibarra, H. (2015b). The authenticity paradox. *Harvard Business Review, Jan–Feb,* 53–59.

Ibarra, H., & Morten, H. (2011). Are you a collaborative leader? *Harvard Business Review, August,* 69–74.

Ibarra, H., Ely, R., & Kolb, D. (2013). Women rising: The unseen barriers. *Harvard Business Review, 91*(9), 60–66.

6.2   The Practice Gap

For an introduction to the restricted or bounded rationality of individuals and organizations, the most celebrated overviews can be found in Kahneman (2011) and March (1994). For interesting treatments of the restricted and 'impractical' nature of reliance on generic rules and technical knowledge as a guide for practice, read accounts highlighting the value of professional knowledge (Schon, 1987), practical wisdom (Schwartz & Sharpe, 2011), phronesis (Flyvbjerg, 2001; Tsoukas, 2005) and metis (Scott, 1999). For an introduction to the unpredictable nature of complex organizations operating in rapidly changing environments, see Brown and Eisenhardt (1998), Stacey and Mowles (2016) and Snowden and Boone (2007). For valuable insights into the importance of being 'mindful' of our limited individual and group perspectives in changing environments, see Weick and Sutcliffe (2011). For considerations of the key significance of creating open, safe and creative learning environments that can attend to the challenges involved, see Edmondson (2011, 2018), Heifetz and Linsky (2017) and Heifetz et al. (2009a, 2009b).

Brown, S., & Eisenhardt, K. (1998). *Competing on the Edge: Strategy as Structured Chaos.* Boston: Harvard Business School Press.

Edmondson, A. (2011). Strategies for learning from failure. *Harvard Business Review*, *89*(4), 48–55.

Edmondson, A. C. (2018). *The Fearless Organization*. Hoboken, NJ: John Wiley.

Flyvbjerg, B. (2001). *Making Social Science Happen*. Cambridge: Cambridge University Press.

Heifetz, R., & Linsky, M. (2017). *Leadership on the Line: Staying Alive through the Dangers of Leading*. Boston: Harvard Business Review Press.

Heifetz, R., Grashow, A., & Linsky, M. (2009). Leadership in a (permanent) crisis. *Harvard Business Review*, July–August, 62–70.

Kahneman, D. (2011). *Thinking, Fast and Slow*. New York: Farrar, Straus and Giroux.

March, J. (1994). *Primer on Decision-Making*. New York: Free Press.

Schon, D. A. (1987). *Educating the Reflective Practitioner*. San Francisco: Jossey-Bass.

Schwartz, B., & Sharpe, K. (2011). *Practical Wisdom: The Right Way to Do the Right Thing*. New York: Riverhead Books.

Scott, J. (1999). *Seeing Like a State*. New Haven: Yale University Press.

Snowden, David J., & Boone, Mary E. (2007). A leader's framework for decision making. *Harvard Business Review*, *85*(11), 68–76.

Stacey, R., & Mowles, C. (2016). *Strategic Management and Organisational Dynamics*. Edinburgh: Pearson Education.

Tsoukas, H. (2005). *Complex Knowledge: Studies in Organizational Epistemology*. Oxford: Oxford University Press.

Weick, K., & Sutcliffe, K. (2011). *Managing the Unexpected* (2nd edition). San Francisco: Jossey-Bass.

6.3   The Power Gap

A classic and accessible statement of the 'power gap' is provided by John Kotter in *Power and Influence* (1985). For a readable introduction to the insidious nature of 'powerlessness' in organizations, see Kanter (1979). For an exploration of the grounding of powerlessness in structural conditions, see Clegg (1989). The most comprehensive overview of these analyses can be found in Buchanan and Badham (2020). Introductions to the importance of being mindful about power deficiencies and the stresses this creates, and mobilizing the energy required to address problems can be found in Boyatzis and McKee (2003) and Bruch and Vogel (2011). For exhortatory and recent re-statements of the need to mobilize power and coalitions and stimulate entre-preneurial energy to overcome the power gap, see Samuel Bacharach's *The Agenda Mover* (2016) and Hamel and Zanini's *Humanocracy* (2020).

Bacharach, S. (2016). *The Agenda Mover: When Your Good Idea is not Enough*. New York: Cornell Publishing.

Boyatzis, R., & McKee, A. (2003). *Resonant Leadership*. Boston: Harvard Business School Publishing.

Bruch, H., & Vogel, B. (2011). *Fully Charged: How Great Leaders Boost Their Organization's Energy and Ignite High Performance*. Boston: Harvard Business Review Press.

Buchanan, D., & Badham, R. (2020). *Power, Politics and Organizational Change* (3rd edition). London: Sage.

Clegg, S. (1989). *Frameworks of Power*. London and Thousand Oaks: Sage.

Hamel, G., & Zanini, M. (2020). *Humanocracy: Creating Organizations as Amazing as the People Within Them*. Boston: Harvard Business Review Press.

Kanter, R. M. (1979). Power failure in management circuits. *Harvard Business Review*, *57*(4), 65–75.

Kotter, J. (1985). *Power and Influence: Beyond Formal Authority*. New York: Free Press.

7.   Paradoxes of change

An ability to embrace new ideas, routinely challenge old ones, and live with paradox will be the effective leader's premier trait. (Tom Peters, *Thriving on Chaos*)

The way of paradoxes is the way of truth. To test reality, we must see it on the tight rope. When the verities become acrobats, we can judge them. (Oscar Wilde, *The Importance of Being Earnest*)

Many popular prescriptions for managing and leading change are in tension and even contradictory. There is, then, a temptation to side with one or the other or settle on a compromise. In this chapter, you will discover the value of adopting a 'paradox mindset' that accepts and works through such tensions and contradictions. A particular focus is on the balancing act required to appreciate, communicate and live with our desire for certainty yet experience of uncertainty in change.

Learning objectives

Head (theory)

7.0 Introduction

7.1 The paradox of rationality

7.2 The paradox of performance

7.3 The paradox of meaning

7.4 Conclusion

7.5 Chapter summary

Heart and hand (practice)

7.6 Cases and exercises

Resources

LEARNING OBJECTIVES

- Understand the nature of paradox and the role of 'both/or' leadership.
- Appreciate and explore the paradoxes of rationality, performance and meaning in leading change.
- Be able to analyse, evaluate and apply strategies for effectively handling ('plumbing') and meaningfully living with ('poetry') the paradoxes of change.

HEAD (THEORY)

7.0   INTRODUCTION

In a *Peanuts* cartoon by Charles M. Schulz, Lucy walks by her brother Linus, who is preparing to launch a snowball.

> Lucy: Life is full of choices. You may choose, if you wish, to throw that snowball at me. You may also choose, if you so wish, not to throw that snowball at me. Now, if you choose to throw that snowball at me, I will pound you right into the ground. If you choose not to throw that snowball at me, your head will be spared.
> Linus: (Throwing the snowball to the ground). Life is full of choices, but you never get any.

In organizations, we often feel like Linus. We are confronted by opportunities we can't take up or feel forced into difficult choices since we cannot achieve one thing without undermining another. Making such choices often feels uncomfortable. Some individuals and groups simply deny the choice exists; others just remain stuck, unwilling to make a necessary sacrifice (Higgs & Rowland, 2010; Lüscher & Lewis, 2008). Ever experienced or feel like that? Well, welcome to the world of paradox.

There are many known tensions, contradictions or paradoxes in change management. Paradoxes exist when there is a 'persistent contradiction between interdependent elements' in our thoughts and actions (Schad et al., 2016, p.10). This chapter is concerned with the major paradoxes leaders face in bringing about change in our purportedly rational organizations. In addressing this topic, we draw strongly on the insights of the most profound and celebrated interpreter of our modern obsession with rationality, James March. As Richard Badham (2017, 2022) identified, we follow March's work in identifying three central paradoxes: a paradox of rationality, a paradox of performance and a paradox of meaning.

- The **paradox of rationality** is created by our commitment to a rational myth that exaggerates organizations' rationality and yet, at the same time, our awareness of the myth and its limitations. Thus, the key question posed by the paradox of rationality is how to be open, critical and reflective about the knowledge we possess while retaining and acting on our faith in its validity and value.
- The **paradox of performance** is the challenge we face in communicating this tension. Assuming and providing certainty about the course and bene-fits of change can stimulate confidence yet appear artificial and unrealistic. On the other hand, being open about uncertainty can enhance credibility yet create anxiety and undermine support. The main challenge identified by the paradox of performance is how to balance these competing expec-tations and demands on the stories we tell and the performances we give.
- The **paradox of meaning** is the reality of 'no guarantees' in the face of accident and circumstance. No matter how effectively we juggle our rational commitments and delicately manage our performance displays, fate can always intervene to thwart our ambitions. The reverse can also be true. How to persist and find meaning in the change enterprise while knowing this lies at the heart of the paradox of meaning.

In this chapter, you will learn about the nature and value of change leaders' accepting and grappling with these tensions, contradictions and paradoxes. It involves appreciating and adopting a *paradox mindset* – one that accepts and grapples with the embedded paradoxes of change. We will also explore the tactics, strategies and value of embracing what we term a 'both/or' leadership approach to these paradoxes. This approach combines the ability to seek solu-tions that *resolve* these paradoxes while adapting to living *with* them.

Handling the Paradoxes

Paradoxes such as those above present themselves as embedded tensions between competing elements we cannot simply wish away. Promoting one part undercuts the other. Exaggerated faith in rationality is unrealistic. Yet, we cannot adopt a more critical view without weakening our motivation to think things through. If we deliver an authoritative unity and certainty in our perfor-mance, we may be naïve, duped or manipulative. Yet, we cannot communicate uncertainty, conflict and chaos without fear of losing credibility, undermining motivation and being judged as a negative resistor or cynic. We are inspired and motivated to act by often unrealistic confidence in and the promise of success. Yet this can create unproductive obstinacy and extreme disappointment. Questioning this 'optimism bias' can destroy the motivation we need to face challenges and persist in overcoming obstacles.

In these ways, the three paradoxes create fundamental dilemmas over how to think and act. How we deal with such quandaries is a strategic and very human challenge. Ignoring or avoiding conflicts and tensions is not an option. We want the best of both worlds, but we cannot have our cake and eat it too. So, what can be done?

Our *traditional logical mindset* responds to such conflicts and tensions by adhering to a simple '*either/or*' managerial strategy. Decision-making entails adopting or advocating one principle, structure or proposal over another or working on a zero-sum compromise or trade-off between the two. We either act from unquestioned faith in rationality, or we don't. We either 'tell it as it is' or silence ourselves. We either wholeheartedly commit to our projects or distance ourselves from them. Or we compromise. In Australia, mongrels are described as 'bitsas' (bits of this, bits of that). Traditional management advocates a pure-bred strategy or living with a mongrel.

Advocates of a paradox mindset advocate an alternative '*both/and*' leadership strategy (Miron-Spektor et al., 2018; Peters, 2012; Smith et al., 2016). This strategy involves adopting frames and creating processes that appreciate the benefits of both sides of whatever dilemma we confront. It pursues both simultaneously despite tensions between the two (Cunha & Putnam, 2019; Putnam et al., 2016; Smith & Lewis, 2011, 2022). It does so by blending two alternative strategies: seeking resolution and pragmatic acceptance. These strategies are quite complicated and, on initial reading, quite difficult to grasp. But bear with us. Once you have thought them through and applied them, you won't look back!

In academic terms and ways we will illustrate later, *resolution* is achieved through either splitting or synthesis. Resolution via splitting involves promoting one side of tension, contradiction or dilemma at one time, in one context, and the other at another or in a different situation. We might express certainty or acknowledge uncertainty to varying groups and in differing environments. Splitting gives expression to both, but at different times and in different places. Resolution via synthesis requires crafting win–win synergies to creatively and simultaneously integrate both poles without succumbing to zero-sum trade-offs. We might adopt a strategy of 'flexible planning' in an attempt to provide order and direction while also adapting to changing circumstances.

Acceptance, in contrast, involves actively recognizing and developing strategies for living with the tensions of adopting and pursuing contradictory perspectives, principles or goals. It accepts that while we seek to incorporate and address both sides or horns of a paradox, we cannot fully resolve the tension between them. We prepare ourselves to:

- creatively 'muddle through',
- act on the basis of presumed certainties,
- be ready to 'cut our losses' when confronted by our flaws, and
- adopt a new set of 'given' assumptions, mindful that these may also be faulty.

Acceptance means exercising resilience in working with and through tensions rather than seeking artificial ways of resolving or removing them (Coutu, 2002; Cunha & Putnam, 2019; Lüscher & Lewis, 2008). This strategy accepts it is impossible to tame what are essentially wicked problems (Grint, 2005).

For some, adopting such a paradox mindset means pursuing a 'both/and' leadership strategy that increases effectiveness and creates a 'dynamic equilibrium' (Schad et al., 2016; Smith & Lewis, 2011). Others are less sanguine and observe that addressing paradoxes is itself paradoxical (Cameron, 1986). These critics argue we need both *either/or* trade-offs **and** *both/and* strategies. Accepting, living with, and working through paradoxical tensions is a complex and challenging strategic juggling act with no guarantees of success (Cunha & Putnam, 2019). Accepting all these elements could be described as a 'both/or' leadership strategy (Westenholz, 1999). Change leaders need to be mindful of such complexities and challenges and willing and able to mobilize energy and support to address them.

Does this sound rather complicated and difficult? Maybe, but it is better than the alternative – suffering from bewildered disappointments and failed strategies. As H. L. Mencken (1920, p.158) put it, 'there is always a well-known solution to every human problem: neat, plausible and wrong'.

7.1   THE PARADOX OF RATIONALITY

Just a few steps from William Shakespeare's birthplace stands a bronze statue of the jester 'Touchstone', from *As You Like It*. Inscribed into the stone plinth beneath are lines from various Shakespearian plays pointing to our fallibility and folly:

> O Noble Fool! A Worthy Fool! (*As You Like It*)

> The fool doth think he is wise, but a wise man knows himself to be a fool. (*As You Like It*)

> Alas! Poor Yorick. I knew him, Horatio: A fellow of infinite jest. (*Hamlet*)

> Foolery, Sir does walk about the orb like the sun: it shines everywhere. (*Twelfth Night*)

A fundamental paradox lies at the heart of our faith in reason and rationality: we are not as rational in thought and action as we think we are or would like to be. Behavioural psychology's insights have found we are 'predictably irrational' (Ariely, 2009). We want to think of ourselves as having God-like qualities of all-knowing wisdom and insight, yet we have feet of clay. We are often mis-led by intuition, emotion, prejudice and unthinking habit (Kahneman, 2011). What rational thought and action can deliver is also not as great as we think or would like. Behavioural theories of the firm have established we all have 'bounded rationality', and get caught up in blinkered, chaotic, messy and often ineffective decision-making processes (March, 1994). What implications does this have for us in practice? It would be stupid of us to ignore how stupid we are! It would be idiotic to expect we will not act like idiots! It would be foolish to think our foolish antics guarantee success! The management guru Tom Peters recounted a reputed employee's response to their manager's complaint of incompetence and resistance to change, 'If we are so stupid, why were you not smart enough to know?'

These insights challenge the myth of organizations (and how they change) as the operation of rational systems in the strategic pursuit of their goals. Instead of viewing organizations in system terms as 'machines' or 'organisms' (Bolman & Deal, 2017; Carlson, 1996; McCabe, 2016; Morgan, 2006), we use metaphors to better capture the ambiguity, chaos and politics. To illustrate, two relevant and valuable counter-images are James March's 'round soccer field' and Rosabeth Moss Kanter's 'Queens croquet game'.

Round Soccer Fields and the Queen's Croquet Game

A rational view of organizations presumes clear and distinct goals, agreed and informed means to reach those goals, and capable members dedicated to pursuing organizational goals using the best means available. This is akin to the traditional view of the soccer field: two goals, two teams, one ball, one referee, and commonly understood and fixed rules. In reality, organizations have multiple, ambiguous and competing goals. There are many diverse and contested means to achieve these goals. And managers, employees and stakeholders' presence and attention shift over time. March advocates using the metaphor of organizations as 'round soccer fields' to capture these conditions (Cohen & March, 1986; March, 1994; Weick, 1976). In such a game there are multiple goals; different balls are thrown into and removed from the game; shifting numbers of players enter into and leave the game; and individuals kick whatever ball comes near them in the direction of a goal they like. Extend the image by including: multiple referees; a sloped playing field that may alter during the game; and shifting rules. In a large minerals company, one manager commented, 'the goalposts move so often that they ought to have wheels on them'. To define what occurs during this process as 'one best way' strategic rationality or to expect such a thing to emerge from the process is naïve and unrealistic.

To describe the effects of changing conditions on this process, Rosabeth Moss Kanter (2001) supplements this imagery with another engaging metaphor: the Queen's Croquet Game from *Alice in Wonderland*. In the game, the flamingo mallets keep moving their heads, and the hedgehog balls frequently unravel and move elsewhere. The hoops, made up of card soldiers, regularly re-position themselves on the orders of a Queen who changes the game's structure at a whim. It illustrates the disruption of previous forms of thought and action by shifts in technology (flamingos), products and preferences (hedgehogs), goals and conditions (card soldiers and whims of the Queen). 'Keeping your eye on the ball' is not enough. There needs to be ongoing attentiveness and adaptation to all the changes in the game.

'Big-R' and 'Little-r' Rationality

A rational appreciation of these conditions does not remove the fundamental tensions. We have inherited two overlapping yet competing views of what it means to be 'rational'. These are constantly at odds, and we live with the tensions these create. The first, Big-R rationality, is the *grandiose* view of rationality and what it can do for us. It proclaims logic, evidence, and systematic reflection provides certain knowledge about the world, ourselves and how we should think and act. It tells us what we should pursue and how we should pursue it. It identifies the 'one best way' of thought and action. It is a comprehensive, omniscient and strategic view of rationality (Badham, 2017). Modern society is grounded in a rational view of progress based on such faith in the benefits and ability of science, technology and growth to provide authoritative solutions to any problems it creates (Badham, 2016). While challenging pre-modern religion and superstition, Big-R rationality simply replaces it with another. It is an uncritical, unreflective and authoritarian view of reason and rationality. It finds expression in scientific authorities pronouncing 'the' truth of their conventional wisdom. It is reflected in bureaucracies taking their rationally determined rules as inviolable and in organizations proclaiming the strategic rationality of their arrangements and endeavours. It is a seductive faith that gives us certainty, meaning and purpose. As individuals, we often relapse into this view when we assume or defend the rightness of our perspectives and causes.

In contrast, we have also inherited what could be described as a little-r view of rationality. It is more reflective (Schon, 1987), critical (Popper, 2011), and limited or bounded in its view of rationality and what it can do for us (Lindblom, 1959; Simon, 1976). While Big-R rationality gives us authority and solutions, little-r rationality uses logic and evidence to challenge and question *any* authoritarian claims of unique access to truth and virtue. Little-r rationality is a more open, liberal and self-critical view of reason. It is pragmatic, tolerant and more sympathetic to craft skills, professional judgement and reflective practice. One of the main concerns of little-r rationality is the danger of uncritical and authoritarian Big-R rationality, as yet another religion.

As a rational version of the optimism bias, the religion of Big-R rationality motivates us. It assumes that if we think and act rationally, we will succeed. We are encouraged by the idea that we have or will uncover and deliver the 'one best way'. Big-R rationality simply seeks to eliminate the mess and impose strategic order in the face of a round soccer field or queen's croquet game. This ethos is profoundly tempting. However, as advocates of little-r rationality reveal, little logic and limited evidence support the view that this is likely to succeed. Strategies and claims based on Big-R rationality mis-lead us into exaggerating what we can do and misunderstanding or covering up what is actually going on (March, 2007; Scott, 1999).

In contrast, little-r rationality advocates working with, rather than against, predictable and unpredictable irrationalities. Yet, it can be discomforting because little-r rationality fails to provide us with clear guidelines and a new certainty. It creates what Popper characterized as the 'strain of civilization' (Popper, 2011). If a new certainty does not give us further confidence, what value does it have? If it cannot show us how to act, how can we find meaning in our pursuit of rational thought and action? Not surprisingly, we often flip-flop or see-saw between these alternative versions in different contexts as individuals and organizations. Given this understanding, then, how should we handle this tension?

Resolution

Splitting: At different times (e.g., in old and new 'eras') and in different contexts (e.g., in more and less uncertain and volatile conditions), the ideas and actions of either a 'one best way' Big-R rationality or a little-r rationality may better align or suit. Big-R rationality provides us with certainty when conditions are stable and uncontested. Little-r rationality is useful in conditions of uncertainty and disagreement on the edge of chaos. The Stacey Matrix Exercise below illustrates some challenges of adopting such a 'contingency' strategy.

Synthesis: It is possible to view the recommendations for 'strategic ambiguity' by Eric Eisenberg (1984, 2006) as advocating a novel synthesis. It supports a general commitment to a broad strategic 'Big-R' rationality that is deliberately vague so as to create the possibility for little-r discussions on how people interpret, approach and implement them.

Living with and working through

Michael Tushman and his colleagues provide a classic example of attempts to 'live with' this tension in organizations in their analysis of *ambidextrous* organizations and leaders (Tushman, 1997; Tushman et al., 2011). They advocate creating cultures and developing leaders who can accept and seek to creatively handle tensions between more 'exploitative' and 'exploratory' forms of innovation. Similar strategies and capabilities are addressed in discussions of the simultaneous handling of 'sustaining' and 'disruptive' innovation (Bower & Christensen, 1995).

Following their lead, we might advocate and explore a more ambidextrous approach to change. This could involve creating structures and cultures able to cope with the tensions of separating and integrating two strategies. These include 'splitting' confident and strategically rational 'Big-R' strategies for public consumption, legitimation and motivational direction; while also adopting self-critical, experimental, exploratory and reflective little-r strategies to adapt to situations in practice and get things done.

7.2 THE PARADOX OF PERFORMANCE

> '*But he has got nothing on,' said a little child.*
>
> '*Oh, listen to the innocent,' said its father; and one person whispered to the other what the child had said. 'He has nothing on, a child says he has nothing on!'*
>
> '*But he has nothing on!' at last cried all the people.*
>
> *The Emperor writhed, for he knew it was true, but he thought 'the procession must go on now,' so held himself stiffer than ever, and the chamberlains held up the invisible train.* (Hans Christian Andersen, 1907, p.220)

An analysis of decision-making in organizations exposes a world more uncertain, chaotic and even foolish than is expected or admitted (Badham, 2017; March, 1994). Like the small boy who asserts the Emperor to be naked, 'telling it as it is' should end the foolishness and pretence. Simply point to the evidence to debunk the ignorance and collusion. Then, replace it with informed thought and action. Oh, if it were that simple!

The (overly) rational model of organizational life is an embedded rational myth or a symbolic performance. Those who challenge this myth risk being condemned as troublemakers or damned as heretics. Failing to take this into account is a recipe for ineffective action and personal disillusion, and even damaged careers. While rational analysis exposes the limited role of rationality in human affairs, it also uncovers the challenges of presenting this as the case. If we return to *The Emperor's New Clothes*, it is no accident that while knowing the child's words are accurate, the Emperor continues 'stiffer than ever' because 'the procession must go on'.

The Managerial Dilemma

Leaders, managers and those working in modern organizations face a fundamental performative dilemma. It is the 'managerial dilemma of speaking a rhetoric of decisiveness, certainty and clarity while experiencing a life of doubt, paradox and contradiction' (March, 2010, p.68). That is, performing with confidence when still uncertain and conflicted. We live in organizations where there is an expectation that we will act with confidence and certainty, secure in our knowledge and ability to achieve explicit goals and objectives. In practice, however, situations and events are often more complex and ambiguous, and outcomes more uncertain than this suggests. A degree of pragmatism, improvisation and exploration is accepted as necessary in coping with the 'mess'. Yet, despite this acceptance, the dominant expectation and display remains one of thinking and acting with knowledge and certainty. In a real sense, we are then forced to be hypocritical (Brunsson, 2002; Christensen et al., 2013; March, 1994). We know there is a degree of uncertainty and irrationality in how we think and act, yet we cannot fully admit it. Since the dilemma is real, moral condemnation of this hypocrisy is futile. Embracing it, however, can have productive outcomes and lies at the heart of a constructive approach to the paradox of performance (Aronson, 1989; Aronson & Aronson, 2018; March, 1994; Pondy, 1977).

A Productive Hypocrisy

There are genuine reasons why organizations and their leaders proclaim how rational and strategic they are in pursuing operational excellence, innovation and change. External institutional regulators, resource providers, customers and suppliers expect organizations to be rational in their organization and efficient and effective in delivering on their promises. Apart from such required displays, confidence in and commitment to organizational enterprises is also an important motivator. 'Great commitments', as March (2007) puts it, 'require great hopes'. We may obtain more if we struggle to attain unrealistic yet desirable aspirations, even if it is impossible to fully realize them in practice (Christensen et al., 2013).

However, this does not remove the performance dilemma managers and leaders face. It is necessary to retain and promote a dubious mythology to generate commitment and garner support. Yet, there are dangers in doing so. Exaggerated expectations and claims about the strategic rationality of actions and programs mis-lead and delude. They encourage hubris and pathological optimism, often followed by excessive cynicism when hopes are dashed. If leaders wish to be authentic and retain credibility, there is a need to acknowledge some of the confusion and ambivalence involved. Failing to do so encourages self-promotion, social manipulation and cover-up. So, caught up on the horns of a performative dilemma, managers and leaders spend considerable time and effort on symbolic juggling. Justifying hope and optimism while acknowledging uncertainty and realism is an ongoing challenge. Doing so, while denying one's own rhetorical performance, is a 'careful dance along a narrow beam, [but] there is the possibility of much grace in it' (March, 1986, p.287).

Resolution
Splitting: One approach to this tension is to split performances over time. For example, March and Olsen (1983) document the presence of what they term a 'reorganization saga'. Leaders encouraged by their previous success and new demands tend to adopt a 'rhetoric of administration' at the start of their tenure. They promise rationalization and successful re-organization. Later in their tenure, after experiencing the complexities and problems of reform, they relapse into a 'rhetoric of realpolitik'. This means blaming bureaucratic inertia and vested or siloed interests for watering down or abandoning projects. In the earlier stage, leaders evangelize and promote omniscient and beneficial reform. It is, at times, a valuable aspirational quest. In the latter stage, they inject a healthy dose of pragmatic realism. In doing so, they confirm our suspicion of naivety and appreciation of human weakness. Deliberately fitting in with and exploiting the existence of this saga using different rhetoric and performances over time is one form of 'splitting'.

Strategies for 'splitting in space' may accompany this 'splitting over time'. One type of rhetorical performance may, for example, be given in 'public' venues and at 'official' events, espousing the official line of unity, certainty and optimism. Another may be delivered in private, on the 'backstage', in 'private' and 'personal' comments and asides. The latter involves admitting, even highlighting, confusion, self-interest, careerism and cynicism (Buchanan & Badham, 2020; Burns, 1961; Goffman, 1959 [2022]). All forms of 'splitting' involve juggling different performances to meet different audiences' expectations.

Synthesis: Erving Goffman (1961) describes the creation of synergies in addressing conflicts and tensions in the performances we are required to give. He argues that in such instances, role distance can be invaluable. In practice, strategic role distance is not a matter of separating ourselves from the roles we play but maintaining a socially expected and approved degree of embracement of them and distancing from them. Goffman argues a vital part of role performance is attaining the proper balance to not appear as either a 'stuffed shirt' or an irresponsible saboteur. As he poetically describes it, 'The image that emerges of the individual is that of a juggler and synthesizer, an accommodator and appeaser, who fulfils one function while he is apparently engaged in another; he stands guard at the door of the tent but lets all his friends and relatives crawl in under the flap' (Goffman, 1961, p.139). Does this need to simultaneously display commitment to and distance from a job and enterprise resonate with you?

Living with and working through

In his collaborations with Olsen (March & Olsen, 1983) and Sutton (March & Sutton, 1997), March provides different illustrations of what is involved in accepting and living with this irremovable performative tension. While noticing the splitting of performances over time by US Presidents, March and Olsen (1983) use the case to advocate embracing the tensions rather than simply alternating between the rhetoric of administration and realpolitik. They recommend an ongoing view of change initiatives or reforms as an exercise in 'civic education'. Civic education requires committing to strategic incrementalism, legitimacy building and leveraging opportunities to move discussion and action forward while accepting the importance yet unpredictability of long-term outcomes. It is a humble and reflective form of what Lindblom (1959) described as 'muddling through'. In the context of leadership in business schools, March and Sutton (1997) recommended a similar approach to coping with the tension in business schools, as both a 'culture of advice-givers' and a 'culture of research workers'. Rather than siding with one or the other, they point to the value and limitations of each as well as being resilient enough to operate in the face of such tensions. Avoiding the temptation to relapse into 'neat solutions' or the 'pathologies' of siding with one or the other, they advocate ongoing acceptance of the 'tension between saying more than we know and understanding how little we can know' (March & Sutton, 1997, p.704).

7.3   THE PARADOX OF MEANING

[A leader is] a bit like the driver of a skidding automobile. The marginal adjustments he makes, his skill, and his luck may possibly make some difference to the survival prospects for his riders. As a result, his responsibilities are heavy. But whether he is convicted of manslaughter or receives a medal for heroism is largely out of his control. (Cohen & March, 1986, p.20)

Once we appreciate the paradoxes of rationality and performance, we are better positioned to handle them. But what does handling involve? In the previous chapter, leaders were encouraged to be mindful of the challenges of change and mobilize the energy and support necessary to address them. The chapter highlighted 'gaps' between what we aspire to and what we achieve and identified strategies and advice for 'plugging the gap'. It involves what March referred to as the 'plumbing' part of the role of managers and leaders. This is the essential craft of working creatively and persistently to overcome the gaps and make things happen in uncertain, complex and conflictual settings.

However, the paradox of meaning surfaces questions and faces the challenges of 'living with the gap' given the various 'knowing–doing' gaps are, to a degree, unavoidable. This paradox highlights the challenge of finding meaning in change activities and projects *when we know careful thought and action do not guarantee success*. It recognizes and accepts a world where 'victory is elusive, and virtue is not reliably rewarded' (March, 2007).

Addressing the paradox of rationality forces us to reconcile our faith in rationality with a critical awareness of its limitations. We have faith but know its limits. The paradox of performance means we must cope with the challenge of communicating this in public. We are expected to demonstrate confidence, which does not allow public doubt. The paradox of meaning takes us deeper, however. While we may tackle these first two paradoxes well, leading change remains inherently risky. There are no guarantees. Machiavelli describes the 'bitch [sic] goddess Fortuna' who undermines all our activities. How do we find meaning and purpose in such an enterprise? How do we learn to 'live with the gap' between what we hope for and what we can achieve? How do we communicate this challenge in an engaging and attractive way? How do we create and explore new meanings that are both imaginative and inspiring?

Resolution

Splitting: As an example of a strategy of splitting, we may adopt a pragmatic and optimistic 'both/and' leadership strategy in one place or context – at work – assuming it is of central importance for our organizations and careers. Meanwhile, we might hold to more existential speculative reflections on the meaning of it all in private and personal situations or contexts, expressing and even railing against the vicissitudes of fortune. This may be something discussed with family and friends in the evenings, on holidays or at the week-ends. The latter may also occur 'backstage' *within* organizations, as a topic of water-cooler gossip or after-work drinks at the bar.

We may also shift the meaning we attribute to events over time. As our projects and careers go well in 'good times', we might embrace the perspective and entrepreneurial ethos of an optimistic 'both/and' leadership strategy. In 'bad times', when failures result, when projects collapse and careers go awry, we may reflect on the naivety of such an approach, appreciate the broader issue of our lack of control over our fate, and speculate on the meaning of the unfairness and injustice that can result.

Synthesis: While there may be inherent limitations on our ability to control events and guarantee outcomes, we *can* align our purposes with an acceptance of this situation. Advocates of 'technologies of foolishness' and 'serious play-fulness' in the innovation process, for example:

- recognize the uncertainty of our actions while remaining committed to 'trying it out',
- view actions as 'experiments', and
- encourage playful and creative 'improvisation'.

They also appreciate that we do not merely pursue and then succeed or fail to realize our goals and purposes. Rather, it highlights the sense of freedom (and possible discomfort) that arises from recognizing we discover our goals and purposes in the course of our actions.

Another synthetic stance is to find meaning in change pursuits by separating the uncertain achievement of outcomes from the personal value of embarking on the journey. Having a transcendent 'why' can help inspire the pursuit of pragmatic goals by providing this pursuit with meaning separate from achieving hoped-for outcomes. In *Man's Search for Meaning*, Viktor Frankl (1959) famously pronounced that 'He who has a "why" to live for can bear almost any how' and illustrated this with the experiences of those who survived the German prison camps in World War II. Simon Sinek (2011) has produced a managerial version of this insight urging individuals and organizations to pursue their 'big why' as an inspiration and guide.

Living with and working through

There is also an aesthetic elegance, artistry and grace, and authenticity in a refined appreciation that pursuing pragmatic goals may not work out in the end. Finally, there is a resonant romantic dimension to the stoicism (Spillane & Joullie, 2015), resilience (Coutu, 2002) and lightness (Weick, 2007) that comes from accepting this is 'a game that can only be played, not won' (*The Legend of Bagger Vance*, 2000). This stance accepts the irreducible nature of this feature of human striving while continuing to grapple with the struggle to find meaning in the process. It is illustrated in different ways in Reinhold Niebuhr's praise of serenity, William Shakespeare's nobility in suffering the slings and arrows of outrageous fortune and Rudyard Kipling's treatment of Triumph and Disaster as two imposters.

The Serenity Prayer (Reinhold Niebuhr)

God, grant me the serenity to accept the things I cannot change, courage to change the things I can, and wisdom to know the difference.

Hamlet's Soliloquy (William Shakespeare)

To be or not to be, that is the question. Whether it is nobler in the mind to suffer the slings and arrows of outrageous fortune, or to take up arms against a sea of troubles, and by opposing end them.

The Poem *'If'* (Rudyard Kipling)

If you can meet with Triumph and Disaster and treat those two impostors just the same ... If you can watch the things you gave your life to, broken, and stoop and build 'em up with worn-out tools ... you'll be a Man [sic], my son.

Accepting and working through such conditions requires a fundamental shift in perspective from the rational model or myth of what is involved in influencing change. When this is fully appreciated, we can no longer find purpose in mechanistic notions of alignment, effectiveness and success alone. These mechanistic notions are not only restricting; they are unreasonable. Recognizing this state of affairs, Karl Weick argues that 'change poets are a little like "Sisyphus, who was doomed eternally to roll up a hill a vast stone that would always fall back just as he was about to reach the top. The dignity of life derives from mankind's continual perseverance in projects for which the universe affords no foothold or encouragement" (MacIntyre, 1967, p. 150)' (quote and citation in Weick, 2011, p.18).

Such poetic insights are essential to us as humans and of central significance in looking after ourselves and others in the change process. In the next chapter, we will explore the ironic stance required to combine this 'poetry' with the pragmatic wisdom of the 'plumber' in developing our capabilities and improving our chances of success as managers and leaders of change.

7.4   CONCLUSION

From Either/or To a Paradox Mindset

There are embedded contradictions confronting managers and leaders in the change enterprise. *Chapter 4. Masks and Performance* outlined the tensions between different views of how to control change, i.e., views on the appropriate and best forms of control. This chapter has addressed three tensions lying even deeper. They involve tensions and contradictions in our approach to:

1. the **knowledge** we apply (seeking certainty yet acknowledging ambiguity),
2. the **performances** we give (appearing authoritative and decisive yet demonstrating humility and reflexivity), and
3. the **meanings** we hold (committed to achieving the purposes we set while also discovering them in the face of uncertainty and serendipity).

When handling these contradictions, traditional 'Either/Or mindsets' are dominated by what Collins and Porras describe as the 'Tyranny of the Or'. This is a 'fixed mindset' approach (Dweck, 2017). Adherents move between being stuck in the face of an irresolvable dilemma, denying its existence and searching for a zero-sum trade-off.

Dilemma Mindset

- 'solutions are seen as either/or choices in which one alternative must be selected among mutually attractive (or unattractive) options'
- 'assumes incompatibility of two poles, and hence as a response, the actor prioritises one pole over another.'

Source: Zheng et al. (2018), p.587.

Typical responses of a dilemma mindset to the identified paradoxes range between two extremes.

1. Search and commit to an objective 'one best way' to think and act directly. Then, persuasively communicate the 'solution' to stakeholders while upholding the faith this best solution will win out.
2. Being sceptical about the 'evidence base' of adopted strategies. Then, communicate the uncertainty, associated anxiety, suspicion and cynicism about the outcomes and likely failure.

In between these two extremes, the dilemma mindset is characterized by an immobilizing and unproductive 'flip-flop' between contradictory forms of thought, performance and meaning. The result is rigid adherence to one-sided thinking, defensiveness and denial in the face of ambiguity and ambivalence, and the pain and exhaustion resulting from unreflective stress-inducing cognitive and emotional dissonance.

In contrast, contemporary advocates of a 'paradox mindset' recommend an alternative 'growth mindset' approach (Dweck, 2017). This mindset adopts a creative, non-zero-sum 'both/and' strategy. It accepts and explores ways to work through or resolve apparent contradictions (Heracleous & Robson, 2020; Miron-Spektor et al., 2018; Smith et al., 2016, 2020; Smith & Lewis, 2011, 2022). Typical responses of such a paradox mindset to the dilemmas of leading change are:

1. Appreciate both views of rationality and creatively explore strategies for resolving or coping with the differences and tensions between them.
2. Acknowledge the need for a certain degree of hypocrisy in communicating and displaying adherence to these views, exploring ways to maintain public confidence while retaining a reputation for honesty and authenticity.

3.   Respect the importance of keeping faith in the confident pursuit of purpose while appreciating the significance of creating meaning for oneself and others in the face of uncertainty, adversity and chance.

Contrary to the dilemma mindset's stressful dissonance and energy-sapping repression, the paradox mindset fosters what we describe as a greater lightness of being – a lightness of thought, heart and touch. The perspectives we adopt, the prejudices we adhere to, and our actions are committed to but reflectively, provisionally and experimentally. For those with such a mindset, irrationalities of thought and decision-making are anticipated, the need to balance contradictory performances is expected, and the challenge of finding meaning in the change enterprise is appreciated as a fundamentally human endeavour.

Mindful mobilizing of a paradox mindset

While the advantages of a paradox mindset are relatively straightforward, its adoption is not without challenges. A cognitive 'paradox frame' must be adopted mindfully and mobilized effectively. A considered and reflective stance is needed, as suggested by recent warnings against a simplistic 'naïve paradoxicality' (Cunha et al., 2021, p.33) and an uncritical acceptance of 'faux paradoxes' (Cole & Higgins, 2022, p.41).

Appreciating the complexities and challenges of applying this mindset recognizes that paradoxes do not come in simple pre-packaged forms. Diagnosing whether tensions are inherent dilemmas, irreconcilable contradictions or addressable paradoxes is complex and challenging. The nature and shape of paradoxes also shift over time and between contexts, and we stereotype them at our peril.

How best to address paradoxes is equally complex. Earlier black-and-white contrasts between 'either/or' thinking ('the Bad') and 'both/and' thinking ('the Good') has been replaced by a clearer understanding of the broad 'strategic repertoire' available (Cunha & Putnam, 2019). It includes paying attention to the tensions between strategies: for resolution, for acceptance and working through, the situational necessity of combining either/or and 'both/and' in 'both/or' strategies, and extending consideration to include 'neither/nor' and 'more/than' approaches (Langley, 2021; Li, 2019, 2021).

Finally, mobilizing energy and support for 'paradox frames' that 'recognise and embrace contradictions' (Leung et al., 2018, p.444) requires going beyond cognitive awareness and appreciation. Cognitive complexity and integrative thinking is a predisposition that aptly recognizes inconsistencies, mixed motives, conflicting goals and the need for regular updating of assumptions and beliefs in the face of ongoing change (Bartunek & Moch, 1987; Bartunek et al., 1983; McCauley et al., 2006; Tetlock et al., 1993; Zerubavel, 1991). But it is not enough to accept their existence. It is also necessary to be energized to address them (Miron-Spektor et al., 2018). The emotional predisposition or capability required to create a productive 'virtuous' rather than debilitating 'vicious' cycle of response to paradox is described by Giorgi (2017) as 'resonance' or a 'personal connection with a frame'. It includes the emotional equanimity necessary to handle the anxieties involved and the emotional complexity needed to appreciate and work with conflicting mores and prejudices. Finally, as Gaim and Cunha succinctly put it (in Pradies et al., 2021), it is one thing to know how paradoxes should be handled; it is quite another to have the behavioural capabilities necessary to bring this about (Cameron, 1986; Hooijberg et al., 1997) and to possess or mobilize the power to ensure they could be handled in this way (Berti et al., 2021; Cunha et al., 2021). The mindful mobilization of the paradox frames we have identified is a critical leadership capability.

7.5   CHAPTER SUMMARY

In *Chapter 7. Paradoxes of Change* you have:

* Been introduced to the idea that there are embedded contradictions in leading change that cannot be resolved by either/or black-and-white strategies.
* Learned that tackling these contradictions requires a 'both-or' leadership approach that combines strategies for both resolving and living with the paradoxical tensions these contradictions create.
* Been informed that the 'paradox mentality' required to appreciate and work through these tensions and contradictions has to be resourcefully mobilized and mindfully applied to be effective.

7.1   The Paradox of Rationality

* We are not as rational in thought and action as we think we are or would like to be. As individuals and institutions, we live with this tension.
* We may partially resolve the tension by either (a) in different contexts being more certain or more sceptical about what rational thought and action can deliver or (b) being deliberately ambiguous about our expectations.
* We live with and work through the tension by creating resilient cultures, structures and capabilities that can recognize and cope with the tensions.

7.2   The Paradox of Performance

* Managers are required to be hypocritical, demonstrating their strategic rationality while acknowledging ambiguity and doubt.

- This tension is partially resolved by giving performances that are (a) different in one place and at one point in time, or (b) simultaneously embrace and yet reveal distance from formal etiquette.
- Living with and working through the dilemmas the tension creates is possible by adopting a perspective of humbly 'muddling through' rather than avoiding or dismissing them.

7.3   The Paradox of Meaning

- Addressing the paradoxes of rationality and performance does not guarantee success. The 'plumber's' mastery must be accompanied by a 'poetic' reflection on 'living with the gap'.
- The tension may be partially resolved by (a) being more confident and more reflective in different times and places, (b) seeking purpose beyond instrumental success or (c) acknowledging we find rather than pursue purpose in innovation.
- We may live with and work through this tension by adopting a stoic and ironic stance.

HEART AND HAND (PRACTICE)

7.6   CASES AND EXERCISES

7.6.1   Paradox of Rationality: The Story of the Stacey Matrix

In 1996, Ralph Stacey produced a matrix designed to capture the complexity and tensions in organizational life. It was commonly described as the 'Stacey Diagram' and was an accessible and popular way to communicate some of the limitations of traditional management when confronted by uncertainty and conflict. It has now been frequently cited and used by academics and consultants as the 'Stacey Matrix'.

The Stacey Matrix uses two dimensions: certainty and conflict. When close to certainty and agreement, traditional planning and control systems and management strategies are more appropriate. Conversely, when there is greater uncertainty and agreement, they are no longer appropriate. Figure 7.1 below provides a recent version.

The Matrix itself provides us with useful suggestive insights. However, what is equally interesting and valuable are the ways it has been used differently from what Ralph Stacey first intended. This illustrates the challenge of encouraging paradoxical thinking about organization and change.

Case material

AdaptKnowledge. (2016). *The Stacey Matrix*. http://www.gptraining.net/training/communication_skills/consultation/equipoise/complexity/stacey.htm (accessed 12 June 2020)

Buckley, F., & Monks, K. (2004). Developing meta-qualities: Outcomes and implications for HR roles. *HRMJ, 14*(4), 41–56.

Stacey, R. D. (2012). The tools and techniques of leadership and management: Meeting the challenge of complexity. In R. Stacey, *The Tools and Techniques of Leadership and Management: Meeting the Challenge of Complexity* (Appendix). London: Routledge. (copy available on the book's website)

Stacey, R. (2015). *Ralph Stacey: Complexity and paradoxes 2015*. https://www.youtube.com/watch?v=Ee_3Pg5zvRg (accessed 12 June 2020)

Task 1

Read the summary of *The Stacey Matrix* in Adapt Knowledge (2016), then answer the following questions:

1. What do you believe are the main characteristics of a world on the 'edge of chaos'?
2. What capabilities do you think are required to operate effectively in this world?

Task 2

Read Buckley and Monks' (2004) discussion of 'meta-qualities' to further inform a discussion of capabilities, and address the following two questions:

1. What kind of 'meta-qualities' are required for managing change on the 'edge of chaos'?
2. What kind of changes are needed to management education to help create these?

Task 3

Watch Ralph Stacey's (2015) short video on complexity and paradox. (Watch up to 2.37 mins.)

1. After watching this video, clarify your understanding of what he means when he advises not getting 'trapped' in your perspective or and advocates viewing organizations as relationships, not systems.
2. Discuss how appreciating the paradox of 'predictable unpredictability' unsettles established views on organizational change and its management. What needs to be done about this?

Task 4

Stacey only used the Matrix diagram once, in 1996, and as documented in the case material reading (Stacey, 2012), he later came to regret ever having developed it. Before looking for an explanation on the website answer, try to second-guess why. Discuss the following.

1. Why do you think this is the case?
2. What do you think is his main criticism of many of those who have used the Matrix?

Now, read Stacey (2012) and discuss:

3. Why do you think the misinterpretation he points to is so widespread and predictable?
4. What challenges does this create for management education?

An updated version of the Stacey Matrix is provided in Figure 7.1. This version emphasizes the importance of capabilities identified in further reading as mindful sensemaking (Weick, in Coutu, 2002), emotional intelligence (Goleman, 2000, 2009), cognitive and behavioural complexity (Denison et al., 1995) and political entrepreneurship (Buchanan & Badham, 2020).

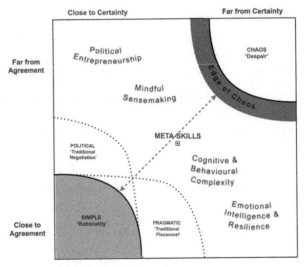

Source: Badham (2004b).

Figure 7.1   *The Stacey Matrix updated*

7.6.2 Paradox of Performance: *Braveheart* Revisited

This exercise draws up and extends the *Braveheart* exercise in Chapter 4. In it, we explore how William Wallace handles the paradox of rationality and the degree to which his persuasiveness and appeal derive from this success in this enterprise.

In the *Braveheart* clip, note the following:

1. The nobles' faith in the effectiveness of conscripting their subjects for battle and focus on achieving a beneficial 'negotiated' outcome exemplifies a narrow and exaggerated view of the formal rationality of organizations.
2. The men on the battlefield reveal an exaggerated faith in William Wallace's ability to solve their problems and lead them to victory.
3. The followers argue to leave the battlefield based on evidence they are outnumbered by the English and are, therefore, highly likely to die. So, to survive, they should leave.

Case material
Braveheart (Director: Gibson, M.) (1995). *Braveheart* leadership speech (1.12.30–1.19.00 mins).

Can be accessed in short form at: *Braveheart Leadership Speech* https://www.youtube.com/watch?v=hyqoC3wHMwY (accessed 5 January 2022)

Task 1
Begin your review of the *Braveheart* Leadership Speech by describing how William Wallace acknowledges and demonstrates:

a. the value of the nobles' efforts as well as their limitations,
b. his personal capabilities as well as the flaws in exaggerating them, and,
c. the valid yet partial and mis-leading nature of the evidence they consider and the strategy they adopt.

Task 2
Discuss how in addressing these issues, he succeeds in establishing rather than undermining his credibility in moving in and out of a more formal 'frontstage' presentation of his authority and a more informal 'backstage' questioning of that authority.

Task 3

Evaluate the success of his performance in motivating those on the battlefield. Then, answer the following question:

1. What lessons might be drawn from this for leaders seeking to communicate the real challenges of change to their staff while energizing them to help address and overcome them?

7.6.3   Handling Paradox: Nimble Leadership at W.L. Gore

W.L. Gore and Associates, inventors of Gore-Tex, have become a famous example of ongoing successful innovation (Hamel, 2012). This is often attributed to a culture and structure that removes traditional management and hierarchy. As such, it provides a leading model of an innovative company that has retained its ethos and structure while thriving over time.

This model may be difficult for others to imitate, as Bill Gore and others have observed (Shipper & Manz, 1998). Rather than providing a simple 'one best way' example of a solution to ongoing innovation, it represents a structure and culture that grapples effectively with the paradoxical tensions of 'designed chaos' (Vera & Rodriguez-Lopez, 2007). Terri Kelly, CEO of Gore, talks of the need for separate structures for innovation and day-to-day operations (Smith et al., 2016, p.65). These are, however, supported by a culture and leadership that values and reinforces both activities while also ensuring the proper connection between them to ensure ideas are not rejected and key talents are used.

In 'Nimble Leadership', Ancona et al. (2019) emphasize the ambivalence of high-level executives towards the changes in behaviour that are required. While recognizing their companies need to be more innovative, they are also terrified of the chaos that might ensue from pushing power and responsibility lower down the organization. W.L. Gore, they argue, provides one example of the leadership and culture required to resolve this tension.

Case material

Ancona, D., Backman, E., & Isaacs, K. (2019). Nimble leadership: Walking the line between creativity and chaos. *Harvard Business Review*, *July–August*, 2–11.

Hamel, G. (2012). *What Matters Now: How to Win in a World of Relentless Change, Ferocious Competition and Unstoppable Innovation*. San Francisco: Jossey-Bass.

Shipper, F., & Manz, C. (1998). Classic Case 6: W.L. Gore and Associates. In A. Thompson, & A. Strickland (Eds.), *Strategic Management: Concepts and Cases* (pp.491–513). Burr Ridge, IL: Irwin. https://www.researchgate.net/publication/ 260943692_CLASSIC_CASE_6_W_L_GORE_ASSOCIATES_INC (accessed 12 June 2020)

Smith, W. K., Lewis, M. W., & Tushman, M. L. (2016). 'Both/and' leadership. *Harvard Business Review*, *May*, 62–70.

Vera, D., & Rodriguez-Lopez, A. (2007). Leading improvisation: Lessons from the American revolution. *Organizational Dynamics*, *36*(3), 303–319.

Task 1

Read Shipper and Manz (1998) on W.L. Gore, then read Ancona et al. (2019) to answer the questions below.

1. List the qualities Ancona et al. (2019) argue are required for 'entrepreneurial', 'enabling' and 'architecting' leaders.
2. Discuss the importance of each in addressing the tensions involved in combining innovation and order.

Task 2

Read the short statement by the W.L. Gore CEO Terri Kelly in Smith et al. (2016), and consider two further questions:

1. What do you think is the value of continually surfacing tensions and discussing them in terms of balance rather than choice?
2. What tensions do you think these entrepreneurial qualities will not resolve but must continue to be 'worked through'?

The general implications of this analysis for the leadership of change are clear. If you have time, however, further your discussion in addressing:

1. What key tensions require ongoing attention from 'entrepreneurial', 'enabling' and 'architecting' change leaders during an initiative?
2. What kinds of cultural and structural supports are required to enable them to play this role?

7.6.4   Practice and Rhetoric: Barack Obama

James March and Johan Olsen documented the cultural ritual of re-organization in the life of US Presidents and the rhetorical duality of that ritual in 'Organizing Political Life' (1983). The 'reorganization saga' shifts over time from a 'rhetoric of administration' ('voice of the prologue') to a 'rhetoric of realpolitik' ('voice of the epilogue'). A similar saga can be identified in the appointment and careers of CEOs and many of their change initiatives. March and Olsen (1983) recommend embracing the inevitability of this saga in both the ***practice and the rhetoric of leadership***.

Case material
March, J., & Olsen, J. (1983). Organizing political life: What administrative reorganization tells us about government. *The American Political Science Review*, *77*(2), 281–296.

Obama, B. (2015). *President Barack Obama (FULL) Interview.* BBC News, 24 July. https://www.youtube.com/watch?v=YdU7fUXDLpI (accessed 5 January 2022)

Key video segments:

- 'Tail End' of his Presidency as a 'Dead Man Walking' (14.23–16.13).
- Turning 'Yes We Can' into 'Yes We Did' (16.15–17.15).

Task 1
Read the following summary of March and Olsen (1983), then read the actual article. It is dense but illuminating.

March and Olsen (1983) observe the **practice of leadership and change** *depends on the following:*

- **the 'problematics of attention':** the variety of actors involved in change will pay attention to the change at different times, in different ways and pursue different goals, and
- **'incremental adaptation':** those involved in promoting change have to make things happen in the context of these shifting and variable interests, solutions available and changing circumstances and interpretations of events.

March and Olsen (1983) recommend viewing the practice of re-organizing more in terms of gardening than engineering, gathering rather than hunting, and evolving 'coral islands' more than heroic human victories. They recognized a shift in the interpretation of events during change, directing our attention towards the rationales yet changing roles of the rhetoric of administration and realpolitik over time. The rhetoric of administration (the 'voice of the prologue') builds on and reinforces our belief in the meaningfulness of human endeavour and the value of virtuous pursuits. The rhetoric of realpolitik (the 'voice of the epilogue') captures our suspicion of high-minded idealism and our lived experience of frustration at bureaucracy, ineffectiveness and narrow-minded self-interest. Both resonate and are both parts of the re-organization saga. March and Olsen (1983, p.292) conclude quite radically, that this is not an argument that 'symbols are important to politics, although they certainly are' but that 'politics is important to symbols, that a primary contribution of politics to life is the *development of meaning*'.

On civic education
These views of the practice and rhetoric or re-organization come together in their recommendations for viewing re-organization as 'civic education'. Such a perspective looks beyond short-term success or failure. Instead, it considers how initiatives educate the public and change public opinion climate in greater

significance than attaining specific short-run objectives. The emphasis is on things such as injecting ideas into debates, creating precedents, developing a logic of the argument that carries over beyond the initial re-organization, creating 'solutions' that others may take up and attach to their 'problems' later, and influencing background support and motivation for change.

Task 2

Having completed Task 1, Task 2 involves considering how March and Olsen's (1983) article informs our understanding of the perspective and rhetoric of Barack Obama. View two segments of Barack Obama's BBC Interview (2015) where he reflects on his presidency (precisely, 14.23–18.02) and discuss the questions below:

   Part 1: 'Tail End' of his Presidency as a 'Dead Man Walking' (14.23–16.13) In this clip, Obama refers to his 'even temperament', looking beyond the '24-hour news cycle' and 'serendipity' and 'convergence' as well as 'robust exertion of Presidential authority' in considering his 'successes'.

1. How does this align with March and Olsen's view of the 'problematics of attention' and 'incremental adaptation'?
2. What do Obama's qualities and experiences suggest about the kind of capabilities required from leaders?

   Part 2: Turning 'Yes We Can' into 'Yes We Did' (16.15–17.15) In this clip, Obama talks of what he did and didn't 'promise', cultural and political 'fault-lines', 'moving the ball forward' and his 'daughter's generation'.

1. How does this align with March and Olsen's arguments about 'civic education'?
2. What do Obama's reflections indicate about the meaning? Is it essential for leaders to find and give to make re-organization a meaningful exercise?

7.6.5   Change Habit 7: Work Through Tension

The senior executive team in charge of building a new patient-centred cancer care hospital could not decide when the opening should occur. Each of the executives had their own different agendas, clients and timelines. They couldn't agree on 'the date' and kept avoiding the issue. As academic consultant-facilitators, we were to help them address the issue. Prior to the big meeting, we interviewed each participant, found out their different views and interests and turned these into 'briefs'. On the day of the event, each executive was asked to present the brief we gave them. The 'twist' was that they were given the briefs with opposing views to those they held and were lobbying for! So, for example, the finance person concerned about costs was asked to present the value of investing in 'doing it properly' and creating a world-class facility. The customer service person who was strongly committed to creating a patient-centred re-organization was asked to make a case for a 'safety-first business as usual' first stage. And so on ... . There was much enthusiasm and laughter, as each participant threw themselves into their task with some gusto. One of the participants remarked at the close of the session, 'It was such a relief from taking a break in just arguing again for my position'. A few days later, they settled on an opening day. Ensuring the full appreciation, acceptance and constructive consideration of competing viewpoints is a creative challenge. Working through the tensions is an intellectual, emotional and practical endeavour.

Task 1

Let's illustrate and explore these issues through a similar exercise.

1. Identify an issue that concerns you and one or more additional friends or colleagues and over which you, quite 'reasonably', disagree.
2. Using what you already know about the different views, or after a conversation to highlight these, craft out what the opposing views would be.
3. Now hold a meeting where each of you presents the opposing view as persuasively as possible (make this as creative and fun as possible).

Task 2

After the meeting, reflect on and discuss with the other person(s):

1. Has this made a difference to how you understand and appreciate each other's views?
2. Do you now find it easier to appreciate the differences and explore solutions with them?

Task 3

3. Consider how, in the future, you might decide to creatively work through conflicting views and attitudes when there are contradictory principles and competing interests at stake.

RESOURCES

The literature on paradox is vast, complex and growing. To make this accessible, we will focus on five sets of key readings.

1.   Managing and Leading Change and Paradox

The most accessible introduction to paradox and change that addresses many of the concerns of managing and leading change is provided by Samuel Beer and Nitin Nohria (Beer & Nohria, 2000a, 2000b). The overview is provided in their 2000 HBR article 'Cracking the Code of Change' and edited book *Breaking the Code of Change* published in the same year.

Beer, M., & Nohria, N. (Eds.) (2000a). *Breaking the Code of Change.* Boston: Harvard Business Review Press.
Beer, M., & Nohria, N. (2000b). Cracking the code of change. *Harvard Business Review, 78*(3), 133–141.

This is usefully supplemented by a review more tightly linked to the paradox perspective introduced below.

Lüscher, L. S., Lewis, M., & Ingram, A. (2006). The social construction of organizational change paradoxes. *Journal of Organizational Change Management, 19*(4), 491–502.

An accessible overview and introduction to the 'paradox mindset' required can be found in the following *Worklife* blog by Heracleous and Robson (2020).

Heracleous, L., & Robson, D. (2020). Why the 'Paradox Mindset' is the key to success. *BBC Worklife, November,* 1–8. https://www.bbc.com/worklife/article/20201109 -why-the-paradox-mindset-is-the-key-to-success. (accessed 5 January 2022)

2.   Paradoxes of Rationality, Performance and Meaning in Modern Organizations

The foundations of these three paradoxes can be found in Richard Badham's (2017) chapter in the *Oxford Handbook of Organizational Paradox,* and his article (2022) in the *Journal of Management History.* In the former, he argues that the work of James March captures and focuses on these three paradoxes in modern organizations. In the latter, he extends this analysis in exploring the 'plumbing' and the 'poetry' of leadership, and the case James March makes for a poetry of leadership that addresses the three paradoxes.

Badham, R. J. (2017). Reflections on the paradoxes of modernity : A conversation with James March. In W. Smith, M. Lewis, P. Jarzabkowski, & A. Langley (Eds.),

The Oxford Handbook of Organizational Paradox (pp.277–295). Oxford: Oxford University Press.

Badham, R. (2022). James March and the poetry of leadership. *Journal of Management History*, *28*(1), 46–65.

3.   A Paradox Perspective

The most widely influential view of organizational paradoxes is Wendy Smith and Marianne Lewis' (2011) 'dynamic equilibrium' model, updated and reviewed in Gail Fairhurst et al.'s (2016) article, Wendy Smith et al.'s (2017) edited volume *The Oxford Handbook of Organizational Paradox* and Wendy Smith and Marianne Lewis' 2022 book.

Fairhurst, G. T., Smith, W. K., Banghart, S. G., Lewis, M. W., Putnam, L. L., Raisch, S., & Schad, J. (2016). Diverging and converging: Integrative insights on a paradox meta-perspective. *The Academy of Management Annals*, *10*(1), 173–182.

Smith, W. K., & Lewis, M. W. (2011). Toward a theory of paradox: A dynamic equilibrium model of organizing, *36*(2), 381–403.

Smith, W., Lewis, M., Jarzabkowski, P., & Langley, A. (Eds.) (2017). *The Oxford Handbook of Organizational Paradox*. Oxford: Oxford University Press.

Smith, W., & Lewis, M. (2022), *Both/and thinking: Embracing creative tension to solve your toughest problems*. Boston: Harvard Business Review Press

For a constructive yet critical questioning of this approach and the field of research it generates, the article by Miguel Cunha and Linda Putnam (2019) is a valuable addition.

Cunha, M. P. e., & Putnam, L. L. (2019). Paradox theory and the paradox of success. *Strategic Organization*, *17*(1), 95–106.

In addition, the following recent book-length overviews are extremely valuable:

Berti, M., Simpson, A., Cunha, M., & Clegg, S. (2021). *Elgar Introduction to Organizational Paradox Theory*. Cheltenham, UK and Northampton, MA, USA: Edward Elgar Publishing.

Cunha, M. P. e., Clegg, S., Rego, A., & Berti, M. (2021). *Paradoxes of Power and Leadership*. London and New York: Routledge.

4.   Both/And Leadership and Working through Paradox

While the reviews of paradox above review the various strategies for handling paradox, two significant articles (Lüscher & Lewis, 2008; Smith et al., 2016) address the key strategies of seeking to both resolve and live with or work through paradox.

Lüscher, L. S., & Lewis, M. W. (2008). Organizational change and managerial sensemaking: Working through paradox. *Academy of Management Journal*, *51*(2), 221–240.

Smith, W. K., Lewis, M. W., & Tushman, M. L. (2016). 'Both/and' leadership. *Harvard Business Review, May*, 62–70.

Overviews of paradox and change, that are less directly and simply aligned with the themes addressed in this book, can be found in addition included in the references at the end of this book (e.g., Cunha et al., 2021; Peters, 2012; Schad et al., 2016; Sharma et al., 2021; Smith et al., 2016; Sparr, 2018).

5. Paradox in Strategy: Strategic Ambiguity, Janus Strategy and the Icarus Paradox

In recent years, there have been several seminal contributions to applying the idea of diversity, tension, contradiction and paradox to strategy. Eric Eisenberg (2006) explores the value of 'strategic ambiguity' in creating 'unified diversity' out of different interests and viewpoints. Loizos Heracleous (2020) outlines the elements of 'Janus strategy' in embracing the need for alignment while accepting and working through paradox (drawing on the myth of the Roman God Janus able to look in multiple directions simultaneously). Finally, Dan Miller (1992) highlights the dangers of an 'Icarus paradox' in the potential failures bred by success (also drawing on ancient mythology, this time the brash son of Daedalus, Icarus, who fell to his death when he over-confidently flew too close to the sun with wings held together by wax).

Eisenberg, E. (2006). *Strategic Ambiguities. Essays on Communication, Organization and Identity*. London and Thousand Oaks, CA: Sage.
Heracleous, L. (2020). *Janus Strategy*. London: KDP.
Miller, D. (1992). *The Icarus Paradox: How Exceptional Companies Bring About Their Own Downfall*. New York: HarperCollins.

7.1 The Paradox of Rationality

Further readings on the paradox of rationality can be found in the chapter by Badham (2017). However, Dan Ariely's talk provides an accessible and entertaining video on our 'predictable irrationality' (2008).

Ariely, D. (2008). *Are we in control of our own decisions?* Ted Talks. https://www.youtube.com/watch?v=9X68dm92HVI

More lengthy treatments of decision-making and our pursuit yet betrayal of individual and organizational irrationality can be found in the following books by Dan Ariely (2009), Dan Kahneman (2011) and James March (1994).

Ariely, D. (2009). *Predictable Irrationality: The Hidden Forces that Shape our Decisions*. New York: HarperCollins.
Kahneman, D. (2011). *Thinking, Fast and Slow*. New York: Farrar, Straus and Giroux.
March, J. (1994). *Primer on Decision-Making*. New York: Free Press.

7.2   The Paradox of Performance

The main paradoxical challenges of managing change by being both participative and coercive, both planned and emergent, are addressed in Beer and Nohria (2000b). The nature of change as 'drama' and managing change as a performing art was addressed above in Chapter 4, and an academic review can be found in Badham et al. (2012b).

Badham, R., Mead, A., & Antonacopoulou, E. (2012b). Performing change: A dramaturgical approach to the practice of managing change. In D. Boje, B. Burnes, & J. Hassard (Eds.), *Routledge Companion to Organizational Change* (Vol. 1, pp.187–205). London and New York: Routledge.

Three illustrations of the paradoxes facing leaders in their change performances are provided by: Grint (2005) in his analysis of three cases of leaders handling 'wicked problems'; Christensen et al. (2013) in addressing hypocrisy and aspirational talk in the case of CSR; and March and Olsen's (1983) discussion of the 'organizational saga' characterizing the rhetoric of US Presidents.

Christensen, L. T., Morsing, M., & Thyssen, O. (2013). CSR as aspirational talk. *Organization, 20*(3), 372–393.
Grint, K. (2005). Problems, problems, problems: The social construction of 'leadership'. *Human Relations, 58*(11), 1467–1494.
March, J., & Olsen, J. (1983). Organizing political life: What administrative reorganization tells us about government. *American Political Science Review, 77*(2), 281–296.

7.3   The Paradox of Meaning

This paradox is most interestingly addressed by James March in his discussion of plumbing, poetry and the meaning of leadership in his book *On Leadership* (March & Weil, 2005).

March, J. G., & Weil, T. (2005). *On leadership*. Oxford: Blackwell.

An accessible brief background to the work of James March and his concern with the meaning of leadership is provided by his HBR Interview (Coutu, 2006) and a relatively dry yet very insightful talk on 'Management and Don Quixote' to the HEC in Paris (March, 2007).

Coutu, D. (2006). Ideas as art: A conversation with James G. March. *Harvard Business Review, October*, 83–89.
March, J. (2007). *Management and Don Quixote*. HEC Paris. YouTube. https://www .youtube.com/watch?v=bztgYMoTEjM (accessed 5 January 2022)

Again, rather abstract, and academic, the article by Karl Weick (2011) on 'change poets' also captures some of the creativity of change agents in how they interpret change, form 'hunches' and avoid being entrapped by the illusion of having to capture what is 'really going on'.

Weick, K. E. (2011). Reflections: Change agents as change poets – on reconnecting flux and hunches. *Journal of Change Management, 11*(1), 7–20.

8.   Ironies of change

Beyond the yellow brick road of naïvete and the muggers' lane of cynicism, there is a narrow path, poorly lit, hard to find, and even harder to stay on once found. People who have the skill and the perseverance to take that path serve us in countless ways. We need more of these people. Many more. (John Kotter, *Power and Influence*)

How can leaders be mindful of the challenges of change, mobilize energy and resources to address them, *and* handle the paradoxes of the change enterprise? Unfortunately, addressing such issues effectively and with meaning is often hampered by deeply embedded 'deficit thinking' in managing and leading change. In this chapter, we advocate a more positive strength-based approach. Unlike naïvely 'gung-ho' versions of this approach, we make a case for one grounded in an engaged ironic sensibility.

Learning objectives
Head (theory)
8.0 Introduction
8.1 An ironic perspective
8.2 An ironic performance
8.3 An ironic temperament
8.4 Chapter summary
Heart and hand (practice)
8.5 Cases and exercises

Resources

LEARNING OBJECTIVES

- Understand and appreciate the weaknesses of a 'deficit approach' to change.
- Examine and explore the value of a strength-based ironic sensibility.
- Be able to analyse and debate the importance of an ironic sensibility as a perspective (ironic gaze), performance (ironic mask), and temperament (ironic temper).

HEAD (THEORY)

8.0   INTRODUCTION

Many of us have experienced change projects going awry, the irrelevance of box-ticking change managers, and those initiating and leading initiatives unaware of what is really going on. We often, in private, partake in *Dilbert* and *The Office*-style ironic reflections on the stupidities we experience. Small wonder popular recommendations for the study of 'stupidology' (Suter, [2007] 2018; Bensoussan, 2021) have been accompanied by academic studies and insights into the 'stupidity paradox' (Alvesson & Spicer, 2017). When asked about the inspiration for his cartoons, Scott Adams, the creator of *Dilbert*, simply stated he observed managers doing stupid things for most of their time and spending much of the rest trying to cover up! Under pressure, however, we often fail to see Adams' humour in the situation. Instead, we become emotional, frustrated, and even angry when confronted by narrow-minded, self-centred, and counter-productive behaviour. Does this resonate? How well have such reactions worked for you? Is there a better way?

A key theme of this book is that change initiatives are bedevilled by gaps we cannot fully surmount and tensions and contradictions we have to live with. The effect of these challenging conditions is the potential for what could be termed a *deficit in meaning*. There are no guarantees of success in a complex and uncertain world where outcomes are never entirely under our control. Doing the right and intelligent thing will not necessarily result in the success we desire and often believe we deserve. So, if our hopes and expectations may be dashed by fortune, accident, or the play of power – what makes our enterprise a meaningful one? How can we avoid experiencing a deficit in the meaningfulness of the change enterprises we embark upon?

This is a difficult topic to raise and talk about in public. When we adhere to a rational myth of how organizations operate, our default reaction is to expect things will work out if only avoidable errors are not made, and irresponsibility does not occur. The attitude of '*Just do it!*' and '*It will be alright on the night!*' is a common default approach, one we are all frequently guilty of. Then, if things do not work out, we become unproductively angry and frustrated, allocate blame, and seek punishment for those who are 'at fault'. Our lives become a stressful rollercoaster ride. We teeter between a dangerous and irresponsible over-optimism and a cynical and debilitating pessimism.

This chapter introduces and advocates an alternative approach marked by a positive, resilient and seriously playful ironic sensibility. Following a discussion of the dangers of deficit thinking, we identify and elaborate on the three main elements of such a sensibility:

1. **An Ironic Perspective**, a lens or gaze aware and accepting of the inherent tensions and challenges of change,
2. **An Ironic Performance** that controls rather than being controlled by the masks we wear and can adopt an ironic mask in communicating the ironies of change, and
3. **An Ironic Temperament** with the tempered discipline and commitment necessary to sustain an ironic perspective and performance.

In conclusion, we summarize the main elements of an ironic sensibility and how it connects to the lightness of being advocated in the Epilogue.

Beyond deficit thinking

In the face of systematic barriers, debilitating knowing–doing gaps and embedded contradictions, leading change might appear to be a frustrating and thankless task. This is not what we wish to suggest. Anyone wishing to achieve personal and institutional outcomes, advance their careers and realize their aspirations has no choice but to accept the challenge. The challenge can be exciting and the enterprise inspiring. Triumphing over odds and opposition can be extremely satisfying. Further developing one's leadership qualities can be immensely fulfilling.

The established rational myth of how organizations operate is, however, mis-leading and counter-productive when it comes to this. It holds a firmly embedded expectation that the right character with the correct mindset, appropriate strategy, and quality tools can 'lead from the front', 'take charge' of change, and guarantee success. When this does not happen, and exaggerated expectations are dashed, this viewpoint encourages a search for those responsible, commonly described as a 'blame the victim' or form of 'deficit thinking'.

In its established form, deficit thinking begins by identifying an 'achievement gap' or 'chasm' (Valencia, 2020, p.1). This gap or chasm is then attributed to the individuals' deficiencies and the groups or cultures in which they are embedded. This is closely followed by quasi-scientific and self-interested recommendations for compensatory initiatives to upskill and re-educate those involved (Davis & Museus, 2019; Valencia, 2012, 2020). Sound familiar?

There is more than a little truth in the jocular description of the first five phases of a project: (1) Enthusiasm, (2) Disillusionment, (3) Panic and Hysteria, (4) Search for the Guilty, and (5) Punishment of the Innocent! (cf. Holland, 2001, p.5). In the case of change initiatives, the initial identification of high 'failure rates' is frequently attributed to management's lack of leadership skills, rigid mindsets, and adaptive capabilities. This is supplemented by imputing psychological weaknesses, inadequacies, and selfish pursuit of self-interest to 'resistors'. This deficit approach is extended beyond individuals to include their 'disadvantaged' situation. Individual deficiencies are located in the narrow and defensive orientations of the groups they are part of and the lack of creativity, innovativeness, and agility in their embedded cultures. This perspective encourages denial, defensiveness, and deceit from all involved who wish to avoid being stigmatized by the failures. As a result, it hinders an open, constructive, and meaningful approach to facing the challenges of change.

In this chapter, we advocate a different approach to understanding and addressing the challenges of change. It is a stoic, strength-based, and seriously playful approach to change involving what we term an 'ironic sensibility'. This approach builds on the recognition of systemic biases against successful change, the existence of knowing–doing gaps, and embedded contradictions in leading change. It accepts and highlights that this creates a potential 'meaning deficit' in change. In the face of such challenges, it is not unreasonable to raise the issue of whether embarking on the change enterprise is worth it. It is worthwhile repeating and remembering Machiavelli's ([1514] 2005, p.22) cautionary observation that

> there is nothing more difficult to execute, nor more dubious of success, nor more dangerous to administer, than to introduce new political orders. For the one who introduces them has as his enemies all those who profit from the old order, and he has only lukewarm defenders in all those who might profit from the new order.

However, acknowledging this reality does not have to be a source of weakness and pessimism. On the contrary, brutal honesty in admitting to the presence of such challenges can be a source of strength and resourceful creativity.

If we take the inevitability of complexity, uncertainty, paradoxical tensions and barriers to success seriously, we may conclude we *cannot fully justify investing ourselves in projects on the hoped for outcomes alone!* Aware of this, an ironic sensibility combines striving to achieve results with an appreciation of the importance of pursuing an initiative for its own sake because it is the right or appropriate thing to do. This may sound somewhat odd as an ethos in our organizational world of system and management speak, but it resonates strongly in our modern culture. The idea that the 'journey is the thing' and that we do something because it is an expression of 'who we are' or because the cause is a moral or just one ('holy war') is commonly recognized. If we pursue a change because it is something we believe in, if it is an expression of who we think we are or would like to be, if the process of pursuing the objective is intrinsically valuable and enhances the well-being of oneself and others, then we can find meaning in the enterprise beyond the play of chance and circumstance. In academic terms, this is often described as moving from an instrumental to a substantive rationale for one's actions or, as we saw in the discussion of James March's paradoxes of modernity , a shift towards combining a 'logic of consequences' with a 'logic of appropriateness' (Badham, 2017, 2022).

While deficit thinking expects success and blames participants when failures occur, an ironic sensibility advocates a creative and resourceful pragmatism in facing them. It develops confidence by highlighting and developing our available strengths.

It is *positive* in focusing on the contribution and meaningful value for those involved in further developing positive identity traits (e.g., self-confidence, self-worth, self-awareness), abilities (e.g., ingenuity, creativity, resourcefulness), developmental opportunities (e.g., for exploration, expression, creativity, relational growth, etc.), and strategic social supports (e.g., camaraderie, coaching, networks, etc.) (Cameron et al., 2003; Cameron, 2008).

It is *resilient* in tempering naïve approaches to 'being positive' or exaggerated views of 'strengths' with a realistic pragmatism in the face of significant challenges. Tempered resilience expects, prepares for and responds to adversity in ways that ameliorate the problems and enhance the ability to 'bounce back' (Boin & Van Eeten, 2013; Hartwig et al., 2020).

It is *seriously playful* in encouraging a lightness of being in response to these challenges. We further elaborate on this in the Epilogue. It involves a lightness of *thought, heart,* and *touch* in accepting and working with the limitations of our knowledge, the partiality of our feelings and commitments and the uncertainty of our actions (Beech et al., 2004; Statler et al., 2009, 2011).

The remainder of this chapter will address how an ironic sensibility that combines, exemplifies and develops such qualities has three dimensions: an ironic perspective, an ironic performance, and an ironic temperament.

8.1   AN IRONIC PERSPECTIVE

Irony has been described as the 'devil's mark or a snorkel of sanity' (Barnes, 1990; Hutcheon, 1994). The view of irony as a 'devil's mark' is quite common. It sees irony as lightweight flippancy or disengaged sarcasm, something wielded by the arrogantly superior or the disillusioned cynic. We do not use this heavily criticized view of irony, advocating instead for the alternative view of irony as a 'snorkel of sanity'.

This view of irony encourages us to accept and enjoy living in a world where we are often mistaken. Plans frequently go awry, and our wants and desires are often frustrated, illusory or unattainable. Its scope ranges from how we grapple on a day-to-day basis with 'life's little ironies' (Thomas Hardy, in Hoyle & Wallace, 2008, p.1429) to how we approach making plans and pursuing strategies, to the 'cosmic irony' of how we create meaning in our lives. It advocates a *reasonable* stance acknowledging the limits to what we can know and control, a *cosmopolitan* appreciation of the contribution and joining of diverse views and sympathies, and a *seriously playful* approach to how we act and what we expect from it. It is an outlook on life that is mature and sympathetic, humble and playful. It steers a considered and careful path between romantic naïvety and negative cynicism, pathological optimism, and debilitating pessimism.[1] As a form of thought, it has a long and notable history.

The Ironic Drama

Irony is an involvement in and engagement with the drama of embracement and distancing towards human striving in the face of the inevitable gap between human hopes, aspirations, and expectations on the one hand and results and achievements on the other (Badham, 2004a).

Fallibility and Folly in Organizational Change

An ironic perspective on organizational change has two dimensions. First, it directs our attention to the *fallibility* of holding onto a rational myth that neglects the irrational aspects of change. The fallibility increases when we fail to see the problems created by the insidious and continuing influence of the rational myth. Second, an ironic perspective also exposes the habitual *folly* of individuals and organizations. Those blinded by an unquestionable commitment to the rational myth rarely disappoint. They arrogantly continue to impose their views, respond defensively to criticism and repress alternative viewpoints – at a cost to everyone. Expecting such thoughts and actions, exposing them, and avoiding them in ourselves are the traditional hallmarks of an ironic perspective.

Since the Middle Ages, this form of irony has been a feature of discussions of *situational ironies*. These exist when actions have an outcome counter or opposite to what was intended. They occur when there is a gap between what people think they know and what they actually know; what they believe themselves to be doing and what they are doing; what they intend to bring about and what they actually bring about; or what they aspire to do or be and what they achieve. An ironic perspective expects and works with these gaps rather than denying, being surprised or outraged at them. Within change, the central situational irony is the gap between how we hope and expect to understand and control organizational change yet experience a world of ambiguity, uncertainty and conflict that often thwarts our expectations and achievements.

The ironic perspective is also a common feature of discussions of *dramatic irony*. This form of irony exists when characters are unaware of what's happening, but observers or the audience can see it. The dramatic irony increases when it is clear to others that the characters' defensiveness, arrogance, and self-interest prevent them from understanding what is happening. Within change, this is a common feature of individuals and organizations when it is quite apparent to observers how they adhere to exaggerated expectations about how rational thought and action create certainty and guarantee outcomes. The irony is made more dramatic the more they can be observed as highly reluctant or failing to see the partiality, limitations, and unintended consequences of their perspectives, programs, and prejudices.

Snorkel of Sanity

Explaining Barnes' (1990) metaphor of irony as a 'snorkel of sanity' may help to clarify the value of an ironic perspective.

The Snorkel

A snorkel helps us breathe while swimming on the surface *and* observe what is going on below the surface. The ironic snorkel allows us to view the 'tip' of the organizational iceberg (above the waterline) and 'bulk' of the iceberg (below). It encourages us to look below the waterline and view the dangers and delights usually obscured from view. It makes it possible for us to appreciate how mis-leading the tip is as a guide to the nature and size of the overall iceberg. However, for our safety, we keep our eye on the tip while discovering what lies below while snorkelling. Collisions can be painful!

The Sanity

'Insanity', as Albert Einstein is frequently misquoted, 'is repeating the same mistakes and expecting different results'. Without an ironic perspective on change, we exaggerate the rationality of individuals and organizations and act based on these assumptions. When these turn out to be mistaken, we frequently become disappointed, angry and frustrated. The outcome is often ineffective and counter-productive fight or flight responses (which we often regret). Seduced by public displays of rationality and our implicit assumptions and commitments to the rational 'tip', we re-enact this reality day after day after day, much like Bill Murray in the movie *Groundhog Day* (1993). An ironic perspective allows us to break the pattern. It encourages us to 'expect the expected'. As a result, we can respond (rather than react) and creatively address such challenges after we assess what lies below and above the surface.

From an effectiveness standpoint, the ironic perspective can help us 'plug the gap' between our aspirations and achievements. Expecting less and persisting more, we can move from a reactive 'culture of complaint' to a constructive 'culture of proactivity'. From a human viewpoint, the ironic perspective also keeps us sane by helping us to 'live with the gap'. It reminds us of the inevitability of gaps between our aspirations and achievements and the degree to which we ultimately cannot control events. It helps us consider and reflect on the meaning of pursuing change, over and above the instrumental achievement of outcomes. It also, somewhat ironically, puts us in a frame of mind and state of being that can help our pragmatic attempts to 'plug the gap'. When the English Professor Eric Wilson (2015) approvingly cites Bill Murray's chant in the movie *Meatballs* (1979), 'It just doesn't matter', there is a constructive dose of humble irony in the quite serious humour! This theme is reiterated in the second book of the popular self-help guru Mark Manson (2019): *Everything is F*****. A Book about Hope*).

8.2   AN IRONIC PERFORMANCE

According to the rational myth of how organizations should change, tensions, contradictions, and errors are unfortunate problems. We are surprised and frustrated by them, allocate blame, and seek solutions. The ironic perspective counters this myth by revealing the inherent tensions, challenges, and multiple meanings in change. Uncertainty, irrationality, and hypocrisy are expected, lived with, and worked through. They are even, at times, to be enjoyed as part of what makes us uniquely human.

An ironic performance communicates this perspective in word and deed. This is an ongoing challenge in an organizational world where the rational myth dominates. The Turkish proverb proclaims, 'He who would tell the truth, should have one foot in the stirrup.' People and organizations are expected to be rational, purposive, and efficient, and they (and we) must display such characteristics. So, calling the game on the chaotic nature of the 'human barn-yard' (Hill, 2008) can be risky. Officials with responsibilities and interests in promoting change programs are frequently expected to give and pursue the official strategic line. They are often over-sensitive to criticism, viewing it as a sign of negative 'resistance'. Those targeted or affected by a change are anxious, disinterested, or disturbed and are frequently disaffected and cynical. They are often more ready to demonize and blame those imposing these changes than participate constructively in addressing problems. Informed by an ironic perspective, these reactions are only to be expected. What is required is a performance that expertly navigates through the tensions involved, captures the different viewpoints and perspectives, and generates support for solutions to problems that arise. While not a simple 'fix', the tradition of thought and practice on what we term an 'ironic performance' can help communicate an ironic perspective's insights.

The Ironic Mask

The ironic performance originates in the educational strategy adopted by Socrates in Ancient Greece (Claydon, 2013; Vlastos, 1991). Rather than educating through informed instruction, Socrates donned a mask of ignorance. Under this guise, he asked seemingly naïve but challenging questions to reveal levels of ignorance and false certainties in conventional wisdom. For his critics, particularly authorities threatened by such questions, Socratic irony, as it is termed, was condemned as an arrogant and manipulative form of deceit. In Ancient Greece, the translation of 'eiron', a person using such methods, was a 'dissembler'. However, for the supporters of Socratic irony, it is engaging and developmental in drawing out knowledge ('educeo') rather than forcing it in ('indoco'). As we present it here, the ironic performance builds on this tradition in questioning the rational myth by drawing out what people 'always, already' know through their lived experience of the uncertainties, conflicts, and challenges of change (Long, 2010).

Implicit in Socratic irony is scepticism and questioning of the arrogance and proclamations of established authority. There is a reason why Socrates was described as the 'gadfly' (horsefly) of Athens, 'stinging' the backside of the horse of authority. The strategy is to conform on the surface, while undermining beneath, reassuring yet unsettling, reaffirming yet questioning. This communication of a double meaning, where what is implicit contradicts what is explicit, lies at the heart of what is now broadly understood as 'verbal irony'. Verbal irony is commonly referred to when we say one thing but mean another. When two people pass each other on a wet and cold night, and one says, 'Nice weather we are having, isn't it!', this is verbal irony. As an overall performance, it may be recognized as an 'irony of manners'. The contrast between 'what is said' and 'what is meant' may be conveyed through winks, shrugs, costumes, or actions of various kinds.

The most sophisticated, and from our point of view, the most interesting and valuable, ironic performance builds on and extends the idea of deliberately communicating several meanings simultaneously. What George Vlastos (1991) has called 'complex irony' and Richard Claydon (2013) 'third-way irony' deepens and shares our common understanding by sympathetically surfacing multiple meanings. Rather than an explicit message being false and an implicit one real, an ironic performance appreciates both and creates a richer and deeper experience by acknowledging and communicating both. In so doing, irony shows the fallibility of one-dimensional interpretations of events, reveals the existence of diverse meanings, and works with the tensions between them. In so doing, an ironic performance has an 'edge' (Hutcheon, 1994). It is not an uncritical appreciation of all perspectives. On the contrary, it invites questioning the authority of dominant or surface meanings and disrupts the pride and arrogance of those purveying or identifying with them.

Back to our simple weather example, the claim that the weather is nice when it is not is only interesting if both the speaker and audience know they really want nice weather but are both suffering from the fact it is not. Part of their discomfort is due to a shared mistake about what the weather would be like or an unrealistic hope or expectation that it will be fine. The smile or laughter the comment evokes is from mutual recognition of this tension and a shared appreciation of the fallibility and folly of their mistaken or unrealistic hopes or action (Piskorska, 2016). An ironic performance achieves such outcomes by communicating the richness of our experience in situations with multiple and overlapping meanings and tensions. Let's now explore what this looks like in organizational change.

The Cosmopolitan Performance

The ironic perspective captures the tensions of our unrealistic expectations of change and ability to control the process and outcomes, yet lived experiences of ambiguity, conflict, and unpredictable results. The ironic performance communicates expectations for the former, experience with recognition of the latter, and accepting, working with and through this tension in collaboration with others. It also expresses a cosmopolitan appreciation of the tension between diverse viewpoints during change and the importance of bringing them together to achieve shared outcomes.

A cosmopolitan performance that effectively communicates this appreciation is a carefully crafted display of five overlapping qualities:

1. *Diversity*. Recognizing multiple and partial perspectives and tensions in change
   In situations and changes where there are ongoing differences and disagreements, the only sustainable common ground is shared recognition of such a 'heterogeneity of dissensions' (Bauman, 1998, p.251). By finding common ground in recognizing difference and appreciating diversity, a cosmopolitan outlook creates what could be described as a 'resonance of dissonance' (Badham & Rhodes, 2018; Rhodes & Badham, 2018).
2. *Toggling*. Standing inside and outside one's viewpoint in change
   This entails an ability to 'look through' and 'look at' one's interests and perspective. It communicates how the performer is both 'in' and 'out', 'actor' and 'spectator', of whatever perspective, role, or action they are

employing or undertaking (McCloskey, 1994). It enables those promoting a change to be both enthusiastic and reflective. It makes it possible to confidently engage people with the change project, while also bringing along those who might be perceiving or experiencing costs by being sensitive to flaws and limitations.

3. **Duality**. Appreciating three types of 'doubleness' in change
   a. Using '*double meanings*' – as a protective cover; as a means of creating identification amongst diverse audiences; as a source of relief from irreconcilable tensions and demands; and as a basis for creative collaboration amongst those with contradictory views and demands (Westwood, 2004),
   b. Playing a '*double part*' – being flexible and adaptive by being able to observe our actions while acting, laughing at others and events while also being able to laugh at ourselves (Rhodes & Badham, 2018), and
   c. Reconciling '*double plots*' – recognizing and addressing 'double plots' in organizational life. These include 'dominant' and 'subordinate' views of events, 'frontstage' and 'backstage' performances, and institutionalized 'rites' and more or less licensed 'anti-rites' (Berger, 1986; Douglas, 1969; Gusfield, 2015).

4. **Humour**. Embracing the playful, comic and humorous dimension of change
   This includes wry scepticism and a sense of comic delight at surfacing idiocy rather than blaming and punishing the wicked. It can use wit and parody to ridicule arbitrary authority and human folly and enjoy playful creativity and experimentation in uncertainty. Humour can facilitate cooperation between diverse views and interests, help cope with the conflict and stress of dissonance, and be a form of 'undercover' resistance (Badham & McLoughlin, 2005; Westwood & Rhodes, 2007).

5. **Humility**. Displaying a humble and unifying will and skill
   Entails the ability to create identification with others by expressing a deep appreciation of one's limited perspective, partial interest and lack of control.

The start and endpoint of an ironic performance is a general awareness of multiple perspectives and interests, appreciation of the tensions between them, respectful acknowledgement of each, and taking action to include them.

8.3   AN IRONIC TEMPERAMENT

ELEPHANTS IN THE MIST

A Discipline and Temper

As we have defined it, managing and leading change *is the discipline of influencing oneself and others to achieve a purpose.* Like the martial arts expert, this discipline involves retaining balance and maintaining poise when under pressure and threat. As outlined above, the ironic perspective and ironic performance have many desirable qualities. However, maintaining and applying these in challenging times requires more than a simple appreciation. It demands ongoing discipline. It requires the existence or development of a particular type of temperament.

Described as a particular type of 'self', 'personality', 'disposition', or 'habitus', the ironic temperament is fashioned and re-fashioned as an ongoing 'strategy for living'. This ironic temperament is tolerant, humble, liberal, and reflective of its supporters and promoters. It captures 'the sweet spot between arrogance and despair' (Kanter, 2004, p.8). It involves being sensitive to one's limitations, aware of, and tolerant of the shortcomings of others. It is charitable but not gullible, realistic yet confident, observing and participating in the carnival of human life with a wry scepticism and sense of the comic. The ironist, in these terms, is the deployer of an irony characterized by, as Anatole France put it, the 'gaiety of reflection and the joy of wisdom' (Johansson & Woodilla, 2005, p.15).

A Type of Actor

There have been various approaches and studies of people with such an ironic temperament within organizational studies. These include investigations of 'tempered radicals' (Meyerson & Scully, 2007), 'principled infidels' (Hoyle & Wallace, 2008), 'creative resistors' (Clegg et al., 2006), 'outsider-insiders' (Klein, 2007), 'engaged ironists' (Badham & McLoughlin, 2005), 'gypsies of reason' (Moeller, 2011), 'ironic managers (Badham & Claydon, 2012); and 'ironic leaders' (Lichtenstein et al., 1995; Torbert, 1987); 'enlightened cynics' (Fleming & Spicer, 2003) and even the 'good soldier Svejk' (Fleming & Sewell, 2002). In each case, albeit in very different ways, the temperament of those studied involves an ability to accept, handle and play with the ambiguities and ambivalences, tensions, and contradictions, of organizational life.

Meyerson's studies of 'tempered radicals' capture 'the heat, passion, torment' of those who try to combine the pursuit of their career with a commitment to broader social causes. They point to the challenges such people face in grappling with isolation, the stigma of hypocrisy and pressures for co-option. Hoyle and Wallace (2008) are more focused on the 'principled infidelity' of professionals, 'professional mediators' who craft out ways to maintain their autonomy and ethic of service in the face of managerialist rhetoric and policies for standardization and control. In contrast, Klein (2007) and Badham and McLoughlin (2005) are centrally concerned with change agents and organizational change.

Klein (2007, p.4) focuses on change agents who, like many maverick 'boundary spanners', can 'step back and wear two hats'. As insiders, they can understand the daily ins and outs of the organization, care about it, and mobilize this understanding as well as their credibility and networks within the organization. At the same time, they can stand back and see where internal assumptions get in the way of performance and use ideas and connections 'outside' to question the status quo and shift established frames of thought and action. Badham and McLoughlin (2005) direct their attention to the 'ironic engagement' of line managers and employees involved in change. In contrast to uncritical supporters of change ('zealots') and disillusioned critics ('cynics'), Badham and his colleagues identified the existence of a range of 'ironically engaged' personnel (Badham et al., 2012a; Badham & McLoughlin, 2005). Their stance was of blended distance and commitment, informed by regular observations of situational ironies and the reflective and often humorous use of verbal irony to communicate their outlook.

A Set of Qualities

The ironic temper we advocate is liberal, practical, and seriously playful. It is liberal in that it acknowledges and respects we live in a 'world in which ends collide' (Berlin, 1969, p.149) and a society in which there are competing 'orders of worth' (Jagd, 2011). During change, we must grapple with multiple tensions and contradictions between the ideals we espouse and the strategies we adopt (Rorty, 1989). There is, for example, an aspirational romance in the change enterprise that needs to be tempered, not undermined by a 'cooler' sense of irony and change paradoxes (Jacobs & Smith, 1997; Turner, 2002).

The ironic temper also has a strong practical focus. It includes an enthusiastic grappling with 'experiments in living' (see Isaiah Berlin and Richard Rorty in McClean (2016)). These involve the 'practical wisdom' of bending, adapting, and blending multiple, competing, and ambiguous ends and means (Schwartz & Sharpe, 2011). They also involve adopting a 'situational ethics' that avoids getting stuck in 'thin' moral generalities and grapples with how they intertwine in 'thick' practical contexts.

Finally, the ironic temper is seriously playful (Millan-Zaibert, 2007; Statler et al., 2009). It involves not merely seriously 'working at' but also having fun 'playing with':

- different intellectual perspectives and imaginative experiments,
- established and future identities and careers, and
- improvisation and judgement in uncertain, complex and contested situations.

It consists of the kind of morality that Joseph Schumpeter praised when he stated, 'To realise the relative validity of one's convictions and yet stand for them unflinchingly, is what distinguishes a civilized man from a barbarian' (cited in Rorty, 1989, p.46).

As we understand and advocate it here, the ironic temper brings together all these qualities.

An alternative, far less sympathetic view of irony regards it as a form of ridicule, a 'smirk and a sneer' (Barnes, 1990, p.155; Hutcheon, 1994). Those with an ironic temper are viewed as ineffective, superficial, empty and confused 'drama queens' (Kunda, [1992] 2006; Badham & McLoughlin, 2005). This is **not** the ironic temperament that we are concerned with here.

An Ironic Stance is…

the best defense we have yet devised…It's a shabby thing by the standard of the Platonic forms or natural right, I admit, with their lovely if blinding uniformity of light. But it's all we've got. Like democracy, which it defends, [it] is the worst

> form of wisdom, except those others that have been tried from time to time. (McCloskey, 1994, p.95)

8.4   CHAPTER SUMMARY

In *Chapter 8. Ironies of Change* you have learned about:

- The value of adopting a proactive approach to grappling with the potential 'meaning deficit' in change.
- What is involved in moving from a deficit to a strengths-based approach to change that is positive, resilient, and seriously playful, and
- The nature and value of cultivating an ironic sensibility that combines an ironic perspective, performance, and temperament.

8.1   An Ironic Perspective

- An ironic outlook is reasonable, cosmopolitan, and seriously playful.
- An ironic gaze is a 'snorkel of sanity' that makes it possible to appreciate the formal frontstage as well as informal backstage dimension of organizational life.
- An ironic perspective appreciates situational and dramatic ironies, acknowledging both our fallibility and frequent folly in failing to recognize or denying this to be the case.

8.2   An Ironic Performance

- Calls the game on overly rational views of organizational change in an appealing way and avoids backlash.
- Adopts an ironic mask that highlights and questions dominant, overly rational views. It accepts the existence of such multiple meanings, reveals their partiality, and plays with the tensions between them.
- Communicates a cosmopolitan appreciation of the diverse and selective nature of all viewpoints, the existence of double meanings, double parts, and double plots in change, and does so with humour and humility.

8.3   An Ironic Temperament

- As a strategy for living, irony requires the cultivation of a particular type of disposition or temper.

- Within organizational studies, the ironic disposition is captured in various studies of the temperament of types of organizational actors, including tempered radicals, insider-outsiders, and ironic leaders.
- The ironic temper consists of a set of qualities that are liberal, cosmopolitan pragmatic and seriously playful.

In the Epilogue, we conclude and draw it all together in making a case for adopting a bearable Lightness of Being incorporating a lightness of thought, heart, and touch in the face of the challenges of leading change.

HEART AND HAND (PRACTICE)

8.5   CASES AND EXERCISES

8.5.1   Institutional Irony: Greenwashing and 'Dieselgate'

This exercise explores a current corporate issue (the Volkswagen emissions scandal, aka 'Dieselgate') through an 'institutional' lens. The classical rational myth views organizations as more or less integrated systems with components effectively aligned to attain formal goals and purposes (Meyer & Rowan, 1977; Schultz et al., 2014).

Institutional theories provide an alternative view of the nature of organizations and how they operate in modern regulated environments (Bromley & Powell, 2012; Meyer & Rowan, 1977). In this view, organizations are far from being integrated systems. They are, instead, a set of 'loosely coupled' elements with diverse characteristics and interests that are often in tension. The varied and contradictory demands placed upon them in an environment of multiple competing stakeholders and regulatory institutions exacerbate these tensions. Consequently, organizations are inevitably 'hypocritical' (Brunsson, 2002). Organizations are forced to juggle competing agendas and requirements while portraying themselves as strategically rational entities catering to their specific demands (Dick, 2015). This view of an organization is an illustration and example of adopting an ironic perspective on organizational life.

A key contemporary debate within the institutional view concerns the challenges facing this juggling act in an era of increased competition and a more pervasive and intrusive 'audit society'. In the late 1970s, Meyer and Rowan (1977) argued that modern institutions exercise 'sagacious conformity', separating their core operations and practices from their formal structures and policies. In what has come to be described as a 'smoke and mirrors' strategy, they 'uncouple' policies and practices, appearing to be conforming to stakeholder/institutional demands while operating in a way that effectively delivers its core products and services. However, Bromley and Powell (2012) have argued that increased competition and auditing are forcing organizations to 'walk the talk' and implement the rules and regulations the environment demands. The result is a different challenge, what they describe as a 'means/ends decoupling'. This means organizations are forced to adhere to regulations, create sub-units, initiate ongoing reforms, and use resources in ways that undermine their ability to deliver their goods and services effectively. While Meyer and Rowan (1977) appeared to be advocating a 'fake it' strategy, Bromley and Powell (2012, p.519) 'encourage leaders to focus thoughtfully on shaping tools, such as systems of reporting, monitoring, and evaluation, in ways that are more directly linked to their organization's core activities, and to search for ways to influence the nature of external standards in the environment'.

In light of the growing interest in sustainability, attention is on conforming to increasing government regulation and creating 'win–win' strategies that improve economic performance through sustainability initiatives. However, corporate 'greenwashing' projects the pursuit of sustainability objectives but fails in practice, thereby appearing deviant, unethical and unproductive – even 'sinful' (UL Insights, 2020; Lyon & Montgomery, 2015). The auto industry's recent 'Dieselgate' scandals align with this perspective.

Amelang and Wehrmann (2020) documented the scandal which broke in September 2015, when Volkswagen (VW) was found to have installed 'defeat devices' in several of their diesel cars. These devices were designed to mis-lead regulators about the actual emissions. Between 2015 and now, the scandal spread to several other automakers (e.g., Daimler, BMW), leading to investigations and lawsuits from a range of regulatory institutions and customers. VW claims the scandal has cost the company over 30 billion euros in fines, penalties, financial settlements, buyback costs and loss of sales (Ruzic, 2019). Moral outrage, fines, lawsuits, and well-publicized firings at various levels of VW have been the dominant theme. Another has been a dramatic level of interest, investment and publicity by VW and other carmakers in developing electricity-driven vehicles. The reputational impact on the 'Made in Germany' brand cost the other German carmakers over $5.2 billion in US sales in 2015 alone (Ruzic, 2019).

In this three-part case, we will discuss what an institutional approach to 'Dieselgate' looks like and explore this 'fake it' or 'make it' debate.

Case material
Theoretical Articles
A summary of Meyer and Rowan (1977) and Bromley and Powell (2012) is included on the website. Relevant theoretical articles are:

Bromley, P., & Powell, W. W. (2012). From smoke and mirrors to walking the talk: Decoupling in the contemporary world. *Academy of Management Annals, 6*(1), 483–530.

Brunsson, N. (2002). *The Organization of Hypocrisy*. Copenhagen: Copenhagen Business School Press.

Dick, P. (2015). From rational myth to self-fulfilling prophecy? Understanding the persistence of means-ends decoupling as a consequence of the latent functions of policy enactment. *Organization Studies, 36*(7), 897–924.

Meyer, J. W., & Rowan, B. (1977). Institutionalized organizations: Formal structure as myth and ceremony. *American Journal of Sociology, 83*(2), 340–363.

Schultz, F., Suddaby, R., & Cornelissen, J. (2014). The role of the business media in constructing rational myths of organizations. In J. Pallas, & L. Stranegard (Eds.), *Organizations and the Media* (pp.13–33). Milton Park and New York: Routledge.

Readings

Amelang, S., & Wehrmann, B. (2020). Dieselgate – a timeline of the car emissions fraud scandal in Germany. https://www.cleanenergywire.org/factsheets/dieselgate-timeline-car-emissions-fraud-scandal-germany (accessed 25 May 2020)

CBS. (2017). *Faster, higher, farther. Delves deep into the Volkswagen emissions scandal.* https://www.cbsnews.com/news/volkswagen-emissions-scandal-faster-higher-farther-author-jack-ewing/ (accessed 12 June 2020)

Ewing, J. (2019). *Dieselgate: Inside the air pollution scandal of the century.* https://medium.com/dyson-on/dieselgate-inside-the-air-pollution-scandal-of-the-century-2e462f430025 (accessed 12 June 2020)

Ewing, J. (2017). *Faster, Higher, Farther, the Inside Story of the Volkswagen Scandal.* New York: Norton.

McLean, B. (2017). *Driven off course: How Volkswagen got on the road to scandal.* https://www.nytimes.com/2017/06/05/books/review/volkswagen-scandal-faster-higher-farther-jack-ewing.html (accessed 5 January 2022)

Rhodes, C. (2015). *Volkswagen outrage shows limits of corporate power.* https://theconversation.com/volkswagen-outrage-shows-limits-of-corporate-power-48302 (accessed 12 June 2020)

Rhodes, C. (2016). Democratic business ethics: Volkswagen's emissions scandal and the disruption of corporate sovereignty. *Organization Studies, 37*(10), 1501–1518.

Rhodes, C. (2018). *Volkswagen, #monkeygate and the sham of corporate social responsibility.* https://independentaustralia.net/business/business-display/volkswagen-monkeygate-and-the-sham-of-corporate-social-responsibility,11152 (accessed 12 June 2020)

Ruzic, D. (2019). *How the Volkswagen scandal turned 'Made in Germany' into a liability.* https://knowledge.insead.edu/economics-finance/how-the-volkswagen-scandal-turned-made-in-germany-into-a-liability (accessed 10 January 2023)

Task 1
Read and reflect upon the insights of Meyer and Rowan (1977) and Bromley and Powell (2012) and discuss the questions below. The articles are lengthy and complex, so the website case support summarizes their central arguments.

1. To what extent do you think organizations tend to separate their formal structures and policies from how they actually operate?
2. To what degree do you think this is inevitable, desirable, or optional and to be avoided?

Task 2
To make the case accessible, the main case materials are available in short summaries.
    Read:

*   Amelang and Wehrmann (2020) for the overview and timeline,
*   CBS (2017), Ewing (2019) and McLean (2017) for an overview of Jack Ewing's (2017) book on the issue, and
*   Rhodes (2015, 2018) for an introduction to Carl Rhodes' (2016) argument that the VW scandal illustrates the need for 'democratic business ethics'.

Task 3
Discuss two key issues and questions:

1. **'Greenwashing vs Walk the Talk'**
    a. In what ways was VW involved in a 'smoke and mirrors' strategy or 'greenwashing'?
    b. Could VW have avoided scrutiny and influenced external standards and views more effectively? Is this a justifiable strategy?
    c. Can you think of ways VW and other car manufacturers would have been (and are) able to seek synergies between environmental demands and corporate performance?

Background Note: Bromley and Powell (2012) argue a 'smoke and mirrors' strategy is not viable, and organizations need to either (i) seek synergies between what external regulators demand and how they effectively achieve their objectives, or (ii) influence the external standards imposed on them.

2. **Changing Ethics?**
    a. What external competitive, internal cultural, and project performance pushed VW managers and employees to 'cheat'?
    b. Considering what we have discussed about an ironic perspective, what strategies would you suggest if you were given responsibility

for bringing about a change in VW that faces up to the challenge of creating a sustainable strategy?

Background Note: Rhodes (2015) argues that corporations cannot be relied upon to adopt an ethical stance.

8.5.2   Leadership transformation: Fire, Snowball, Mask and Movie

We now move from an ironic perspective (recognizing the ironies in organizational life) to consider how an ironic outlook can spark creativity and imagination. This case study is based on the HBR article 'Fire, snowball, mask and movie: how leaders spark and sustain change' by Peter Fuda and Richard Badham (2011), which introduces several metaphors leaders can use to help organize their reflection and make their actions more considered and purposeful. There is a temptation to see these metaphors as simple techniques and rules. However, Fuda and Badham emphasize they are designed to stimulate rather than instruct (Parker, 2010). The metaphors capture lessons from the stories of change told by successful change CEOs, so they are more than idle speculation. They are, however, intended to be explored and used in a generative fashion, more like a stimulating Rorschach 'inkblot' than a programmed change manual.

Let's explore an 'ironic' take on the generative leadership metaphors proposed for this exercise. It involves exploring how Fuda and Badham unpack the metaphors as well as critiquing the partiality of their view and exploring others. Feel free to make one or more selections from the first four metaphors. The 'Fire' metaphor is embedded in the HBR link (Fuda & Badham, 2011) and links to the Snowball, Mask and Movie metaphors provided below 2011; 2011a, 2011b, 2011c, 2011d).

Case material

Fuda, P. (2011a). *Mask: How leaders conceal imperfections and adopt a persona* (Leadership Transformation). YouTube & The Alignment Partnership. https://www.youtube.com/watch?v=lol1cky8dm8 (accessed 5 January 2022)

Fuda, P. (2011b). *Movie: A leader's process of self-awareness and reflection.* Australia: YouTube & The Alignment Partnership. https://www.youtube.com/watch?v=QFX6UDtYW0M (accessed 5 January 2022)

Fuda, P. (2011c). *Fire metaphor: From 'burning platform' to 'burning ambition'.* Australia: YouTube & The Alignment Partnership. https://www.youtube.com/watch?v=Tfn6vD4yyC4

Fuda, P. (2011d). *Snowball of accountability (leadership transformation).* Australia: YouTube & The Alignment Partnership. https://www.youtube.com/watch?v=Ep_1nluEkiY

Fuda, P., & Badham, R. (2011). Fire, snowball, mask, movie: How leaders spark and sustain change. *Harvard Business Review*, *89*(11), 145–148, 167.

Oswick, C., Keenoy, T., & Grant, D. (2002). Metaphor and analogical reasoning in organization theory: Beyond orthodoxy. *The Academy of Management Review, 27*(2), 294.

Parker, H. (2010). *Aussies guide to recovery*. Australia: News.com.Au.

Within organization studies, exploring metaphors has been encouraged to throw additional light on phenomena by viewing one thing in terms of another and reflecting on the implications (Morgan, 2006). Irony has, however, been advocated as an alternative approach. Irony encourages us to identify and question how metaphors underlie our thinking or are deployed to stimulate new ideas (Oswick et al., 2002). However, the mature ironic perspective we advocate and adopt is aware that all views are partial and flawed. So, the purpose is not to simply 'debunk' a dominant metaphor but to enrich our understanding by exploring the implications of this view, counter-views and the value of an expansive approach that embraces multiple meanings. As Linda Hutcheon (1994) observes, irony always has an 'edge' in that it destabilizes and questions established views and certainties. However, it can be used for generative re-construction rather than simple destruction. Let's explore what this looks like here.

Task 1

For each selected metaphor(s):

1. *Watch* the video(s), and write down how the metaphor is 'unpacked' to provide insight and advice.
2. *Imagine* different or alternative ways the metaphor might be unpacked, focusing on elements or implications that might contradict some features of the initial message. For example, you might explore the fact that 'fire' may burn out and consume what is available, the 'snowball' may not pick up momentum if conditions are 'icy', the taking off of one 'mask' may simply reveal or be another, and our 'movie' may never get 'produced' or be abandoned because of the 'critics'.
3. *Creatively* combine the initial insights *and* these ironic twists. Explore the implications for advice on how to lead change. As part of this exercise, you might draw a picture or cartoon of this more extended and critical metaphor and what it implies.
4. *Present* your findings.

8.5.3   Cosmopolitan Performances: Humility, Parody and Power

Traditional verbal irony is often presented as an either/or performance (saying one thing but meaning another). A complex third-way irony, however, includes a both/and strategy. It resonates by communicating multiple meanings and contradictory tensions which people know but often ignore or deny rather than address. This ironic performance faces complexity and various audiences and points to the 'wicked' nature of the world, its problems, and the diversity of viewpoints.

As part of this performance, a display of cosmopolitanism can be persuasive, engaging, and effective. Such displays reveal an appreciation of diversity while searching for unity that includes mutual respect. This exercise will explore how this is done in very different contexts. Drawing on the richness of popular culture rather than relying on the more one-dimensional management cases, this exercise uses three popular video clips to illustrate different dimensions of such a performance. It illustrates the serious playfulness of our advocacy of irony. The clips, selected for their richness and humour, should open discussion and debate rather than offer prescriptive 'how to' illustrations. In exploring each of the three parts, the main discussion question is: *How and how well does the main protagonist display a cosmopolitan sensibility?*

Case material

Connery, S. (2009). *Sir Sean Connery accepts AFI life achievement award in 2006* (p.12 February). https://www.youtube.com/watch?v=y4Z1BXALdwI (accessed 5 January 2022)

Kubrick, S. (2009). *Full Metal Jacket born to kill peace button duality of man* (p.12 January). USA: YouTube. https://www.youtube.com/watch?v=KMEViYvojtY (accessed 5 January 2022)

Stewart, J., & O'Reilly, B. (2013). *Bullshit mountain – O'Reilly vs Jon Stewart* (p.23 October). https://www.youtube.com/watch?v=yT5fzEL8Vrc (accessed 5 January 2022)

Task 1

Parts A + B + C

In exploring each incident, the main discussion question is: *How and how well does the main protagonist display a cosmopolitan sensibility?*

Use the five main elements described in The Ironic Performance as displaying cosmopolitanism:

1. *Appreciation of Diversity* – a recognition of multiple viewpoints.
2. *Ability to Toggle* – standing inside and outside one's own perspective and interests.
3. *Handling of Duality* – the 'doubleness' in what we say, how we act and situations we are in.
4. *Sense of Humour* – to encourage playfulness, alleviate stress and as a useful cover.

5. *Attitude of Humility* – creating identification by admitting and sharing one's limitations.

Part A

How one receives recognition is a complex challenge of balancing acceptance and appreciation with humility and distance. It also involves recognizing and including those who might be critical of who you are and what you have done, as well as those who might be less successful, less experienced, or younger and your peers who have achieved success and are more experienced.

Task 2

Watch the Sean Connery clip (Connery, 2009) and answer the questions below.

1. In addressing the main discussion question (*How and how well does the main protagonist display a cosmopolitan sensibility?*), consider how Sean Connery balances humorous humility by communicating confidence, purpose, and lack of ingenuousness.
2. What lessons might you draw from this on enhancing your reputation as a change agent in handling praise and success?

Part B

In this clip, Jon Stewart (American comedian, writer, producer, activist, and television host) takes on Bill O'Reilly (American journalist, author, and former television host). Faced with O'Reilly's conservative populism ('Debt is bad'), Stewart does not take on O'Reilly's argument directly. Instead, he undermines O'Reilly's authority and credibility through what is presented as a sincerely motivated playfulness to make key points, for example, timely gestures and distractions ('raised platform'), questioning motives through popular and accessible ridicule ('Bullshit Mountain', 'alternative reality' and 'Big Bird') while reframing the terms of debate (not the 'problem' but the 'problem-solving mechanism').

Task 3

Watch the Jon Stewart and Bill O'Reilly clip and answer the questions below.

1. In addressing the main discussion question (*How and how well does the main protagonist display a cosmopolitan sensibility?*), explore what you believe resonates with the audience in such a performance, that is, why it is accepted as a valid contribution to the debate rather than superficial play.
2. How do you think such methods might be used to engage those affected by or being enrolled in change?

Part C

Arguably less successful as a performance, this clip from *Full Metal Jacket* (Director Stanley Kubrick) provides a humorous example of a soldier (The Joker played by Matthew Modine) attempting to convey the soldier's dilemma of fighting for peace by killing through buyng a 'Peace' badge while having 'Born to Kill' on his helmet.

Task 4

Watch 'Speaking truth to power – the 'Joker' in *Full Metal Jacket* (Kubrick, 2009) and answer the questions below.

1. In exploring the main discussion question (*How and how well does the main protagonist display a cosmopolitan sensibility?*), consider the following issues.
   a. How effectively do you think his message communicated the 'duality of man' to his fellow soldiers and superiors?
   b. Given the one-dimensional response of the superior, how might he have been more effective in 'speaking truth to power'?
   c. What lessons might you draw from how change agents may protect themselves and engage others when challenging established authority?

8.5.4   Poise and Performance: Gandhi

Leadership can be defined and approached in many ways. However, two pervasive and valuable desirable leadership qualities relate strongly to our discussion of the ironic temperament. These are poise and performance.

1. *Poise* is the ability to productively respond to and effectively handle conditions that traditional managers find threatening. These conditions include uncertainty and complexity, diverse and contradictory perspectives, conflict, and tension.
2. *Performance* is the ability to tell stories and give performances that influence and persuade others who may have very different mindsets from one's own. Leaders need to mobilize superiors, colleagues and subordinates who often have different perspectives, interests, and abilities to cope with the threatening conditions outlined above.

David Rooke and William Torbert (2005) documented that 'post-conventional' leaders possessing such capabilities represent only 5% of managers.

In this exercise, you will be using the case of Mahatma Gandhi's leadership performance to explore how an ironic temperament fosters such capabilities.

Case material

Mahatma Gandhi arrives in the UK (1931). British Pathe (3.30). https://www.youtube
.com/watch?v=P6njRwz_dMw (accessed 5 January 2022)

Gandhi on the Salt March (1982). From the movie *Gandhi* (Director: Attenborough,
R.). https://www.youtube.com/watch?v=WW3uk95VGes (4.46) (accessed 5 January
2022)

In the early twentieth century, Gandhi led the Indian people in their liberation
from rule by the British. Gandhi employed various tactics and strategies
designed to unite a diverse Indian continent, mobilize the different factions
against the British Empire, and win back the continent in the face of the
superior military strength of the British. His ethical philosophy of *Ahimsa*
('compassion') and political strategy *of Satyagraha* ('nonviolent resistance'
or 'civil disobedience') led him to advocate tactical subversion rather than
armed struggle, and highly symbolic acts of persuasion rather than vengeance
(Carlson, 1986).

   While a prolific speech giver, Gandhi symbolized the liberation movement
through his non-verbal communication. Gonsalves (2010) documents that
Gandhi used silence, fasting, clothing, and presence to great effect. Gandhi's
use of the symbolism of wearing the Indian hand-woven natural fibre loincloth
woven out of *khadi* has become a distinctive trademark and was wielded by
Gandhi to great effect. When he arrived in India in 1915, he chose to wear
the clothing of his native Kathiawad region, which cheered those from his
hometown. By 1917, he changed to wearing the khadi-woven *kurta-pyjama*
or *kurta-dhoti*, more common throughout India. From 1921 on, he turned to
a waist-covering *dhote* or loincloth to identify more strongly with the poor,
who could only afford limited sparse clothing. His changing attire 'spun
a yarn' of great significance. It symbolized both his rejection of the British
Empire with its 'Manchester cloth' English clothing and his reaching out to
unite the diverse Indian sub-continent (Gonsalves, 2010; Kapoor, 2017).

   The end-product we see, 'Gandhi, as a personal global symbol of liberation',
was not achieved quickly or easily. Gandhi stresses this in his autobiography
with humility and self-awareness. His approach and practice were 'experiments', his ideas and strategies shifting over time, often contradictory and
frequently contested and often rejected at the time and remain a subject of
controversy (Gandhi, 1925; McGivering, 2015; Mistry, 2017; Orwell, 1949;
Stone II, 1990).

Task 1

Watch the video *Mahatma Gandhi Arrives in the UK* (1931) and discuss the
questions below.

In *Mahatma Gandhi Arrives in the UK*, the 'half-naked fakir' and 'malignant subversive fanatic' (as Winston Churchill described him) communicates several things to the British media and population without speaking a word.

1. What were the messages this 'bizarre little man' communicated without saying a word?
2. How did Gandhi's performance make critical points that cut across the cultural divide between his supporters and critics? How did he do this yet avoid a repressive response from authorities?
3. Issues for discussion: how he makes his entrances; his accoutrement of 'pots and pans' and 'loincloth, spinning wheel and goats' milk'; refusal to speak to the microphone; and the publicity from which the commentator 'understood he shrank'.
4. Discuss significant actions not included in the video clip, e.g., Gandhi staying in the East End of London and visiting the Lancashire cotton mills during his stay.

Task 2
Watch *Gandhi on the Salt March* (1982) and discuss the questions below.
In the second clip, note the difference between Gandhi's 'passive resistance' strategy and 'peaceful nonviolent non-cooperation' and how he handles the symbolic dimensions of his nationwide protest a new ('salt') law.

1. In what ways does Gandhi use or turn a 'pinch of salt' into a compelling and provocative form of action?

Gandhi has been described as a man of contradictions and tensions: a conservative radical, a moderate extremist and forcefully humble.

2. How does Gandhi display an ability to handle tensions in making his criticisms acceptable in incidents with the waiter and the governor?

Task 3
Discuss whether and in what form Gandhi has an ironic temperament.

1. In what sense do you think Gandhi possessed an *ironic perspective*, i.e., to what degree did he accept and work with the fallibility and folly of the British, his fellow Indians and himself?
2. How did Gandhi deliver *ironic performances* capturing multiple perspectives and protecting himself from reprisals while criticizing others?
3. What kind of applied philosophy and discipline (*temperament*) do you think allowed Gandhi to consistently and effectively retain this perspective and give these performances?

To improve the depth of the discussion, you can select from the set of further readings provided below. Also, feel free to draw on any material you find valuable for this exercise, as multiple YouTube clips and written materials are available.

For further information, see:

Carlson, C. A. (1986). Gandhi and the comic frame: 'Ad Bellum purificandum'. *Quarterly Journal of Speech, 72*(4), 446–455.
Gonsalves, P. (2010). *Clothing for Liberation*. New Delhi: Sage.
Kapoor, P. (2017). MK Gandhi's most 'indelicate' gift for Queen Elizabeth (and other stories about Khadi). https://scroll.in/article/852143/mk-gandhi-s-most-indelicate -gift-for-queen-elizabeth-and-other-stories-about-khadi (accessed 5 January 2022)
McGivering, B. J. (2015). Is Gandhi still a hero to Indians? https://www.bbc.com/news/ world-asia-31847578 (accessed 5 January 2022)
Mistry, R. (2017). Gandhi: The myths behind the Mahatma. *In Defense of Marxism* (16 August), 1–12. https://www.marxist.com/gandhi-the-myths-behind-the-mahatma .htm (accessed 5 January 2022)
Orwell, G. (1949). *Reflections on Gandhi*. Partisan Review, (January), 1–7. https:// www.orwell.ru/library/reviews/gandhi/english/e_gandhi (accessed 5 January 2022)
Rooke, D., & Torbert, W. R. (2005). Seven transformations of leadership. *Harvard Business Review*, (April), 1–12.
Stone II, J. H. (1990). M. K. Gandhi: Some experiments with truth. *Journal of Southern African Studies, 16*(4), 721–740.

8.5.5   Change Habit 8: Keep Steady

In his analysis of Bill Murray's performance in the comedy film, *Meatballs* (1979), Professor Eric Wilson (2015) points to the humorous way Murray (a camp counsellor) shifts dramatically from an inspirational coach enthusing his team to win to a caring trickster reflecting on the superficiality of the obsession with winning, to an evangelical preacher of embracing an 'anything goes' philosophy. Much like Lynne Segal (2017) advocates in her book on radical happiness and collective joy, the shared recognition of the absurdity of too narrow an obsession with winning ultimately enthuses the team. While on the surface a slapstick scene, it is actually an artful and meaningful performance and sophisticated stance! You will find the video entertaining, and it can be located at: It Just Doesn't Matter! *Meatballs* movie clip (1979).

Professor Wilson uses this scene to illustrate how when things really do matter, one must keep in mind that, ultimately and fundamentally, 'It just doesn't matter!'. Such a stoic ability to remain optimistic, persistent, and even-tempered in the face of frustrating setbacks is the final change habit that it is essential to cultivate. Developing a steady and tempered commitment to change is essential to retain optimism and hope and not lash out dysfunctionally when challenged.

Task 1

As an illustrative, hold steady or 'It just doesn't matter!' activity, select **one** frustrating situation (from work or home life) that can be described as A, B, or C:

A. **The Dilemma of the 'Tempered Radical'** (Meyerson & Scully, 2007)
   You feel that sticking to your commitment to the group/organization and what they require from you challenges who you think you are and want to be, but you are committed to both.
B. **The Challenge of 'Outsider–Insiders'** (Klein, 2007)
   You feel that those 'inside' a group do not understand the importance of things that must be done, and you are forced into balancing credibility with them and insights and advice you have from 'outside'.
C. **The Stance of 'Principled Infidelity'** (Hoyle & Wallace, 2007)
   You feel that externally imposed rules and regulations undermine your ability to act or do your work, and you are considering ways you might 'bend the rules' to follow what is imposed yet get the job done.

Task 2

Reflect on how you addressed such issues and situations in the past? What has gone well and what hasn't? What personal traits do you have that led you to handle these effectively or not?

Task 3

1. **Act Now.**
   Develop a strategy to address the current issue/situation. Carry it out! Keep in mind how you balance the fact that the issue/situation 'matters' to you, and yet, in the broader scheme of things, 'it just doesn't matter'.
2. **Reflect on Future Aspirations.**
   Analyse what went well and what did not go so well in the moment and afterwards. Consider the challenges of committing to an endeavour while keeping in mind that ultimately 'it just doesn't matter'. Are there ways you might improve how you achieve this balance in the future?

RESOURCES

For a summary and more extended discussion of the nature and weaknesses of 'deficit thinking', see:

Davis, L. P., & Museus, S. D. (2019). What is deficit thinking? An analysis of conceptualizations of deficit thinking and implications for scholarly research. *NCID Currents*, *1*(1), 117–130.

Valencia, R. R. (2012). *The Evolution of Deficit Thinking: Educational Thought and Practice*. London and New York: Routledge.
Valencia, R. R. (2020). *International Deficit Thinking*. London and New York: Routledge.

For a general introduction and then critical discussion of the promotion of 'positive' strength-based approaches to motivation, organization, and change, see:

Bushe, G. R., & Marshak, R. J. (2009). Revisioning organization development. *The Journal of Applied Behavioral Science, 45*(3), 348–368.
Bushe, G., & Marshak, R. (2015). *Dialogic Organizational Development: The Theory and Practice of Transformational Change*. Oakland: Berrett-Koehler.
Cameron, K. S. (2008). Paradox in positive organizational change. *Journal of Applied Behavioral Science, 44*(1), 7–24.
Cameron, K., Dutton, J., & Quinn, R. (2003). *Positive Organizational Scholarship: Foundations of a New Discipline*. Oakland: Berrett-Koehler.
Cameron, K., & McNaughtan, J. (2014). Positive organizational change. *Journal of Applied Behavioral Science, 50*(4), 445–462.
Cunha, M. P. e., Clegg, S., & Rego, A. (2013). Lessons for leaders: Positive organization studies meets Niccolò Machiavelli. *Leadership, 9*(4), 450–465.
Dixon, M., Lee, S., & Ghaye, T. (2016). Strengths-based reflective practices for the management of change: Applications from sport and positive psychology. *Journal of Change Management, 16*(2), 142–157.
Peterson, C., & Seligman, M. (2004). *Character Strengths and Virtues. A Handbook and Classification*. Oxford: American Psychological Association and Oxford University Press.

For constructive, and at times playful, recommendations for appreciating the role of stupidity in organizational life, see:

Alvesson, M., & Spicer, A. (2017). *The Stupidity Paradox*. London: Profile Books.
Bensoussan, B. (2021). *Stupidology*. Reproduced by Marie-Luce, 6 October 2021. https://ibis.co.za/ci/index.php/news-footer/158-stupidology-by-babette-bensoussan (accessed 1 August 2022)
Suter, K. ([2007] 2018). *Stupidology: The study of stupidity*. 13 February 2018. https://onlineopinion.com.au/view.asp?article=19566 (accessed 1 August 2022)

Research on irony in organizational life is often complex and inaccessible. However, a useful general introduction to irony in organization studies is provided by Eric Hoyle and Mike Wallace (2008) and the relevant sections in Carl Rhodes and Richard Badham (2018). An edited book-length overview can be found in Ulla Johansson and Jill Woodilla (2005). For a more popular and accessible discussion of the role of irony in organizations, listen to the ABC radio podcast by Richard Badham and Richard Claydon discussing 'The Ironic Manager' (Aedy, 2017), the LSE Business Review blog post by Richard Badham and Carl Rhodes (2018) on the 'Bearable lightness of being' on organizations and Richard Badham and Richard Claydon's (2012) short play 'The dance of identification'.

Aedy, R. (2017). The ironic manager. ABC This Working Life. https://www.abc.net.au/radionational/programs/this-working-life/ironic-manager/8614352

Badham, R., & Claydon, R. (2012). The dance of identification: Ambivalence, irony and organizational selfing. *Problems and Perspectives in Management, 10*(4), 80–97.

Badham, R., & Rhodes, C. (2018). Mis-leading ethics: Towards a bearable lightness of being. *LSE Business Review*. 6 June. https://blogs.lse.ac.uk/businessreview/2018/06/06/misleading-ethics-towards-a-bearable-lightness-of-being/ (accessed 5 January 2022)

Hoyle, E., & Wallace, M. (2008). Two faces of organizational irony: Endemic and pragmatic. *Organization Studies, 29*(11), 1427–1447.

Johansson, U., & Woodilla, J. (2005). *Irony and Organizations*. Copenhagen: Copenhagen Business School Press.

Rhodes, C., & Badham, R. (2018). Ethical irony and the relational leader: Grappling with the infinity of ethics and the finitude of practice. *Business Ethics Quarterly, 28*(1), 71–98.

For a debate over the value or not of adopting an ironic stance towards organizational life, see the point and counterpoint in papers by Fleming and Spicer (2003) and Badham and McLoughlin (2005).

Badham, R. J., & McLoughlin, I. (2005). Ambivalence and engagement: Irony and cultural change in late modern organizations. *International Journal of Knowledge, Culture and Change Management in Organisations, 5*, 1–15.

Fleming, P., & Spicer, A. (2003). Working at a cynical distance. *Organization, 10*(1), 157–179.

For more general sociological reflections on the central importance of irony in modern polity, ecological thinking, feminism, and the anti-nuclear movement, see:

Ferguson, K. (2003). *The Man Question*. Berkeley: University of California Press.

Jacobs, R., & Smith, P. (1997). Romance, irony, and solidarity. *Sociological Theory, 15*(1), 60–80.

Jessop, B. (2003). Governance and meta-governance: On reflexivity, requisite variety and requisite irony. In H. P. Bang (Ed.), *Governance as Social and Political Communication* (pp.111–116). Manchester: Manchester University Press.

Seery, J. (2019). *Political Returns: Irony in Politics and Theory from Plato to the Antinuclear Movement*. London: Routledge.

Turner, B. (2001). Cosmopolitan virtue: On religion in a global age. *European Journal of Social Theory, 4*(2), 131–152.

Turner, B. S. (2002). Cosmopolitan virtue, globalization and patriotism. *Theory, Culture and Society, 19*(1–2), 45–63.

For a fun and insightful addition to this debate, see:

Brassett, J. (2009). British irony, global justice: A pragmatic reading of Chris Brown, Banksy and Ricky Gervais. *Review of International Studies, 35*(1), 219–245.

8.1   An Ironic Perspective

For discussions of the ironic perspective, see the overviews above, and Rhodes and Badham (2018) and Hoyle and Wallace (2008):

Hoyle, E., & Wallace, M. (2008). Two faces of organizational irony: Endemic and pragmatic. *Organization Studies, 29*(11), 1427–1447.
Rhodes, C., & Badham, R. (2018). Ethical irony and the relational leader: grappling with the infinity of ethics and the finitude of practice. *Business Ethics Quarterly, 28*(1), 71–98.

8.2   An Ironic Performance

For a general research overview of what this involves, see the section on 'Ironic Performance' in Rhodes and Badham (2018). For a case illustration of the use of humour as a performance in a management team, see Mary Jo Hatch (1997), and for a follow-up but rather academic discussion about the importance of understanding how people enact 'dramatic irony' in organizations, see Gylfe, Franck and Vaara (2019). Finally, for a rather theoretical yet interesting treatment of cosmopolitan irony as a key dimension of citizenship in diverse contexts, see Turner (2002), particularly from page 55.

Gylfe, P., Franck, H., & Vaara, E. (2019). Living with paradox through irony. *Organizational Behavior and Human Decision Processes, 15*(5), 68–82.
Hatch, M. J. (1997). Irony and the social construction of contradiction in the humor of a management team. *Organization Science, 8*(3), 275–288.
Rhodes, C., & Badham, R. (2018). Ethical irony and the relational leader: Grappling with the infinity of ethics and the finitude of practice. *Business Ethics Quarterly, 28*(1), 71–98.
Turner, B. S. (2002). Cosmopolitan virtue, globalization and patriotism. *Theory, Culture and Society, 19*(1–2), 45–63.

8.3   An Ironic Temperament

For examples of the ironic temperament and how it is exercised in organizations, see Deborah Meyerson and Maureen Scully's (2007) research on 'tempered radicals', Eric Hoyle and Mike Wallace's work on 'principled infidelity' (2007) in educational institutions, and Linda Trethewey's (1999) analysis of irony as a means of living with paradox in the Women's Social Services Organization (WSSO).

Hoyle, E., & Wallace, M. (2007). Educational reform: An ironic perspective. *Educational Management Administration and Leadership, 35*(1), 9–25.

Meyerson, D. E., & Scully, M. A. (2007). Tempered radicalism and the politics of ambivalence and change. *Organization Science, 6*(5), 585–600.

Trethewey, A. (1999). Isn't it ironic: Using irony to explore the contradictions of organizational life. *Western Journal of Communication, 63*(2), 140–167.

An excellent recent contribution to the debate is provided by Daniel Newark (2018) in his reworking of the work of James March to capture the 'logic of absurdity' in leadership. Further reflections are provided by Richard Badham (2022) in his recognition of the contributions of March to the 'poetry of leadership'.

Badham, R. (2022). James March and the poetry of leadership. *Journal of Management History,* 28(1), 46–65.

Newark, D. (2018). Leadership and the logic of absurdity. *Academy of Management Review,* 43(2), 198–216.

For some interesting, sophisticated, and valuable broader reflections on the social and existential issues touched on by the ironic temperament, see:

Berlant, L. (2011). *Cruel Optimism.* Durham and London: Duke University Press.

Nagel, T. (1979). The absurd. In T. Nagel (Ed.), *Mortal Questions* (pp.11–23). Cambridge: Cambridge University Press,.

Segal, L. (2017). *Radical Happiness: Moments of Collective Joy.* London and New York: Verso.

NOTE

1.   Established in Ancient Greece, it has been the kind of irony advocated by such literary and philosophical giants as Socrates (470–399 BC), Johan Wolfgang von Goethe (1749–1832), Friedrich Schlegel (1772–1829), Soren Kierkegaard (1813–1855), Oscar Wilde (1854–1900), Kenneth Burke (1897–1993) and Richard Rorty (1931–2007). It is a form of irony captured and reviewed in overviews by such critics as Gregory Vlastos (1991), Kathy Ferguson (1993), Linda Hutcheon (1994), Claire Colebrook (2004), James Fernandez and Mary Huber (2001), and Peter Sloterdijk (2020). It has been explored in organizational studies by Gideon Kunda ([1992] 2006), Linda Trethewey (1999) with Karen Ashcraft (2004), Barry Turner (2002), Cliff Oswick, Tom Keenoy and David Grant (2002), Ulla Johansson and Jill Woodilla (2005), Edward Hoyle and Mike Wallace (2008), Richard Claydon (2013). For discussions of irony in the public sphere, see Ronald Jacobs and Paul Smith (1997), Jeffrey Guhin (2013) and Peter Sloterdijk (2020).

Epilogue

Although not sure they were on the right track, the crew
anticipated that the journey ahead could be a lot of fun.....

After the red pill
What we leave behind
A lightness of being
Encore

AFTER THE RED PILL

Down the Rabbit Hole
I almost wish I hadn't gone down that rabbit-hole – and yet – and yet – it's rather curious, you know, this sort of life! I do wonder what can have happened to me!
(Carroll, 2009, p.33)

In this book, you have been encouraged to see 'how deep the rabbit hole goes' with a particular 'Red Pill' to explore what is truly involved in leading change management. In *Re-Imagining Change*, you were shown how the easy, mundane and 'surface' 'Blue Pill' view of organizational change is heavily steeped in rational mythology of how organizations operate and how they transform. You were then introduced to the idea of an embedded 'Change Problem', as the systemic 'Lord's Slope' makes realizing change a challenging enterprise in organizations mis-led by this myth. The counter-metaphors of the 'iceberg' and the 'rollercoaster' were presented to help open up thought and action, freeing you of the restrictions of overly rational images of what change involves and how it should be managed. We also quickly ran through the history of change management thought, revealing how some of the thinking of Kurt Lewin has been and can be used to help create an alternative view of change management.

We argued for and illustrated the advantages of this approach. However, it is essential to keep in mind that these views are heresy from the perspective of narrowly rational expectations of how change does and should occur. In a formally Blue Pill world, communicating and acting on Red Pill insights requires consideration and care. The Red Pill metaphor is used to help support such a re-imagining of change management. It does so by providing a value-laden contrast. It highlights the difference between conventional and reassuring views of the world and more subversive and challenging views that can better capture what is really going on. As Yeffeth (2003) observed, this contrast also acknowledges the discomforts that might arise from 'taking the Red Pill'. However, it portrays these as an unavoidable yet worthwhile cost in taking responsibility for one's own thoughts and actions and experiencing the joys of adventure and achievement that follow.

In the *Cycle of Change*, we addressed adopting this 'Red Pill' approach in practice. It is one thing to open up creative thought and action with counter metaphors and methods, and it is another to embed them in how we think and act. The Cycle of Change spells out what is involved in this new approach. It uses the classic PDCA cycle since it is a commonly understood and widely used rational approach to learning and innovation. In contrast to linear views of the world, however, it performs the valuable task of emphasizing the importance of continuous experimentation and learning in innovation. This occurs through ongoing processes of Planning, Doing, Checking and Action. The Change Cycle is similar in that it is an iterative and cyclical approach to ongoing Planning, Executing and Evaluating change. The Cycle of Change section gave you some of the concepts, tools, insights and processes involved in completing a productive cycle. In contrast to the PDCA's overly rational and task-based view of what is required, however, the Cycle of Change also extends the analysis. It includes culture and meaning in Orienting, Performing and Reflecting upon the change enterprise and its progress.

Rather than Planning, we explored Mapping as an Orienting device. Rather than Executing, we encouraged the donning of Masks in Performing change. Rather than Evaluating, we pursued the use of Mirrors for ongoing Reflection. These terms were deliberately chosen to capture and highlight the interpretive, meaningful and cultural nature of change. Change is not just tasks and activities. It is also about narratives, stories and sensemaking, sensegiving, sensereceiving, and even sensecensoring (Maitlis & Lawrence, 2007; Sonenshein, 2010; Vaara et al., 2016; Whittle et al., 2016). The practice of change is an interactive, cultural and political process, and the Cycle of Change captures this character.

We have endeavoured to make this cycle as straightforward as possible, grounding it in many established views of what managing and leading change involves. Again, however, it can be perceived as somewhat heretical by those with a narrow and blinkered view of change management. Rather than viewing change as progress through fixed stages, it directs attention to the fluid, complex, overlapping and iterative nature of the chain of activities that make up the change journey. Rather than focusing on formal, cognitive and project-like views of 'management' as an exercise in prediction and control, it highlights the informal, emotive, cultural and political dimensions of change as a discipline of influence. This understanding is essential for capturing and influencing change in practice and is a critical component in your change agent's 'toolkit'. But, recalling the *Lord's Slope*, it is vital to be aware many others will not share or appreciate your insights. What regularly and routinely happens in organizations is something other than a productive Change Cycle, and you will encounter mindsets, habits and prejudices that run counter to it. These are a fundamental part of the Change Problem.

To address such issues, we went further and deeper into exploring the *Leadership of Change*. Establishing and maintaining an effective change cycle can sometimes feel less like kicking goals on a level playing field and more like the labours of Sisyphus, the Greek mythological figure punished for his trickery. Zeus condemned Sisyphus to endlessly roll a boulder uphill only to have it roll back down again. On the surface, an essential part of handling such experiences and challenges is expecting them first, being mindful of them and being prepared to mobilize energy and resources to address them. These capabilities are qualities embedded in the 'heads, hearts and hands' of mindful, agile and adaptive leaders.

The leadership challenge begins but does not end here. Our individualistic and modernist ethos tempts us to view such qualities through an ultimately debilitating grandiose, romantic, heroic lens. Mindfulness is often restricted to techniques for enhancing our effectiveness (Purser et al., 2016). However, a deeper level of mindfulness requires accepting and attending to paradoxes and ironies of change that cannot be 'fixed' or solved (King & Badham, 2019, 2020). We need the resilience, courage and wisdom to learn to live with and work through them (Badham & King, 2021). Mobilizing energy and resources to address challenges must be done, knowing they may not be overcome. Finding and communicating meaning and purpose in a world where 'victory is elusive, and virtue is not reliably rewarded' is a profoundly human endeavour. It goes far beyond commando-style 'take the hill' exhortations and purpose-driven corporate vision statements.

In such circumstances, a mature leader's elegant, balanced and poised stance inspires enthusiasm for and commitment to worthwhile causes while acknowledging limits to our understanding, ethics, and endeavours. From the perspective of the expert technician or novice 'plumber', this is profoundly disappointing and highly demotivating. However, it humanizes the enterprise for the professional craftsperson and the 'change poet' (Weick, 2011). It allows us to both 'look at' and 'look through' our perspectives and endeavours, deepening our appreciation of our struggles, relationships and achievements without succumbing to naïve optimism or debilitating cynicism. As Barrack Obama put it, it is about 'moving the ball forward'. This is, ultimately, how 'deep the rabbit hole' goes.

WHAT WE LEAVE BEHIND

In pursuit of knowledge, every day something is acquired; In pursuit of wisdom, every day, something is dropped. (Lao Tzu, cited in Muller, 1999, p.134 and Weick, 2007, p.5)

When management education is viewed as providing instruction manuals or accessible practical 'takeaways', it ignores an important insight from the change literature. That is, every new order is built out of the destruction of an old one. To free up our thoughts, emotions and actions, we need to appreciate the limitations of our established habits and prejudices. To bring about a deliberate transformation, those requested or required to change must be encouraged and supported to 'leave behind' conventional wisdom and patterns of behaviour. As Karl Weick (2007, p.6) puts it in his review of management education, 'human potential is realised as much by what we drop, as what we acquire'. A central theme of the *Ironies of Organizational Change* has been to encourage and support you to 'drop' or 'let go' of a critical barrier lying in the way of creatively grappling with the challenges of change. The barrier is the overly rational myth of organizations and the models of change that this generates.

'Letting go' of this mythology is no simple task, however. It is a bit like peeling an onion. We move from discarding an obvious external skin to uncovering and peeling back multiple layers. If we do this deftly, it is a precise and effective enterprise. If we do it clumsily, it ends in tears.

The first layer is the Just Do It or '*Nike*' approach to change. It takes the form of a standard and automatic reflex response. We tell others what to do, and if they don't do it, we tell them again, only louder. If this doesn't work, we metaphorically 'hit them'. We approach change with our heads and believe in the unquestioned rightness of our cause. We focus on the rational 'tip' of whatever change we address and then look for tools and techniques to manage the process. Conflict, resistance and chaos are all signs that something has gone wrong, and we look for and seek to impose certainty, predictability and control.

The second layer is the *Humanistic Transition* view of change. When confronted by the limitations and weaknesses of the first layer, it is also a reflex and automatic response. It combines recognizing the heart as well as the head with the need to persuade rather than simply instruct. It sees change as a psychological and cultural transition where interests, values and identities demand attention. It seeks effective ways to persuade people to change. However, the overly rational ethos is retained, and it similarly attempts to plan and control the change process. At this second level, change management involves gaining and applying knowledge of the stages of change and methods for effectively moving individuals and institutions through these stages. It also assumes that expert analysis or diagnosis reveals a common purpose for change and 'one best way' for achieving it.

The third layer is the *Entrepreneurial Hero* tradition, which is now a widespread and familiar response to the static and even naïve assumptions of the second. It identifies change management with agile and adaptive leadership. It considers the head, the heart and the hand. Change agents are viewed as entrepreneurial heroes facing the challenges of overcoming bureaucratic inertia in the face of a VUCA world (Volatile. Uncertain. Complex. Ambiguous). It advocates developing adaptive and agile capabilities, leaders, cultures and structures that embrace uncertainty, adapt rapidly and mobilize the energy and power to overcome the forces of inertia. Traditional 'rational' views of change management ignore the challenges of dismantling established bureaucracies. They avoid uncertainty and restrict exploration and improvisation. And they fail to understand and address the emotional and political dimensions of making change happen in practice. The humanistic transition views are regarded as too slow, rigid, expert-driven, and apolitical to inform the improvisation, experimentation, and innovation needed to act rapidly and effectively in uncertain and contested situations.

For many, there is a temptation to stop here, celebrating the 'end of change management' as traditionally defined and siding with this new agile and adaptive approach. There is a romance to this quest that is highly seductive. But yet, it too has its restrictions as a deeper layer of our onion. Despite its celebration of uncertainty and complexity, it still proposes what looks like a prescriptive 'one best way' of thought and action. While accepting the fluidity of change and the challenging nature of the practice of 'getting things done', it provides us with a stereotyped view of the 'evil' past (and the thoughts and institutions that preserve it) and a one-dimensional view of the 'good' future (the era of 'post-bureaucracy' and even the arrival of 'humanocracy' (Hamel & Zanini, 2020). While recognizing the significance of emotion and the play of politics and power, the entrepreneurial hero perspective fails to address the challenges of preserving personal well-being and finding meaning in the face of the inevitable struggles and frustrations of change.

Each of these layers of the onion continues to operate within a deeper set of assumptions constituting what could be defined as the final layer: a 'Fix-It' approach to change management. This approach assumes that acquiring knowledge of change dynamics and applying it through appropriate methods, processes, and tools will ensure the desired outcomes. Similar to traditional communication models, IT implementation and medical cures, there is a background faith in and search for a 'magic bullet' (Markus & Benjamin, 1997; Sproule, 1989). It is expected that applied technical knowledge will solve all problems, that there is 'one best way' solution, and once uncovered, it could be directly communicated or 'injected' into the head of the necessary audiences.

In crude terms, the 'Fix-It' approach to change management accepts there are 'problems in how we manage change', yet seeks and is confident of being able to 'tame' them and find 'solutions'. In part, this is a really important and valuable activity. Much of this book has been focused on helping you in this enterprise, clarifying the challenges you are likely to confront and provide guidelines and insights on how to address them better. However, this is not the whole story for you as a person. Just as therapists warn of the dangers of counsellors attempting to 'fix the problems' of their clients, similar problems face this 'fix-it' change mentality. As seen in the chapters on the paradoxes and ironies of change, not everything can be 'fixed'. There are enduring contradictions and challenges in change, and 'wicked' problems (Waddock et al., 2015) that we must accept, endure and work through. We have to 'live with' tensions and dilemmas since there are 'no guarantees' or 'final solutions' (Badham, 2017; Lüscher & Lewis, 2008).

Moreover, as in the case of therapy, too great a commitment to a 'fix-it' mentality may end up undermining its own enterprise. Those with such an attitude are highly prone to stress, disappointment, frustration and burnout. When this occurs, a relapse into a counter-productive authoritarian instruction-based 'just do it' mode is an ever-present temptation.

The unpeeling of these layers of the onion does *not* involve merely rejecting their views as false. *How* we unpeel the onion matters. The Ancient Greece philosopher Plato stated the difference between the bad and the good butcher is that the former hacks and shatters the meat and the bones, while the latter cuts with precision along the natural joints. In deciding what to 'leave behind' and how we do so, we need to be similarly skilled. Each of the above layers of the rational model has both insights and limitations. Gareth Morgan (2006) notes all these perspectives in his celebrated *Images of Organization*, in 'creating ways of seeing, they create ways of *not* seeing' (p.348). An essential component of the lightness of being, as detailed further below, is the ability to both 'look through' and 'look at' the perspectives we employ (Kegan & Lahey, 2009; Lanham, 1995; McCloskey, 1994), appreciating both insights and limitations, and working with both. What we need to 'leave behind' is unreflective and exaggerated faith in each of these levels of the onion. We replace this with a clear insight into their partiality and restrictions. In so doing, a greater appreciation is needed of both the 'plumbing' and 'poetry' of change, as discussed in the *Leadership of Change*.

The plumbing in change management involves dealing with the known and addressing it using existing technical knowledge and expert techniques, whether these are mechanistic project management methods, mapping techniques, leadership styles or the creation of learning environments. However, as with any craft, it requires more than technical knowledge and expert techniques. It involves the craft wisdom and creative artistry of a professional making judgement calls in often uncertain, complex and ethically ambiguous situations. From this perspective, the layers of 'just do it', 'humanitarian transition', 'entrepreneurial hero' and 'fix-it' approaches provide the cultural context, and standard prescriptions change professionals have to work with and within. Each has its limitations. Yet, they provide us with heuristics we can use and a language we have to work with. They do **not** offer complete solutions. To think they do, or will, detracts from and undermines focused and mindful attention on the practical challenges of change.

The poetry of change management goes even further in transcending the rational myth. Understanding what this means helps us identify the partiality and limitations of its deeper forms. Poetry, as we know it, is a far cry from engineering. A poetic approach to leading change appreciates how our perspectives impose order on the flux of change. It appreciates how the language, and the images that we use, do not reflect the world. In an important sense, they construct it. A poetic sensibility recognizes the existence of choice in how we do so and the value of evocative imagery in guiding our actions and enriching our experience and our lives. In the face of the ambiguous and uncertain flux in change, 'change poets', as Karl Weick (2011) describes them, create and act on 'hunches'. In so doing, they recognize that, at least in part, we 'talk' change into existence. Within the rational model, 'poetry' tends to be understood in instrumental terms, as the use of inspirational and persuasive imagery, rhetoric and narrative to 'sell' the change agenda. As such, it remains within a rational 'fix-it' agenda. From a deeper poetic perspective, however, how we think about and act within 'change' is something we bring to it, and it may be more or less aesthetic and meaningful. As James March and Johan Olsen (1983, p.13) put it, 'it is not that symbols are important to change, although they certainly are. Rather the argument is the reverse – that change is important to symbols, that a primary contribution of change to life is in the development of meaning.' This is a fundamental shift in understanding, and possibly one of the reasons why the Greek philosopher Plato excluded poets from his authoritarian Republic! As we will now illustrate, it is part of the 'lightness of being' that this book supports and encourages you to adopt in the face of the challenges of change.

A LIGHTNESS OF BEING

Learning to drop one's tools to gain lightness, agility, and wisdom tends to be forgotten in an era where leaders and followers alike are preoccupied with knowledge management, acquisitions, and acquisitiveness. (Weick, 2007, p.6)

In *The Unbearable Lightness of Being*, Milan Kundera (2009) recounts the tragedies that befall those locked into the heavy seriousness of a life dictated by the pursuit of 'Es Muss Sein' ('It Must Be'). As managers, leaders and participants in change initiatives, we are all too often the unfortunate and unwitting dupes of a particular brand of this heaviness. Formally prescribed or self-designated 'agents of change', we can become caught up in a managerial mystique that believes organizational life should be an efficient and orderly enterprise. We identify ourselves and our projects as heroic agents or saviours on a grand march to salvation. It encourages us to expect and strive for a productive and harmonious journey. Leaders proclaim this, clients demand it, employees expect it, consultants advise it, academics study it, and we come to impose it upon ourselves. Unfortunately, when we internalize these expectations, we become victims of the 'whips inside men' (Mills, 1969, p.110) and dupes of our modern institutional hubris (Alvesson & Gabriel, 2016).

Muhammed Ali, arguably one of the world's greatest boxers of all time, famously promised boxing fans he'd 'Float like a butterfly, sting like a bee...' against his opponent. Unfortunately, most people tend to float more like bees and sting like butterflies! Filled with expectations that people and things ought to be more rational than they are, we frequently lash out unproductively in frustration and anger, particularly when under pressure. Caught up in the subsequent conflicts, we become bogged down in angry ruminations and self-justifications at the expense of our health and effectiveness. A quest to 'make things right' weighs upon us. We see ourselves as agents of reason and light, solving the problems others are too ignorant to understand, too incompetent to address or too uncommitted to resolve. We then often end up 'pushing' change in ways that only feed resistance and opposition. It causes suffering and burnout (in ourselves and others), as we lose all sense of proportion regarding what is realistically and sensibly attainable. Preoccupied with such problems, we are less likely to be mindfully strategic and less inclined to focus on what is possible and achievable in the current circumstance. We 'float like a bee and sting like a butterfly'.

The organizational costs of this phenomenon have been documented (King & Badham, 2019), and a recent conversation with the CEO of an Asia-Pacific IT company reminded us of the personal dimension of this phenomenon. Following a discussion about the importance of ability and adaptability in VUCA environments, she exclaimed, 'It is all very well being flexible, reflective and able to operate on the "edge of chaos", but when it comes down to it, we will all be out on stress relief.' Small wonder that the demand for relaxation, resilience and mindfulness has increased in a high-velocity 'attention economy' where distraction, lack of concentration, and mental strain and illness indicators are rising.

There is, however, another way. Freed up from the rational myth of how organizations operate and change, we can better respond and even take some comic delight in the predictable and unpredictable irrationalities of managing and leading change. It requires a bearable 'lightness of being' that goes beyond a 'lightness of thought' to include a 'lightness of heart' and a 'lightness of touch'. Each of these is essential as our reflex response to the frustrations and challenges of change is an embodied one. While intellectual awareness is crucially important, it has to be accompanied by emotional intelligence and practical wisdom to combat our habitual responses.

Therefore, rather than providing you with specific methods and tools as final takeaways, we will briefly outline what is involved in translating the content of *Ironies of Organizational Change* into a strategy for living on the rollercoaster of change.

Encore

A lightness of thought means adopting a *reasonable* rather than rational approach to managing and leading change. Rather than presuming strategically rational thought and action, this stance acknowledges and accepts predictable irrationality and the partial nature of our understanding and control. It involves an ability to ongoingly 'look at' as well as 'look through' the beliefs, values and strategies of oneself and others. It recognizes the limitations of the information we work with, the incompleteness of our knowledge, the ambiguities and ambivalences embedded in the perspectives we adopt and the moralities that we deploy, and the ongoing potential within change for unintended consequences to occur and the role of chance, accident or external influences on the course of events. It expects fallibility and folly in oneself as well as others. For some, this might be described as recognizing the comic nature of the human carnival (Berger, 1986; Carlson, 1986), while for others, it is merely a case of 'not taking oneself too seriously' or 'having a sense of humour' that can ease tensions and lubricate relationships (Westwood, 2004). However, lightness should not be equated with superficiality or lack of commitment. On the contrary, it is a capable, proactive, flexible and agile lightness brought about by letting go the weighty burden of inflated claims, unrealistic aspirations, institutional denials and the 'blame game' ruminations of overly rational views of change.

Lightness of Heart

Lightness of heart means a deep-seated appreciation of *cosmopolitan* diversity (Levy et al., 2016; McClean, 2016). It is one thing to recognize the partiality of competing viewpoints intellectually. It is another to 'take this to heart' and, when confronted by irreconcilably different views, not relapse into prejudiced denial or aggression. The lightness of heart includes what is commonly regarded as 'emotional intelligence,' that is, both the *awareness* of the morally, politically and emotionally charged nature of our viewpoints as well as others and the *ability to handle* these differences in interests and emotions (Goleman, 2000; Huy, 1999).

Turner (2001, 2002) characterizes such capabilities as a form of 'cosmopolitan irony'. What he means by this is a 'cool' approach to the passionate moral and political divides we confront. It is an ability to appreciate diversity and difference while putting one's cultural programming to one side for a while, or at least 'turning down the volume' of the voices in our head that re-tell and reinforce our narratives when confronted by opposing ones. But, again, similar to the lightness of thought, there are common sense injunctions to adopt such an approach. Many of us are often advised, or advise others, 'to get over oneself', to 'stand back and look at the other point of view', to adopt a 'third position' (separate from a protagonist and an antagonistic viewpoint), to 'look at things from the other's point of view', and recognize there are 'at least two sides to every story' (O'Connor & Seymour, 2011).

The lightness of heart involves a deep appreciation of what this means when emotions are aroused, values threatened, and crises are imminent. In the change process, it consists of considering:

- the views and feelings of those promoting and receiving a change,
- the perspectives and prejudices of winners and losers, and
- enthusiastically persisting in promoting one's ideas and views.

… All while remaining flexible and appreciative that one can only do so much in a world where much is out of our control.

Lightness of Touch

The lightness of touch means a *seriously playful* approach to one's initiatives and actions (Badham & Claydon, 2012; Schrage, 1999). While recognizing its partial nature and limited role, committing to action marks such an approach. For Karl Weick (2007), this includes an awareness of the need to move beyond 'superficial simplicity' and 'confused complexity' and towards a more 'profound simplicity'. The profound simplicity includes the flexibility, confidence, and courage to improvise and experiment. It accepts the partial and provisional nature of one's assumptions and yet is ready to make judgement calls in complex and uncertain situations. It includes a degree of mindful attention and wary consideration that the best-laid plans may go awry. A lightness of touch also involves, at least in part, thinking and acting according to the popular phrase: *'Never get into something you cannot get out of'*. It is a resourceful enterprise. In combining 'serious' and 'playful', we also consider the 'serious' value of creative and entertaining 'play'. It supports invention and exploration by encouraging and supportive 'flow' like experiences amongst creative enthusiasts rather than grudging compliance from organizational conscripts (Küpers, 2017; March, 1981; Statler et al., 2009).

Supported by a lightness of thought, heart, and touch, managing and leading change can be a joyful experience while being seriously committed to the enterprise.

ENCORE

The challenges of change cannot be simply 'managed away'. However sophisticated our theories, refined our techniques and practical our insights, the issues, complexities and uncertainties remain. This makes grappling with the realities of change both anxious and exciting. A figurative illustration of what can be achieved, however, is provided by David Viney (2020) in his classic J-Curve. As exemplified in the cartoon representation above, our overly rational managerial hopes and expectations for instant success are frequently countered by disaster stories of chaos and disaster as initiatives crash and burn in the 'valley of death'. What an informed and capable approach can do, however, is increase the likelihood of a successful flight with a less deep and costly 'dip' in performance and motivation in getting there.

Over the last fifteen years, professional managers at many levels have attended classes designed to achieve this outcome. They enjoy the 'ah, ha' moments as the ideas capture their lived experiences and allow an open, informed and enjoyable discussion. While individuals and groups vary, a pattern evolved across the approximately 4,000 mature professionals introduced to this way of addressing the subject of change. At the outset, there is a surprise – for some, excitement and a degree of anxiety for others. During the learning experience, they gain confidence as the clear implications are spelt out, and practical advice is given. And then, after applying the ideas in practice, there are regular comments about 'life-changing experiences' and 'I never thought I would get something so personal and valuable out of a change course' (Badham et al., 2015). It's like they all went through their own change journey – unfreezing, moving and refreezing.

In his book *What Got you Here, Will not Get you There*, Marshall Goldsmith (2008) illustrated how the skills and capabilities required to become a traditional middle manager are not enough to take you further into becoming an influential and successful leader. The *Ironies of Organizational Change* has been designed to help you take up Goldsmith's challenge. In contrast to instruction manuals and textbooks that focus on communicating basic concepts and methods of planning change, we have introduced you to a far deeper look at how you might lead change in organizations, how this might apply to your personal lives and the meaning you might find or create in the enterprise. We hope we have at least in part succeeded in this enterprise and wish you luck on your further journey.

Resource guide: force field analysis – a comprehensive guide to forces, fields and analyses

If you are to influence change, you need to be able to understand it.

Introduction
Part A: The field
Part B: The forces of change
Part C: The force field analysis
Part D: Forces for and against change – the force field matrix

INTRODUCTION

In Chapter 3, you were introduced to the key change mapping tools that included a force field analysis. In the Intermission, you were provided with an illustrative case in the form of Jamie Oliver's School Dinners. This Resource Guide is an essential supplement in that it provides a comprehensive yet accessible introduction to the complex 'field' of change, the 'forces' within them, and the individual and organizational factors that foster readiness or create resistance to change. We advocate and support a broad, pragmatic, and reflective stance to exploring the nature of change and the conditions to be taken into account by those seeking to influence or bring it about. The Resource Guide supports such a stance by reviewing the literature to help you effectively map out change, reflect on the assumptions you have made and evaluate the progress you have achieved.

The approach adopted is one of 'simplexity' (Colville et al., 2016). This is an attempt to shift insight and focus from 'confused complexity' to the creation of 'profound simplicity' (Weick, 2011). It highlights the complexities that need to be considered while providing concepts and heuristics that are simple enough to be practical and valuable. This is, inevitably, a balancing act and one we hope we have successfully achieved.

For accessibility, Chapter 3 and the Intermission omitted some of the complexities involved in identifying the nature and context of change and the character of the forces affecting it. As a counter-balance, this Resource Guide is provided as a supplemental guide. It provides a deeper analysis of the main factors and issues that need to be considered. We hope to have done so in as accessible a form as possible.

Unfortunately, standard textbooks frequently address the nature of change in one chapter, history and approaches in another, tools and techniques in yet another and introduce readiness and resistance as separate topics. Although this makes the sprawling literature manageable, it has the unfortunate effect of artificially separating overlapping ideas, concepts, and issues. This unwittingly contributes to an undesirable degree of intellectual fragmentation and practical confusion.

We seek to avoid this by integrating and simplifying the issues without being narrowly prescriptive or over-simplistic. We show how the approaches to change can be usefully viewed as contributions to defining change as a 'field' and exploring the 'forces' within it. We use this framework to integrate such discussions with tools such as force field analysis and investigations of both individual and organizational 'readiness' and 'resistance' to change.

Reading and thinking through the issues covered in this Resource Guide is critical to deepening your understanding of change and informing your leadership practice.

From Iceberg to Field

We analyse change as a field ('field analysis') to shift the focus away from achieving a discrete 'technical' change (e.g., implementing a CRM system, creating 'agile' structures, enhancing 'sustainability') and onto the set of social relationships within which 'the change' is embedded. There are various ways to discuss this shift in focus. For some, it is 'systems thinking' (Nadler & Tushman, 1989; Roth & DiBella, 2015; Scharmer & Kaufer, 2013). For others, it is a 'processual' focus on context and process in change (Dawson, 2019; Tsoukas & Chia, 2002). In this Resource Guide, however, we draw on what we view as the most comprehensive, insightful and useful approach. It regards *change as action within a socio-material 'field'* (Fligstein & McAdam, 2012).

As with the 'iceberg' metaphor (introduced in Chapter 2), this approach to field analysis directs our attention onto *both* the more formal, rational, and strategic 'above the surface' dimensions of change *and* the more informal, identity and emotional, cultural, and political, dimensions 'below the surface'. The iceberg metaphor acts as an initial guide and helpful ongoing reminder that:

- there are formal and rational aspects and forces of change (the 'Tip'),
- these are accompanied by more informal, cultural, and political elements and forces ('the 'Bulk'), and
- there is often limited understanding and silencing of discussion of 'what lies below' (the 'Waterline').

The iceberg is a noteworthy heuristic since our individual and organizational tendency is to focus on the 'tip', underestimate the significance of the 'bulk' and implicitly or explicitly collude in maintaining this status quo. Keeping this ('iceberg') bias in mind is crucial when embarking upon a comprehensive and worthwhile 'force field analysis' of the terrain change agents and initiatives must cross.

The iceberg metaphor only takes us so far, however. The forces of change are more fluid, interactive, complex, and dynamic than often represented in rigid and restrictive views of the 'iceberg'. To create a useful route map, we need a deeper understanding of the force field.

What follows makes a case for the relevance of such an analysis. We begin by grounding force field analysis in an in-depth understanding of what a field is ('field theory'), how we define specific fields, the nature of forces of change and the process of conducting a force field analysis, and define what is meant by (1) fields, (2) forces of change and (3) force field analysis.

USING THIS RESOURCE GUIDE

Each section of the Resource Guide helps you map out change using the latest research insights. Because this is a comprehensive summary, the explanation is inevitably somewhat dense. Below is our recommended approach to help you navigate and use this Guide:

(i)   *Part A: The Field*

Read this section before you begin mapping change. It briefly introduces why a systematic approach is required to analyse change and recommends using the term 'field' to describe what is being changed. Approaching change as a 'field' is useful, flexible, and practical.

(ii)   *Part B: The Forces of Change*

Read this section before listing the forces for and against change in a force field analysis. It recommends the use of a Strategic-TLC classification to help order the different forces in a way that is sufficiently complex yet not overwhelmingly so. So long as you think it through, creating your own classification is also helpful.

(iii)   *Part C: The Force Field Analysis*

Before you and others conduct a formal analysis of the forces for and against change, read this section carefully. It recommends careful consideration of *who* does the analysis as well as *when* and *how* it is done. It is also a reminder that you are studying a dynamic set of processes and every attempt to map it out is inevitably abstract and simplified. Be prepared to reconsider and update your assumptions.

(iv)   *Part D: Forces For and Against Change – The Force Field Matrix*

This section can be used at two points. First, before conducting a preliminary force field analysis, it can provide you with ideas and pointers about common sources of readiness and resistance to change. After an initial force field analysis, it can be used a second time to evaluate what you have come up with and provide suggestions for further consideration. This is the longest section of the Resource Guide and arguably the one of most use. Good luck!

PART A: THE FIELD

The idea of a field has its historical origins in the *physical sciences*. It is an essential reminder to all those who unreflectively seek to 'push' change. Similar to an electromagnetic field, if your change initiative is an uninformed 'push', then you will likely get an 'equal and opposite' 'push back'!

The fundamental principles of treating change as a field lay in the work of Kurt Lewin in the 1930s. His famous equation

$B=f(P,E)$

pointed to the key notion:

B (individual behaviour) is a function (f) of the person (P) and their environment (E).

How people behave, Lewin argued, is a function of what he termed their 'life space' formed by their situated interactions and relationships. Thus, as Lewin (1935, p.41) put it, 'the dynamics of the processes is always to be derived from the relations of the concrete individual to the concrete situation' (cited in Hilgers & Mangez, 2015, p.4).

This idea of a field was taken up and politicized by the French sociologist Pierre Bourdieu (Swartz, 2016). Neo-institutional researchers have subsequently used it to explore the influence and dynamics of the institutional fields within which organizations are embedded (Greenwood et al., 2020; Powell & DiMaggio, 1991; Smets et al., 2012). A field approach has also been advocated as a key change management method (Burnes & Cooke, 2013; Swanson & Creed, 2014) and as a valuable integrative approach to studying social and organizational life (Fligstein & McAdam, 2011, 2012; Martin, 2003).

The notion of a field directs us to the interdependence of the forces affecting a change. In his book *The Closing Circle* ([1971], 2020), Barry Commoner's first of his four famous laws of ecology was 'Everything is connected to everything else.' This could aptly be described as a central principle of all field analysis. When we think of a defined or proposed change in field terms, we look at the web of relationships that constitute the change and within which it is embedded. John Kotter (1996) illustrated this using a metaphor of an office where each item of furniture is attached to the others. The metaphor introduces us to some features of a field analysis, however, but not all.

Kotter's Office

Imagine walking into an office and not liking the way it is arranged. So, you move one chair to the left. You put a few books on the credenza. You get a hammer and rehang a painting. All of this may take an hour at most since the task is relatively straightforward. Indeed, creating change in any system of independent parts is usually not difficult. Now imagine going into another office where a series of ropes, big rubber bands, and steel cables connect the objects to one another. First, you'd have trouble even walking into the room without getting tangled up. After making your way slowly over to the chair, you try to move it, but find that this lightweight piece of furniture won't budge. Straining harder, you do move the chair a few inches, but then you notice that a dozen books have been pulled off the bookshelf, and that the sofa has now moved slightly in a direction you don't like. You slowly work your way over to the sofa, to try to push it back into the right spot, which turns out to be incredibly difficult. After thirty minutes, you succeed, but now a lamp has been pulled off the edge of the desk and is precariously hanging in mid-air, supported by a cable going in one direction and a rope going in the other. (Kotter, 1996, p.135)

Another source of our current notion of the field has military origins, viewing it as a *field of conflict or battlefield*. In line with this perspective, strategic endeavours, conflicts, and tension within any field demand careful consideration.

In line with its military origins, the idea of a field also captures the existence of tension and conflict between the interdependent forces. While fields may be patterned by many common and agreed-upon expectations, habits, rules, and regulations, they are often also chaotic, conflictual, and antagonistic. As further illustrated in Bourdieu's field analysis, the 'field of forces' includes uncertain, contradictory and contested 'rules of the game'. A field is, often, a 'field of struggle' (Savage & Silva, 2013), in which the struggle may be deliberate, conscious or embedded in habits, routines and practices.

Finally, while fields may be consensual or conflictual, organized, or disorganized, the interaction between the different forces is often patterned and directional. From the perspectives of those attempting to influence the field and bring about change, this pattern and direction may be supportive or opposed to what they intend. As Kurt Lewin (2009, p.74) emphasized, the field is not static but more akin to a river flowing in a certain direction.

From what has been just discussed, it is clear that by a state of 'no social change' we do not refer to a stationary but to a quasi-stationary equilibrium; that is, to a state comparable to that of a river which flows with a given velocity in a given direction during a certain time interval. A social change is comparable to a change in the velocity or direction of that river. (Lewin, 2009, p.74)

Capturing the momentum of the field or its overall trajectory is akin to 'a slope (a gradient) down which an object will "roll"' (Martin, 2003, p.8). As in our discussion of the 'Lord's Slope' in change, for example, modern organizations have systemic biases towards prioritizing strategy formation over execution, design over implementation, and initiating rather than realizing reforms.

In combining these ideas, a field perspective is a practical, open, and flexible way of capturing the many interactions and relationships that shape a course of events. Particular field theories are more prescriptive in how they define the main constituents of fields and how they interact, and they do so in order to provide more detailed and focused advice (Grenfell, 2008; Lounsbury & Zhao, 2017; Savage & Silva, 2013). For our present purposes, however, an open and flexible approach is most desirable in establishing the groundwork for a field analysis. Effectively applying such an approach combines:

1. a systemic, rather than a systems approach,
2. a relational, situational, and dynamic view of events, and
3. consideration of fields within fields.

Systemic, not just Systems

It makes sense to view change as a 'system', but only as a starting point. If 'no person is an island', neither is any change, and the idea of a 'system' points to this. What we often presume to be 'the change' (e.g., the introduction of a new software system) is affected by and involves altering a variety of other conditions and relationships (e.g., operational processes, habitual routines, jobs and careers, reward systems, identities, power relations, rituals, and stories). As one engineer from a large steel company put it after attending our course, 'I always thought I was improving equipment. Now, I know I was redesigning jobs.'

Yet, while systems thinking captures the embedding of change in a web of connections and relationships, it still has several limitations. We often view systems rather narrowly as machines or organisms, a set of more or less well-oiled or healthy parts performing required functions (see Morgan, 2006). Yet organizations are often far more chaotic, contradictory, and dynamic than this suggests. Consider the following two important points to go beyond a 'narrow' view of systems in viewing change as a 'systemic' web of relationships:

- Some things are more 'tightly coupled' than others, so more attention needs to be paid to those relationships.
- The different elements in the web of relationships may conflict with each other.

Unlike mechanical and organic systems, social fields may be integrated and riven by tension, contradiction, and diverse political interests. For example, in *Jamie's School Dinners*, how children responded to the changes in food was immediately affected by their peers, and increasingly throughout the change, Jamie realized this and adapted his strategies accordingly. How children responded was also influenced by a more general view of Jamie's 'cool' status as a celebrity chef, but this turned out to have relatively little effect on their responses when it conflicted with peer group pressure. On a side note, this is also a warning against exaggerating the degree of influence a charismatic, transformational leader has on people's responses to change.

Connections, Contexts and Dynamics

We all know, relationships and connections change over time and take varying forms in different contexts. In different situations, we see things differently and are subject to different influences. As Fred Emery and Eric Trist (1965), p.26) famously put it, 'the field itself. The "ground is in motion"' (cf. Scott & Meyer, 1992, p. 142; cited in Martin, 2003, p.27). While this sounds relatively common-sense, it is based on a profound insight. The world can be viewed as interacting forces and relations, with events conditioned by context. However, our atomistic and mechanistic view of the world tends to see separate elements that have precise and general causative effects on each other. When applied to organizational life, this approach blinkers us to the situational dynamics affecting events. It also encourages an exaggerated belief in what generic 'scientific' knowledge can provide. '*Knowing how*' to act within a field requires wisdom that extends beyond '*knowing that*' certain elements are present and impact each other.

The lesson here is clear. Any specific change affects and is affected by its relationship with other things, and these relationships shift over time and between situations. These need to be considered in assessing the nature and role of forces for and against a proposed change.

Defining Fields

Next, we consider how to characterize or define a specific 'field'. This involves:

1. drawing the line, or establishing 'boundaries', between different fields,
2. capturing the nature and role of 'fields within fields', and
3. exploring how one field interacts with others.

Quite often, what we take to be 'fields' are defined by common sense notions of social and organizational life identifiable and different from other areas. For example, an organization is itself a field of interacting elements distinguished from the 'outside'. However, it is also embedded in a specific industry sector and economic, geographical, and cultural regions. When we explore inside organizations, references are made to sub-units and workgroups as relatively independent and identifiable collective entities. Underlying what we might take to be 'fields' are assumptions that they involve a fairly dense web of interactions between people and elements in the area, that there are observable and relatively enduring patterns of behaviour, and a recognizable shared set of values and beliefs (even if ambiguous, contradictory or contested).

Determining such issues is far from being simply an academic enterprise. To capture what is involved in a 'change', we need to identify the relationships within which it is embedded. An analysis cannot capture all relationships, so there is a need to focus on the main ones, that is, those that constitute the main characteristics of a 'field', and what these involve is often far from obvious and requires the making of judgement calls. 'Getting it right' has practical outcomes. If we focus on one set of relationships, assuming these are the 'field' while neglecting others, then we will have effects we did not foresee and meet opposition (or find support) that we did not expect. An important part of effective field analysis is to be explicit about the boundaries of the 'field' you are assuming to be in place, treat this as a hypothesis and be ready to shift in the face of contrary evidence and experience.

One of the intuitively most obvious and important challenges in defining the nature and boundaries of fields is the existence of fields within fields. Every field can be broken up into sub-fields and, in turn, are part of a broader field. Fligstein and McAdam (2011, 2012) aptly represent this as the 'Russian dolls' challenge as one 'field' of change is nested in another. Fuda and Badham (2011) capture the reflections of transformational CEOs on this issue, noting the importance of interlinked changes in the CEO at work, their executive team, their extended leadership team, and the overall organization (Fuda, 2013). These are, in turn, situated in broader changes ranging from the deeply personal (the CEO's individual personality and family life) to the broader upline environment (international parent, Board, government, sector). Studies of readiness and resistance to change confirm this approach by recommending a 'multi-level' analysis of the nature and sources of attitudes to change. This means combining an investigation within the organization (individual, workgroup, sub-unit, organization culture and structure) and outside (organizational type, market sector, broad institutional field, a socio-political and economic-technical environment more generally).

For our present purpose, fields are defined by the density of interactions and patterns of behaviour rather than formal designations. So, defining 'boundaries', exploring 'interactions' with other fields and deciding whether these are 'nested' within broader fields depends on the density and what we are interested in. The focus is, ultimately, a judgement call. As illustrated by the dilemma faced by John Steinbeck's tenant below. The focus and interventions that follow from them are decisions made on pragmatic grounds.

Who Should We Shoot?

Scene drawn from John Steinbeck's *Grapes of Wrath*

In John Steinbeck's *Grapes of Wrath*, there is a scene in which a tenant farmer gets a frustrating lesson in the field of forces responsible for change. Bank representatives have advised the tenants they must get off the land because 'sharecropping' is no longer profitable, and the bank has bought the land to farm. A tractor driver is charged with demolishing the structures, and the tenant threatens to shoot him. The driver responds there is no point shooting him, he has his instructions and another driver will just replace him. There is then a cascade of questions from the tenant about the level of person responsible so he can shoot him or her. The list seems endless, running through the immediate superior, the president of the bank and the board of directors. The driver suggests perhaps there is no-one responsible such that shooting them will help! The tenant exclaims in frustration that if it is something people have created, we should be able to change it…while watching his house being demolished!

Source: For the original, see Steinbeck, John (1951). *The Grapes of Wrath*. Harmondsworth: Penguin p.155.

PART B: THE FORCES OF CHANGE

Field analysis, and any application of force field analysis, requires a deter-mination of the 'forces' at play. The advantage of the open and flexible field analysis we have described above is not tying us down to a pre-determined model of 'the' nature, driver, or process of change. Yet in avoiding 'superficial simplicity', there is a danger that we merely end up in 'confused complexity'. What is required, therefore, is to supplement a general view of the nature of 'fields' by making judgement calls about the set of important and relevant 'forces' to consider in the 'swamp' of multiple shifting factors at play. It is important to be ever-mindful, however, that this is a judgement call. It should be done reflectively, aware that any perspective is just that, and avoid being lulled into a false sense that one has captured objective reality. The 'map is not the territory'!

So, what is a 'force'?

Action, Context and Forces

In a field analysis of organizational stability and change, we look at action in context, and include in the context both social and material influences. For this reason, we refer to the interaction of action and context in 'socio-material fields' as constituting and influencing organizational change (Badham, 2009; Feldman & Orlikowski, 2011; Fligstein & McAdam, 2012; Savage & Silva, 2013).

The interaction of action and context that make up the forces in a field of change is described by neo-institutional scholars as 'embedded agency'. This re-describes a phenomenon nicely captured in the famous comment below by Karl Marx:

> Men [sic] make their own history, but they do not make it just as they please: they do not make it under circumstances chosen by themselves, but under circumstances directly encountered, given, and transmitted from the past. The tradition of dead generations weighs like a nightmare on the brain of the living. (Marx, 1972, orig.1852, p.10)

In contemporary change parlance, this notion goes back to Lewin's formula about people acting but doing so in particular environments. Other people, distributions of power, available resources, established cultures, formalized structures, physical, technological, and material environments and so on, are circumstances or conditions that shape, enable and constrain what people *strive* to do. These conditions do not determine how we act, but they can also not be overcome through the simple exercise of will. We cannot ignore that we occupy particular positions in any social field, but what these positions are is affected by what we bring to those positions, how we interpret them and, within limits, our use of the scope and potential to re-position ourselves. As Owen-Smith and Powell (2012) describe it, 'fields of forces' are intertwined with 'fields of play'.

While individual and collective behaviour may be habitual and unreflective, patterned, and constrained, there is an irreducibly purposeful and meaningful dimension to human action that makes it necessary to include agency and intentionality in any characterization of social forces. If we ignore the contextual or environmental factors that condition and shape what we want and can do, we blinker ourselves to the social realities we must work with and within. If we fail to appreciate the realm of choice, intention, creativity and striving in human action, we limit our options, ignore a crucial part of our experience, and may even create self-fulfilling prophecies of an inability to change things. A balanced view is needed, one that recognizes social conditioning yet appreciates individual enterprise. As such, it is necessary to characterize and explore social forces, and the fields they combine to create, as 'fields of endeavour' (Owen-Smith & Powell, 2012, p.601), 'strategic action fields'(Fligstein & McAdam, 2011) or 'organized striving' (Martin, 2003, p.20).

Interestingly, material forces also come into play in ways that are frequently either over-emphasized or under-appreciated. They take the form of variable configurations of raw materials, equipment, plant and buildings, IT systems, ecological events, and so on. They exist, in part, independently of interpretations of them, yet the force they exert cannot be separated from how people 'make sense' of them and act based on these interpretations. Sometimes, the role of material factors is overplayed, as people react to perceptions rather than realities, and individuals and groups find it in their interests to make attributions that are not accurate. For example, in one large manufacturing company we worked with, senior management commonly attributed reductions in workforce headcount to 'technology' rather than managerial strategy, as the union agreement allowed for technological unemployment to occur without negotiations being required. Established lenses, paradigms or frames for viewing technology may be as important as the material factors themselves.

Key Forces

When considering the types of forces involved, it quickly becomes apparent that there are as many views of the different forces of change as theories of organization and views of human nature and social life. As James March (1981, p.563) put it, 'Theories of change in organizations are primarily different ways of describing theories of action in organizations, not different theories.' Each of these theories captures and priorities different social forces.

How these forces are best divided and parcelled out in a force field analysis is a critical judgement. This can be done in multiple ways, and decisions must be made on what is useful and relevant. Our 'iceberg' image, for example, identifies the key division as lying between the more official, formal, public, frontstage, and structural or technical forces and the unofficial, private, backstage, and cultural and political forces. This plays a useful role in pointing to contrasts between what we say and what we do and what is explicit and tacit, what is common and possible to talk about and what is less common and more challenging to discuss. In an organizational world in which the 'tyranny of the tangible' (Reynolds & Lewis, 2017) is active, this acts as an important source of insight and as a reminder that change involves both above the surface strategically rational components of an organization and the below the surface influence of culture, power, and emotion. Such a rough division, sometimes characterized as between the 'hard' and the 'soft' dimensions of change

(Senior & Fleming, 2006), is quite common in popular parlance and academic analysis, and plays a useful role.

One of the limitations of this simple bi-polar iceberg model, however, is its failure to break down these different factors in a way that makes them more amenable to analysis and intervention. Therefore, to go further and beyond the simple hard/soft image, below are several classic and popular classifications of the forces of change illustrated in the diagrams at the end of this section.

Popular Classifications of Forces of Change

1. *The McKinsey '7S' Model* (Waterman et al., 1980).
2. *The Galbraith 'Star' Model* (Galbraith, 2009).
3. *The Johnson and Scholes 'Cultural Web' Model* (Johnson, 1992; Johnson et al., 2017).
4. *The Tushman and Nadler 'Congruency' Model* (Tushman & Nadler, 1980).
5. *The Wheatley 'Above and Below the Green Line' Model* (Wheatley, 2006; Zuieback, 2020).
6. *Weisbord's 'Six Box' Organizational Model* (Weisbord, 1976) introduced in http://www.marvinweisbord.com/index.php/six-box-model (accessed 21 May 2022).

Note: Each model provides a different framework for exploring the more formal structural, rational, and strategic and the more informal cultural, behavioural and leadership dimensions of an organization.

While the model you select is up to you, the need for a model is not optional. To be useful, a force field analysis must make judgement calls about the types of forces involved – their character, weight, relations, and effects. Ultimately, whatever choice is made is an inevitable yet necessary simplification of the 'blooming, buzzing confusion' of a complex world (James, 2007, p.314 original published 1890).

Our personal preference is for a relatively simple characterization that draws on the insights of the 'iceberg' as well as the dominant approaches (or 'prejudices') that inform many theories of organizational 'changing' (Bennis, 1966; Bennis & Nanus, 1985; Caldwell, 2006). Thus, while traditional organizational development models are well known for drawing on iceberg imagery and advocating attending to culture, this approach deepens and enriches what is considered by breaking down forces into:

- Strategy-Structure
- Technology-Innovation

- Leadership-Power
- Culture-Meaning (see Figure 10.1).

FORCES	DRIVERS ➝	FORCES FOR AND FORCES AGAINST ◄───	
Type	Goals	Disruptions & Misalignments	Embedded Frames & Powers
Strategy	*Performance*	Institutional/ Structure-Strategy	Frames (Strategic)/ Dominant Coalition/ Organizational Slack
Technology	*Efficiency*	Technology / External Best Practice -Internal Capabilities	Frames (Technology)/ Routine Practices/ Sunk Costs
Leadership	*Power*	Political / Innovative-Established Leadership	Hierarchy & Interests/ Fragmentation/ Lack of Will & Skill
Culture	*Meaning*	Cultural/ Old v New Purpose & Commitment	Frames (Cultural)/ Diverse Identities/ Denial, Fear & Cynicism

Figure 10.1   Strategic TLC (S-TLC) framework

Above the Surface

Strategy-Structure: At the apex of widespread strategic discussions of organizational change lie performance considerations and the need to adapt the organizational structure to environmental demands. Commonly described as a 'rational adaptation' (Demers, 2007) or 'performance-driven' (Donaldson, 1998) approach, the dominant focus is on:

- formal organizational structures,
- the degree to which they are integrated, aligned, or misaligned to market and regulatory demands in the environment, and
- the creation of strategies to create greater integration and alignment (Child, 1972, 1997).

Exploring such forces captures many of the key economic and governmental drivers and restraints on change. Additional pressures are created by many organizations' 'S-shaped' development as they grow and develop over time (Tushman & O'Reilly, 1997). This is a phenomenon emphasized by 'punctuated equilibrium' models of change as evolving through 'evolutionary' and 'revolutionary' periods (Gersick, 1991) and those arguing that in dynamic contexts 'ambidextrous organizations' are necessary to sustain 'business as usual' while also exploring and initiating more 'disruptive' forms of innovation and change (O'Reilly III & Tushman, 2004; Tushman et al., 2011). The dynamics of the 'S-curve' results in:

- growth and maturity undermining the effectiveness of organic structures established and best suited for smaller and start-up organizations,
- bureaucratic mechanistic structures of large and mature companies being challenged as gains from process standardization and mass production decline and greater flexibility, diversification and innovativeness are required in their products and adaptability, and
- internal organizational differentiation taking place or being required, making established forms of integration inefficient and ineffective.

At the heart of structural and strategic approaches emphasizing these factors lies the view that 'organizational performance drives organizational change and adaptation. For an organization that is maladapted, the adaptive change it needs tends to occur when poor organizational performance leads to a crisis' (Donaldson, 1998, p.1). The misalignments and misfits described above are key contributors to such a performance crisis, yet they are not the only ones.

On the one hand, the organizational environment is broader than economic markets and governmental regulations. In the popular PESTLE analysis, economic, political, and legal factors are accompanied by social and environmental ones (Morrison & Daniels, 2010). Moreover, the driving effect of performance challenges brought about by maladaptation may be ameliorated or counter-balanced (Child, 1997; Lehman & Hahn, 2013; Singh, 1986) by:

- 'loose coupling' with the environment, creating a degree of 'organizational slack' in requiring adaptation to its demands,
- the performance costs of changing brought about by sunk costs, as well as the time, attention and resources needed to deal with complex and disruptive transformations, and
- lack of strategic understanding or ability to respond to environmental changes brought about by senior management's established frames, vested interests, and inability to collaborate effectively.

In contrast, the driving effect of performance challenges is enhanced when organizations and their senior managers effectively scan the environment, are competent and effective in strategy development and execution, and are agile and adaptable in their structural response-ability.

Technology-Innovation: The next most commonly identified social forces are those associated with technological change in both products and processes.

These are driven by the alignment or misalignment between 'external' 'best practice' and 'internal' capabilities. In this case, the dominant focus is on:

- the increased cost-effectiveness, capabilities and disruptive consequences of new product and process technologies,
- in the face of these demands and new environmental conditions, the relatively uncompetitive nature of established products and/or the relative inefficiency of the equipment, processes and capabilities within the organization's existing operations, and
- the development and implementation of technology and innovation strategies that ensure that the new, more competitive product and process innovations are introduced.

Such factors are recognized and promoted as a driving force for change when organizations have:

- an innovative culture and structure that values and rewards innovation, and
- capabilities and resources to develop and implement effective innovation strategies (Tidd & Bessant, 2021).

Similar to the strategic drivers for change, however, the strength and impact of technology and innovation as a driving force can be weakened or counter-balanced by 'core rigidities' (Leonard-Barton, 1992). Past success can mean that previous 'core capabilities' (knowledge and skills, technical systems, managerial systems, values and norms) become difficult to change. Key restraining elements are:

- Established technological frames that define useful capabilities and desirable directions (Cornelissen & Werner, 2014; Kaplan & Tripsas, 2008; Orlikowski & Gash, 1994);
- Embedded and sunk costs in knowledge and skills, equipment and configurations, and processes and routines (Sydow et al., 2009); and
- Limitations on the degree to which product innovation and operational efficiency are key in ensuring organizational survival (Singh, 1986).

Below the Surface

Leadership-Power: The importance of leadership and power in change has been aptly captured by Jeffrey Pfeffer (1992, p.135) in his renowned observation:

> There are politics involved in innovation and change. And unless and until we are willing to come to terms with organizational power and influence and admit that the

skills of getting things done are as important as the skills of figuring out what to do, our organizations will fall further and further behind.

The emphasis on leadership and politics as a social force highlights:

*   the significance of power and agency in bringing about change,
*   the degree to which willing and able change agents and leaders are present and available, and
*   the existence and viability (or not) of a political process of creating and supporting the actions of change entrepreneurs and aligned coalitions (Bacharach, 2016; Buchanan & Badham, 2020; Kanter, 1985).

A key consideration is whether there is alignment between the leadership capabilities and power resources available and those required to bring about the change.

Power is the 'capacity to mobilize people and resources to get things done' (Kanter, 1981, p.221). In the face of the opportunities and challenges created by other forces of change, the possession and ability to exercise power is of crucial significance (Greenwood & Hinings, 1996). The ability to bring about change is severely compromised, for example, when leaders' political capabilities are inadequate, coalitions fragmented, weak or unstable, and there are powerful vested interests in the status quo.

Culture-Meaning: Peter Drucker's purported phrase 'Culture eats strategy for breakfast' nicely captures how people individually and collectively interpret and make sense of themselves, others, and the world around them. There is no evidence that Peter Drucker coined the phrase, but popular, less dramatic references are often made to culture 'beating', 'trumping' or at least 'determining and limiting' strategy in bringing about change (Quora, 2020). Strategic demands and technological requirements must be interpreted, and the purpose of achieving strategic goals and developing technological capabilities must be established. The central focus in attending to this social force is whether the existing culture aligns with what is necessary to make people believe the change is needed and motivates them to support it.

The focus on culture and meaning as a social force emphasizes how people make sense of initiatives and events through the cognitive frames and value-laden prejudices they inherit, share, take for granted, espouse, and adhere to. Whether the goals of change initiatives are regarded as meaningful, and whether ends and means are understood or misunderstood, unclear or contested, depends on the assumptions and expectations, perspectives and values, identities and storylines that people hold or adhere to (Rhodes & Brown, 2005; Brown et al., 2009; Cunliffe & Coupland, 2011; Giorgi et al., 2015; Sonenshein, 2010; van Dijk & van Dick, 2009; Werner & Cornelissen, 2014).

Such interpretations are influenced by cultural conditions external as well as internal to organizations involved (e.g., 'best practice' templates in an industry, innovation fads and fashions, labour market conditions such as levels of employment and entry of 'Gen X' or 'Gen Z' employees, popular commitment to causes such as climate change, sustainability and so on).

Cultural factors inside an organization are likely to support change when the change:

- is regarded as purposeful and meaningful,
- aligns with a strong positive organizational identity,
- is supported by existing and new societal norms and expectations,
- is compatible with individual and sub-group identities, statuses, and self-narratives,
- works with rather than against existing psychological contracts,
- is seen as being introduced by capable, supportive, and trusted leaders, and
- is part of an open, dynamic, confident, and innovative culture.

When such conditions are absent, cultures are fragmented, cynical, competitive, and defensive and the intervention contradicts deeply held values, identities and beliefs, or with contemporary cultural developments, then change is likely to generate significant resentment and opposition (Anthony, 1994; Bushe & Marshak, 2015; Martin, 2002; Quinn, 1988).

PART C: THE FORCE FIELD ANALYSIS

An established method for undertaking a field analysis addressing these social forces is described in Chapter 3 and the 'Intermission' as 'force field analysis'. Derived initially from the work of Kurt Lewin, the method is premised on the basic assumptions of a 'field' approach, that is, that social forces have to be explored systemically and dynamically, considered in context and in interaction with each other as they evolve over time and space. This is, however, often forgotten.

Context of a Force Field Analysis

A simple force field analysis has become an established method to identify forces for and against a change within a field. It commonly takes the form of a list of promoting and resisting forces of varying strengths, with the strengths of each represented by shorter/longer or thinner/thicker lines on a force field diagram (see Chapter 3). An additional factor, commonly associated with force field analysis, emphasizes considering and addressing the social forces keeping the field in its existing state. As the ex-British prime minister Tony Blair (2010, p.271) put it:

> They [reasons not to change] are always there for a reason and historically at least, often for a good reason. Changing [the system] can be even harder. A whole web of custom, practice and interest has been created around them; yet for the organisation to make progress, they must be changed.

Because of the power and influence of such factors, Kurt Lewin (1947b, p.26) prescribed the removal of restraining forces as a primary and key element of change management.

Talk of an 'existing state' does not, however, mean that a field is static. As we observed above, Lewin makes it clear that actions and events within a field have a particular direction and momentum (like a 'river'). The forces affecting this direction support a certain pattern of action or trajectory. When an intervention is made to bring about changes in this field, these forces will either promote or prevent shifts in patterns or direction. A force field analysis interrogates these forces and their implications for those seeking to bring about a change. The change agent seeks guidance on the appropriate route to take across the change terrain by analysing these forces, their direction, how strong they are, how they interrelate, and how they evolve over time.

Despite the initial sophisticated work of Kurt Lewin, however, much of the current academic and consultancy literature provides us with a superficial or restricted understanding of such a force field analysis. Superficial consultancy approaches tend to give overly simplified, static, and atomistic 'lists' of forces. Little, if no, attention is paid to how they shift over time, intertwine with each other, and are affected by context (Burnes & Cooke, 2013; Swanson & Creed, 2014).

Academic research has also tended to reduce promoting and hindering forces to psychological attitudes of 'readiness' or 'resistance' (Dent & Goldberg, 1999). While this research has been extended in recent times, it often fails to direct our attention to (or provide us with an analysis of) the complex social field within which these attitudes are embedded (Ford & Ford, 2008; Patalano, 2011; Piderit, 2000). Relying on diagnostic questionnaires and a 'variance'-based search for decontextualized evidence-based causal generalizations betrays many of the processual base assumptions of field theory (Burnes & Cooke, 2013; Fligstein & McAdam, 2011). Moreover, despite extensive studies, there remains no commonly agreed definition of resistance or readiness, limited and uncertain knowledge of general conditions promoting either, and few reliable tools for measurement (Bouckenooghe, 2010; Bouckenooghe et al., 2009; Weiner et al., 2020).

　　The good news, however, is we do not have to analyse the forces for and against a change with a blank slate. There is a swathe of useful academic and practitioner-based research and experience on the social forces that promote or obstruct change. As we have seen above, as these routinely reference sets of structural, technological, cultural and leadership forces, they are quite manageable. Moreover, numerous important insights are provided into elements or variants of these forces. This literature also provides some important insights into elements or variants of these forces promoting change and others acting as hindrances. The final section of this Resource Guide provides you with an accessible overview of the literature and some useful heuristic guidelines.

Danger: A Babel of Competing Discourses!

Conducting a force field analysis is a challenging task and should be approached with care. Unfortunately, the academic and practitioner literature on change management does not lend itself easily to this enterprise. The research and advice are as fragmented and inconclusive as it is voluminous. It is essential to be mindful of this situation when scanning through the now massive and growing literature on managing and leading change. There are, as one wit put it, 'many approaches but few arrivals'. This is a well-established, persistent, and ongoing problem. There is no sound, acceptable, and accessible agreement on defining the nature of change or managing and leading it. Following Kurt Lewin's recommendation to be wary of the barriers to change, the depth of this problem and its likely continuation should be appreciated. To create a useful force field analysis you will have to be selective, pragmatic, and ready to make judgement calls.

　　Does this seem to be too radical or critical a claim? Not if we take academic authorities' opinions on the literature seriously. In 2003, for example, Pettigrew, Woodman, and Cameron (2001, p.697) re-iterated Kahn's (1974, p.487) assertion that the literature on change was restricted to 'a few theoretical propositions...repeated without additional data or development; a few bits of homey advice...reiterated without proof or disproof; and a few sturdy empirical observations...quoted with reverence but without refinement or explication' (Kahn, 1974, p.487).

　　Some contemporary scholars consider that the assessment remains sadly accurate. As Pettigrew ([1985] 2011, p.86) confirmed:

> the field of organisational change and development is characterised by limited attempts at theoretical development, few theoretical debates, highly focused kinds of conceptualisation, and minimal empirical findings. All this adds up to some rather poor descriptive theories of change which beyond a shopping list

of prescriptive do's and don'ts, sometimes qualified by contextual riders, could hardly be described as adequate guides to informed action.

By, Burnes and Oswick's review (2011, p.5) used more colourful language in noting that:

> when we look at the field of change, we do not see a single community of scholars and practitioners attempting to understand and develop the study and practice of change. Instead, we see a sea populated with islands, atolls, reefs, and a lot of individuals madly paddling boats between them who are frustrated by the fact that no one seems to speak the same language or see the world in the same way.

Finally, in 2020, in *Changing Change Management*, Darren McCabe (2020, p.187) noted that this fragmentation continues to obscure the fact that much of the change literature continues to operate, often tacitly, within overly rational, managerialist and depoliticized views of the forces of change. The result, he warns, is an ongoing 'circularity' as 'prescriptions are offered irrespective of the failings of earlier initiatives...with change initiatives simply perpetuating disengagement, prompting yet more change efforts aimed at enlisting the support of those on the receiving end of them'.

Following Caldwell (2006, pp.162, 167), our aim in this book is 'finding a way out of the Babel of competing discourses' by appreciating that 'there are not only dangers of fragmentation, but also enormous possibilities for creative pluralism and the reinvention of practice'. The purpose of this review is to help you navigate through the change literature. The aim is to help you draw on its insights in mapping out change reflectively and practically, rather than being confused by its fragmentation, complexity and often incoherence.

Content and Process

Keep in mind when analysing the forces of change that the '*map is not the territory*'. Any decision about how to divide up the force field, interpret the nature and strength of elements and speculate how they intertwine to create effects is a judgement call. Traditional academics would like to find evidence-based generalizations to determine corrective action, and practitioners yearn for simple to apply and practical tools in their outcomes. Yet, both ignore or deny the inherently uncertain and complex nature of the 'swampy lowlands' or 'mangle' of practice (Pickering, 1995; Schon, 1983). Appreciating the importance of keeping these yearnings under control is a key requirement for a reflective change practitioner. As Karl Weick (2007) emphasizes, it is essential not to run away from recognizing this complexity. He captures this advice in his slogan to 'Complicate yourself!' However, Weick also adds that we need to move from 'Confusing Complexity' to 'Profound Simplicity' for practical purposes. We cannot rest on our laurels content with our maturing in understanding the complexity of change. We need to make intelligent and sometimes courageous judgements about simplifying and imposing order on this 'mess' to act more effectively.

Appreciating uncertainty, complexity, and interdependence is vital in analysing fields and forces of change and their management. As Ian Mitroff and his colleagues (2012, p.96) put it:

> Today's executives need to be able to address complex, messy problems. As the late organizational scholar, Russell L. Ackoff once put it, 'Managers don't solve simple, isolated problems; they manage messes.' Ackoff was also instrumental in defining the nature of such messes. According to him, a mess is a system of constantly changing, highly interconnected problems, none of which is independent of the other problems that constitute the entire mess. As a result, no problem that is part of a mess can be defined and solved independently of the other problems.

Consequently, when we analyse the forces of change in detail, we must be mindful that they are separated for analytical purposes only. They are defined, categorized and examined as distinct forces yet then put back together again to examine their overlaps, interactions and interdependence in context. This tangled web is commonly acknowledged in detailed innovation studies, with Joe Tidd and John Bessant (2021) describing it as the 'spaghetti model of innovation'. So, while we identify and explore different forces for analysis, it is vital to re-examine them to capture overlaps and interactions. In her review of organizational change as 'transformation or evolution', Demers (2007) notes how the structure-strategy analysis of 'punctuated equilibrium' was intertwined with cognitive, cultural, and political analyses of frames, expectations and vested interests facilitating or preventing radical change. As Badham (2013, p.62) put it:

> Change is always contextual, and such forces are always inter-dependent. It makes no more sense to talk of one force or fact as 'the' cause of change than it does to try and identify the taste of one strand of spaghetti in a Bolognese separate from the rest. Change is always changing in or of a force field, a nested set of interdependent and fluid processes, all moving, often in tension, and in context difficult to separate.

Such realities are commonly recognized by practitioners as well as academics. The popular cartoon of a change manager pointing at a 'change project' depicted as a straight line at the beginning, and a tangled web of lines in the middle, a box entitled 'And a Miracle Happens Here', and then a clear arrow at the end, makes that point. The book *The Messy Middle* by Scott Belsky (2018), former Chief Product Officer of Adobe, expands upon this point. One of the books' endorsers remarks that creating something new is 'like jumping off a cliff and sewing a parachute on the way down'. Ongoing and iterative force field analyses inform the stitching and the re-stitching.

Analysing the forces of change requires making judgement calls about what it is useful to identify as different forces, separate these out, and then explore how they interact with others and alter as circumstances change. If such judgement calls are wrong and unhelpful, then a change version of GIGO (Garbage In. Garbage Out.) occurs. Conversely, a superficial or inaccurate analysis of the force field is of little value and can be mis-leading and distracting. The Greek philosopher Plato called attention to such skills in his metaphor of the good and bad butcher in *The Phaedrus* (2013). The good butcher works with the bones, sinews, and tissues, cutting effectively and precisely where appropriate. The bad butcher hacks away without understanding, thought or success. In the hands of the 'good butcher', a force field analysis is sufficiently complex and informed to grasp the key features of change, yet mature and straightforward enough to grasp the essential elements in a way that is of practical use, in time and in context. A key to an effective force field analysis requires being aware of our prejudices and simplifications, being ready (even excited) about acting while being aware of them, being ongoingly mindful about the need to test them out, and potentially revising.

In doing so, attention needs to be paid to three main issues:

Who

The appropriate people need to be selected for the force field analysis. Conditions also need to be actively generated for effective dialogue and interactive communication within the selected group. Representation of knowledge and interests must be balanced against the need to create collective interest and involvement and the practical need to make valid decisions. Building a team that is operationally effective and politically credible is essential. The 'group' may be as small as one or two individuals, a working group of change agents or formal change team, or a larger group of those involved and affected. Consideration should also be given to establishing a formal or informal 'steering committee' and 'working group' and how the creation of the team undertaking a force field analysis will help in establishing a good working relationship between the two. This is, in itself, a crucial change project!

When

A force field analysis is not a 'one-off' event conducted by an expert group in the initial 'diagnostic phase'. When undertaken early on in a change project, a blend of insider and outsider insights are required to surface and critically analyse the often taken-for-granted nature of the field of forces (inside and outside the organization). Expect initial agreement and disagreement areas, and these need to be surfaced and further explored. There are twin dangers of achieving a 'superficial consensus' or getting bogged down in 'analysis paralysis', so opening up critical thought while also focusing on achieving practical insights and outcomes is essential. As the change project proceeds, revisiting the force field is imperative. It is, as we have mentioned, part of an iterative 'GPS'. Every set of conclusions underlying the next action stage is also a hypothesis, and action is an experiment. Any force field analysis is always a 'best guess at the time'. It is provisional, revisable and should be tested out throughout the change process. Force field analysis is an ongoing work-in-progress, not a static output. In the process, be ready for the challenge that time is often scarce and resourcing a force field analysis and re-analysis will often meet resistance.

How

The Gap, Force Field and Route Analyses are iterative, cyclical, and ongoing, providing revisable insights into progress and guidelines for action. Therefore, be aware that a force field analysis:

- **Depends on a Gap Analysis**. Depending on how you define the change, the field of forces will be different. If, for example, the change involves a major political shift, then diagnosing the state of power and politics will be a crucial part of the force field analysis. When you explore the forces in more detail, you may become aware that the 'gap' you initially identified was mis-leading or misrepresenting the degree of change in different areas (often the cultural and political dimensions). So, be ready to revise the gap analysis.
- **Informs a Route Analysis**. The focus of the force field analysis is to identify relevant forces for the route you plan to take, that is, how they affect your initial preparation, persisting through the 'difficult middles', and embedding change in a way that prevents 'slipping back'. So, take the force field analysis seriously in defining the details of what you will do on your defined route.
- **Is an intervention in itself**. Recognize that every diagnosis is an intervention, and every intervention a diagnosis. How you and your group collect, analyse, and communicate your force field analysis is already a 'change intervention'. Attend to this and learn from it. In addition, every time you act, it is testing out of hypotheses, so use action for diagnosis. Kurt Lewin

is attributed as saying, 'you cannot understand a system until you try to change it' (Schein, 1996, p.34).

- **Is both quantitative and qualitative.** Use qualitative and quantitative indicators, objective measures, and intuitive judgements, official statements, and informal stories. As a rule, the more technical, certain and less contentious the force or issue, the more it is relevant to use quantitative data and formal statements. The more taken-for-granted and emotive, the less certain and more political the force or issue, the more appropriate qualitative analysis, observation of behaviour, and listening to stories. Putting a 'quantitative' frame around 'fuzzy' data can, however, ignite discussion and, in many cases, help 'sell' the change agenda.

PART D: FORCES FOR AND AGAINST CHANGE – THE FORCE FIELD MATRIX

To make a broad range of academic and practitioner research accessible and manageable, we summarize key insights in a simple two-by-two matrix that captures the established literature's varying focus and key contributions (*Figure 10.2 The Force Field Matrix*). The two main axes of the matrix represent the different levels of analysis (psychological or structural forces) and direction (promoting or hindering forces).

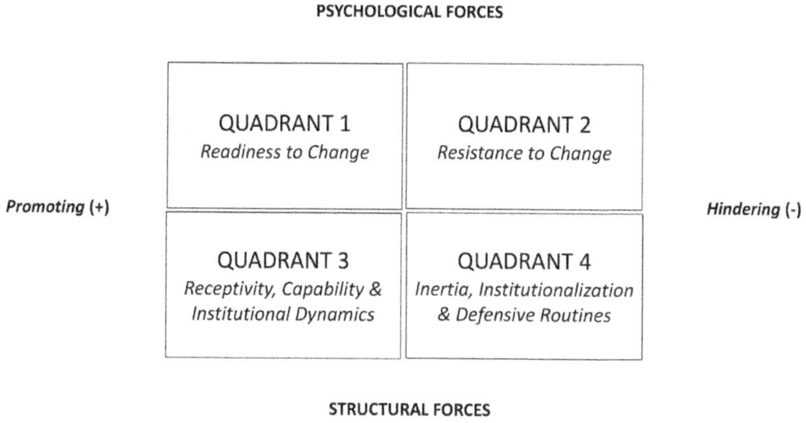

PSYCHOLOGICAL FORCES

	QUADRANT 1 *Readiness to Change*	QUADRANT 2 *Resistance to Change*	
Promoting (+)			Hindering (-)
	QUADRANT 3 *Receptivity, Capability &* *Institutional Dynamics*	QUADRANT 4 *Inertia, Institutionalization* *& Defensive Routines*	

STRUCTURAL FORCES

Figure 10.2   *The force field matrix*

The literature on forces for and against change is dominated by psychological assessments of attitudes to change. These are most often represented in terms of attitudes of 'readiness' (as an individual and collective psychological forces 'for' change) and 'resistance' (as individual and collective psychological forces 'against' change). There is also a substantial body of research on the structural and organizational forces for and against changes. The forces for change are most addressed in the literature on change receptivity, readiness, and institutional dynamics. The forces against change are most frequently captured in the literature on change inertia, institutionalization, and defensive routines.

Quadrant 1: Readiness to Change

Research on readiness to or for change provides valuable insights into the forces for and against change. As indicated by the title of change articles such as 'Are you ready?' (Holt et al., 2010) and 'Ready or not' (By, 2007), individuals and organizations may be viewed as being more or less ready for change, with readiness for change being 'a complex multi-dimensional construct including psychological and structural factors that occur at both the individual and organizational level. In practical terms, readiness for change requires both a willingness and capability to change' (Weiner, 2009, p.2). A key focus in readiness to change has been on *attitudes to change* at the individual, group, and organizational level (Weiner, 2009). Much of the literature on readiness for change has been an attempt to elaborate on what these involve (Armenakis & Bedeian, 1999; Armenakis & Harris, 2009; By, 2007; Cunningham et al., 2002; Holt et al., 2007a, 2007b, 2010; Oreg et al., 2011; Rafferty et al., 2013; Vakola, 2013; Weiner, 2009; Weiner et al., 2020).

At the centre of psychological readiness is whether people are *willing* and *able* to change. We use the general term 'people' deliberately, as the relevant beliefs, emotions, and intentions can occur at *multiple levels* – the individual, the group, the sub-unit, the organization or beyond (Armenakis et al., 1993; Bouckenooghe, 2010; Rafferty et al., 2013; Weiner, 2009). Each level has its importance and is *multi-dimensional* in character. It also includes the 'head' (cognitive/beliefs), the 'heart' (affect/feelings) and the 'hand' (intentional behaviour).

As a set of cognitive beliefs, readiness involves both 'change valence' (willing) and 'change efficacy' (able) (Weiner, 2009). *Change valence* is whether people value the specific change. For example, do they believe it is necessary, beneficial, or worthwhile for themselves or others? A classical analysis of readiness beliefs by Armenakis and Harris (2009) emphasizes three central beliefs informing a willingness to change. First, there is a 'discrepancy' (i.e., the change is necessary and significant), second, it is 'appropriate' (i.e., it will address the discrepancy in the current situation), and finally, it has personal 'valence' (i.e., there is something of benefit in it for them). *Change efficacy* is whether people believe they can bring about the change as individuals or a collective. Weiner (2009) relates change efficacy to beliefs about having the necessary knowledge, resources, and support (e.g., time, political backup). In their conceptualization of the final two readiness beliefs, Armenakis, Bernerth, Pitts, and Walker (2007) emphasize the importance of two components: 'efficacy' beliefs (i.e., they and the organization can successfully implement the change), and belief in 'principal support' (i.e., formal leaders and opinion leaders are committed to the change).

Change readiness goes beyond the cognitive. It includes feelings about the change, such as hope, confidence, excitement and even relaxation (Bouckenooghe, 2010; Rafferty et.al., 2013). Weiner et al. (2020) discuss such feelings in terms of current and future positive affect, emotions that incline people towards change based on their current emotional state and their future imaginings. Finally, readiness involves an intentional behavioural prepared-ness to change. Readiness consists in believing the change is desirable and feeling it to be so, but also an intention to act to support it. Change commit-ment is *a resolve* to pursue the course of action involved in change implemen-tation. As Weiner (2009) and Weiner et al. (2020) note, change commitment is clearly affected by and intertwined with beliefs about change valence and change efficacy.

The diagnosis of change readiness involves exploring whether such attitudes exist at various organizational levels. These levels intertwine. Individual atti-tudes are affected by those of the group, a group by the organization, and the

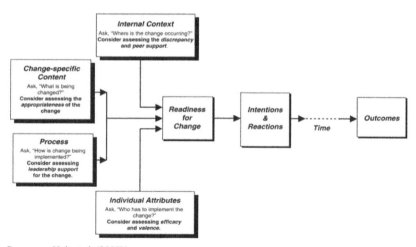

Source: Holt et al. (2007b).

Figure 10.3 *An integrated model of readiness for change*

organization by the institutional context and culture in which it is embedded. Notably, for example, an individual and group's 'efficacy' beliefs are clearly affected by confidence in their own abilities as well as those of the organization and its leaders (Vakola, 2013).

Along with this psychological focus is a recognition of the effect of *individual and organizational conditions* on readiness attitudes. A useful and well-established framework used to explain these effects explores the impact of the *content, context* and *process* of change, and *individual* attributes (Holt et al., 2007a, 2007b) (see Figure 10.3).

The literature on this topic is voluminous, however, we select key identified conditions affecting attitudes of practical use in a force field analysis (see Table 10.1).

Table 10.1   Factors influencing readiness to change attitudes

Content of the Change	*Range, depth, and speed of the change.* Where the change is more radical, disruptive, and transformational, shifting established mindsets is more likely to be a major challenge. The greater costs and uncertainties may increase a reluctance to change. These effects may be exaggerated if these changes are undertaken more rapidly, thereby polarizing change agents and recipients.
	Impact on work. When the content of the change questions established (taken for granted) assumptions, habits and practices, similar challenges are created, particularly if these are intertwined with the identities of those involved.
	Personal impacts. The effect of the specific content of the change on personal values and interests clearly has a major effect (e.g., downsizing and job insecurity, career enhancement or disruption, perceptions of fairness and justice). However, such issues tend to be explored much more deeply in the resistance to change literature.
Context of Change	The readiness literature is quite general on the influence of the external context in 'triggering' change and pays more attention to the 'internal organizational' context. Factors in the internal context influencing attitudes to change are:
	Levels of organizational commitment and perceived organizational support
	General trust in leadership and immediate supervisors as well as their perceived support
	Degree of openness, involvement and interaction in organizational communication and participation
	Organizational capabilities and competencies in innovation and change
	Past experiences with change
	Levels of formalization and centralization in structures, policies and procedures
	Amount of job enrichment and autonomy in jobs and work systems.

Process of Change	The main process elements influencing attitudes include:
	Structural issues such as adequate clarity of goals, adequacy of resourcing and a relevant implementation plan
	Issues of level of information and communication, degree of participation and interactional and procedural justice, and
	Level of trust in and support from leaders and change agents for the change, their change capabilities, and the congruity of change agent and recipient values.
The Individual	In terms of individual personality, readiness is influenced by:
	Needs for personal initiative and mastery, higher-order achievement and growth
	Traits of generalized self-efficacy, tolerance for ambiguity and openness to experience, proneness to positive affectivity and thoughts, flexible or growth mindset
	Coping styles of problem-solving and adaptation, absence of defensiveness and avoidance
	Group, sub-culture, union and professional affiliation
	Sex, age and level of education
	Organizational circumstances such as tenure, status, network and work orientation.

On a methodological note, readiness to change attitudes and influences upon them should be regarded as:

- *Heuristics*. These are general influences and conditions. They need to be set in context and creatively explored as suggestive insights and heuristic guides.
- *Ongoing*. Readiness can be assessed and reassessed at all stages of the change process and should include all forms of continuing change, not just formally planned initiatives, and
- *Complex*: While several useful readiness assessment tools are available, it is important to be mindful of the partial nature of the insights they produce.

Quadrant 2: Receptivity, Capability, and Institutional Dynamics

The readiness for change literature focuses on attitudes and beliefs in creating psychological readiness for change. The structures and contexts creating organizational readiness to change are more directly and extensively addressed in literature on organizational change receptivity, capability, and institutional dynamics.

Organizational receptivity to change is a well-established notion (Pettigrew et al., 2001; Newton et al., 2003). It includes multi-level attitudes to change (Clarke et al., 1996; Frahm & Brown, 2007; Huy, 1999) and more structural conditions (Butler, 2012; Newton et al., 2003; Weiner, 2009). However, the most influential explicit model of organizationally receptive contexts is the '8-factor' model of Pettigrew, Ferlie and McKee (1992a, 1992b). Butler (2003, 2012) provided an updated '5-factor' model, and Frahm and Brown (2007) explicitly linked organizational receptivity to research on 'continuously changing organizations'.

Pettigrew and Whipp (1991) initially created a '5-factor' model of the organizational dimensions of 'managing change for corporate success' attributing significance to: Environment, Leadership, Human Resources, Linked Strategy and Operations, and Coherence (see **Figure 10.4**). This was followed shortly by their '8-factor' model of receptive and non-receptive organizational contexts (Pettigrew et al., 1992a, 1992b) (see **Figure 10.5**).

A different approach to diagnosing change receptivity is provided by those exploring the idea of variable *organizational change capacity (OCC)*. Judge and Douglas (2009) identify eight (8) dimensions of such a capacity from the change literature (see Table 10.2).

Table 10.2   Factors influencing organizational change capacity

FACTOR	DEFINITION
1. Trustworthy leadership	The ability of senior executives to earn the trust of the rest of the organization and to show organizational members the way to meet its collective goals.
2. Trusting followers	The ability of the non-executive employees to constructively dissent with and/or willingly follow a new path advocated by its senior executives.
3. Capable champions	The ability of an organization to attract, retain, and empower change leaders to evolve and emerge.
4. Involved mid-management	The ability of middle managers to effectively link senior executives with the rest of the organization.
5. Innovative culture	The ability of the organization to establish norms of innovation and encourage creative activity.
6. Accountable culture	The ability of the organization to carefully steward resources and successfully meet pre-determined deadlines.
7. Effective communication	The ability of the organization to communicate vertically, horizontally, and with customers.
8. Systems thinking	The ability of the organization to focus on root causes and recognize the interdependencies within and outside the organizational boundaries.

Alternative and updated approaches have been provided by Buono and Kerber (2010) and Buono and Subbiah (2014), in their focus on organizational members, structure and culture, and Soparnot's (2013) model of context,

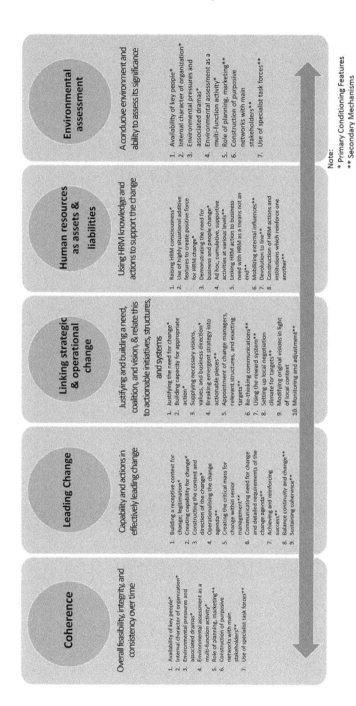

Source: Drawn from Pettigrew and Whipp (1991).

Figure 10.4 Five-factor model of managing change for success

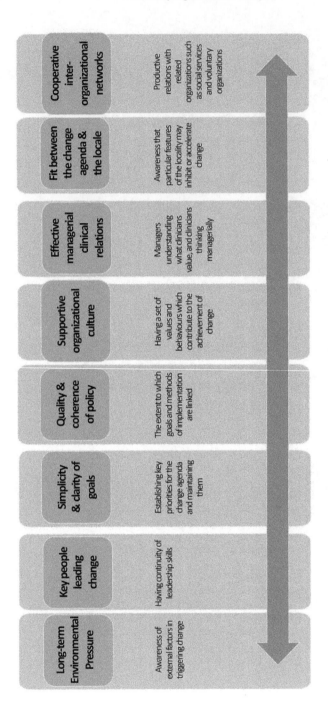

Source: Drawn from Pettigrew, Ferlie and McKee (1992a, 1992b).

Figure 10.5   *Receptivity to change: eight factor model*

process and learning dimensions. In reviewing the development and use of the concept of OCC, Heckmann, Steger and Dowling (2016) document the significance of its emphasis on:

- establishing routines for initiating, managing, and implementing change, grounded in experience,
- capacity to lead and manage a cascade of change initiatives, and
- the positive contribution of external technological turbulence.

Research on institutions and institutional fields provides additional insights into institutional dynamics and field characteristics creating a greater readiness to change. Oliver (1992) emphasizes the importance of 'deinstitutionalization' through political, functional, and social pressures for change in both the organization and its environment (see also Maguire & Hardy, 2009) (see Table 10.3).

Table 10.3   Pressures for deinstitutionalization

FACTOR	DEFINITION
1. Political pressures	Intra-organizational factors eroding political agreement and environmental pressures leading to questioning of practices, e.g., performance crisis, inter-organizational conflict, political dissensus with shifting power, and shifts in external dependence
2. Functional pressures	Perceived instrumental or technical value brought about by declining economic utility of practices, greater technical clarity about routine processes and requirements and external shifts in definitions of performance, heightened competition for resources and dissonant information or unexpected events
3. Social pressures	Normative fragmentation, disruption of organizational continuity and changes in laws and societal expectations, and disaggregation of external constituents and their demands (social pressures)

Greenwood and his colleagues (Greenwood & Hinings, 1996; Smets et al., 2012) argue that for institutional change to occur, the forces for 'deinstitutionalization' need to be analysed as combining:

1. *External or 'contextual' factors*: changing market conditions and institutional or regulatory changes, exogenous 'shocks' and contradictions within industry/field in which organizations are located, and
2. *Intraorganizational' factors*: precipitating and enabling change. 'Precipitating Dynamics':
   - pressures for change from interest dissatisfaction with existing arrangements, and

- changes or conflicts in value commitments towards the necessity and value of these arrangements.

'Enabling Dynamics':
- ability to respond to these pressures as a result of a shift in
- power dependencies (altering the balance of power), and
- capacity for action (based on an understanding, set of skills and available resources for managing the transition).

Battilana and her colleagues (2009; Leca et al., 2008) address these issues in exploring the conditions in organizations that influence the ability of institutional entrepreneurs to bring about change. They highlight:

1. *External Context and Organizational Fields*
   - jolts, crises, or resource problems within an organizational field that promote change,
   - heterogeneity or fragmentation in the organizational field, i.e., contending templates or models, tensions, and contradictions, that may support change,
   - degree of institutionalization of the organization, i.e., low degrees characterized by higher uncertainty, enabling change initiatives,
   - institutional status of the organization, i.e., both high and low low-status organizations being more capable and supportive of transformation depending on the change being considered, and
   - location of organizations at the intersection of fields, i.e., this allows and enables experimentation.
2. *Internal Context and Social Position of Institutional Entrepreneurs*
   - formal position, higher status helps to legitimate divergent ideas, and framing of stories, and
   - informal social capital, enabling allowing them to network more effectively, and give them the legitimacy to bridge different stakeholders.

A recent comprehensive overview of institutional entrepreneurship, reviewing the nature of institutional entrepreneurs and institutional factors affecting their ability to bring about change is provided by Hardy and Maguire (2017).

A word of caution and advice on how to use these insights. First, create your own framework rather than simply bundling these together. The different concepts employed by the varying approaches are general, vague, and overlapping. Second, the different elements they point to should not be treated as a checklist of separate and distinct elements. They are interdependent, dynamic, and situational in character. Their meaning and effects are interpreted and negotiated locally, shift over time and, as Pettigrew and Whipp (1991) and Pettigrew, Woodman and Cameron (2001) advise, should be considered more as 'signs and symptoms' than fixed causes.

Quadrant 3: Resistance to Change

The vast majority of studies on resistance focus on 'attitudes to change' (Bouckenooghe, 2010) and 'change recipient reactions' (Oreg et al., 2018). While there is no authoritative definition of resistant attitudes, popular definitions refer to an 'intentional/behavioral component as a driving force behind maintaining the status quo and hindering successful implementation of change' (Bouckenooghe, 2010, p.504).

There are multiple possible sources of psychological resistance to change. Drawing on Kurt Lewin's idea of a force field, Lester Coch and John French (1948) attributed resistance to change to lack of participation and involvement in change. This reflected and reinforced the popular idea that people do not resist change per se so much as 'being changed'. In the 1960s and 70s, the focus of attention was extended. As Johns (1973, p.60) puts it, citing Sayles and Strauss (1966, p.303), 'It is not change itself which causes the resistance, but the meaning of the change for the people involved.'

In a classic HBR piece, Paul Lawrence (1954) attributed resistance to:

- perceived threats to social relationships,
- the self-preoccupation by staff or change initiators with their interest and concerns,
- change agents overlooking the know-how of front-line change recipients, and
- false and mis-leading accusations by staff and change initiators of operator resistance.

Johns (1973) extended the critical analysis of the influence of change initiators in pointing to a resistant 'chain reaction' that can occur when change initiators:

- ignore the meaning change has for recipients (often treating the change as a 'trivial' or 'technical' issue),
- withhold information due to fear of potential resistance, and
- fail to recognize the positive value of resistance in:
  - pinpointing communication issues,
  - stimulating greater consideration of human relations issues,
  - helping to identify areas of low morale, and
  - productively questioning the appropriateness of the change.

In their influential HBR article, John Kotter and Leonard Schlesinger (1979) built on such notions in recommending strategies for overcoming resistance tailored to whether the source of resistance lay in:

- parochial self-interest,
- misunderstanding and lack of trust,
- different assessments of change by initiators and recipients, and
- low tolerance of change.

In more recent years, in the face of a vast proliferation of research and advice on sources of resistance to change, it has become popular to draw up 'resistance lists' (e.g., see Table 10.4).

Table 10.4   Sources of resistance

Dent & Goldberg (1999)	Kanter (2006)	Palmer, Dunford & Buchanan (2021)
Surprise	Loss of control	Dislike of change
Inertia	(being done to you, not involved)	Discomfort with uncertainty
Misunderstanding	Excess uncertainty	Perceived negative effect on interests
Emotional side-effects	(not knowing enough about what it	Attachment to established culture/ways
Lack of trust	will mean)	of doing things
Fear of failure	Surprise, surprise	Perceived breach of psychological
Personality conflicts	(suddenly springing change without	contract
Poor training	notice)	Lack of conviction that change is
Threat to job status/	Difference effect	needed
security	(require becoming conscious of/	Lack of clarity as to what is expected
Work group breakup	question familiar routines and	Belief that the specific change being
Fear of poor outcome	habits)	proposed is inappropriate
Faults of change	Loss of face	Belief that the timing is wrong
Uncertainty	(old ways were wrong)	Excessive change
	Concerns about future competence	Cumulative effect of other changes in
	(can I do it?)	one's life
	Ripple effects	Perceived clash with ethics
	(affects other projects, personal	Reaction to the experience of previous
	life etc.)	changes
	More work	Disagreement with the way change is
	Past resentments	being managed
	(anyone with a gripe)	
	Sometimes the threat is real	
	(winners and losers)	

Such lists are a useful 'sensitising device' in breaking down commonly recognized sources of opposition to change at the individual, group, and collective levels. Yet, they represent a somewhat 'scattergun' approach, listing multiple elements that may be significant and have different effects in varying contexts. Various attempts have, however, been made to group such lists of elements into more systematic categories.

Johns (1973) used Maslow's hierarchy of needs as a heuristic aid, attributing individual motivation to resist threats to:

- basic physiology,
- safety and security,
- belongingness,
- status and self-esteem, and
- self-actualization, self-realization and sense of achievement.

Dubrin and Ireland (1993) grouped sources of resistance as lying in:

- fear of poor personal outcomes (e.g., earn less money, personal inconvenience, more work),
- fear of the unknown, and
- fear of organizational problems (e.g., inappropriateness of the change, anxiety about 'fallout').

George and Jones (2012) separated individual, group and organizational level sources of resistance.
At the *individual* level, they attribute resistance to:

- uncertainty and insecurity,
- selective perception, and
- retention and habit.

At the *group* level, they emphasize:

- group norms (e.g., informal pressures), and
- group cohesiveness (e.g., priority of the group, groupthink and escalating commitment when challenged).

At the *organizational* level, key factors are seen to be:

- differences in functional orientation and goals,
- power and conflict,
- mechanistic, formalized, and centralized structures, and
- habituated organizational cultures.

Oreg (2006) attributed resistance to three main factors:

- personality (dispositional resistance to change),
- outcomes (negative effect on power and prestige, job security and intrinsic rewards), and
- the process of change (trust in management, social influences, available information).

Drawing on the content, context, process, and individual personality model commonly employed in the readiness literature, Shaul Oreg and Jacob Goldenberg (2015) provide one of the most systematic overviews. They attribute resistance to change to individual personality, process, content, and context (see Table 10.5).

Table 10.5   Factors influencing resistance to change

1. Individual Personality Factors	Reluctance to lose control; cognitive rigidity; lack of psychological resilience; intolerance towards the adjustment period; preference for low levels of stimulation and novelty; reluctance to give up old habits
2. Process Factors	Lack of information and communication, inadequate participation and involvement, low levels of management support, change management incompetence, and absence of interactional and procedural justice
3. Content Factors	Specific change elements that create: risk barriers (physical harm, economic costs, functional concerns, social ostracism); threats to status, expertise and job security concerns; effects on job conditions such as increased complexity and greater demands; and undermining of self-concept and identity. They could have included: challenging cognitive reframing.
4. Context Factors	Internal (lack of a supportive and trusting environment, absence of trust in colleagues and supervisors, low levels of organizational commitment, narrow and restrictive jobs, and perceptions of other people's likely resistance to change) and external (timing cf. competitors viewed as too early or too late, social factors such as level of cosmopolitanism, religiosity and population density, economic variables such as the wealth of the nation, and cultural issues such as those captured by Gert Hofstede (2001) (e.g., degree of power distance, uncertainty avoidance, collectivism v individualism, femininity v masculinity, and short-termism).

Source: Drawn from Oreg and Goldenberg (2015).

When considering the nature and sources of resistance, we must keep in mind five factors (see Table 10.6).

Table 10.6   Nature and sources of resistance

1. Forms and degrees of resistance exist.	Resistance lies on a continuum, from apathy at one end, characterized by indifference, foot-dragging and lack of motivation, to aggressive resistance involving overt blocking, campaigning, subversion and sabotage. In between, as Coetsee (1999) defines it, lie a range of forms of 'passive' resistance (negative perceptions and attitudes, voiced in communications and negotiations) and 'active' resistance (voicing strong opposing views, sceptical about dialogue, formal lobbying and direct action).
2. Resistance is multi-faceted and multi-levelled.	Similar to readiness, resistant attitudes are 'multi-faceted' or 'tripartite', including a combination of beliefs, feelings and intentions (Oreg, 2006; Piderit, 2000). Furthermore, even if there is a full intention to resist (or not), other factors also determine final behaviour (Burnes, 2015; Burnes & Cooke, 2013; Webb & Sheeran, 2006).
3. Resistance is often ambivalent.	Rather than being one-dimensionally 'resistant' or not, individuals, groups and organizations may be both 'for' or 'against'. What we believe, feel and intend may be in tension with each other and with actual behaviour. Moreover, there may be costs and gains from the change, different reactions to the change itself and the change agent, and different views of the value of the change for oneself and the collectivity (Ford et al., 2008; Larson & Tompkins, 2005; Oreg & Sverdlik, 2011; Piderit, 2000).
4. Resistance includes change agents.	Resistant attitudes are held by change initiators and agents as well as change recipients. In various significant and damaging ways the former may 'resist resistance' (Ford et al., 2008)
5. Resistance can be positive.	Resistant attitudes and behaviours may be valuable and positive as well as costly and negative (Courpasson et al., 2012; Dent & Goldberg, 1999; Oreg, 2018). They may be based on well-informed reasoning and commitments, generate useful ideas and stimulate a level of constructive debate and dialogue that improves understanding and commitment.

Consideration needs to be given, therefore, to:

- the specific forms of resistance considered,
- consistency and inconsistency between different elements and across different levels,
- resistance amongst initiators as well as recipients to change, and
- the degree to which forms of resistance should be seen as promoting or obstructing change.

Quadrant 4: Inertia, Institutionalization and Defensive Routines

The broader organizational features acting as obstacles or barriers to change are addressed in views of institutions as 'recalcitrant tools' (Selznick, 1948) embedded in organizational populations or institutional fields that create numerous obstacles and barriers to successful deliberate change (DiMaggio & Powell, 1983; Hannan & Freeman, 1984). In contrast to rational and strategic views of organizations as adapting effectively to their environments ('rational adaptation' theory), research on population ecology, institutional fields and defensive routines identifies how obstacles to achieving effective change can be embedded in organizations and their contexts.

Structural inertia

One of the most well known yet frequently misunderstood approaches are theories of the resistant effects of 'structural inertia' embedded in organizations and the population of organizations of which they are a part (Baum & Shipilov, 2012; Hannan et al., 2007; Hannan & Freeman, 1977, 1984; Hannan et al., 2003; Kelly & Amburgey, 1991). In contrast to superficial interpretations of this research, structural inertia does *not* refer to a condition of 'no change'. Nor does its presence mean that organizations are *unable to change in any way*. It highlights, however, the real costs incurred in making substantial change and the dangers of initiating change while ignoring or underestimating these costs and the risks involved. Michael Hannan and John Freeman even go so far as to suggest that these factors are so significant that organizations initiating substantial changes are less likely to survive than those who do not (Hannan & Freeman, 1984, p.159).

Identifying sources of structural inertia range from relatively common-sense lists of internal and external barriers to transforming what is or altering direction to more tightly defined and comprehensive explanations of central factors making significant change difficult. For example, Hannan and Freeman (1977) provided a helpful initial list of four (4) internal and four (4) external constraints (see Table 10.7).

Table 10.7   *Sources of structural inertia*

Internal Barriers	1. *Sunk costs*: investment in plant and equipment and personnel
	2. *Limited internal information*: received by decision-makers
	3. *Political constraints*: vested interests (specific short term costs cf. General long-term benefits)
	4. *Organizational history*: normative agreement on procedure, tasks and authority, provides principled justification of resisting, and inhibits consideration of options
External Barriers	1. *Legal and economic barriers* to entry in new areas
	2. *Constraints on external information*, turbulence, and limited internal specialists
	3. *Established legitimacy assets* are undermined, loss of institutional support
	4. The *problem of collective rationality*, satisfying *all* stakeholders

Source: Drawn from Hannan and Freeman (1977).

Hannan and Freeman (1984) embed this 'list' in a more systematic framework. They observed that for organizations to survive over time, they dedicate considerable time and resources to ensuring their structural methods for coordinating and delivering outcomes are maintained. Change undermines this investment and requires new forms. They emphasize three ways in which organizations reproduce themselves and consequently make significant change difficult to achieve (see Table 10.8).

Table 10.8   *Ways in which organizational reproduction makes change difficult*

1. Reliability and Accountability:	What makes organizations operate effectively is their ability to reliably deliver and legitimate the resources and rules they deploy as 'rational'. Unfortunately, significant change undermines this capability.
2. Institutionalization and Routines:	Reproduction is enhanced by (a) assumptions becoming taken-for-granted and then morally and politically sanctioned, and (b) possessing an established repertoire of standardized routines. Both are difficult to change, as change threatens the ability of the former to release thought and energy for other tasks, and the latter becomes embedded in sunk expertise, processes, and practices.
3. Hierarchy of Inertia:	Some parts of an organization are slower and more difficult to change. For example, changes in the technical system are easier to achieve than the managerial and institutional systems controlling it and governing the relationship with the broader society. The most inflexible and unresponsive institutional elements are, in hierarchical order, goals, forms of authority, core technology, and marketing strategy.

Source: Drawn from Hannan and Freeman (1977).

More recently, Hannan, Polos and Carroll (2002a, 2002b, 2003, 2007) have added a new framework for capturing the dynamics of structural inertia (see Table 10.9).

Table 10.9   Updated framework for capturing dynamics of structural inertia

1. Code Violations and Sanctions:	Significant change is seen as creating serious 'architectural' and 'cultural' code violations. The term 'code' is used to capture the established arrangements as both a 'genetic code' or blueprint for acting and a 'penal code' in which there are punishments for violating rules of conduct. When code violation imposes high costs, challenges official sanctions and cultural norms or results in strong punishment, then change is less likely to receive support
2. Centrality of Change and Costs:	Significant and complex changes impose greater: direct and indirect costs (when they involve changing relations between sub-units and have greater cultural significance); and opportunity costs (diverting time and resources from operations and routine strategic responses to environmental opportunities and threats)
3. Fog of Change and Risks:	The increasingly uncertain, problematic and time/resource consuming nature of significant change given: (a) the 'cascade of change' it creates, as code violations and adjustments spread unpredictably across sub-units; and (b) 'intricacy, opacity and asperity' as it is challenging to compute effects, sub-units are often inscrutable 'enclaves' and opposition is created when challenging shared and deeply held commitments.

Source: Drawn from Hannan et al. (2002a, 2002b, 2003, 2007).

These ideas and concepts can be used to address the forms and degrees of 'structural inertia' obstructing significant change. As a general approach, four contributions are essential to consider (see Table 10.10).

Table 10.10   *Key forms and degrees of structural inertia obstructing significant change*

1. Institutional Inertia:	The degree to which there are commitments and threats to *reliability and accountability, institutionalization and routines*, and *the architectural and cultural codes* they embody.
2. Process Challenges and Costs:	How central and 'deep' intended change is; how complex and uncertain the 'cascade of change', the 'intricacy' involved and the 'viscosity' (sluggishness) it creates; what level of 'sunk costs' have to be foregone; how substantial are the direct, indirect and opportunity costs of handling the challenges that result; and to what degree are these challenges underestimated.
3. Momentum:	The nature of structural inertia. It is not static but sluggish regarding the speed of change in the environment and involves a 'path dependent' tendency to respond in established and conservative ways (Hannan & Freeman, 1984; Kelly & Amburgey, 1991; Patalano, 2011). It is, consequently, helpful to ask to what degree an intended change is hindered by: 'repetitive momentum' (repeating past behaviour because of previous success or as a cognitive defence), 'positional momentum' (sunk costs and pervasive influence of past experience, skills, knowledge and cognition), and 'contextual momentum' (a structure or culture that is biased to conservatism) (Amburgey & Miner, 1992).
4. Liability of Newness:	Tendencies towards structural inertia also reside in the development of an organization over time and the centrality of its established character. Liability of newness: if the organization is relatively small and newly created, structural inertia may derive from a 'liability of newness' (stretched resources, lack of external legitimacy, compliance challenges, etc.). Liability of adolescence: if the organization is more established, the change may confront a 'liability of adolescence' (change depletes the initial 'buffer' of stock of goodwill, assets, and, initially, there are no new constituents or stakeholders). Liability of ageing: finally, if it is a mature and well-established organization, change encounters the 'liability of ageing' ('senescence' of old age reflecting outdated foundations, accumulation of out-of-date routines and structures, internal political frictions, blinkered frames etc.).

Institutionalization

Research on structural inertia is vital in sensitizing us to the costly nature of significant change and the risks of underestimating such costs. Contemporary 'neo-institutional' research adds to this notion by extending and deepening our understanding of the nature of institutionalization and the role it can play in obstructing change (Zucker, 1977, 1983, 1987).

In the early work on institutionalization, a distinction was made between the 'technical' and 'economic' side of an organization's nature (formal, structural, rational, and efficiency-oriented) and its 'institutional' character as, what Selznick (1948) termed, an 'adaptive social structure' (informal, unwritten, meaningful, and legitimacy oriented). Following on from the work of Zucker (1977), DiMaggio and Powell (1983), and Scott (2014), research on institutions has focused attention on three key dimensions or 'pillars' of this institutional character (see Table 10.1).

Table 10.11   Three pillars of institutionalization

1. The regulative pillar	Refers to the 'rules of the game' sanctioned by powerful actors within institutions and the field in which they are located. They are the formal and informal rules that regulate behaviour, and institutional regulators have the power to establish such rules, inspect conformity to them and manipulate sanctions to ensure compliance.
2. The normative pillar	Refers to the tacit and explicit values and norms that specify how things should be done. They define appropriate goals, legitimate means for pursuing these goals, the conduct required by those following the 'rules of the game', and the desirable and required identities of those involved.
3. The cultural-cognitive pillar	Involves shared perceptions of taken-for-granted reality. It includes individual mindsets and institutional schemata shaping interactions by defining 'what is going on here'. Interactions are shaped by shared views of the social world and our place in it. These views are often taken for granted as descriptions of reality itself, perceived as objective and external 'facts' of social life.

Source: Drawn from Scott (2014).

Each of these forms of institutionalization can obstruct institutional change. Early research on institutionalism focused on the normative dimension of institutionalization and its regulative forms within organizations. More recent 'neo-institutional' analysis has concentrated on cultural-cognitive dimensions, particularly taking-for-granted frames and reifying assumptions and relationships (Greenwood et al., 2020; Powell & DiMaggio, 1991). In recent years, however, with the rise of interest in institutional entrepreneurship, social movements, and institutional work in general, this tendency of neo-institutional research to highlight the key role of 'cool' cultural-cognitive factors has been countered by greater consideration of the role of 'hot' agency and politics in the regulative sphere (Fligstein & McAdam, 2012; Powell & DiMaggio, 1991, p.15).

These general features of institutionalization are commonly drawn on in research on the degree to which organizational change is restricted in scope and depth by established institutional 'archetypes' (Greenwood & Hinings,

1988), 'frames' (Cornelissen & Werner, 2014; Nadler et al., 1995; Werner & Cornelissen, 2014) or 'path dependent' forms of innovation (Pierson, 2000; Sydow et al., 2009). In each case, it is argued that 'deep structures' (Gersick, 1991) constrain innovation, thought and action within a set of institutional parameters. For example, Greenwood and Hinings (1988) argue that organizational change tends to proceed along restricted and predictable 'tracks' set by established institutional 'archetypes'. These archetypes form a coherent structural pattern supported by underpinning interpretative schemes that define the proper domain of the institution, its mode of organization and criteria of evaluation. Organizations often tend to 'adjust' to such archetypes rather than 'reorient' them for three reasons (see Table 10.12).

Table 10.12   *Why organizations adjust to archetypes not reorient them*

1. Recognition of Need:	Organizations do not recognize the need for reorientation as they are caught within existing means and structural forms. As a result, they selectively monitor their environment, and often miss or fail to detect critical information. Interpretations are made in terms of established solutions and existing behavioural routines.
2. Cost–Benefit Calculations:	Even if the need is recognized, it is subject to cost–benefit calculations, which often delay action until the threats are so great that the costs of disruption to existing patterns of thought and behaviour are overcome.
3. Vested Interests and Power:	Constituencies of interests and patterns of privilege within the archetype seek to sustain or advance their established claims on scarce and valued resources.

Source: Drawn from Greenwood and Hinings (1988).

Beyond the individual institution, pressures to conform within established patterns are exerted by the broader 'institutional field' within which they are embedded. Drawing on the pathbreaking work of DiMaggio and Powell (1983), key significance is commonly attributed to three mechanisms (see Table 10.13).

Table 10.13   Pressures to conform to the institutional field

1. Coercive:	Formal and informal pressures exerted on an organization by: other organizations on which they are dependent and cultural expectations in the society in which organizations function. This is felt as force, persuasion, or an invitation to collude with government mandates, laws, rules of the state, standard operating procedures required by HQs, service infrastructures etc., or more subtle expectations of how the organization should conform to the practices of others.
2. Mimetic:	Given the existence of uncertain technologies, goals and environmental changes and demands, this represents pressure upon an organization to model itself on others, copying the more legitimate and successful.
3. Normative:	This involves normative standards, principles, and injunctions about how to behave, most prominently represented in institutional fields by the role of professional associations in defining knowledge and standards and establishing and maintaining influential networks.

Source: Drawn from DiMaggio and Powell (1983).

However, explanations for how institutions become 'locked in' to narrow change trajectories by such phenomena vary considerably. These range from the very real costs of changing and increasing returns from the established arrangement to various self-reinforcing mechanisms (Pierson, 2000; Sydow et al., 2009). Unsurprisingly, specific explanations vary according to different views of institutional stability and change and path dependency factors.

This is partly due to the weight attributed to regulative, normative, and cognitive-cultural features of institutionalization. It also reflects different views of the institutional field within which organizations are embedded, as these can be considered as autonomous from other fields, based on common meanings and consensus, or riven by conflict, contradiction, and ambiguity, and exert a constraining effect on the organizations within it. Recent reconsiderations of institutional fields and path dependency have tended to reassert the presence of multiple and conflicting 'organizational logics' within a field (Fligstein & McAdam, 2012; Micelotta et al., 2017; Thornton & Ocasio, 2008; Thornton et al., 2012), rather than one uniform paradigm, frame, or archetype (Schneiberg, 2007).

As we saw in the earlier discussion of receptivity, capability and institutional dynamics, institutional theory has been variously used to investigate the dynamics of institutional change. As a useful aid to understanding obstructions to or restraints on change, however, the above contributions can be applied in:

- reviewing institutional constraints on change initiatives and proposals – through embedded and established regulative, normative, and cultural processes inside and outside the organization;
- considering whether the identified changes challenge established archetypes or restricted path-dependent models of innovation, shaped by these factors inside and outside the organization; and
- assessing the degree to which the institutionalization effects are influential and whether they are influenced by an embedded consensus within a relatively autonomous institutional field or the state of play of conflicting, contradictory and ambiguous 'logics' and in more permeable and overlapping institutional fields.

Defensive routines

As David Buchanan and Richard Badham (2020) outline in their chapter on 'Speaking Up', individuals and organizations are frequently caught up in 'cycles of denial' and 'spirals of silence' when faced with challenges and threats. As structural inertia and institutionalization analysis reveals, change initiatives frequently challenge established cognitive, normative, and political views and interests and are often obstructed or restrained by them.

When this challenge is perceived as psychologically or socially threatening:

- individuals are often 'over-protective' of embedded ideas and habits, and
- organizations establish 'defensive routines' to prevent the surfacing and discussion of challenging issues and questions ('making the undiscussable undiscussable').

When the challenges directly threaten individual and collective interests:

- individuals protect themselves through 'displays of conformity' and
- institutions protect themselves through an embedded 'mobilizations of bias' (this 'bias' ensures that acceptable issues and concerns are 'built in' to decision-making protocols and unacceptable ones are 'built out').

An assessment of organizational barriers to change must include whether such individual and collective thoughts, behaviours and patterns are present within the organization where the intended or identified change is to occur. For example, patterns of cover-up and pretence, rigidity, and embarrassment avoidance may be more or less extensive and deeply embedded in an organization's culture and structure and reinforced by structures of power.

As Zerubavel (2006) notes, such institutional barriers mean that requirements for change are often:

- just *not noticed,*
- more or less consciously *ignored,* or
- their *recognition is discouraged.*

Serious consideration and assessment of such factors is warranted (see
'How Defensive is your Organization', in Buchanan and Badham, 2020,
pp.217–221).

Bibliography

Abrahamson, E. (2004). Avoiding repetitive change syndrome. *MIT Sloan Management Review*, (Winter), 93–95.

A Bug's Life (Director: Lasseter, J.) (1998). Going around the leaf scene (2.00–2.30). https://www.youtube.com/watch?v=qTQJdGp4F34 (accessed 23 May 2022).

Accenture. (2018). *Transformation GPS: Take the guesswork out of your change journey* (2 May), 1–6. https://www.accenture-insights.be/en-us/articles/transformation-gps-take-the-guesswork-out-of-your-change-journey (accessed 23 May 2022).

AdaptKnowledge. (2016). *The Stacey matrix*. http://www.gptraining.net/training/communication_skills/consultation/equipoise/complexity/sstace.htm (accessed 12 June 2020).

Aedy, R. (2017). *The ironic manager*. ABC This Working Life. https://www.abc.net.au/radionational/programs/this-working-life/ironic-manager/8614352 (accessed 21 May 2022).

Aeschylus. (2012). *Prometheus bound*. Indianapolis: Hacket Publishing.

Aguirre, D., Von Post, R., & Alpern, M. (2013). *Culture's role in enabling organizational change*. Booz and Company, PWC. https://www.strategyand.pwc.com/gx/en/insights/2011-2014/cultures-role-organizational-change.html (accessed 21 May 2022).

Aiken, C. (now Dewar), & Keller, S. (2009). *The irrational side of change management*. McKinsey Quarterly, (2), 101–109. https://www.mckinsey.com/business-functions/people-and-organizational-performance/our-insights/the-irrational-side-of-change-management (accessed 21 May 2022).

Alvesson, M., & Einola, K. (2019). Warning for excessive positivity: Authentic leadership and other traps in leadership studies. *Leadership Quarterly*, *30*(4), 383–395.

Alvesson, M., & Gabriel, Y. (2016). Grandiosity in contemporary management and education. *Management Learning*, *47*(4), 464–473.

Alvesson, M., & Spicer, A. (2017). *The stupidity paradox*. London: Profile Books.

Amabile, T. M., & Kramer, S. J. (2011). The power of small wins. *Harvard Business Review*, *89*(5), 1–17.

Amburgey, T. L., & Miner, A. S. (1992). Strategic momentum: The effects of repetitive, positional, and contextual momentum on merger activity. *Strategic Management Journal*, *13*(5), 335–348.

Amelang, S., & Wehrmann, B. (2020). Dieselgate – a timeline of the car emissions fraud scandal in Germany. https://www.cleanenergywire.org/factsheets/dieselgate-timeline-car-emissions-fraud-scandal-germany (accessed 25 May 2020).

Amis, J. M., & Janz, B. D. (2020). Leading change in response to COVID-19. *The Journal of Applied Behavioral Science*, *56*(3), 272–278.

Ancona, D. (2005). Leadership in an age of uncertainty. *Center for Business Research Brief*, *6*(1), 1–3.

Ancona, D., Backman, E., & Isaacs, K. (2019). Nimble leadership: Walking the line between creativity and chaos. *Harvard Business Review*, *July–August*, 2–11.

Ancona, D., Malone, T. W., Orlikowski, W. J., & Senge, P. M. (2007). In praise of the incomplete leader. *Harvard Business Review, 85*(2), 92–100, 156.

Anderson, H. C. (1907). *Fairy tales from Hans Christian Andersen* (3rd edition). London: J.M. Dent & Co.

Anthony, P. (1994). *Managing culture.* Milton Keynes: Open University Press.

Appelbaum, S. H., Habashy, S., Malo, J. L., & Shafiq, H. (2012). Back to the future: Revisiting Kotter's 1996 change model. *Journal of Management Development, 31*(8), 764–782.

Argyris, C. (1986). Skilled incompetence. *Harvard Business Review, September–October,* 1–7.

Argyris, C. (1993). *Knowledge for action: A guide to overcoming barriers to organizational change.* San Francisco: Jossey-Bass.

Argyris, C. (2010). *Organizational traps: Leadership, culture, organizational design.* Oxford and New York: Oxford University Press.

Argyris, C., & Schon. D. A. (1978). *Organizational learning: A theory of action perspective.* Reading, MA: Addison-Wesley.

Ariely, D. (2008). *Are we in control of our own decisions?* US: Ted Talks. https://www .youtube.com/watch?v=9X68dm92HVI (accessed 21 May 2022).

Ariely, D. (2009). *Predictable irrationality: The hidden forces that shape our decisions.* New York: Harper Collins.

Armenakis, A. A., & Bedeian, A. G. (1999). Organizational change: A review of theory and research in the 1990s. *Journal of Management, 25*(3), 293–315.

Armenakis, A. A., Bernerth, J. B., Pitts, J. P., & Walker, H. J. (2007). Organizational change recipients' beliefs scale: Development of an assessment instrument. *The Journal of Applied Behavioral Science, 43*(4), 481–505.

Armenakis, A. A., & Harris, S. G. (2009). Reflections: Our journey in organizational change research and practice. *Journal of Change Management, 9*(2), 127–142.

Armenakis, A. A., Harris, S. G., & Mossholder, K. W. (1993). Creating readiness for organizational change. *Human Relations, 46*(6), 681–703.

Armstrong, S., & Fukami, C. (2009). *The Sage handbook of management learning, education and development.* London and Thousand Oaks: Sage.

Aronson, E. (1989). The rationalizing animal. In H. Leavitt, L. Pondy, & D. Boje (Eds.), *Readings in managerial psychology* (pp.134–144). Chicago: University of Chicago Press.

Aronson, E., & Aronson, J. (2018). *The social animal.* Worth: Macmillan.

Ashcraft, K., & Trethewey, A. (2004). Special Issue Synthesis. Developing tension: An agenda for applied research on the organization of irrationality. *Journal of Applied Communication Research, 32*(2), 171–181.

Avishai, B. (2020). The pandemic isn't a black swan but a portent of a more fragile global system. In *The New Yorker,* 21 April. https://www.newyorker.com/news/ daily-comment/the-pandemic-isnt-a-black-swan-but-a-portent-of-a-more-fragile -global-system (accessed 21 May 2022).

Bacharach, S. (2016). *The agenda mover: When your good idea is not enough.* New York: Cornell Publishing.

Badham, R. (1985). The dangers of technospeak. In Jura Books (Ed.), *1984 and social control* (pp.27–35). Sydney: Jura Books.

Badham, R. (1990). *Circuits of change: Report on workshops with sociotechnical change agents in Denmark, the Netherlands and the UK.* Wollongong: University of Wollongong Working Paper.

Badham, R. (2000). Human factors, power and politics. In W. Karwowski (Ed.), *International encyclopedia of ergonomics and human factors* (pp.94–97). New York: John Wiley.

Badham, R. (2003). 'Living in the blender of change': The carnival of control in a culture of culture. *Tamara*, *2*(4), 22–38.

Badham, R. (2004a). *Disciples, ratbags and ironists: In defense of irony* (unpublished seminar paper, University of Queensland Business School, 13 August).

Badham, R. (2004b). Leading change. Unpublished MGSM 866 Powerpoint Pack. Sydney: Macquarie Graduate School of Management.

Badham, R. (2006). Mudanças not removalists: Rethinking the management of organizational change. *Human Factors and Ergonomics in Manufacturing*, *16*(3), 229–245.

Badham, R. J. (2009). Technology and the transformation of work. In S. Ackroyd, R. Batt, P. Thompson, & P. S. Tolbert (Eds.), *The Oxford handbook of work and organization* (pp.115–137). Oxford: Oxford University Press.

Badham, R. (2011). *Experiencing Change: The Death Valley Roller-Coaster*, Leaflet 2 Location: Ironies of Organizational Change: Book Website @ https://reimaginingchange.com/.

Badham, R. (2013). *Short change: An introduction to managing change*. Suny: Business Perspectives.

Badham, R. (2016). *Theories of industrial society*. London and New York: Routledge.

Badham, R. (2017). Reflections on the paradoxes of modernity: A conversation with James March. In W. K. Smith, M. W. Lewis, P. Jarzabkowski, & A. Langley (Eds.), *The Oxford handbook of organizational paradox* (pp.277–295). Oxford: Oxford University Press.

Badham, R. (2022). James March and the poetry of leadership. *Journal of Management History*, *28*(1), 46–65.

Badham, R., Bridgman, T., & Cummings, S. (2020). The organization-as-iceberg as a counter-metaphor. In M. Maclean, S. Clegg, R. Suddaby, & C. Harvey (Eds.), *Historical organization studies: Theory, methods and applications* (pp.55–77). London and New York: Routledge.

Badham, R., Cançado, V., & Darief, T. (2015). An introduction to the 5M framework: Reframing change management education. *Brazilian Administration Review*, *12*(1), 22–38.

Badham, R., & Claydon, R. (2012). The dance of identification: Ambivalence, irony and organizational selfing. *Problems and Perspectives in Management*, *10*(4), 80–97.

Badham, R., Claydon, R., & Down, S. (2012a). The ambivalence paradox in cultural change. In D. Boje, B. Burnes, & J. Hassard (Eds.), *Routledge companion on organizational change* (pp.404–424). London and New York: Routledge.

Badham, R., & Hafermalz, E. (2019). Using parody in transforming a health care organization in Australia. In E. Antonacopoulou, & S. Taylor (Eds.), *Sensuous learning for practical judgment in professional practice: Volume 2: Arts-based interventions* (pp.109–135). London: Palgrave.

Badham, R., & King, E. (2021). Mindfulness at work: A critical re-view. *Organization*, *28*(4), 531–554.

Badham, R., & McLoughlin, I. (2005). Ambivalence and engagement: Irony and cultural change in late modern organizations. *International Journal of Knowledge, Culture and Change Management in Organisations*, *5*, 1–15.

Badham, R., Mead, A., & Antonacopoulou, E. (2012b). Performing change: A dramaturgical approach to the practice of managing change. In D. Boje, B. Burnes,
& J. Hassard (Eds.), *Routledge companion to organizational change* (Vol. 1,
pp.187–205). London and New York: Routledge.

Badham, R., & Rhodes, C. (2018). Mis-leading ethics: Towards a bearable lightness
of being. *LSE Business Review*. 6 June. https://blogs.lse.ac.uk/businessreview/2018/
06/06/misleading-ethics-towards-a-bearable-lightness-of-being/ (accessed 5 January
2022).

Bain. (2018). *Results delivery*. http://www.bain.com/consulting-services/results
-delivery/index.aspx (accessed 21 May 2022).

Bakken, T., & Hernes, T. (2006). Organizing is both a verb and a noun: Weick meets
Whitehead. *Organization Studies*, *27*(11), 1599–1616.

Bandits (Director: Levinson, B.) (2001). Bandits 2001 vs RED 2010. 20 October 2016.
https://www.youtube.com/watch?v=VrSscuReTQA (9.00–12.30) (accessed 21 May
2022).

Barends, E., Janssen, B., ten Have, W., & ten Have, S. (2014). Effects of change interventions: What kind of evidence do we really have? *Journal of Applied Behavioral
Science*, *50*(1), 5–27.

Barnes, J. (1990). *Flauberts parrot*. New York: Vintage.

Barrett, F. J. (2003). Coda: Creativity and improvisation in jazz and organizations:
Implications for organizational learning. *Organization Science*, *9*(5), 605–622.

Barrett, F. J. (2012a). *If Miles Davis taught your office to improvise*. https://www
.fastcompany.com/3000340/if-miles-davis-taught-your-office-improvise (accessed
21 May 2022).

Barrett, F. J. (2012b). *Yes to the mess: Surprising leadership lessons from jazz*. Boston:
Harvard Business Review Press.

Barton, M., & Sutcliffe, K. (2017). Contextualized engagement as resilience-in-action:
A study of expedition racing. *Academy of Management Conference* (Vol.
Sub-Theme). Atlanta Georgia. http://hub.jhu.edu/2017/08/08/backwoods-resilience
-business-organizational-theory (accessed 2 August 2022).

Bartunek, J., Gordon, J., & Weathersby, R. (1983). Developing complicated understanding in administrators. *Academy of Management Review*, 8(2), 273–284.

Bartunek, J. M., & Jones, E. B. (2017). How organizational transformation has been
continuously changing and not changing. *Research in Organizational Change and
Development*, *25*, 143–169.

Bartunek, J. M., & Moch, M. K. (1987). First-order, second-order, and third-order
change and organization development interventions: A cognitive approach. *The
Journal of Applied Behavioral Science*, *23*(4), 483–500.

Bass, B., & Riggio, R. (2006). *Transforming leadership*. Mahwah, NJ: Lawrence
Erlbaum Associates.

Battilana, J., Leca, B., & Boxenbaum, E. (2009). How actors change institutions:
Towards a theory of institutional entrepreneurship. *Academy of Management
Annals*, *3*(1), 65–107.

Baum, J. A., & Shipilov, A. V. (2012). Ecological approaches to organizations. In
Clegg, S., & Hardy, C. (Eds.), *The Sage handbook of organization studies* (2nd
edition, pp.55–110). London: Sage.

Bauman, Z. (1998). *Modernity and ambivalence*. Cambridge: Polity Press.

Bazerman, M., & Watkins, M. (2004). *Predictable surprises: The disasters you should
have seen coming and how to prevent them*. Boston: Harvard Business School Press.

Beavan, C. (2013). *Who's afraid of Machiavelli?* BBC (YouTube). https://www .youtube.com/watch?v=wsMs-DuGy1o (accessed 23 May 2022).

Beckhard, R., & Harris, R. (1985). *Organizational transitions: Managing complex change*. Reading, MA: Addison-Wesley.

Beech, N., Burns, H., De Caestecker, L., MacIntosh, R., & MacLean, D. (2004). Paradox as invitation to act in problematic change situations. *Human Relations*, *57*(10), 1313–1332.

Beer, M., Eisenstat, R., & Foote, N. (2009). *High commitment, high performance*. San Francisco: Jossey-Bass.

Beer, M., & Nohria, N. (Eds.) (2000a). *Breaking the code of change*. Boston: Harvard Business Review Press.

Beer, M., & Nohria, N. (2000b). Cracking the code of change. *Harvard Business Review*, *78*(3), 133–141.

Belot, M., & James, J. (2011). Healthy school meals and educational outcomes. *Journal of Health Economics*, *30*(3), 489–504.

Belsky, S. (2018). *The messy middle: Finding your way through the hardest and most crucial part of any bold venture*. Harmondsworth: Penguin.

Bennett, J. (2009). Cultivating intercultural competence: A process perspective. In D. Deardorff (Ed.), *The Sage handbook of intercultural competence* (pp.121–141). Thousand Oaks and London: Sage.

Bennis, W. (1966). *Changing organisations*. New York: McGraw Hill.

Bennis, W., & Nanus, B. (1985). *Leaders: The strategies for taking charge*. New York: Harper & Row.

Bensoussan, B. (2021). *Stupidology*. Reproduced by Marie-Luce, 6 October 2021. https://ibis.co.za/ci/index.php/news-footer/158-stupidology-by-babette-bensoussan (accessed 1 August 2022).

Berger, P. (1986). *Invitation to sociology: A humanistic perspective*. Harmondsworth: Penguin.

Berlant, L. (2011). *Cruel optimism*. Durham, NC: Duke University Press.

Berlin, I. (1969). *Four essays on liberty*. Oxford and New York: Oxford University Press.

Berti, M., Simpson, A., Cunha, M., & Clegg, S. (2021). *Elgar introduction to organizational paradox theory*. Cheltenham, UK and Northampton, MA, USA: Edward Elgar Publishing.

Bhattacharjee, D., Gilson, K., & Yeon, H. (2016). Putting behavioral psychology to work to improve the customer experience. McKinsey, (March). https:// www.mckinsey.com/business-functions/marketing-and-sales/our-insights/putting -behavioral-psychology-to-work-to-improve-the-customer-experience (accessed 22 May 2022).

Blair, T. (2010). *A journey: My political life*. New York: Vintage.

Bohemian Rhapsody (Director: Singer, B.) (2018). Queen meeting with Ray Foster scene (43.00–46.50). https://www.youtube.com/watch?v=C1XOQTcW5f4 (accessed 23 May 2022).

Boin, A., & Van Eeten, M. J. G. (2013). The resilient organization : A critical appraisal. *Public Management Review*, *15*(3), 429–445.

Bolman, L. G., & Deal, T. E. (2017). *Reframing organizations*. San Francisco: Jossey-Bass.

Bookstein, F. L. (2015). *The map is not the territory*. https://fs.blog/2015/11/map-and -territory/ (accessed 22 May 2022).

Boorstin, D. (1983). *The discoverers: A history of man's search to know his world and himself.* New York: Random House.

Boorstin, D. J. (1992). *The creators: A history of heroes of the imagination.* New York: Random House.

Boorstin, D. (1998). *The seekers: The story of man's continuing quest to understand his world.* New York: Random House.

Borgen (2010). TV, Series 1 Episode 1, 'Decency in the Middle' (58.30) Election Debate: 'Vote for a New Denmark' (46.10–48.25). https://www.youtube.com/watch?v=Y3eLn3JHcjw&list=PLVIshZFGP-z2KQ1sP9q7R6QqQOHzQJyE8 (accessed 3 January 2022).

Bouckenooghe, D. (2010). Positioning change recipients' attitudes toward change in the organizational change literature. *The Journal of Applied Behavioral Science*, *46*(4), 500–553.

Bouckenooghe, D., Devos, G., & Van den Broeck, H. (2009). Organizational change questionnaire – climate of change, processes, and readiness: Development of a new instrument. *The Journal of Psychology*, *143*(6), 559–599.

Bowden, D. E., & Smits, S. J. (2011). Understanding the multifaceted nature of change in the healthcare system. In J. Wolf, H. Hanson, & M. Moir (Eds.), *Organization development in health care: High impact practices for a complex and changing environment* (pp.3–23). New York: Informati.

Bower, J., & Christensen, C. M. (1995). Disruptive technologies : Catching the wave. *Harvard Business Review, January–February*, 1–20.

Boyatzis, R., & McKee, A. (2003). *Resonant leadership.* Boston: Harvard Business School Publishing.

Brassett, J. (2009). British irony, global justice: A pragmatic reading of Chris Brown, Banksy and Ricky Gervais. *Review of International Studies*, *35*(1), 219–245.

Braveheart (Director: Gibson, M.) (1995). Braveheart leadership speech (26 January 2018). https://www.youtube.com/watch?v=hyqoC3wHMwY (3.53) (accessed 23 May 2022).

Bridges, W., & Bridges, S. ([1991] 2016). *Managing transitions* (4th edition). New York: Hatchett.

Bridges, W., & Mitchell, S. (2000). Leading transition: A new model for change. *Leader to Leader*, 1–8. https://doi.org/10.1002/1531-5355(200021)2000:16<1::AID-LTL1>3.0.CO;2-K (accessed 23 May 2022).

Briner, W., Geddes, M., & Hastings, C. (1990). *Project leadership.* New York: Van Nostran Reinhold.

Brockling, U. (2016). *The entrepreneurial self: Fabricating a new type of subject.* London and New York: Sage.

Bromley, P., & Powell, W. W. (2012). From smoke and mirrors to walking the talk: Decoupling in the contemporary world. *Academy of Management Annals*, *6*(1), 483–530.

Brown, A. (1998). *Organizational culture.* London and New York: Prentice Hall Financial Times Management.

Brown, A.D., Gabriel, Y., & Gherardi, S. (2009). Storytelling and change: An unfolding story. *Organization*, *16*(3), 323–333.

Brown, M., & Hosking, D. (1986). Distributed leadership and skilled performance as successful organization in social movements. *Human Relations*, *39*(1), 65–79.

Brown, S., & Eisenhardt, K. (1998). *Competing on the edge: Strategy as structured chaos.* Boston: Harvard Business School Press.

Bruch, H., & Vogel, B. (2011). *Fully charged: How great leaders boost their organization's energy and ignite high performance*. Boston: Harvard Business Review Press.

Brunsson, N. (2002). *The organization of hypocrisy*. Copenhagen: Copenhagen Business School Press.

Brunsson, N. (2009). *Reform as routine: Organizational change and stability in the modern world*. Oxford and New York: Oxford University Press.

Buchanan, D. (2015). I couldn't disagree more: Eight things about organizational change that we know for sure, but which are probably wrong. In B. Burnes, & J. Randall (Eds.), *Perspectives on change: What academics, consultants and managers really think about change* (pp.5–22). London and New York: Routledge.

Buchanan, D., & Badham, R. (2008). *Power, politics and organizational change*. London and New York: Sage.

Buchanan, D., & Badham, R. (2020). *Power, politics and organizational change* (3rd edition). London: Sage.

Buchanan, D., & Boddy, D. (1992). *The expertise of the change agent*. New York: Prentice Hall.

Buckley, F., & Monks, K. (2004). Developing meta-qualities: Outcomes and implications for HR roles. *HRMJ, 14*(4), 41–56.

Buono, A. F., & Kerber, K. W. (2010). Creating a sustainable approach to change: Building organizational change capacity. *SAM Advanced Management Journal, 75*(2), 4–21.

Buono, A. F., & Subbiah, K. (2014). Internal consultants as change agents: Roles, responsibilities, and organizational change capacity. *Organization Development Journal, 32*(2), 35–53.

Burnes, B. (1996). No such thing as … a 'one best way' to manage organizational change. *Management Decision, 34*(10), 11–18.

Burnes, B. (2004a). Kurt Lewin and complexity theories: Back to the future? *Journal of Change Management, 4*(4), 309–325.

Burnes, B. (2004b). Kurt Lewin and the planned approach to change: A re-appraisal. *Journal of Management Studies, 41*(6), 977–1002.

Burnes, B. (2015). Understanding resistance to change – building on Coch and French. *Journal of Change Management, 15*(2), 92–116.

Burnes, B. (2017). *Managing change*. Harlow: Pearson Education.

Burnes, B., & Bargal, D. (2017). Kurt Lewin: 70 years on. *Journal of Change Management, 17*(2), 91–100.

Burnes, B., & Cooke, B. (2012). The past, present and future of organization development: Taking the long view. *Human Relations, 65*(11), 1395–1429.

Burnes, B., & Cooke, B. (2013). Kurt Lewin's field theory: A review and re-evaluation. *International Journal of Management Reviews, 15*, 408–425.

Burns, T. (1961). Micropolitics: Mechanisms of institutional change. *Administrative Science Quarterly, 6*(3), 257–281.

Bushe, G. R., & Marshak, R. J. (2009). Revisioning organization development. *The Journal of Applied Behavioral Science, 45*(3), 348–368.

Bushe, G., & Marshak, R. (2015). *Dialogic organizational development: The theory and practice of transformational change*. Oakland: Berrett-Koehler.

Business Balls. (2019). *Nudge theory: A complete overview*. https://www.businessballs.com/improving-workplace-performance/nudge-theory/ (accessed 6 October 2019).

Butler, M. J. (2003). Managing from the inside out: drawing on 'receptivity'to explain variation in strategy implementation. *British Journal of Management, 14*, 47–60.

Butler, M. (2012). Establishing organizational receptivity for change. In C. Rathbone (Ed.), *Ready for change: Through turbulence to reformation and transformation* (pp.29–52). Basingstoke: Palgrave Macmillan.

By, R.T. (2007). Ready or not.... *Journal of Change Management, 7*(1), 3–11.

By, R. T., Burnes, B., & Oswick, C. (2011). Change management: The road ahead. *Journal of Change Management, 11*(1), 1–6.

Byrne, E. (2006). Ed Byrne slates Alanis Morrissette. 12 September 2006. https://www.youtube.com/watch?v=nT1TVSTkAXg (accessed 22 July 2022).

Caldwell, R. (2003). Models of change agency: A fourfold classification. *British Journal of Management, 14*(2), 131–142.

Caldwell, R. (2006). *Agency and change: Rethinking change agency in organisations.* London: Routledge.

Cameron, K. S. (1986). Effectiveness as paradox: Consensus and conflict in conceptions of organizational effectiveness. *Management Science, 32*(5), 539–553.

Cameron, K. S. (2008). Paradox in positive organizational change. *Journal of Applied Behavioral Science, 44*(1), 7–24.

Cameron, K., Dutton, J., & Quinn, R. (2003). *Positive organizational scholarship: Foundations of a new discipline.* Oakland: Berrett-Koehler.

Cameron, K., & McNaughtan, J. (2014). Positive organizational change. *Journal of Applied Behavioral Science, 50*(4), 445–462.

Carlson, C. A. (1986). Gandhi and the comic frame: 'Ad Bellum purificandum'. *Quarterly Journal of Speech, 72*(4), 446–455.

Carlson, R. V. (1996). *Reframing and reform: Perspectives on organization, leadership, and school change.* White Plains: Longman.

Carroll, L. (2009). *Alice's adventures in wonderland and through the looking glass.* Oxford and New York: Oxford University Press.

CBS. (2017). *Faster, higher, farther. delves deep into the Volkswagen emissions scandal.* https://www.cbsnews.com/news/volkswagen-emissions-scandal-faster-higher-farther-author-jack-ewing/ (accessed 12 June 2020).

Chia, R. (2014). Reflections: In praise of silent transformation – allowing change through 'letting happen'. *Journal of Change Management, 14*(1), 8–27.

Chia, R., & Langley, A. (2004). The first organization studies summer workshop: Theorizing process in organizational research (call for papers). *Organization Studies, 25*(8), p.1486.

Chicken Run (Directors: Lord, P., & Park, N.) (2000). A better place scene (16.37–18.45). https://www.youtube.com/watch?v=GKjA8F4ruvg (accessed 21 May 2022).

Child, J. (1972). Organizational structure, environment and performance: The role of strategic choice. *Sociology, 6*(1), 1–22.

Child, J. (1997). Strategic choice in the analysis of action, structure, organizations and environment: Retrospect and prospect. *Organization Studies, 18*(1), 43–76.

Child, J. (2015). *Organization: Contemporary principles and practice.* Chichester: Wiley.

Christensen, L. T., Morsing, M., & Thyssen, O. (2013). CSR as aspirational talk. *Organization, 20*(3), 372–393.

Clark, K., & Collins, C. J. (2002). Strategic decision-making in high velocity environments: A theory revisited and a test. In M. Hitt, R. Amit, C. Lucrier, & R. Nixon (Eds.), *Creating value: Winners in the new business environment* (pp.213–239). Oxford: Blackwell.

Clark, T. (2007). *Starbucked: A double tall tale of caffeine, commerce, and culture.* New York and London: Little Brown and Company.

Clarke, J. (and others) (1996). Faculty receptivity/resistance to change, personal and organizational efficacy, decision deprivation and effectiveness in Research 1 Universities, ASHE Annual Meeting Paper ED 402846 HE 029763, November 39p Paper presented at the Annual Meeting of the Association for the Study of Higher Education (21st, Memphis) 31 October–3 November.

Claydon, R. (2013). *Towards a complex third-way irony*. Unpublished PhD, Macquarie University.

Clegg, C. W. (1993). Social systems that marginalize the psychological and organizational aspects of information technology. *Behaviour and Information Technology*, *12*(5), 261–266.

Clegg, S. (1989). *Frameworks of power*. London and Thousand Oaks: Sage.

Clegg, S. R., Kornberger, M., Carter, C., & Rhodes, C. (2006). For management? *Management Learning*, *37*(1), 7–27.

Clemmer, J. (1995). *Pathways to performance*. Toronto: Macmillan.

Coch, L., & French, J. (1948). Overcoming resistance to change. *Human Relations*, *1*(1), 512–532.

Coetsee, L. (1999). From resistance to commitment. *Public Administration Quarterly*, *23*(2), 204–222.

Cohen, M., & March, J. (1986). *Leadership and ambiguity*. Boston: Harvard Business Review Press.

Cole, M., & Higgins, J. (2022). *Leadership unravelled: The faulty thinking behind modern management*. London and New York: Routledge.

Colebrook, C. (2004). *Irony*. London and New York: Routledge.

Collins, D. (1998). *Organizational change: Sociological perspectives*. London and New York: Routledge.

Collinson, D., Smolović Jones, O., & Grint, K. (2018). 'No more heroes': Critical perspectives on leadership romanticism. *Organization Studies*, *39*(11), 1625–1647.

Colville, I., Pye, A., & Brown, A. D. (2016). Sensemaking processes and Weickarious learning. *Management Learning*, *47*(1), 3–13.

Commoner, B. ([1971] 2020). *The closing circle: nature, man and technology*. New York: Dover.

Connery, S. (2009). *Sir Sean Connery accepts AFI life achievement award in 2006* (p.12 February). https://www.youtube.com/watch?v=y4Z1BXALdwI (accessed 5 January 2022).

Cook, G. et al. (2008). *The Discourse of the School Dinners Debate: Full Research Report* ESRC End of Award Report, RES-000-22-1947. Swindon: ESRC. https://kipdf.com/report-the-discourse-of-the-school-dinners-debate-1-background_5ae8 ef557f8b9aba7d8b460e.html (accessed 25 May 2022).

Cook, R. (2008). *Has Jamie's Ministry of Food worked in Rotherham*. Saturday 15 November, *The Guardian*. https://www.theguardian.com/lifeandstyle/2008/nov/15/jamie-oliver-ministry-food-rotherham (accessed 25 May 2022).

Cooley, C. H. ([1902] 2009). *Human nature and the social order*. New York: Cornell University Press.

Cooperrider, D. L., & Whitney, D. (2005). *Appreciative inquiry:Key themes and dimensions in AI research*. San Francisco: Berrett-Koehler.

Cornelissen, J. P., & Werner, M. D. (2014). Putting framing in perspective: A review of framing and frame analysis across the management and organizational literature. *Academy of Management Annals*, *8*(1), 181–235.

Courpasson, D., Clegg, F., & Clegg, S. (2012). Resisters at work: Generating productive resistance in the workplace. *Organization Science*, *23*(3), 801–819.

Coutu, D. L. (2002). How resilience works. *Harvard Business Review, May*, 1–8.

Coutu, D. L. (2003). Sense and reliability: A conversation with celebrated psychologist Karl E. Weick. *Harvard Business Review, April*, 84–90.

Coutu, D. (2006). Ideas as art: A conversation with James G. March. *Harvard Business Review, October*, 83–89.

Covey, S. R. (2020). *The seven habits of highly effective people* (Anniversary edition). New York: Simon & Schuster.

Crainer, S. (1997). *The Tom Peters phenomenon: Corporate man to corporate skunk.* New York: Capstone.

Cronshaw, S. F., & McCulloch, A. (2008). Reinstating the Lewinian vision: From force field analysis to organizational field assessment. *Organization Development Journal, 26*(4), 89–103.

Cummings, S., Bridgman, T., & Brown, K. G. (2016). Unfreezing change as three steps: Rethinking Kurt Lewin's legacy for change management. *Human Relations, 69*(1), 33–60.

Cunha, M. P. e., Clegg, S., & Rego, A. (2013). Lessons for leaders: Positive organization studies meets Niccolò Machiavelli. *Leadership, 9*(4), 450–465.

Cunha, M.P. e., Clegg, S., Rego, A., & Berti, M. (2021). *Paradoxes of power and leadership.* London and New York: Routledge.

Cunha, M. P. e., & Putnam, L. L. (2019). Paradox theory and the paradox of success. *Strategic Organization, 17*(1), 95–106.

Cunliffe, A. L. (2001). Managers as practical authors: Reconstructing our understanding of management practice. *Journal of Management Studies, 38*(3), 351–371.

Cunliffe, A. L. (2002). Social poetics as management inquiry: A dialogical approach. *Journal of Management Inquiry, 11*(2), 128–146.

Cunliffe, A., & Coupland, C. (2011). From hero to villain to hero: Making experience sensible through embodied narrative sensemaking. *Human Relations, 65*(1), 63–88.

Cunningham, C. E., Woodward, C. A., Shannon, H. S., Macintosh, J., Lendrum, B., Rosenbloom, D., & Brown, J. (2002). Readiness for organizational change: A longitudinal study of workplace, psychological and behavioural correlates. *Journal of Occupational and Organizational Psychology, 75*(4), 377–392.

Cyert, R., & March, J. (1963). *A behavioral theory of the firm.* Englewood Cliffs, NJ: Prentice Hall.

Czarniawska, B. (2017). The fate of counter-narratives: In fiction and in actual organizations. In S. Frandsen, T. Kuhn, & M. W. Lundholdt (Eds.), *Counter-narratives and organization* (pp.195–208). New York and London: Routledge.

Czarniawska, B., & Joerges, B. (1996). Travels of ideas. In B. Czarniawska, & G. Sevon (Eds.), *Translating organizational change* (pp.13–47). Berlin and New York: De Gruyter.

Davis, L. P., & Museus, S. D. (2019). What is deficit thinking? An analysis of conceptualizations of deficit thinking and implications for scholarly research. *NCID Currents, 1*(1), 117–130. http://dx.doi.org/10.3998/ currents.17387731.0001.110 (accessed 5 January 2022).

Dawson, P. (1994). *Organizational change.* London and New York: Sage.

Dawson, P. (2019). *Reshaping change: A processual perspective* (2nd edition). London: Routledge.

De Keyser, B., Guiette, A., & Vandenbempt, K. (2021). On the dynamics of failure in organizational change: A dialectical perspective. *Human Relations, 74*(2), 234–257.

Dellinger, S. (1996). *Communicating beyond our differences: Introducing the psycho-geometrics system.* New York: Jade Link.

Demers, C. (2007). *Organizational change theories: A synthesis*. London: Sage.

Deming, W. E. (2000). *Out of the crisis*. Boston: MIT Press.

Denison, D. R., Hooijberg, R., & Quinn, R. E. (1995). Paradox and performance: Toward a theory of behavioral complexity in managerial leadership. *Organization Science, 6*(5), 524–540.

Denning, S. (2011). *The leaders guide to storytelling*. San Francisco: Jossey-Bass.

Dent, E. B., & Goldberg, S. G. (1999). Challenging resistance to change. *Journal of Applied Behavioral Science, 35*(1), 25–41.

Dessen, S. (2009). *Along for the ride*. New York: Viking.

De Ven, A. van, & Johnson, P. E. (2006). Knowledge for theory and practice. *Academy of Management Review, 31*(4), 802–821.

Dhingra, N., Emmett, J., Samo, A., & Schaninger, B. (2020). Igniting individual purpose in times of crisis. *McKinsey Quarterly, 25*(7), 1–11.

Dick, P. (2015). From rational myth to self-fulfilling prophecy? Understanding the persistence of means–ends decoupling as a consequence of the latent functions of policy enactment. *Organization Studies, 36*(7), 897–924.

DiMaggio, P., & Powell, W. (1983). The iron cage revisited: Institutional isomorphism and collective rationality in organizational fields. *American Sociological Review, 48*, 147–160.

Dixon, M., Lee, S., & Ghaye, T. (2016). Strengths-based reflective practices for the management of change: Applications from sport and positive psychology. *Journal of Change Management, 16*(2), 142–157.

Donaldson, L. (1998). *Performance-driven organizational change*. London: Sage.

Dopson, S. (1997). *Managing ambiguity and change* (7th edition). London: Palgrave Macmillan.

Douglas, M. (1969). The social control of cognition: Some factors in joke perception. *Man, 3*(3), 361–376.

Du Gay, P. (2000). *In praise of bureaucracy: Weber, organization, ethics*. London: Sage.

Du Gay, P., & Vikkelso, S. (2017). *For formal organization*. Oxford: Oxford University Press.

Dubrin, A., & Ireland, R. (1993). *Management and organization* (2nd edition). Nashville: South- Western Publishing.

Duckworth, A. (2016). *Grit: The power of passion and perseverence*. New York and London: Scribner.

Dunn, S. (1990). Root metaphor in the old and new industrial relations. *British Journal of Industrial Relations, 28*(1), 1–31.

Dunoon, D., & Langer, E. (2011). Mindfulness and leadership: Opening up to possibilities. *Integral Leadership Review, 11*(5), 1–15.

Dunphy, D. (2000). Embracing paradox: Top-down versus participative management of organizational change: A commentary on Conger and Bennis. In M. Beer, & N. Nohria (Eds.), *Breaking the code of change* (pp.123–136). Boston: Harvard Business Review Press.

Dunphy, D. C., & Stace, D. A. (1988). Transformational and coercive strategies for planned organizational change: Beyond the O.D. model. *Organization Studies, 9*(3), 317–334.

Dweck, C. (2014). The power of believing that you can improve. Ted@Norrkoping. https://www.ted.com/talks/carol_dweck_the_power_of_believing_that_you_can _improve (Accessed 10 January 2023).

Dweck, C. (2017). *Mindset: Changing the way you think to fulfil your potential* (6th edition). New York: Robinson.

Easterby-Smith, M., & Lyles, M. A. (Eds.) (2011). *Handbook of organizational learning and knowledge management* (pp.453–476) (2nd edition). Oxford: Blackwell.

Economist Intelligence Unit. (2008). *A change for the better: Steps for successful business transformation.* www.eiu.com/report_dl.asp?mode=fi&fi=1003398485.PDF (accessed 23 May 2022).

Edgley, C. (Ed.) (2013). *The drama of social life: A dramaturgical handbook.* Farnham: Ashgate.

Edmondson, A. (2011). Strategies for learning from failure. *Harvard Business Review,* *89*(4), 48–55.

Edmondson, A. C. (2018). *The fearless organization.* Hoboken, NJ: John Wiley.

Eisenberg, E. (1984). Ambiguity as strategy in organizational communication. *Communication Monographs, 51*(3), 227–242.

Eisenberg, E. (2006). *Strategic ambiguities. Essays on communication, organization and identity.* London and Thousand Oaks: Sage.

Elrod, P. D., & Tippett, D. D. (2002). The 'death valley' of change. *Journal of Organizational Change Management, 15*(3), 273–291.

Ely, R. J., Ibarra, H., & Kolb, D. M. (2011). Taking gender into account: Theory and design for women's leadership development programs. *Academy of Management Learning and Education, 10*(3), 474–493.

Emery, F., & Trist, E. (1965). The causal texture of organization environments. *Human Relations, 18*(1), 21–32.

Etzioni, A. (1975). *A comparative analysis of complex organizations: On power, involvement and their correlates.* New York: Free Press.

Ewing, J. (2017). *Faster, higher, farther: The inside story of the Volkswagen scandal.* New York: Norton.

Ewing, J. (2019). *Dieselgate: Inside the air pollution scandal of the century.* https://medium.com/dyson-on/dieselgate-inside-the-air-pollution-scandal-of-the-century-2e462f430025 (accessed 12 June 2020).

Faeste, L., Reeves, M., & Whitaker, K. (2021). The science of organizational change. *BCG Henderson Institute Newletter,* 2 May, 1–16. https://www.bcg.com/publications/2019/science-organizational-change (accessed 24 May 2022).

Fairhurst, G. T., Smith, W. K., Banghart, S. G., Lewis, M. W., Putnam, L., Raisch, S., & Schad, J. (2016). Diverging and converging: Integrative insights on a paradox meta-perspective. *The Academy of Management Annals, 10*(1), 173–182.

Farnham Street (2015). The map is not the territory. Https://fs.blog/2015/11/map-and-territory (accessed 22 January 2020).

Feed Me Better Campaign (2004). *Jamie's School Dinners.* https://en.wikipedia.org/wiki/Jamie%27s_School_Dinners (accessed 20 January 2023).

Feldman, M. S., & Orlikowski, W. J. (2011). Theorizing practice and practicing theory. *Organization Science, 22*(5), 1240–1253.

Fellner, K. (2008). *Wrestling with Starbucks: Conscience, capital, cappuccino.* New Brunswick and London: Rutgers University Press.

Ferguson, K. (1993). *The man question: Visions of subjectivity in feminist theory.* San Francisco: University of California Press.

Ferguson, K. (2003). *The man question.* Berkeley: University of California Press.

Fernandez, J., & Huber, M. (Eds.) (2001). *Irony in action: Anthropology, practice, and the moral imagination.* Chicago: University of Chicago Press.

Fineman, S., Gabriel, Y., & Sims, D. (2010). *Organizations and organising* (4th edition). London: Sage.

Fischer, B. (2016). The leadership advantage of Bezos, Musk, Ma and Zhang: An explorer's mindset. *Forbes*, 1–6. https://www.forbes.com/sites/billfischer/2016/03/26/the-leadership-advantage-of-bezos-musk-ma-and-zhang-an-explorers-mindset/#41bc00537046 (accessed 23 May 2022).

Fischer, B., Lago, U., & Liu, F. (2013). *Reinventing giants: How Chinese global competitor Haier has changed the way big companies transform.* San Francisco: Jossey-Bass.

Flash (2014-present). *Flash – 4 rules – throw away the plan* (20 May 2017). https://www.youtube.com/watch?v=l3FcbZXn4jM (accessed 24 May 2022).

Fleming, P. (2013). Resisting work: The corporatization of life and its discontents. *Journal of Chemical Information and Modeling* (Vol. 53). Philadelphia: Temple University Press.

Fleming, P., & Sewell, G. (2002). Looking for the good soldier, Svejk. *Sociology, 36*(4), 857–873.

Fleming, P., & Spicer, A. (2003). Working at a cynical distance. *Organization, 10*(1), 157–179.

Fleming, R., & Colizzi, N. (2017). It's 8-to-1 against your change program: How to beat the odds. https://www.bain.com/insights/its-8-to-1-against-your-change-program-how-to-beat-the-odds/ (accessed 23 June 2019).

Fligstein, N., & McAdam, D. (2011). Toward a general theory of strategic action fields. *Sociological Theory, 29*(1), 1–26.

Fligstein, N., & McAdam, D. (2012). *A theory of fields.* Oxford: Oxford University Press.

Flowers, R., & Swan, E. (Eds.) (2015). *Food pedagogies.* London: Routledge.

Flyvbjerg, B. (2001). *Making social science happen.* Cambridge: Cambridge University Press.

Ford, J. D., & Ford, L. W. (2008). Resistance to change: The rest of the story. *Academy of Management Review, 33*(2), 362–377.

Ford, J. D., Ford, L. W., & D'Amelio, A. (2008). Resistance to change: The rest of the story. *Academy of Management Review, 33*(2), 362–377.

Fox, A. (1974). *Beyond contract: Work, power and trust relations.* London: Faber.

Fraher, A. M. Y. L., Branicki, L. J., & Grint, K. (2017). Mindfulness in action: Discovering how U.S. navy seals build capacity for mindfulness in high-reliability organizations (HROS). *Academy of Management Discoveries, 3*(3), 239–261.

Frahm, J. (2016). Of myth busting, babies and bathwater. *Conversations of Change*, (1 May), 1–11. https://conversationsofchange.com.au/of-myth-busting-babies-and-bathwater (accessed 22 May 2022).

Frahm, J. (2017). *Conversations of change: A guide to implementing workplace change.* Melbourne: Jennifer Frahm Collaborations.

Frahm, J., & Brown, K. (2007). First steps: Linking change communication to change receptivity. *Journal of Organizational Change Management, 20*(3), 370–387.

Frankl, V. (1959). *Man's search for meaning.* Boston: Beacon Press.

Franssen, T. (2014). *Prometheus through the ages:From ancient trickster to future human.* Exeter: University of Exeter.

Freeland, G. (2020). Pandemic accentuates two problems with change management: One is change, the other is management. *Forbes*, 29 *June*, 1–5. https://www.forbes.com/sites/grantfreeland/2020/06/29/pandemic-accentuates-two-problems-with

-change-management-one-is-change-the-other-is-management/?sh=5bd301b46969 (accessed 22 May 2022).

French, W., & Bell, C. (1973). *Organization development: Behavioral science interventions for organization develpment.* Englewood Cliffs, NJ: Prentice Hall.

Fuda, P. (2011). Master chef, coach, Russian dolls: How leaders spark and sustain change, Part 2. *Harvard Business Review, 21 October,* 1–4. https://hbr.org/2011/10/master-chef-coach-russian-doll (accessed 22 May 2022).

Fuda, P. (2011a). *Mask: How leaders conceal imperfections and adopt a persona* (Leadership Transformation). YouTube & The Alignment Partnership. https://www.youtube.com/watch?v=lo11cky8dm8 (accessed 5 January 2022).

Fuda, P. (2011b). *Movie: A leader's process of self-awareness and reflection.* Australia: YouTube & The Alignment Partnership. https://www.youtube.com/watch?v=QFX6UDtYW0M (accessed 5 January 2022).

Fuda, P. (2011c). *Fire metaphor: From 'burning platform' to 'burning ambition'.* Australia: YouTube & The Alignment Partnership. https://www.youtube.com/watch?v=Tfn6vD4yyC4 (accessed 10 January 2023).

Fuda, P. (2011d). *Snowball of accountability (leadership transformation).* Australia: YouTube & The Alignment Partnership. https://www.youtube.com/watch?v=Ep_1nluEkiY (accessed 10 January 2023).

Fuda, P. (2013). *Leadership transformed: How ordinary managers become extraordinary leaders.* Las Vegas: Amazon Publishing.

Fuda, P. (2014). *Master Chef.* TAP. Ironies of Organizational Change Book @ www.reimaginingchange.com (with permission).

Fuda, P. (2016). *Coach: In the context of sport and how it applies to business transformation* (12 April). YouTube & The Alignment Partnership. https://www.youtube.com/watch?v=0cHTfZ6xyX8 (accessed 22 May 2022).

Fuda, P., & Badham, R. (2011). Fire, snowball, mask, movie: How leaders spark and sustain change. *Harvard Business Review, 89*(11), 145–148, 167.

Fulop, L., & Linstead, S. (1999). *Management: A critical text.* Basingstoke: Macmillan.

Fulop, L., & Rifkin, W. (1999). Management knowledge and learning. In L. Fulop, & S. Linstead (Eds.), *Management: A critical text* (pp.14–48), Basingstoke: Macmillan.

Furness., H. (2015). Jamie Oliver admits school dinners campaign failed because eating well is a middle-class preserve. *The Telegraph,* August, 1–6. https://www.telegraph.co.uk/news/celebritynews/11821747/Jamie-Oliver-admits-school-dinners-campaign-failed-because-eating-well-is-a-middle-class-preserve.html (accessed 25 May 2022).

Furr, N., Nel, K., & Ramsoy, T. (2018). *Leading transformation: How to take charge of your company's future.* Boston: Harvard Business Review Press.

Galbraith, J. R. (2009). *The Star Model summary.* The Star Model. http://www.jaygalbraith.com/images/pdfs/StarModel.pdf (accessed 22 May 2022).

Gandhi, M. K. (1925). *An autobiography or the story of my experiments with the truth* (translation. Desai, M.). Bombay: Gandhi Book Centre, Navajivan Publishing House.

Gandhi (1983). (Director: Attenborough, R.).

Gandhi on the Salt March (1982). From the movie *Gandhi* (Director: Attenborough, R.). https://www.youtube.com/watch?v=WW3uk95VGes (4.46) (accessed 5 January 2022).

Gardner, H. (1995). *Leading minds.* New York: Basic Books Harper Collins.

Garrety, K., Badham, R., Morrigan, V., Rifkin, W., & Zanko, M. (2003). The use of personality typing in organizational change: Discourse, emotions and the reflexive subject. *Human Relations, 56*(2), 211–235.

George, J., & Jones, G. (2012). *Understanding and managing organizational behavior.* Englewood Cliffs, NJ: Prentice Hall.

Gerschman, J., Finger, H., & Goldman, A. (2017). *The mindful entepreneur.* New York: Xoum.

Gersick, C. J. G. (1991). Revolutionary change theories: A multilevel exploration of the punctuated equilibrium paradigm. *Academy of Management Review, 16*(1), 10–36.

Ghislanzoni, G., Heidari-Robinson, S., & Jermiin, M. (2010). Taking organizational redesigns from plan to practice. *McKinsey Global Survey Results*, 1–9. https://www .mckinsey.com/business-functions/people-and-organizational-performance/our -insights/taking-organizational-redesigns-from-plan-to-practice-mckinsey-global -survey-results (accessed 22 May 2022).

Gibbons, P. (2015). *The science of successful organizational change: How leaders set strategy, change behavior, and create an agile culture.* New York and London: Pearson.

Gino, F. (2018). Why curiosity matters. *Harvard Buiness Review*, (October), 1–27.

Giorgi, S. (2017). The mind and heart of resonance: The role of cognition and emotions in frame effectiveness. *Journal of Management Studies, 54*(5), 711–738.

Giorgi, S., Lockwood, C., & Glynn, M. A. (2015). The many faces of culture: Making sense of 30 years of research on culture in organization studies. *Academy of Management Annals, 9*(1), 1–54.

Goffman, E. (1961). *Encounters. Two studies in the sociology of interaction.* Harmondsworth: Penguin University.

Goffman, E. ([1959] 2022). *The presentation of self in everyday life.* New York: Anchor Books: Doubleday.

Goldsmith, M. (2008). *What got you here won't get you there: How successful people become even more successful.* New York: Profile Books.

Goleman, D. (2000). Leadership that gets results. *Harvard Business Review*, March–April: 78–90.

Goleman, D. (2009). *Emotional intelligence: Why it can matter more than IQ.* New York: Bloomsbury Press.

Gonsalves, P. (2010). *Clothing for liberation.* New Delhi: Sage.

Govindarajan, V. (2016). Planned opportunism: Using weak signals to spur innovation. *Harvard Business Review*, May, 1–9.

Graham, D.W. (2021). Heraclitus. In Edward N. Zalta (Ed.), *The Stanford encyclopedia of philosophy* (Summer 2021 edition). https://plato.stanford.edu/archives/sum2021/ entries/heraclitus/ (accessed 20 June 2022).

Grahame, K. (2022). *The wind in the willows.* Seoul: Compass Publishing.

Greenwood, R., & Hinings, C. R. (1988). Organizational design types, tracks and the dynamics of strategic change. *Organization Studies, 9*(3), 293–316.

Greenwood, R., & Hinings, C. R. (1996). Understanding radical organizational change: Bringing together the old and the new institutiionalism. *The Academy of Management Review, 21*(4), 1022–1054.

Greenwood, R., Oliver, C., Lawrence, T. B., & Meyer, R. (Eds.) (2020). *The Sage handbook of organizational institutionalism* (2nd edition). London: Sage.

Grenfell, M. (2008). *Pierre Bourdieu.* Utrecht, Netherlands: Acumen.

Grey, C. (2003). The fetish of change. *Tamara: Journal of Critical Postmodern Organization Science, 2*(2), 1–19.

Grint, K. (2000). *The arts of leadership*. Oxford: Oxford University Press.

Grint, K. (2005). Problems, problems, problems: The social construction of 'leadership'. *Human Relations*, *58*(11), 1467–1494.

Guhin, J. (2013). Is irony good for America? The threat of nihilism, the importance of romance, and the power of cultural forms. *Cultural Sociology*, 7(1), 23–38.

Guillet de Monthoux, P., & Czarniawska-Joerges, B. (2005). Introduction: Management beyond case and cliché. In B. Czarniawska-Joerges, & P. Guillet de Monthoux (Eds.), *Good novels, better management: Reading organizational realities* (pp.1–17). Chur, Switzerland: Harwood.

Gulati, B. R., Huffman, S., & Neilson, G. (2002). The barista principle – Starbucks and the rise of relational capital. *Strategy + Business*, *28*(3), 1–12. https://www.strategy-business.com/article/20534?gko=eb786 (accessed 3 January 2022).

Gusfield, J. (2015). *Performing action: Artistry in human behaviour and social research*. London and New York: Routledge.

Gylfe, P., Franck, H., & Vaara, E. (2019). Living with paradox through irony. *Organizational behavior and human decision processes*, *15*(5), 68–82.

Hamel, G. (2000). *Leading the revolution: how to thrive in turbulent times by making innovation a way of life*. Boston: Harvard Business School Press.

Hamel, G. (2012). *What matters now: How to win in a world of relentless change, ferocious competition and unstoppable innovation*. San Francisco: Jossey-Bass.

Hamel, G. (2018). *Why change management is an oxymoron*. http://www.garyhamel.com/video/why-change-management-oxymoron (accessed 23 May 2022).

Hamel, G., & Zanini, M. (2020). *Humanocracy: Creating organizations as amazing as the people within them*. Boston: Harvard Business Review Press.

Hannan, M., & Freeman, J. (1977). The population ecology of organizations. *American Journal of Sociology*, *82*(5), 929–964.

Hannan, M., & Freeman, J. (1984). Structural inertia and organizational change. *American Sociological Review*, *49*(2), 149–164.

Hannan, M., Polos, L., & Carroll, G. (2002a). *Structural inertia and organizational change revisited II: Complexity, opacity and change* (Research Paper 1733; Issue April).

Hannan, M., Polos, L., & Carroll, G. R. (2002b). *Structural inertia and organizational change revisited III: The evolution of organizational inertia* (Research Paper 1734; Issue April).

Hannan, M., Polos, L., & Carroll, G. R. (2003). The fog of change: Opacity and asperity in organizations. *Administrative Science Quarterly*, *48*(3), 399–432.

Hannan, M., Polos, L., & Caroll, G. (2007). *Logics of organization theory*. Princeton: Princeton University Press.

Hardy, C., & Maguire, S. (2017). Institutional entrepreneurship and change in fields. In R. Greenwood, C. Oliver, T. Lawrence, & R. Meyer (Eds.), *The Sage handbook of organizational institutionalism* (2nd edition) (pp.261–281). London: Sage.

Hart, C. (2003). Summary of Beer & Nohria (2000). Cracking the code of change. https://maaw.info/ArticleSummaries/ArtSumBeerNohria2000.htm (accessed 23 May 2022).

Hartwig, A., Clarke, S., Johnson, S., & Willis, S. (2020). Workplace team resilience: A systematic review and conceptual development. *Organizational Psychology Review*, *10*(3–4), 169–200.

Hatch, M. J. (1997). Irony and the social construction of contradiction in the humor of a management team. *Organization Science*, *8*(3), 275–288.

HBR Editors. (2014). How companies can profit from a 'growth mindset'. *Harvard Business Review*, 28–29.

Heckmann, N., Steger, T., & Dowling, M. (2016). Organizational capacity for change, change experience, and change project performance. *Journal of Business Research*, *69*(2), 777–784.

Heifetz, R., Grashow, A., & Linsky, M. (2002). A survival guide for leaders. *Harvard Business Review* (June), 65–74.

Heifetz, R., Grashow, A., & Linsky, M. (2009a). Leadership in a (permanent) crisis. *Harvard Business Review*, *July–August*, 62–70.

Heifetz, R. A., Grashow, A., & Linsky, M. (2009b). *The practice of adaptive leadership*. Boston: Harvard Business Review Press.

Heifetz, R., & Linsky, M. (2017). *Leadership on the line: Staying alive through the dangers of leading*. Boston: Harvard Business Review Press.

Helin, J., Hernes, T., Hjorth, D., & Holt, R. (Eds.) (2014). *The Oxford handbook of process philosophy and organization studies*. Oxford: Oxford University Press.

Hemerling, J., Kilmann, J., & Matthews, D. (2018). The head, heart and hands of transformation. *BCG Henderson Institute* (Vol. November). https://www.bcg.com/en-au/publications/2018/head-heart-hands-transformation.aspx (accessed 23 May 2022).

Heracleous, L. (2020). *Janus strategy:* London: KDP.

Heracleous, L., & Bartunek, J. (2021). Organization change failure, deep structures and temporality: Appreciating Wonderland. *Human Relations*, *74*(2), 208–233.

Heracleous, L. & Robson. D. (2020). Why the 'paradox mindset' is the key to success. *BBC Worklife*, November, 1–8. https://www.bbc.com/worklife/article/20201109-why-the-paradox-mindset-is-the-key-to-success.(accessed 5 January 2022).

Heracleous, L., Yniguez, C., & Gonzalez, S. A. (2019). Ambidexterity as historically embedded process: Evidence from NASA, 1958 to 2016. *The Journal of Applied Behavioral Science*, *55*(2), 161–189.

Higgs, M., & Rowland, D. (2000). Building change leadership capability: The quest for change competence. *Journal of Change Management*, *1*(2), 116–130.

Higgs, M., & Rowland, D. (2005). All changes great and small: Exploring approaches to change and its leadership. *Journal of Change Management*, *5*(2), 121–151.

Higgs, M., & Rowland, D. (2010). Emperors with clothes on: The role of self- awareness in developing effective change leadership. *Journal of Change Management*, *10*(4), 369–385.

Higgs, M., & Rowland, D. (2011). What does it take to implement change successfully? A study of the behaviors of successful change leaders. *Journal of Applied Behavioral Science*, *47*(3), 309–335.

Hilgers, M., & Mangez, E. (2015). *Bourdieu's theory of social fields*. London: Routledge.

Hill, I. (2008). The 'human barnyard' and Kenneth Burke's philosophy of technology. *K.B. Journal*, *5*(1), 1–13.

Hindshaw, I., & Gruin, A. (2017). *Reenergize change programs to escape the valley of death. Forbes (Bain Insights)*, 10, 4–7. https://www.forbes.com/sites/baininsights/2017/06/27/reenergize-change-programs-to-escape-the-valley-of-death/#31a929ce5bbe (accessed 22 May 2022).

History Channel (2018). Martin Luther King Jr: Leader of the 20th century civil rights movement – biography (3: 51) (accessed 3 January 2022).

Hofstede, G. (2001). *Culture's consequences comparing values, behaviors, institutions, and organizations across nations* (2nd edition). London: Sage.

Holland, W. (2001). *Red zone management*. Chicago: Dearborn Press.

Hollingworth, P. (2016). *The light and fast organization*. Melbourne: Wiley.

Holt, D., Armenakis, A., Feild, H., & Harris, S. (2007a). Readiness for organizational change: The systematic development of a scale. *Journal of Applied Behavioral Science*, *43*(2), 232–255.

Holt, D. T., Armenakis, A. A., Harris, S. G., & Feild, H. S. (2007b). Toward a comprehensive definition of readiness for change: A review of research and instrumentation. *Research in Organizational Change and Development*, *16*(6), 289–336.

Holt, D. T., Helfrich, C. D., Hall, C. G., & Weiner, B. J. (2010). Are you ready? How health professionals can comprehensively conceptualize readiness for change. *Journal of General Internal Medicine*, *25*(SUPPL. 1), 50–56.

Hooijberg, R., Hunt, J. G., & Dodge, G. E. (1997). Leadership complexity and development of the leaderplex model. *Journal of Management*, *23*(3), 375–408.

Hot Fuzz (Director: Wright, E.) (2007a). Hot Fuzz opening scene (22 January). https://www.youtube.com/watch?v=7Lqd-UwZmJ4 (accessed 23 May 2022).

Hot Fuzz (Director: Wright, E.) (2007b). Hot Fuzz good luck Nicholas scene (28 June). https://www.youtube.com/watch?v=faMh6OYfuNE (accessed 23 May 2022).

Hougaard, R., & Carter, J. (2018). *The mind of the leader*. Boston: Harvard Business Review Press.

Hougaard, R., Carter, J., & Coutts, G. (2016). *One second ahead: Enhance your performance at work with mindfulness*. Basingstoke and New York: Palgrave Macmillan.

Hoyle, E., & Wallace, M. (2007). Educational reform: An ironic perspective. *Educational Management Administration and Leadership*, *35*(1), 9–25.

Hoyle, E., & Wallace, M. (2008). Two faces of organizational irony: Endemic and pragmatic. *Organization Studies*, *29*(11), 1427–1447.

Huczynski, A., & Buchanan, D. (2006). Feature films in management education. *Journal of Organizational Behavior Education*, 1, 73–94.

Hughes, M. (2011). Do 70 per cent of all organizational change initiatives really fail? *Journal of Change Management*, *11*(4), 451–464.

Hughes, M. (2016). Leading changes: Why transformation explanations fail. *Leadership*, *12*(4), 449–469.

Hughes, M. (2019). *Managing and leading organizational change*. London: Taylor & Francis.

Hughes, M. (2022). Reflections: How studying organizational change lost its way. *Journal of Change Management*, *22*(1), 8–25.

Huron Consulting (2021). *COVID-19: Change management and leadership during times of uncertainty*. https://www.huronconsultinggroup.com/insights/covid-19-change-management-leadership (accessed 23 May 2022).

Hustedde, R., & Score, M. (1995). Force-field analysis: incorporating critical thinking in goal setting. *CD Practice*, 4, 1–7. https://files.eric.ed.gov/fulltext/ED384712.pdf (accessed 23 May 2022).

Hutcheon, L. (1994). *Irony's edge: The theory and politics of irony*. London and New York: Routledge.

Huy, Q.N. (1999). Emotional capability, emotional intelligence, and radical change. *Academy of Management Review*, *24*(2), 325–345.

Ibarra, H. (2015a). *Act like a leader, think like a leader*. Boston: Harvard Business Review Press.

Ibarra, H. (2015b). The authenticity paradox. *Harvard Business Review*, *January–February*, 53–59.

Ibarra, H. (2018). *Act like a leader*. HR Congress, Brussels. 28–29 November. https://www.youtube.com/watch?v=4pk9TkHRZmI (accessed 3 January 2022).

Ibarra, H., Ely, R., & Kolb, D. (2013). Women rising: The unseen barriers. *Harvard Business Review, 91*(9), 60–66.

Ibarra, H., & Morten, H. (2011). Are you a collaborative leader. *Harvard Business Review, August*, 69–74.

Ie, A., Ngnoumen, C. T., & Langer, E. J. (2014). *The Wiley Blackwell handbook of mindfulness* (Vols 1–2). Chichester: Wiley-Blackwell.

Ingold, T. (2007). *Lines: A brief history*. London and New York: Routledge.

Inns, D. (1996). Organisation development as journey. In C. Oswick, & D. Grant (Eds.), *Organization development: Metaphorical explorations* (pp.20–34). London: Pitman.

Invictus (Director: Eastwood, C.) (2009a). *Scene 1. Mandela's team motivation. First day in the office*. YouTube. https://www.youtube.com/watch?v=gqhS7t2dyEY (accessed 23 May 2022).

Invictus (Director: Eastwood, C.) (2009b). *Scene 2. Forgiveness*. YouTube. https://www.youtube.com/watch?v=CYSKHgEwkfA (accessed 23 May 2022).

Isaksen, S., & Tidd, J. (2006). *Meeting the innovation challenge: Leadership for transformation and growth*. Hoboken, NJ: Wiley.

Isern, J., Meaney, M. C., & Wilson, S. (2009). Corporate transformation under pressure. *McKinsey and Company* (Voices of Transformation 3), 1–10. https://www.mckinsey.com/business-functions/people-and-organizational-performance/our-insights/corporate-transformation-under-pressure (accessed 21 May 2022).

Isern, J., & Pung, C. (2007). Driving radical change. *McKinsey Quarterly*, (4), 1–12. htts://doi.org/10.1057/9781137492319_5 (accessed 23 May 2022).

Jabri, M. (2017). *Managing organizational change: Process, social construction and dialogue* (2nd edition). London: Palgrave Macmillan.

Jackson, M., & Grace, D. (2018). *Machiavelliana*. New York: Value Inquiry.

Jacobs, R., & Smith, P. (1997). Romance, irony, and solidarity. *Sociological Theory, 15*(1), 60–80.

Jacquemont, D., Maor, D., & Reick, A. (2015). How to beat the transformation odds. *McKinsey & Company*, 1–10. https://www.bing.com/search?q=How%20to%20beat%20the%20transformation%20odds&pc=cosp&ptag=C999N9926A6EFB831429&form=CONBDF&conlogo=CT3210127 (accessed 21 May 2022).

Jagd, S. (2011). Pragmatic sociology and competing orders of worth in organizations. *European Journal of Social Theory, 14*(3), 343–359.

James, W. ([1890] 2007). *The principles of psychology* (Vol. 21, Issue 2). Boston: Harvard University Press.

Jamie's Food Revolution. Seasons 1 & 2. (Directors: Smith, B., & Bartley, M.) (2010, 2011). https://www.amazon.com/Jamies-Sugar-Rush/dp/B01G2IWENE/ref=sr_1_1?crid=3AQMFHIF3IORZ&keywords=jamie%27s+sugar+rush&qid=1653443452&s=instant-video&sprefix=jamie%27s+sugar+rush%2Cinstant-video%2C275&sr=1-1 (accessed 25 May 2022).

Jamie's Kitchen (Director: Scott, S.) (2005). https://www.amazon.com/Jamies-Kitchen-television-Jamie-Oliver/dp/B0007N4AWE/ref=sr_1_3?crid=1GIYQK2CWH4JB&keywords=jamie%27s+kitchen%3A+the+complete+television+series&qid=1653443689&s=movies-tv&sprefix=jamie%27s+kitchen+the+complete+television+series%2Cmovies-tv%2C296&sr=1-3 (accessed 25 May 2022).

Jamie's Ministry of Food (Director: Jones, E.) (2008). https://www.amazon.com/Jamies-Ministry-Food-Episode-2/dp/B074N8VD7Q/ref=sr_1_1?crid=3OY4PBRNVA6JZ&keywords=jamie%27s+ministry+of+food&qid=1653443549&s=instant-video&sprefix=jamie%27s+ministry+of+food%2Cinstant-video%2C271&sr=1-1 (accessed 25 May 2022).

Jamie's Return to School Dinners (Director: Hornby, N.) (2006). https://www.amazon
.com/Jamies-Return-School-Dinners-Hornby/dp/B076CWLFJ1/ref=sr_1_1?crid
=33GPFQ9T8Z4H7&keywords=jamie%27s+return+to+school+dinners&qid=
1653443421&s=instant-video&sprefix=jamie%27s+return+to+school+dinner
%2Cinstant-video%2C278&sr=1-1 (accessed 21 May 2022).

Jamie's School Dinners (Directors: Gilbert, G. & Oliver, J.) (2005). 01 – Ep01. https://
www.stan.com.au/watch/jamies-school-dinners & https://www.justwatch.com/au/tv
-show/jamies-school-dinners/season-1 (accessed 22 May 2022).

Jamie's School Dinners (Director: Gilbert, G.) (2005). https://www.amazon
.com/Jamies-School-Dinners-Episode-2/dp/B074N9FQLC/ref=sr_1_1?crid=
1T0VPIY2AMHXU&keywords=jamie%27s+school+dinners&qid=1653443359
&sprefix=jamie%27s+school+dinner%2Caps%2C339&sr=8-1 (accessed 25 May
2022).

Jamie's Sugar Rush (Director: Cooper, V.) (2015). https://www.amazon.com/Jamies
-Sugar-Rush/dp/B01G2IWENE/ref=sr_1_1?crid=3AQMFHIF3IORZ&keywords=
jamie%27s+sugar+rush&qid=1653443452&s=instant-video&sprefix=jamie%27s+
sugar+rush%2Cinstant-video%2C275&sr=1-1 (accessed 25 May 2022).

Jessop, B. (2003). Governance and meta-governance: On reflexivity, requisite variety
and requisite irony. In H.P. Bang (Ed.), *Governance as social and political communication* (pp.111–116). Manchester: Manchester University Press.

Johansson, U., & Woodilla, J. (Eds.) (2005). *Irony and organizations*. Copenhagen:
Copenhagen Business School Press.

Johns, E. (1973). *The sociology of organisational change*. Oxford: Pergamon Press.

Johnson, G. (1992). Managing strategic change: Strategy, culture and action. *Long
Range Planning, 25*(1), 9–19.

Johnson, G., Whittington, R., Regner, P., Scholes, K., & Angwin, D. (2017). *Exploring
corporate strategy*. London: Pearson.

Joost. (2019a). *Picking the brain of the world's most radical CEO: Zhang Ruimin*, from
https://corporate-rebels.com/interview-zhang-ruimin/ (accessed 19 January 2020).

Joost. (2019b). *The world's most pioneering company of our times*. Corporate Rebels.
https://corporate-rebels.com/haier/ (accessed 19 January 2020).

Jordan, S., & Johannessen, I. A. (2014). Mindfulness and organizational defenses:
Exploring organizational and institutional challenges to mindfulness. In A. Ie, C.
T. Ngnoumen, & E. J. Langer (Eds.),*The Wiley Blackwell handbook of mindfulness*
(pp.424–442).

Jordan, S., Messner, M., & Becker, A. (2009). Reflection and mindfulness in organizations: Rationales and possibilities for integration. *Management Learning, 40*(4),
465–473.

Judge, W., & Douglas, T. (2009). Organizational change capacity: The systematic
development of a scale. *Journal of Organizational Change Management, 22*(3),
635–649.

Kahn, R. L. (1974). Organizational development: Some problems and proposals.
Journal of Applied Behavioural Science, 10, 485–502.

Kahneman, D. (2011). *Thinking fast and slow*. New York: Farrar, Strauss and Giroux.

Kahneman, D., & Tversky, A. (1982). Intuitive prediction: Biases and corrective
procedures. In D. Kahneman, P. Slovic, & A. Tversky (Eds.), *Judgement under
uncertainty: Heuristics and biases* (pp.3-20). London: Cambridge University Press.

Kalina, P. (2020). Change management : COVID-19 and beyond. *Journal of Human
Resource Management, 23*(1), 38–40.

Kanter, R. (2002). Strategy as improvisational theater. *MIT Sloan Management Review*, *43*(2), 76–81.

Kanter, R. M. (1979). Power failure in management circuits. *Harvard Business Review*, *57*(4), 65–75.

Kanter, R. M. (1981). Power, leadership, and participatory management. *Theory into Practice*, *20*(4), 219–224.

Kanter, R. M. (1985). *The change masters: Innovation and entrepreneurship in the American corporation.* New York: Simon & Schuster.

Kanter, R. M. (1999). The enduring skills of change leaders. *Leader to Leader*, *13*(Summer), 15–22.

Kanter, R. M. (2001). *Evolve: Succeeding in the digital culture of tomorrow.* Cambridge MA: Harvard Business Review Press.

Kanter, R. M. (2003). Leadership and the psychology of turnarounds. *Harvard Business Review*, *81*(6), 58–67, 136.

Kanter, R. M. (2004). *Confidence.* New York: Random House.

Kanter, R. M. (2006). *Leading with confidence.* Sydney: Global Leaders Network Seminar.

Kanter, R. M. (2009). *Supercorp: How vanguard companies create innovation, profits, growth and social good.* London: Profile Books.

Kanter, R. M. (2010). Powerlessness corrupts. *Harvard Business Review*, *88*(7–8), 36.

Kanter, R.M. (2011). *The change wheel: Elements of systemic change and how to get change rolling* (Harvard Working Paper No. 9-312–083). Boston.

Kanter, R. M. (2012). Creating a supportive environment for innovation to flourish. https://www.youtube.com/watch?v=MPmQLsRInc0&feature=youtu.be. (accessed 3 January 2022).

Kanter, R. M. (2015). Small wins go a long way in improving U.S. rail transportation. *Harvard Business Review*, *12 May*, 1–4.

Kanter, R. M. (2020). *Think outside the building: How smart leaders can change the world one smart innovation at a time.* New York: Public Affairs.

Kanter, R. M., Stein, B. A., & Jick, T. D. (1992). *The challenge of organizational change: How companies experience it and leaders guide it.* New York: Free Press.

Kaplan, S., & Tripsas, M. (2008). Thinking about technology: Applying a cognitive lens to technical change. *Research Policy*, *37*(5), 790–805.

Kapoor, P. (2017). MK Gandhi's most 'indelicate' gift for Queen Elizabeth (and other stories about Khadi). https://scroll.in/article/852143/mk-gandhi-s-most-indelicate-gift-for-queen-elizabeth-and-other-stories-about-khadi (accessed 5 January 2022).

Kegan, R., & Lahey, L. (2009). *Immunity to change: How to overcome it and unlock potential in yourself and your organization.* Boston: Harvard Business Press.

Kegan, R., & Lahey, L. (2016). *An everyone culture: Becoming a deliberately developmental organization.* Boston: Harvard Business Review Press.

Kehr, H. (2017). *Motivate yourself with visions, goals and willpower.* Munich. https://www.youtube.com/watch?v=iuIisjRIcVI (accessed 23 May 2022).

Keller, S., Meaney, M., & Pung, C. (2010). What successful transformations share. *McKinsey Global Survey Results*, 1–5. https://www.mckinsey.com/~/media/mckinsey/business%20functions/people%20and%20organizational%20performance/our%20insights/what%20successful%20transformations%20share%20mckinsey%20global%20survey%20results/what%20successful%20transformations%20share%20mckinsey%20global%20survey%20results.pdf (accessed 23 May 2022).

Kelly, D., & Amburgey, T. L. (1991). Organizational inertia and momentum: A dynamic model of strategic change. *Academy of Management Journal, 34*(3), 591–612.

Kelly, P., & Harrison, L. (2009). *Working in Jamie's kitchen: Salvation, passion and young*. Basingstoke: Palgrave/Macmillan.

Kim, S., & Ji, Y. (2018). Gap analysis. In R. L. Heath, & W. Johansen (Eds.), *International encyclopedia of strategic communication* (pp.1–6). Chichester: Wiley.

King, E., & Badham, R. (2019). Leadership in uncertainty: The mindfulness solution. *Organizational Dynamics, 48*(4), 1–15.

King, E., & Badham, R. (2020). The wheel of mindfulness: A generative framework for second-generation mindful leadership. *Mindfulness, 11*(1), 166–176.

King, Jr., M. L. (1963, 28 August). *I have a dream* speech, Lincoln Memorial, Washington D.C., USA. [Video file]. Historic Film Archive. https://www.historicfilms.com/tapes/10767 (accessed 3 January 2022).

Klein, J. A. (2007). *True change: How outsiders on the inside get things done in organizations*. San Francisco: Jossey-Bass.

Knowledge@Wharton. (2019). For Haier's Zhang Ruimin, success means creating the future. https://knowledge.wharton.upenn.edu/article/haiers-zhang-ruimin-success-means-creating-the-future/ (accessed 19 January 2020).

Koehn, N. F., McNamara, K., Khan, N., & Legris, E. (2014). *Starbucks coffee company: Transformation and renewal* (Harvard Business School Case Study No. 9-314–068).

Kofman, F., & Senge, P. (1993). Communities and commitments: The heart of learning organizations. *Organization Dynamics, 22*(2), 5–23.

Kogod, T. (2021). The Matrix resurrections reveals the Red Pill's secret truth. 31 December 2021. https://www.cbr.com/matrix-4-revealred-pills-true-meaning/ (accessed 22 July 2022).

Kolb, A., & Kolb, D. (2009). Experiential learning theory: A dynamic, holistic approach to management learning, education and development. In S. Armstrong, & C. Fukami (Eds.), *The Sage handbook of management learning, education and development* (pp.42–69). London and Thousand Oaks: Sage.

Kolb, D. A. (2015). *Experiential learning: Experience as the source of learning and development*. Upper Saddle River, NJ: Pearson Education.

Kotter, J. (1985). *Power and influence: beyond formal authority*. New York: Free Press.

Kotter, J. (1990). *A force for change: How leadership differs from management*. New York: Free Press.

Kotter, J. (1996). *Leading change*. Boston: Harvard Business School Press.

Kotter, J. (2007). Leading change: Why transformation efforts fail. *Harvard Business Review, January*, 96–103.

Kotter, J. (2012). The perils of confusing management and leadership. https://www.youtube.com/watch?v=Dz8AiOQEQmk (accessed 3 January 2022).

Kotter, J. (2014). *Accelerate: Building strategic agility for a faster-moving world*. Boston: Harvard Business Review Press.

Kotter, J. (2018). *8 steps to accelerate change in your organisation*. Kotter Inc. https://www.kotterinc.com/research-and-insights/8-steps-accelerating-change-ebook-2020/ (accessed 23 May 2022).

Kotter, J. P., & Cohen, D. S. (2002). *The heart of change: Real-life stories of how people change their organizations*. Boston, MA: Harvard Business School Press.

Kotter, J. P., & Schlesinger, L. A. (1979). Choosing strategies for change for overcoming it. *Harvard Business Review, 57*(2), 106–114.

Kreuz, R. (2022). What irony is not, *The MIT press reader*. https://thereader.mitpress.mit.edu/what-irony-is-not/ (accessed 22 July 2022).

Kruger, M. (2012). *The arts of leadership by Keith Grint: An executive book summary.* https://keithdwalker.ca/wp-content/summaries/1-c/Arts of Leadership.Grint.EBS.pdf (accessed 23 May 2022).

Kübler-Ross, E. (1969). *On death and dying.* London: Macmillan

Kubrick, S. (2009). *Full Metal Jacket born to kill peace button duality of man* (p.12 January). https://www.youtube.com/watch?v=KMEViYvojtY (accessed 5 January 2022)

Kunda, G. ([1992] 2006). *Engineering culture: Control and commitment in a high-tech corporation.* Philadelphia, PA: Temple University Press.

Kundera, M. (2009). *The unbearable lightness of being.* London: Harper.

Küpers, W. (2017). Inter-play(ing) – embodied and relational possibilities of 'serious play' at work. *Journal of Organizational Change Management,* 30(7), 993–1104.

Lahri, G., & Shankar, A. (2020). *Combating COVID-19 with an agile change management approach* (May 2020). https://www2.deloitte.com/content/dam/Deloitte/in/Documents/human-capital/in-hc-consulting-deloitte-change-management-pov-on-covid-noexp.pdf (accessed 24 May 2022).

Lakoff, G., & Johnson, M. (1999). *Philosophy in the flesh: The embodied mind and its challenge to western thought.* New York: Perseus.

Langer, E. ([1989]2009). *Mindfulness.* Cambridge, MA: Perseus.

Langley, A. (2021). Paradox as irony: Inspirations from jazz, linguistics, mathematics, poetry and other stories. In R. Bednarek, M. Cunha, J. Schad, & W. Smith (Eds.), *Interdisciplinary dialogues on organizational paradox: Investigating social structures and human expression. Research in the Sociology of Organizations,* 73(Part B) (pp.163–175). London: Emerald Publishing.

Langley, A. N. N., Smallman, C., Tsoukas, H., & Van de Ven, A. H. (2013). Process studies of change in organization and management: Unveiling temporality, activity, and flow. *Academy of Management Journal,* 56(1), 1–13.

Langley, A., & Tsoukas, H. (Eds.) (2017). *The Sage handbook of process organization studies.* London: Sage.

Lanham, R. A. (1995). *The electronic word: Democracy, technology, and the arts.* Chicago: University of Chicago Press.

Larson, G. S., & Tompkins, P. K. (2005). Ambivalence and resistance: A study of management in a concertive control system. *Communication Monographs,* 72(1), 1–21.

Lawrence, P. R. (1954). How to deal with resistance to change. *Harvard Business Review,* 32(3), 49–57.

Lawrence, T. B., Dyck, B., Maitlis, S., & Mauws, M. K. (2006). The underlying structure of continuous change. *MIT Sloan Management Review,* 47(4), 59–66.

Leca, B., Battilana, J., & Boxenbaum, E. (2008). *Agency and institutions: A review of institutional entrepreneurship* (Working Paper 08-096). Cambridge, MA: Harvard Business School, pp.1–52.

Leggott, J., & Jochsherf, T. (2010). From the kitchen to 10 Downing Street. In J. Taddeo, & K. Dvorak (Eds.), *The tube has spoken: Reality TV and history* (pp.47–65). Louisville: University of Kentucky Press.

Lehman, D. W., & Hahn, J. (2013). Momentum and organizational risk taking: Evidence from the National Football League. *Management Science,* 59(4), 852–868.

Leith, J. M. (2017). '70% of organizational change initiatives fail' – how the myth evolved. http://jackmartinleith.com/70-percent-organizational-change-initi (accessed 23 May 2022).

Leonard-Barton, D. (1992). Core capabilities and core rigidities: A paradox in managing new product development. *Strategic Management Journal,* 13(1), 111–125.

Lesser, E., Fontaine, M., & Slusher, J. (2011). *Knowledge and communities*. London and New York: Routledge.

Leung, A. K. Y., Liou, S., Miron-Spektor, E., Koh, B., Chan, D., Eisenberg, R., & Schneider, I. (2018). Middle ground approach to paradox: Within- and between-culture examination of the creative benefits of paradoxical frames. *Journal of Personality and Social Psychology, 114*(3), 443–464.

Levinson, E. (2015). Thriving on change: Creating a gap analysis (3:01). https://www.youtube.com/watch?v=uc3m_yWAbSk&feature=youtu.be (accessed 23 May 2022).

Levy, O., Peiperl, M. A., & Jonsen, K. (2016). Cosmopolitanism in a globalized world: An interdisciplinary perspective. In J. Osland, M. Li, & M. Mendenhall (Eds.), *Advances in global leadership* (Volume 9, pp.279–321). London: Emerald Publishing.

Lewin, K. (1935). *A dynamic theory of personality*. New York: McGraw-Hill.

Lewin, K. (1947a). Frontiers in group dynamics II: Channels of group life. *Social Planning and Action Research, 1*(2), 143–153.

Lewin, K. (1947b). Frontiers in group dynamics. *Human Relations, 1*(1), 5–41.

Lewin, K. (1997). *Resolving social conflict & field theory in the social sciences*. Washington: American Psychological Association.

Lewin, K. (2009). Quasi-stationary social equilibria and the problem of permanent change. In Burke, W., Lake, D., & Paine, J. (Eds), *Organization change: A comprehensive reader*. San Francisco, CA: Jossey-Bass, pp.73–77.

Lewis, M. (2004). *Moneyball: The art of winning an unfair game*. New York: W.W. Norton.

Lewis, M. W., & Smith, W. K. (2014). Paradox as a metatheoretical perspective: Sharpening the focus and widening the scope. *The Journal of Applied Behavioral Science, 50*(2), 127–149.

Leybourne, S. (2005). Improvisation within management: Oxymoron, paradox, or legitimate way of achieving? In *Academy of Management Conference ODC Division, 5–10 August*. Honolulu.

Leybourne, S. A. (2006). Managing change by abandoning planning and embracing improvisation. *Journal of General Management, 31*(3), 11–29.

Li, X. (2019). Is 'Yin-Yang balancing' superior to ambidexterity as an approach to paradox management? *Asia Pacific Journal of Management, 36*(1), 17–32.

Li, X. (2021). Quantum approach to organizational paradox: A Copenhagen perspective. *Academy of Management Review*, 46(2), 412–415.

Liberman, K. (2013). Following sketched maps. In K. Liberman, *More studies in ethnomethodology* (pp.45–83). Albany: State University of New York Press.

Lichtenstein, B. M., Smith, B., & Torbert, W. (1995). Leadership and ethical development. *Business Ethics Quarterly, 5*(1), 97–116.

Liedtka, J. (2018). Why design thinking works. *Harvard Business Review, September–October*, 1–13.

Lindblom, C. (1959). The science of 'muddling through'. *Public Administration Review, 19*(2), 79–88.

Lindsay, B., Smit, E., & Waugh, N. (2018). How the implementation of organizational change is evolving. *McKinsey & Company*, (February), 1–8. https://www.mckinsey.com/~/media/McKinsey/Business Functions/McKinsey Implementation/Our Insights/How the implementation of organizational change is evolving/How-the-implementation-of-organizational-change-is-evolving.ashx (accessed 23 May 2022).

Lippitt, R., Watson, J., Westley, B., & Spalding, W. B. (1958). *The dynamics of planned change: A comparative study of principles and techniques.* New York: Harcourt Brace.

Litre, P., Michels, D., Hindshaw, I., & Ghosh, P. (2018). *Busting three common myths of change management.* 2 August. Bain and Company. https://www.bain.com/insights/results-delivery-busting-3-common-change-management-myths/ (accessed 21 May 2022).

Lok, J., Badham, R., & de Rond, M. (2022). Why some practices are harder to change than others: Theorizing the substantive contingency of organizational change (Submission to the Academy of Management Review). Sydney.

Long, M. (2010). Derrida and a theory of irony: Parabasis and parataxis. Unpublished PhD *English Studies.* Durham University.

Lounsbury, M., & Zhao, E. Y. (2017). *Neo-institutional theory* (Issue January 2014). Oxford Bibliography.

Love Actually (Director: Curtis, R.). (2003). Billy Mack – Christmas is all around (first scene). https://www.youtube.com/watch?v=_-aMV2xXdpsv

Luecke, R. (2003). *Managing change and transition.* Boston: Harvard Business School Publishing.

Lüscher, L. S., & Lewis, M. W. (2008). Organizational change and managerial sensemaking: Working through paradox. *Academy of Management Journal, 51*(2), 221–240.

Lüscher, L. S., Lewis, M., & Ingram, A. (2006). The social construction of organizational change paradoxes. *Journal of Organizational Change Management, 19*(4), 491–502.

Lyon, T. P., & Montgomery, A. W. (2015). The means and end of greenwash. *Organization & Environment, 28*(2), 223–249.

Maak, T., Pless, N. M., Wohlgezogen, F., & Crisis, C. (2021). The fault lines of leadership: Lessons from the global Covid-19 crisis. *Journal of Change Management, 21*(1), 66–86.

Machiavelli, N. ([1514] 2005). *The Prince.* Translator Peter Bondanella, Oxford: Oxford University Press.

Maguire, S., & Hardy, C. (2009). Discourse and deinstitutionalization: The decline of DDT. *The Academy of Management Journal, 52*(1), 148–178.

Mahatma Gandhi arrives in the UK (1931). British Pathe (3.30). https://www.youtube.com/watch?v=P6njRwz_dMw (accessed 5 January 2022).

Mahler, J. (2009). *Organizational learning at NASA: The Challenger and Columbia accidents.* Washington: Georgetown University Press.

Maitlis, S., & Lawrence, T. B. (2007). Triggers and enablers of sensegiving in organizations. *Academy of Management Journal, 50*(1), 57–84.

Mankins, M. (2017). 5 Ways the best companies close the strategy-execution gap. *Harvard Business Review, 13*(3), 1–6.

Manson, M. (2019). *Everyting is f*****: A book about hope.* New York: Harper.

Manz, C., & Sims, H. (2001). *The new superleadership.* San Francisco: Berrett-Koehler.

March, J. G. (1967). *Handbook of organizations. Revue Française de dociologie* (Vol. 8). London and New York: Routledge.

March, J. G. (1981). Footnotes to organizational change. *Administrative Science Quarterly, 26*(4), 563–577.

March, J. (1986). How we talk and how we act: Administrative theory and administrative life. In M. Cohen, & J. March (Eds.), *Leadership and ambiguity* (pp.273–290). Boston: Harvard Business School Press.

March, J. (1994). *Primer on decision-making*. New York: Free Press.

March, J. G. (2007). *Management and Don Quixote*. https://www.youtube.com/watch ?v=bztgYMoTEjM (accessed 5 January 2022).

March, J. G. (2010). *Ambiguities of experience*. Ithaca: Cornell University Press.

March, J. G., & Olsen, J. P. (1983). Organizing political life: What administrative reorganization tells us about government. *American Political Science Review*, *77*(2), 281–296.

March, J. G., & Olsen, J. P. (2009). The logic of appropriateness. In Moran, M., Rein, M., and Goodin, R. (Eds). *The Oxford handbook of public policy*. Oxford: Oxford University Press, pp.689–709.

March, J. G., & Sutton, R. (1997). Organizational performance as a dependent variable. *Organization Science*, *8*(6), 698–706.

March, J. G., & Weil, T. (2005). *On leadership*. Oxford: Blackwell.

Markus, M. L., & Benjamin, R. I. (1997). The magic bullet theory in IT-enabled transformation. *Sloan Management Review*, *38*(2), 55–68.

Marshak, R. J. (1993). Managing the metaphors of change. *Organizational Dynamics*, *22*(1), 44–56.

Marshak, R. (2004). Morphing: The leading edge of organizational change in the twenty-first century. *Organization Development Journal*, *22*(3), 8–21.

Martin, J. (2002). *Organizational culture: Mapping the terrain*. London: Sage.

Martin, J. L. (2003). What is field theory? *American Journal of Sociology*, *109*(1), 1–49.

Martin, R. (2009). *Design of business: Why design thinking is the next competitive advantage*. Boston: Harvard Business Press.

Martin, R. L. (2010). The execution trap. *Harvard Business Review*, *7*(8), 64.

Martin, R. L., & Golsby-Smith, T. (2017). Management is much more than a science. *Harvard Business Review, September–October*, 128–135.

Marturano, J. (2014). *Finding the space to lead*. London and New York: Bloomsbury Press.

Marx, K. (1972). *The 18th Brumaire of Louis Bonaparte*. Moscow: Progress.

McCabe, D. (2016). 'Curiouser and curiouser !': Organizations as Wonderland – a metaphorical alternative to the rational model. *Human Relations*, *69*(4), 945–973.

McCabe, D. (2020). *Changing change management*. London: Routledge.

McCauley, C. D., Drath, W. H., Palus, C. P., O'Connor, P. M. G., & Baker, B. A. (2006). The use of constructive-developmental theory to advance the understanding of leadership. *Leadership Quarterly*, *17*(6), 634–653.

McClean, D. (2016). *Richard Rorty, liberalism and cosmopolitanism*. London and New York: Routledge.

McCloskey, D. (1994). *Knowledge and persuasion in economics*. Cambridge: Cambridge University Press.

McCurdy, H. E. (1993). *Inside NASA: High technology and organizational change in the U.S. space program*. Baltimore, MD: Johns Hopkins University Press.

McCurdy, H. E. (2001). *Faster, better, cheaper: Low-cost innovation in the U.S. space program*. Baltimore, MD: Johns Hopkins University Press.

McGivering, B. J. (2015). Is Gandhi still a hero to Indians? https://www.bbc.com/news/ world-asia-31847578 (accessed 5 January 2022).

McKinsey and Co. (2019). *McKinsey transformation: Tell a compelling change story to inspire your organization*. https://www.youtube.com/watch?v=4FlP1-5WMyo (accessed 22 May 2022).

McLean, B. (2017). *Driven off course: How Volkswagen got on the road to scandal.* https://www.nytimes.com/2017/06/05/books/review/volkswagen-scandal-faster-higher-farther-jack-ewing.html (accessed 5 January 2022).

McLoughlin, I. P., Badham, R. J., & Palmer, G. (2005). Cultures of ambiguity: Design, emergence and ambivalence in the introduction of normative control. *Work, Employment and Society, 19*(1), 67–89.

Meaney, M., & Pung, C. (2008). McKinsey global survey results: Creating organizational transformations. *McKinsey Quarterly, 7*(3), 1–7.

Meatballs: It Just Doesn't Matter! (Director: Reitman, I.) (1979). https://www.bing.com/videos/search?q=It+Just+Doesn%e2%80%99t+Matter!+(1979)++Meatballs+(6%2f9)+Movie+CLIP+(1979)+HD&view=detail&mid=F5BAC96D89BCB96F2704F5BAC96D89BCB96F2704&FORM=VIRE (accessed 5 January 2022).

Mencken, H. L. (1920). Prejudices. Second series. Ebook. Project Gutenberg Updated 2021. https://www.gutenberg.org/files/53467/53467-h/53467-h.htm (accessed 10 January 2023).

Meyer, J. W., & Rowan, B. (1977). Institutionalized organizations: Formal structure as myth and ceremony. *American Journal of Sociology, 83*(2), 340–363.

Meyerson, D. E., & Scully, M. A. (2007). Tempered radicalism and the politics of ambivalence and change. *Organization Science, 6*(5), 585–600.

Micelotta, E., Lounsbury, M., & Greenwood, R. (2017). Pathways of institutional change: An integrative review and research agenda. *Journal of Management, 43*(6), 1885–1910.

Millan-Zaibert, E. (2007). *Friedrich Schlegel and the emergence of romantic philosophy.* New York: Suny Press.

Miller, D. (1992). *The Icarus paradox: How exceptional companies bring about their own downfall.* New York: Harper Collins.

Miller, P., & Rose, N. (2008). *Governing the present: Administering economic, social and personal life.* Cambridge: Polity.

Mills, C. W. (1969 [1951]). *White collar: The American middle classes.* Oxford: Oxford University Press.

MindTools. (2019). Force field analysis: How to use the tool. https://www.mindtools.com/pages/article/newTED_06.htm (accessed 20 December 2019).

Mintzberg, H., Ahlstrand, B., & Lampel, J. (1998). *Strategy safari: A guided tour through the wilds of strategic management.* New York: Free Press.

Miron-Spektor, E., Keller, J., Smith, W., & Lewis, M. (2018). Microfoundations of organizational paradox: The problem is how we think about the problem. *Academy of Management Journal, 61*(1), 26–45.

Mish, F. et al. (2020). *Merriam-Webster's collegiate dictionary* (11th edition). Springfield, MA: Merriam-Webster.

Mistry, R. (2017). Gandhi: The myths behind the Mahatma. *In Defense of Marxism* (16 August), 1–12. https://www.marxist.com/gandhi-the-myths-behind-the-mahatma.htm (accessed 5 January 2022).

Mitroff, I., Alpaslan, C., & Mason, R. (2012). The messy business of management. *MIT Sloan Management Review, 54*(1), 96.

Moeller, H. G. (2011). *The radical Luhmann.* New York: Columbia University Press.

Moneyball (Director Miller, B.) (2011a). Scene 1 from Moneyball – What is the problem? 13 August 2014. https://www.youtube.com/watch?v=pWgyy_rlmag (accessed 23 May 2022).

Moneyball (Director: Miller, B.) (2011b). Scene 2 from Moneyball – Science vs scouts. 4 November 2016. https://www.youtube.com/watch?v=DtumWOsgFXc (accessed 23 May 2022).

Moneyball (Director: Miller, B.) (2011c). Scene 3 from Moneyball – Adapt or die. 10 December 2014. https://www.youtube.com/watch?v=ugN5aD5p2NU (accessed 23 May 2022).

Morgan, G. (1997). *Imaginization*. London: Sage.

Morgan, G. (2006). *Images of organization*. London: Sage.

Morrison, E., Hutcheson, S., Nilson, E., Fadden, J., & Franklin, N. (2019). *Strategic doing: Ten skills for agile leadership*. Hoboken, NJ: Wiley.

Morrison, M., & Daniels, K. (2010). *PESTLE analysis factsheet*. London: Chartered Institute of Personnel and Development.

Muecke, D.C. (1980). *The compass of irony*. London: Methuen.

Muller, W. (1999). *Sabbath: Restoring the sacred rhythm of rest*. New York: Bantam.

Nadler, D., Shaw, R., & Walton, A. (1995). *Discontinous change: Leading organizational transformation*. San Francisco: Jossey-Bass.

Nadler, D., & Tushman, M. (1989). Organizational frame bending: Principles for managing reorientation. *Academy of Management Executive*, 3(3), 194–204.

Nagel, T. (1979). The absurd. In T. Nagel (Ed.), *Mortal questions* (pp.11–23). Cambridge: Cambridge University Press.

Newark, D. (2018). Leadership and the logic of absurdity. *Academy of Management Review*, 43(2), 198–216.

Newton, J., Graham, J., McLoughlin, K., & Moore, A. (2003). Receptivity to change in a general medical practice. *British Journal of Management*, *14*(2), 143–153.

Nietzsche, F. ([1913] 2011). Human all-too-human part II, Project Gutenberg. https://www.gutenberg.org/files/37841/37841-h/37841-h.html (accessed 10 January 2022).

Noonan, W. R. (2011). Discussing the undiscussable: Overcoming defensive routines in the workplace. *Rotman Magazine*, (Spring), 17–21.

O'Connor, J., & Seymour, J. (2011). *Introducing NLP: Psychological skills for understanding and influencing people*. Newbury Port, MA: Conari Press.

O'Reilly III, C., & Tushman, M. (2004). The ambidextrous organization. *Harvard Business Review*, 82(4), 74–81.

O'Toole, J., & Bennis, W. (2009). What's needed next: A culture of candor. *Harvard Business Review*, June, 2–8.

Obama, B. (2015). *President Barack Obama (FULL) Interview – BBC News*. 24 July 2015. https://www.youtube.com/watch?v=YdU7fUXDLpI (accessed 5 January 2022).

Obama, M. (2018). *Becoming*. New York: Crown, Penguin Random House.

Offereins, J. (2020). Managing the (change) curve. *Eleven 8, 31 March*, 1–5. https://www.eleven8consulting.com/news/managing-the-change-curve (accessed 23 May 2022).

Ohana, D. (2019). *The intellectual origins of modernity*. London: Taylor & Francis.

Oldham, S. (2018). 'To think in enterprising ways': Enterprise education and enterprise culture in New Zealand. *History of Education Review*, *47*(1), 87–101.

Oliver, C. (1992). The antecedents of deinstitutionalization. *Organization Studies*, *13*(4), 563–588.

Oreg, S. (2006). Personality, context, and resistance to organizational change. *European Journal of Work and Organizational Psychology*, *15*(1), 73–101.

Oreg, S. (2018). Resistance to change and performance: Toward a more even-handed view of dispositional resistance. *Journal of Applied Behavioral Science, 54*(1), 88–107.

Oreg, S., Bartunek, J., Lee, G., & Do, B. (2018). An affect-based model of recipients' responses to organizational change events. *Academy of Management Review, 43*(1), 65–86.

Oreg, S., & Goldenberg, J. (2015). *Resistance to innovation.* Chicago: University of Chicago Press.

Oreg, S., & Sverdlik, N. (2011). Ambivalence toward imposed change: The conflict between dispositional resistance to change and the orientation toward the change agent. *Journal of Applied Psychology, 96*(2), 337–349.

Oreg, S., Vakola, M., & Armenakis, A. (2011). Change recipients' reactions to organizational change: A 60-year review of quantitative studies. *Journal of Applied Behavioral Science, 47*(4), 461–524.

Orlikowski, W., & Gash, D. (1994). Technological frames: Making sense of information technology in organizations. *ACM Transactions on Information Systems, 12*(2), 174–207.

Orwell, G. (1949). *Reflections on Gandhi.* Partisan Review, (January), 1–7. https://www.orwell.ru/library/reviews/gandhi/english/e_gandhi (accessed 5 January 2022).

Oswick, C., Grant, D., Michelson, G., & Wailes, N. (2005). Looking forwards: Discursive directions in organizational change. *Journal of Organizational Change Management, 18*(4), 383–390.

Oswick, C., Keenoy, T., & Grant, D. (2002). Metaphor and analogical reasoning in organization theory: Beyond orthodoxy. *The Academy of Management Review, 27*(2), 294.

Owen-Smith, J., & Powell, W. W. (2012). Networks and institutions. In R. Greenwood, C. Oliver, P. Lawrence, & R. Meyer (Eds.), *The Sage handbook of organizational institutionalism* (pp.596–623). London: Sage.

Palmer, I., Dunford, R., & Buchanan, D. A. (2017). *Managing organizational change: A multiple perspectives approach* (3rd edition). New York: McGraw Hill.

Palmer, I., Dunford, R., & Buchanan, D. A. (2021). *Managing organizational change: A multiple perspectives approach* (4th edition). New York: McGraw Hill.

Parker, H. (2010). *Aussies guide to recovery.* Australia. News.com.Au. (copy on Ironies of Organizational Change website).

Parker, S. & Bindl, U. (Eds.) (2017). *Proactivity at work: Making things happen in organizations.* New York and Oxford: Routledge.

Pascal, B., & Krailsheimer, A. J. (1995). *Pensees.* Penguin Classic. Harmondsworth: Penguin Books.

Pascale, R., Sternin, J., & Sternin, M. (2010). *The power of positive deviance.* Boston: Harvard Business School Publishing.

Patalano, R. (2011). Resistance to change: Historical excursus and contemporary interpretations. *Review of Political Economy, 23*(2), 249–266.

Perrow, C. (1983). The organizational context of human factors engineering. *Administrative Science Quarterly, 28*(4), 521–541.

Perry, W. (2015). *Big change, best path: Successfully managing organizational change with wisdom, analytics and insight.* New York: Kogan Page.

Peters, L. (2012). The rhythm of leading change: Living with paradox. *Journal of Management Inquiry, 21*(4), 405–411.

Peters, T. (2018). *The excellence dividend.* New York: Vintage.

Peterson, C., & Seligman, M. (2004). *Character strengths and virtues. A handbook and classification*. Oxford: American Psychological Association and Oxford University Press.

Peterson, R. A. (2005). In search of authenticity. *Journal of Management Studies*, *42*(5), 1083–1098.

Pettigrew, A. (1997). What is a processual analysis? *Scandinavian Journal of Management*, *13*(4), 337–348.

Pettigrew, A. (2000). Linking change processes to outcomes: A commentary on Ghoshal. In M. Beer, & N. Nohria (Eds.), *Breaking the code of change* (pp.243–253). Boston: Harvard Business Review Press.

Pettigrew, A. ([1985] 2011). *The awakening giant: Continuity and change in imperial chemical industries*. London and New York: Routledge.

Pettigrew, A., Ferlie, E., & McKee, L. (1992a). *Shaping strategic change: Making change in large organiztions: The case of the NHS*. London: Sage.

Pettigrew, A., Ferlie, E., & McKee, L. (1992b). Shaping strategic change – the case of the NHS in the 1980s. *Public Money and Management*, *12*(3), 27–31.

Pettigrew, A., & Whipp, R. (1991). *Managing change for competitive success*. Oxford: Blackwell.

Pettigrew, A. M., Woodman, R. W., & Cameron, K. S. (2001). Studying organizational change and development: Challenges for future research. *Academy of Management Journal*, *44*(4), 697–713.

Pfeffer, J. (1992). *Managing with power: Politics and influence in organizations*. Boston: Harvard Business School Press.

Pfeffer, J., & Salancik, G. (1977). Organization design: The case for a coalitional model of organizations. *Organization Dynamics*, *6*(2), 15–29.

Pfeffer, J., & Sutton, G. (2000). *The knowing–doing gap: How smart companies turn knowledge into action*. Boston: Harvard Business School Press.

Pickering, A. (1995). *The mangle of practice*. Chicago: University of Chicago Press.

Piderit, S. (2000). Rethinking resistance and recognizing ambivalence: A multidimensional view of attitudes toward an organizational change. *The Academy of Management Review*, *25*(4), 783–794.

Pierson, P. (2000). Increasing returns, path dependence and the study of politics. *The American Political Science Review*, *94*(2), 251–267.

Pike, J., & Kelly, P. (2014). *The moral geographies of children, young people and food: Beyond Jamie's school dinners*. Palgrave: Macmillan.

Piper, N. (2013). Audiencing Jamie Oliver: Embarrassment, voyeurism and reflexive positioning. *Geoforum*, *45*(November), 346–355.

Pirotti, G., & Venzin, M. (2017). *Resilient organizations: Responsible leadership in times of uncertainty*. Cambridge and New York: Cambridge University Press.

Piskorska, A. (2016). Echo and inadequacy in ironic utterances. *Journal of Pragmatics*, *101*, 54–65.

Plato (2013). *The Phaedrus*. Project Gutenberg ebook. https://www.gutenberg.org/files/1636/1636-h/1636-h.htm (accessed 10 January 2023).

Pondy, L. (1977). Effectiveness: A thick description. In P. Goodman, & J. Pennings (Eds.), *New perspectives on organizational effectiveness* (pp.226–234). San Francisco: Jossey-Bass.

Popper, K. (2011). *The open society and its enemies*. London and New York: Routledge Classics.

Powell, W., & DiMaggio, P. (1991). Introduction. In W. Powell, & P. DiMaggio (Eds.), *The new institutionalism in organizational analysis* (pp.1–41). Chicago: University of Chicago Press.

Pradies, C. et al. (2021). The lived experience of paradox: How individuals navigate tensions during the pandemic crisis. *Journal of Management Inquiry*, *30*(2), 154–167.

Prochaska, J., Prochaska, J., & Levesque, D. (2001). A transtheoretical approach to changing organizations. *Administration and Policy in Mental Health*, 28(4), 247–261.

Prosci. (2018). Measuring the effectiveness of change management. *Thought Leadership Article*. www.prosci.com (accessed 23 May 2022).

Prosci. (2019). *Prosci change management methodology*. https://www.prosci.com/resources/articles/change-management-methodology (accessed 23 May 2022).

Purser, R. E. (2019). *McMindfulness: How mindfulness became the new capitalist spirituality*. London: Repeater Books.

Purser, R E., Forbes, D., & Burke, A. (2016). *Handbook of mindfulness: Culture, context and social engagement*. Berlin: Springer.

Putnam, L. L., Fairhurst, G. T., & Banghart, S. (2016). Contradictions, dialectics, and paradoxes in organizations: A constitutive approach. *Academy of Management Annals*, *10*(1), 65–171.

Quinn, R. (1988). *Beyond rational management: Mastering the paradoxes and competing demands of high performance*. San Francisco: Jossey-Bass.

Quora. (2020). *Did Peter Drucker actually say 'culture eats strategy for breakfast' – and if so, where/when?* https://www.quora.com/Did-Peter-Drucker-actually-say-culture-eats-strategy-for-breakfast-and-if-so-where-when (accessed 23 May 2022).

Quote Investigator (2018). *If you fail to prepare you are preparing to fail*. https://quoteinvestigator.com/2018/07/08/plan/ (accessed 23 May 2022).

Rafferty, A. E., Jimmieson, N. L., & Armenakis, A. A. (2013). Change readiness: A multilevel review. *Journal of Management*, *39*(1), 110–135.

Ramsey, C. (2018). Reflective practice or poetic mindfulness: A role for social poetics in constructing and performing futures. *Action Learning: Research and Practice*, *15*(2), 90–101.

Ratcliffe, S. (2016). Helmuth von Moltke 1800–91 Prussian military commander. In *Oxford Essential Quotations (online)*. Oxford: Oxford University Press.

Rendle, G. (2017). *Gil Rendle – the rollercoaster of change* (3 March). https://www.youtube.com/watch?v=jFXX7OeoTI8 (accessed 23 May 2022).

Rescher, N. (1996). *Process metaphysics: An introduction to process philosophy*. Albany: State University of New York Press.

Reynolds, A., & Lewis, D. (2017). Closing the strategy–execution gap means focusing on what employees think, not what they do. *Harvard Business Review, October*, 2–5.

Reynolds, M., & Vince, R. (2016). *Organizing reflection*. New York and London: Routledge.

Rhodes, C. (2015). *Volkswagen outrage shows limits of corporate power*. https://theconversation.com/volkswagen-outrage-shows-limits-of-corporate-power-48302 (accessed 12 June 2020).

Rhodes, C. (2016). Democratic business ethics: Volkswagen's emissions scandal and the disruption of corporate sovereignty. *Organization Studies*, *37*(10), 1501–1518.

Rhodes, C. (2018). *Volkswagen, #monkeygate and the sham of corporate social responsibility*. https://independentaustralia.net/business/business-display/volkswagen

-monkeygate-and-the-sham-of-corporate-social-responsibility,11152 (accessed 12 June 2020).

Rhodes, C., & Badham, R. (2018). Ethical irony and the relational leader: Grappling with the infinity of ethics and the finitude of practice. *Business Ethics Quarterly*, *28*(1), 71–98.

Rhodes, C., & Brown, A. D. (2005). Narrative, organizations and research. *International Journal of Management Reviews*, *7*(3), 167–188.

Rhodes, C., & Westwood, R. (2008). *Critical representations of work and organizations in popular culture*. New York and London: Routledge.

Rick, T. (2014). *Organizational culture is like an iceberg.* http://www.torbenrick.eu/blog/culture/organizational-culture-is-like-an-iceberg/ (accessed 22 May 2022).

Rick, T. (2015). *The iceberg that sinks organizational change.* https://www.torbenrick.eu/blog/change-management/iceberg-that-sinks-organizational-change/ (accessed 22 May 2022).

Rifkin, W., & Fulop, L. (1997). A review and case study on learning organizations. *The Learning Organization*, *4*(4), 135–148.

Riley, J. (2016). *Lewin's force field analysis model* (8:31). https://www.youtube.com/watch?v=X9ujAtYAfqU (accessed 23 May 2022).

Robinson, K. (2011). *Out of our minds: Learning to be creative*. Chichester: Capstone.

Robinson, S. (2020). *What is an explorer's mindset?* https://www.anexplorersmindset.com (accessed 7 January 2022).

Rogers, E. (2003). *Diffusion of innovations* (5th edition). New York: Free Press.

Rooke, D., & Torbert, W. R. (2005). Seven transformations of leadership. *Harvard Business Review, April*, 1–12.

Rorty, R. (1989). *Contingency, irony and solidarity*. Cambridge: Cambridge University Press.

Rosenbaum, D., More, E., & Steane, P. (2018). Planned organizational change management. *Journal of Organizational Change Management*, 31(2), 286–303.

Roth, G., & DiBella, A. (2015). *Systemic change management*. London: Palgrave Macmillan.

Rothenberg, A. (1979). *The emerging goddess*. Chicago: University of Chicago Press.

Rowland, D., & Higgs, M. (2008). *Sustaining change: Leadership that works*. San Francisco: Jossey-Bass.

Ruzic, D. (2019). How the Volkswagen scandal turned 'Made in Germany' into a liability. https://knowledge.insead.edu/economics-finance/how-the-volkswagen-scandal-turned-made-in-germany-into-a-liability (accessed 10 January 2023).

Ryle, G. (2009). *The concept of mind*. London and New York: Routledge.

Sandberg, S. (2013). *Lean in: Women, work, and the will to lead*. New York: Alfred Knopf.

Savage, M., & Silva, E. B. (2013). Field analysis in cultural sociology. *Cultural Sociology*, *7*(2), 111–126.

Sayles, L., & Strauss, G. (1966). *Human behaviour in organizations*. Englewood Cliffs, NJ: Prentice Hall.

Schad, J., Lewis, M. W., Raisch, S., & Smith, W. K. (2016). Paradox research in management science: Looking back to move forward. *The Academy of Management Annals*, *10*(1), 5–64.

Schaninger, B., Simpson, B., Zhang, H., & Zhu, C. (2020). Demonstrating corporate purpose in the time of the coronavirus. *McKinsey & Company*, *98*(18), 40.

Scharmer, C. O. (2009). *Theory U: Leading from the future as it emerges*. New York: Berrett-Koehler.

Scharmer, O., & Kaufer, K. (2013). *Leading from the emerging future.* New York: Berrett-Koehler.

Schattschneider, E. (1975). *The semi-sovereign people.* New York: Cengage.

Schein, E. H. (1961). *Coercive persuasion.* New York: Norton.

Schein, E. H. (1996). Kurt Lewin's change theory in the field and in the classroom. *Systems Practice, 9*(1), 27–47.

Schein, E. H. (2008). From brainwashing to organization therapy: The evolution of a model of change dynamics. In T. Cummings (Ed.), *Handbook of organization development* (pp.39–53). Thousand Oaks and London: Sage.

Schillinger, A. G. (1984). Man's enduring technological dilemma. *Technology in Society, 6*(1), 59–71.

Schmula (2020). *What does an effective PDCA process require?* https://www.shmula .com/what-does-an-effective-pdca-process-require/24325/ (accessed 12 June 2020).

Schneiberg, M. (2007). What's on the path? Path dependence, organizational diversity and the problem of institutional change in the US economy, 1900–1950. *Socio-Economic Review, 5*(1), 47–80.

Schneider, D., & Goldwasser, C. (1998). Be a model leader of change. *Management Review, March,* 41–45.

Schon, D. (1970). *Change and industrial society.* Reith Lectures: Lecture 2: Dynamic Conservatism. 22 November. BBC 4 UK. https://www.bbc.co.uk/radio4/features/the -reith-lectures/transcripts/1970/ (accessed 23 May 2022).

Schon, D. (1983). *The reflective practitioner: How professionals think in action.* New York: Basic Books.

Schon, D. A. (1987). *Educating the reflective practitioner.* San Francisco: Jossey-Bass.

Schrage, M. (1999). *Serious play: How the world's best companies simulate to innovate.* Boston: Harvard Business Press.

Schultz, F., Suddaby, R., & Cornelissen, J. (2014). The role of the business media in constructing rational myths of organizations. In J. Pallas, & L. Stranegard (Eds.), *Organizations and the Media* (pp.13–33). Milton Park and New York: Routledge.

Schultz, H., & Gordon, J. (2012). *Onward: How Starbucks fought for its life without losing its soul.* New York: Rodale.

Schultz, H., & Yang, D. J. (1999). *Pour your heart into it: How Starbucks built a company one cup at a time.* New York: Hyperion.

Schumpeter, J. (1928). The instability of capitalism. *Economic Journal, 38*(151), 379–380.

Schumpeter, J. (1968). *The theory of economic development.* Cambridge, Boston: Harvard University Press.

Schutz, A. (1943). The problem of rationality in the social world. *Economica, 10*(38), 130–149.

Schwartz, B., & Sharpe, K. (2011). *Practical wisdom: The right way to do the right thing.* New York: Riverhead Books.

Schwarz, G. M., Bouckenooghe, D., & Vakola, M. (2021). Organizational change failure: Framing the process of failing. Special Issue: Introduction and Overview. *Human Relations, 74*(2), 159–179.

Scott, J. (1999). *Seeing like a state.* New Haven: Yale University Press.

Scott, R., & Meyer, J. (1992). *Organizational environments: Rationality and ritual.* London: Sage.

Scott, S., Garden, G., Oliver, J., Halliley, M., & Limited, V. A. (2004). *Jamie's Kitchen: Fifteen lessons on leadership training video.* https://www.arclearn.com/ course/JKL/jamies-kitchen-fifteen-lessons-on-leadership (accessed 23 May 2022).

Scott, W. R. (2014). *Institutions and organizations: Ideas, interests, and identities.* London: Sage.

Seery, J. (2019). *Political returns: Irony in politics and theory from Plato to the antinuclear movement.* London: Routledge.

Segal, L. (2017). *Radical happiness: Moments of collective joy.* London and New York: Verso.

Selznick, P. (1948). Foundations of the theory of organizations. *American Sociological Review*, 13(1), 25–35.

Senge, P. M. (1990). *The fifth discipline: The art and practice of the learning organization.* New York: Currency Doubleday.

Senge, P., Kleiner, A., Roberts, C., Ross, R., Roth, G., & Smith, B. (2007). *The dance of change: the challenges of sustaining momentum in learning organisations.* London: Nicholas Brealey.

Senge, P., Kleiner, A., Roberts, C., Ross, R., & Smith, B. (2010). *The fifth discipline fieldbook: Strategies and tools for building a learning organization.* London: Nicholas Brealey.

Senge, P., & Roth, G. (1999). *The dance of change: The challenges to sustaining momentum in a learning organization.* New York: Currency.

Senior, B., & Fleming, J. (2006). *Organizational change.* Englewood Cliffs, NJ: Prentice Hall.

Senior, B., Swailes, S., & Carnall, C. (2020). *Organizational change* (6th edition). Harlow: Pearson.

Sense, A. (2004). An architecture for learning in projects. *Journal of Workplace Learning*, 16(3), 123–145.

Seville, E. (2016). *Resilient organizations.* New York: Kogan Page.

Sharma, G., Bartunek, J., Buzzanell, P.M., Carmine, S., Endres, C., Etter, M., Fairhurst, G. et al. (2021). A paradox approach to societal tensions during the pandemic crisis. *Journal of Management Inquiry*, 30(2), 121–137.

Sharot, T. (2011). *The optimism bias: A tour of the irrationally positive brain.* New York: Pantheon Books.

Sharot, T. (2012). *The optimism bias – Tali Sharot.* 27 April 2013. https://www.youtube.com/watch?v=vQ6JJjyYHbk (accessed 23 May 2022).

Shipper, F., & Manz, C. (1998). Classic case 6 WL Gore and associates. In A. Thompson, & A. Strickland (Eds.), *Strategic management: Concepts and cases* (pp.491–513). Burr Ridge, IL: Irwin. https://www.researchgate.net/publication/260943692_CLASSIC_CASE_6_W_L_GORE_ASSOCIATES_INC (accessed 5 January 2022).

Shotter, J. (1996). Living in a Wittgensteinian world: Beyond theory to a poetics of practices. *Journal for the Theory of Social Behaviour*, 26(3), 293–311.

Simon, B. (2009). *Everything but the coffee: Learning about America from Starbucks.* Berkeley, Los Angeles and London: University of California Press.

Simon, H. (1976). From substantive to procedural reality. In J. Kastelein et al. (Eds.), *25 years of economic theory* (pp.65–86). Leiden, the Netherlands: Stenfert Kroese.

Sinclair, A. (2016). *Leading mindfully.* Sydney: Allen & Unwin.

Sinek, S. (2011). *Start with why.* New York: Penguin.

Singh, J. V. (1986). Performance, slack, and risk taking in organizational decision making. *Academy of Management Journal*, 29(3), 562–585.

Sinha, P. N. (2010). The dramatistic genre in leadership studies: Implications for research and practice. *Leadership*, 6(2), 185–205.

Sirolli, E. (1999). *Ripples from the Zambezi.* Gabriola Island, BC: New Society Publishers.

Sirolli, E. (2012). *Want to help someone? Shut up and listen!* (27 November). TED Talk (YouTube). https://www.youtube.com/watch?v=chXsLtHqfdM (accessed 23 May 2022).

Sirolli, E. (2015). *The new Victorians the millennial revolution* (21 August). https://www.youtube.com/watch?v=I3YbwLhOWLA (accessed 23 May 2022).

SlideTeam. (2019). Current state/future state. https://www.slideteam.net/powerpoint-presentation-slides/current-state-future-state.html (accessed 23 May 2022).

Slocum, R., Shannon, J., Cadieux, K. V., & Beckman, M. (2011). 'Properly, with love, from scratch': Jamie Oliver's food revolution. *Radical History Review, 110*, 178–191.

Sloterdijk, P. (2020). *Infinite mobilization.* Cambridge: Polity.

Smets, M., Morris, T., & Greenwood, R. (2012). From practice to field: A multilevel model of practice-driven institutional change. *Academy of Management Journal, 55*(4), 877–904.

Smith, D., & Elliott, D. (2007). Exploring the barriers to learning from crisis: Organizational learning and crisis. *Management Learning, 38*(5), 519–538.

Smith, W. K., & Lewis, M. W. (2011). Toward a theory of paradox: A dynamic equilibrium model of organizing. *Academy of Management Review, 36*(2), 381–403.

Smith, W. K., Lewis, M. W., Jarzabkowski, P., & Langley, A. (2017). Introduction: The paradoxes of paradox. In W. Smith, M. Lewis, P. Jarzabkowski, & A. Langley (Eds.), *The Oxford handbook of organizational paradox* (pp.1–27). Oxford: Oxford University Press.

Smith, W., & Lewis, M. (2022). *Both/and thinking: Embracing creative tension to solve your toughest problems.* Boston: Harvard Business Review Press.

Smith, W. K., Lewis, M. W., & Tushman, M. L. (2016). 'Both/and' leadership. *Harvard Business Review, May*, 62–70.

Smollan, R. K. (2014). Control and the emotional rollercoaster of organizational change. *International Journal of Organizational Analysis, 22*(3), 399–419.

Snowden, D. J., & Boone, M. E. (2007). A leader's framework for decision making. *Harvard Business Review, 85*(11), 68–76.

Sonenshein, S. (2010). We're changing – or are we? Untangling the role of progressive, regressive, and stability narratives during strategic change implementation. *Academy of Management Journal, 53*(3), 477–512.

Soparnot, R. (2013). The concept of organizational change capacity. *Journal of Organizational Change Management, 24*(5), 640–661.

Sparr, J. L. (2018). Paradoxes in organizational change: The crucial role of leaders' sensegiving. *Journal of Change Management, 18*(2), 162–180.

Spence, D. (2005). Jamie's school dinners. *BMJ, 330*(7492), p.678.

Spicer, A. (2018). *Business Bullshit.* London: Routledge.

Spillane, R., & Joullie, J.-E. (2015). *Philosophy of leadership.* Basingstoke and New York: Palgrave Macmillan.

Sproule, J. M. (1989). Progressive propaganda critics and the magic bullet myth. *Critical Studies in Media Communication, 6*(3), 225–246.

Stacey, R. D. (2012). The tools and techniques of leadership and management: Meeting the challenge of complexity. In R. Stacey, *The tools and techniques of leadership and management: Meeting the challenge of complexity* (Appendix). London: Routledge.

Stacey, R. (2015). *Ralph Stacey: Complexity and paradoxes.* https://www.youtube.com/watch?v=Ee_3Pg5zvRg (accessed 5 January 2022).

Stacey, R., & Mowles, C. (2016). *Strategic management and organisational dynamics*. London: Pearson Education.

Statler, M., Heracleous, L., & Jacobs, C. D. (2011). Serious play as the practice of paradox. *Journal of Applied Behavioral Science, 47*(2), 236–256.

Statler, M., Roos, J., & Victor, B. (2009). Ain't misbehavin': Taking play seriously in organizations. *Journal of Change Management, 9*(1), 87–107.

Steinbeck, J. (1951). *The Grapes of Wrath*. Harmondsworth: Penguin.

Stewart, J., & O'Reilly, B. (2013). *Bullshit mountain – O'Reilly vs Jon Stewart* (p.23 October). https://www.youtube.com/watch?v=yT5fzEL8Vrc (accessed 5 January 2022).

Stokes, J., & Clegg, S. (2002). Once upon a time in the bureaucracy: Power and public sector management. *Organization, 9*(2), 225–247.

Stone II, J. H. (1990). M. K. Gandhi: Some experiments with truth. *Journal of Southern African Studies, 16*(4), 721–740.

Storey, J. (2004). *Leadership in organizations: current issues and key trends*. London and New York: Routledge.

Storr, W. (2019). *The science of storytelling*. London: William Collins/Harper Collins.

Stouten, J., Rousseau, D. M., & De Cremer, D. (2018). Successful organizational change: Integrating the management practice and scholarly literatures. *Academy of Management Annals, 12*(2), 752–788.

Sull, D., & Eisenhardt, K. M. (2012). Simple rules for a complex world. *Harvard Business Review, 90*(9), 68–74.

Sull, D., & Eisenhardt, K. M. (2015). *Simple rules: How to thrive in a complex world*. Boston and New York: Houghton Mifflin Harcourt.

Sull, D., Homkes, R., & Sull, C. (2015). Why strategy execution unravels – and what to do about it. *Harvard Business Review, 2*(March), 1–10.

Suter, K. ([2007] 2018). *Stupidology: The study of stupidity*. 13 February 2018. https://onlineopinion.com.au/view.asp?article=19566 (accessed 1 August 2022).

Swanson, D. J., & Creed, A. S. (2014). Sharpening the focus of force field analysis. *Journal of Change Management, 14*(1), 28–47.

Swartz, D. (2016). *Bourdieu's concept of field* (April, pp.1–21). Oxford Bibiographies.

Sydow, J., Schreyögg, G., & Koch, J. (2009). Organizational path dependence: Opening the black box. *Academy of Management Review, 34*(4), 689–709.

Szabla, D. B., Pasmore, W., Barnes, M. A., & Gipson, A. N. (2017). *The Palgrave handbook of organizational change thinkers*. London: Palgrave.

Taddeo, J., & Dvorak, K. (Eds.) (2010). *The tube has spoken: Reality TV and history*. Louisville: University of Kentucky Press.

Taleb, N. (2010). *The black swan: The impact of the highly improbable*. New York: Random House.

Tanner, R. (2022). Unfreeze, change, refreeze: Is this a child's game? https://managementisajourney.com/unfreeze-change-refreeze-is-this-a-childs-game/ (accessed 23 May 2022).

Tetlock, P. E., Peterson, R. S., & Berry, J. M. (1993). Flattering and unflattering personality portraits of integratively simple and complex managers. *Journal of Personality and Social Psychology, 64*(3), 500–511.

Thaler, R. (2011). *Nudge: An over*view (30 July). https://www.youtube.com/watch?v=xoA8N6nJMRs (accessed 23 May 2022).

Thaler, R. (2015). *Misbehaving. The making of behavioral economics*. New York and London: W.W. Norton.

Thaler, R. (2019). *A closer look at nudging* (4 June). https://www.youtube.com/watch ?v=nQ_9m7yERUw (accessed 23 May 2022).

Thaler, R., & Sunstein, C. (2008). *Nudge. Improving decisions about health, wealth and happiness.* New Haven and London: Yale University Press.

The Legend of Bagger Vance (2000). (Director Redford, R.).

The Matrix (Directors: Wachowski, L. & L.) (1999). *The Matrix – tumbling down the rabbit hole.* 2 April. https://www.youtube.com/watch?v=TbYirSi08m4 (accessed 30 May 2022).

The Matrix Resurrections (Director: Wachowski, L.) (2021). Red Pill Blue Pill scene (11.12–12.03).

Thomas, J. (1985). Force field analysis: A new way to evaluate your strategy. *Long Range Planning, 18*(6), 54–59.

Thornhill Associates. (2018). *Thornhill Leadership Survey 3.1.* https://www.thornhill .co.za/wordpress/wp-includes/images/resources/Thornhill Leadership Survey 3.1 (TLS) fact sheet.pdf (accessed 23 May 2022).

Thornton, P., & Ocasio, W. (2008). Institutional logics. In R. Greenwood, C. Oliver, R. Sudday, & K Sahlin-Andersson (Eds.), *The Sage handbook of organizational institutionalism* (pp.99–128). London: Sage.

Thornton, P., Ocasio, W., & Lounsbury, M. (2012). *The institutional logics perspective: A new appraoch to culture, structure and process.* Oxford: Oxford University Press.

Thunberg, G. (2021). Greta Thunberg mocks world leaders in 'blah, blah, blah' speech. BBC News. https://www.bing.com/videos/search?q=thornberg+2021+blah+blah+ blah&docid=608010895198521315&mid=E3B47F8FC708860137D6E3B47F8FC7 08860137D6&view=detail&FORM=VIRE (accessed 24 May 2022).

Tichy, N., & Devanna, M. (1986 reprint 1997). *Transformational leader: The key to global competitiveness.* New York: Wiley.

Tidd, J., & Bessant, J. (2021). *Managing innovation: Integrating technological, market and organizational change* (7th edition). Chichester: John Wiley & Sons.

Tollmann, P., Keenan, P., Mingardon, S., Dosik, D., Rizvi, S., & Hurder, S. (2017). *Getting smart about change management.* Boston Consulting Group. https:// www.bcg.com/publications/2017/change-management-getting-smart-about-change -management.aspx (accessed 21 May 2022).

Torbert, W. (1987). *Managing the corporate dream: Restructuring for long-term success.* New York: Dow Jones-Irwin.

Tourish, D. (2013). *The dark side of transformational leadership.* New York: Routledge.

Tourish, D., Collinson, D., & Barker, J. R. (2009). Manufacturing conformity: Leadership through coercive persuasion in business organisations. *Management, 12*(5), 360–383.

Trahms, C. A., Ndofor, H. A., & Sirmon, D. G. (2013). Organizational decline and turnaround: A review and agenda for future research. *Journal of Management, 39*(5), 1277–1307.

TransitionCulture. (2006). *What can we learn from Jamie's school dinners? – 10 insights for energy descent.* TransitionCulture.Org, 4–8. https://www.transitionculture.org/ 2006/07/06/what-can-we-learn-from-jamies-school-dinners-10-insights-for-energy -descent/ (accessed 23 May 2022).

Trethewey, A. (1999). Isn't it ironic: Using irony to explore the contradictions of organ- izational life. *Western Journal of Communication, 63*(2), 140–167.

Trethewey, A., & Ashcraft, K. L. (2004). Special issue introduction – Practicing disorganization: The development of applied perspectives on living with tension. *Journal of Applied Communication Research, 32*(2), 81–88.

Tsoukas, H. (2005). *Complex knowledge: Studies in organizational epistemology.* Oxford: Oxford University Press.

Tsoukas, H., & Chia, R. (2002). On organizational becoming: Rethinking organizational change. *Organization Science, 13*(5), 567–582.

Turner, B. (2001). Cosmopolitan virtue: On religion in a global age. *European Journal of Social Theory, 4*(2), 131–152.

Turner, B. S. (2002). Cosmopolitan virtue, globalization and patriotism. *Theory, Culture and Society, 19*(1–2), 45–63.

Turner, V. (1991). *The ritual process. Structure and anti-structure.* Ithaca: Cornell Paperbacks.

Tushman, M. L. (1997). The ambidextrous organization. *Journal of Business Strategy, July–August,* 42–46.

Tushman, M., & Nadler, D. (1980). A model for diagnosing organizational behavior. *Organizational Dynamics, 9*(2), 35–51.

Tushman, M., & O'Reilly, C. (1997). *Winning through innovation: A practical guide to leading organizational change and renewal.* Boston: Harvard Business School Press.

Tushman, M. L., Smith, W. K., & Binns, A. (2011). The ambidextrous CEO. *Harvard Business Review, 89*(June), 74–80.

Uhl-Bien, M., & Ospina, S. (Eds.) (2012). *Advancing relational leadership research: A dialogue among perspectives.* Charlotte: Information Age Publishing.

UL Insights (2020). Sins of greenwashing. https://www.ul.com/insights/sins-greenwashing (accessed 10 January 2023).

Vaara, E., Sonenshein, S., & Boje, D. (2016). Narratives as sources of stability and change in organizations: Approaches and directions for future research. *Academy of Management Annals, 10*(1), 495–560.

Vaill, P. (1989). *Managing as a performing art.* San Francisco: Jossey-Bass.

Vakola, M. (2013). Multilevel readiness to organizational change: A conceptual approach. *Journal of Change Management, 13*(1), 96–109.

Valencia, R. R. (Ed.) (2012). *The evolution of deficit thinking: Educational thought and practice.* London and New York: Routledge.

Valencia, R. R. (2020). *International deficit thinking.* London and New York: Routledge.

van Dijk, R., & van Dick, R. (2009). Navigating organizational change: Change leaders, employee resistance and work-based identities. *Journal of Change Management, 9*(2), 143–163.

Vargas, R., & Conforto, E. (2019). The innovator's mindset: Radical can-do. *Rotman Magazine,* (Winter), 59–63.

Vera, D., & Rodriguez-Lopez, A. (2007). Leading improvisation: Lessons from the American revolution. *Organizational Dynamics, 36*(3), 303–319.

Video Arts (2012). *Leadership skills training video – Jamie's school dinners: living with change.* https://www.youtube.com/watch?v=gLGUt49a7iQ (accessed 23 May 2022).

Video Arts (2015). *Jamie's school dinners: Managing change – a recipe for manaing and living with change.* https://www.trainingrightnow.com/course/JSDMC1/jamies-school-dinners-managing-change (accessed 22 May 2022).

Video Arts (2020). Jamie's kitchen: *Fifteen lessons on leadership trailer*. https://vimeo .com/376331983 (accessed 22 March 2022).

Vince, R. (2001). Power and emotion in organizational learning. *Human Relations*, *54*(10), 1325–1351.

Vince, R., & Reynolds, M. (2009). Reflection, reflective practice and organizing reflection. In S. Armstrong, & C. Fukami (Eds.), *The Sage handbook of management learning, education and development* (pp.89–104). London and Thousand Oaks: Sage.

Viney, D. (2020). The 'J-curve' of change, 28 January 2020. https://www.linkedin .com/pulse/j-curve-change-david-viney (accessed 22 July 2022).

Vinson, M., Pung, C., & Gonzalez-Glanch, J. (2006). Organizing for successful change management: A McKinsey global survey. *McKinsey Quarterly*, (June), 1–8.

Vlastos, G. (1991). *Socrates: Ironist and moral philosopher*. Cambridge: Cambridge University Press.

Vlastos, G. (1994). *Socratic studies*. Cambridge: Cambridge University Press.

Vonnegut, K. (1980). Hypocrites you always have with you. *The Nation, 230*(15), 469–470.

Waddock, S., Meszoely, G. M., Waddell, S., & Dentoni, D. (2015). The complexity of wicked problems in large scale change. *Journal of Organizational Change Management, 28*(6), 993–1012.

Warburton, N. (2015). Erving Goffman and the performed self (1:58). 15 April. Narrated by Stephen Fry BBC Radio 4. https://www.youtube.com/watch?v=6Z0XS -QLDWM (accessed 22 May 2022).

Warin, M. (2011). Foucault's progeny: Jamie Oliver and the art of governing obesity. *Social Theory and Health, 9*(1), 24–40.

Waterman, R., Peters, T., & Phillips, J. (1980). Structure is not organization. *Business Horizons, 23*(3), 14–26.

Watkins, M., & Bazerman, M. (2003). Predictable surprises: The disasters you should have seen coming. *Harvard Business Review, 81*(3), 72–85.

Watson, G. (1971). Resistance to change. *American Behavioral Scientist, 14*(5), 745–766.

Weale, S. (2015). The new dinner lady: 10 years on, can an Ottolenghi chef prove Jamie Oliver's revolution wasn't a flash in the pan? *The Guardian, 4 April*, 1–9. https:// www.theguardian.com/education/2015/apr/04/school-dinners-revolution-10-years -on (accessed 25 May 2022).

Webb, T. L., & Sheeran, P. (2006). Does changing behavioral intentions engender behavior change? A meta-analysis of the experimental evidence. *Psychological Bulletin, 132*(2), 249–268.

Weick, K. E. (1976). Educational organizations as loosely coupled systems. *Administrative Science Quarterly, 21*(1), 1–19.

Weick, K. (1983). Misconceptions about managerial productivity. *Business Horizons, July–August*, 47–52.

Weick, K. (1995). *Sensemaking in organizations*. Thousand Oaks and London: Sage.

Weick, K. E. (1996). Prepare your organization to fight fires. *Harvard Business Review, 74*(3), 143–148.

Weick, K. E. (1998). Improvisation as a mindset for organizational analysis. *Organization Science, 9*(5), 543–555.

Weick, K. E. (2004). Mundane poetics: Searching for wisdom in organization studies. *Organization Studies, 25*(4), 653–668.

Weick, K. E. (2007). Drop your tools: On reconfiguring management education. *Journal of Management Education*, *31*(1), 5–16.

Weick, K. E. (2011). Reflections: Change agents as change poets – on reconnecting flux and hunches. *Journal of Change Management*, *11*(1), 7–20.

Weick, K. E., & Quinn, R. E. (1999). Organizational change and development. *Annual Review of Psychology*, *50*(1), 361–386.

Weick, K., & Sutcliffe, R. (2011). *Managing the unexpected* (2nd edition). San Francisco: Jossey-Bass.

Weiner, B. J. (2009). A theory of organizational readiness for change. *Implementation Science*, *4*(67), 1–9.

Weiner, B. J., Clary, A. S., Klaman, S. L., & Turner, K. (2020). Organizational readiness for change: What we know, what we think we know, and what we need to know. In B. Albers, A. Shlonsky, & R. Mildon (Eds.), *Implementation science 3.0*. (pp.101–145). Berlin: Springer.

Weisbord, M. (1976). Organizational diagnosis: Six places to look for trouble with or without a theory. *Group & Organization Studies (now Group & Organization Management)*, *1*(4), 430–447.

Werner, M. D., & Cornelissen, J. P. (2014). Framing the change: Switching and blending frames and their role in instigating institutional change. *Organization Studies*, *35*(10), 1449–1472.

Westenholz, A. (1999). From a logic perspective to a paradox perspective in the analysis of an employee-owned company. *Economic and Industrial Democracy*, *20*(4), 503–534.

Westwood, R. (2004). Comic relief: Subversion and catharsis in organizational comedic theatre. *Organization Studies*, *25*(5), 775–795.

Westwood, R., & Rhodes, C. (Eds.) (2007). *Humour, work and organizations*. London and New York: Routledge.

Wheatley, M. (2006). *Leadership and the new science: Discovering order in a chaotic world*. San Francisco: Berrett-Koehler.

Whittle, A., Mueller, F., Gilchrist, A., & Lenney, P. (2016). Sensemaking, sense-censoring and strategic inaction: The discursive enactment of power and politics in a multinational corporation. *Organization Studies*, *37*(9), 1323–1351.

Williams, R. (2010). Jamie Oliver's school dinners shown to have improved academic results. *The Guardian*, *30 March*, 4–7. https://www.theguardian.com/education/2010/mar/29/jamie-oliver-school-dinners-meals (accessed 25 May 2022).

Williams, R. (2015). *Keywords: A vocabulary of culture and society*. Oxford and New York: Oxford University Press.

Wilson, E. (2015). *Keep it fake: Inventing an authentic life*. New York: Sarah Crichton.

Wright, C., & Nyberg, D. (2015). *Climate change, capitalism, and corporations*. Cambridge: Cambridge University Press.

Wright, C., & Nyberg, D. (2017a). An inconvenient truth: How organizations translate climate change into business as usual. *Academy of Management Journal*, *60*(5), 1633–1661.

Wright, C., & Nyberg, D. (2017b). How bold corporate climate change goals deteriorate over time. *Harvard Business Review*, *22 November*, 2–4.

Wucker, M. (2016). *The gray rhino: How to recognize and act on the obvious dangers we ignore*. New York: St Martins Press.

Wucker, M. (2020). Was the pandemic a grey rhino or a black swan? in *The World Ahead: The World in 2021*, 17 November 2020, pp.1–6.

Yanow, D., & Tsoukas, H. (2009). What is reflection-in-action? A phenomenological account. *Journal of Management Studies, 46*(8), 1339–1364.

Yeffeth, G. (2003). *Taking the red pill: Science, philosophy and religion in* The Matrix. Chichester: Summersdale.

Yeganeh, B., & Kolb, D. (2009). Mindfulness and experiential learning. *OD Practitioner, 41*(3), 8–14.

Zerubavel, E. (1991). *The fine line: Making distinctions in everyday life.* Chicago and London: University of Chicago Press.

Zerubavel, E. (2006). *The elephant in the room: Silence and denial in everyday life.* Oxford: Oxford University Press.

Zheng, W., Kark, R., & Meister., A. L. (2018). Paradox versus dilemma mindset: A theory of how women leaders navigate the tensions between agency and communion. *Leadership Quarterly, 29*(5), 584–596.

Zucker, L. (1977). The role of institutionalization in cultural persistence. *American Sociological Review, 42*, 726–743.

Zucker, L. (1983). Organizations as institutions. In R. A. Rothman, P. S. Tolbert, & S. R. Barley (Eds.), *Research in the sociology of organizations* (Vol. 2, Issue 2, pp.1–47). Greenwich, CT: JAI Press.

Zucker, L. G. (1987). Institutional theories of organization. *Annual Review of Sociology, 13*, 443–464.

Zuieback, S. (2020). Below the green line or the 6 circle model: putting theory into practice. Chapter 1: overview. https://stevezuieback.com/site/assets/files/1076/below_the_green_line_-_overview.pdf (accessed 10 January 2023).

Index